UNDERSTANDING
TODAY'S POLICE

Understanding
Today's Police

Second Edition

Mark L. Dantzker, Ph.D.

Taken from:

Understanding Today's Police, Second Edition,
by Mark L. Dantzker
Copyright ©2000, 1995 by Prentice-Hall, Inc.
A Pearson Education Company
Upper Saddle River, New Jersey 07458

This special edition published in cooperation with Pearson Custom
Publishing.

Printed in the United States of America

10 9 8 7 6

Please visit our web site at www.pearsoncustom.com

ISBN 0–536–63509–9

BA 993293

PEARSON CUSTOM PUBLISHING
75 Arlington Street, Suite 300
Boston, MA 02116

CONTENTS

3 PATROL   60

6   POLICE AND THE LAW   160

PREFACE

Policing in the United States has undergone many changes and will continue to change in the future. This appears particularly true in light of the adoption of community policing. An area that continues to experience change is the educational status of police officers, evolving from a time when a high school education was not even required to a time when many police agencies are requiring some level of college education, with a growing contingent supporting the requirement of a bachelor's degree for all police officers. As a result of this push for higher education universities and colleges continue to address the increased educational needs brought about by this change by offering a related curriculum, which in most cases has been labeled *criminal justice*. Most criminal justice programs include courses directly related to policing.

Although the first police science courses were offered in the early 1900s, textbooks were not written to support these course offerings until the late 1960s and early 1970s. Even then, few books were offered, and the few books that were available were similar in content and approach. This situation continued through the 1980s despite the rapid changes occurring in our communities and throughout the nation, mandating new and innovative approaches to policing. Little change was taking place in the textbook field until the early 1990s when many new police-oriented textbooks came on the scene, among which was the first edition of this text. With little difference among the books by content, each text had to present the information in a way that would set it apart from the others. My approach was to offer a mixture of theory and practicality highlighted by real experiences, observations, and anecdotes through a pedagogical tool called "Case in Point." As a believer in "sticking with the one that brung you," the second edition of this text continues the tradition of the first, mixing theory and practicality through many new or updated cases. Furthermore, the second edition contains new photographs and popular cartoons that illustrate the ideas and concepts explored in the text. With that, I present *Understanding Today's Police* (2nd ed.).

Policing has existed in some manner or another in the United States since early colonial times. From the first professionalism movement to today's technological advances, policing has gone through many changes. However, this textbook is designed to focus more on the police of today and tomorrow than on the history of policing. Starting with the role of today's police officer, you will gain an understanding of many facets of policing that will help you to attain greater insight into today's police.

What started as a fairly simple job has grown into a multifaceted quasi-profession. The roles of today's police officer are many, which often leads to unwanted conflict. Chapter 1, The Police Role in Our Society, focuses on the change in the police role, both historically and currently, to provide a better understanding of today's police officer.

Policing is one-third of the criminal justice system and is often discussed as such. Yet, seldom is policing itself examined as a system. Chapter 2, From a Systems Perspective, offers a view of policing as a three-tiered system: local, state, and federal. In addition, the subsystems of each system are explored. Furthermore, it is no secret that police as a group do not think highly of the rest of the criminal justice system. Often, police are blamed for the high crime rates or the failure of criminal convictions. However, police are seldom satisfied with how well the rest of the system supports them or does its justice-related tasks. This chapter also addresses interaction and relationships of police with the courts, probation and parole, and corrections.

The most visible component of policing is patrol. Often considered the most important element of policing, the patrol division is the starting point for most police careers and citizen contacts. The function, services and delivery, dominant features, and effectiveness of patrol are the major areas discussed in Chapter 3, Patrol. Under the rubric of patrol one may find other units such as traffic, K-9, SWAT, and reserves. Furthermore, being a patrol officer is no easy task. This chapter also examines situations that tend to present the greatest difficulty for the police officer because of role frustration, laws, and personal attitudes. Topics include domestic violence, dealing with juveniles, homeless people, and drugs.

The patrol division is not the only component of policing worthy of discussion. Chapter 4, Criminal Investigations and Other Support Units, provides a look at the myth and reality of criminal investigations, why police officers want to be detectives, the investigative process, investigative units, and techniques for conducting an investigation. In addition, this chapter examines other components of the agency that provide vital support to patrol and criminal investigations. These units include communications, training, research and analysis, and other specialized units.

Chapter 5, Organization and Management, focuses on the general organization and management of police agencies. Attention is given to organizational and management theories, styles of management, and such administrative issues as discipline and labor relations. In addition, the definition, measurement, application, and control mechanisms of police accountability are examined.

In the 1960s a variety of landmark Supreme Court cases were handed down that police believed hindered their abilities to enforce the law. Since then several legal situations have arisen that have further put police on the defensive. Insight into the growing legal changes for policing is found in Chapter 6, Police and the

Law. This chapter also discusses what occurs when the police break the law: corruption, which includes types of corruption, theories, typologies associated with corruption, and controls.

Should I make an arrest? Issue a warning ticket? Shoot to kill? These are just a few of the questions a police officer may ask himself or herself during his or her career. The answer is usually the result of the officer's use of discretion. Police officers have broad powers of discretion. Chapter 7, The Use of Discretion, will define discretion and examine its sources, along with the results of improper use and suggestions for controlling it.

An area of great concern, particularly since the 1960s, is how well police and community relate to one another. When the relationship between the police and the community is strained, the ability of police officers to perform their required and expected tasks becomes more difficult. The perceptions, problems, attitudes, and solutions that pertain to police–community relations are discussed in Chapter 8, Relating to the Community. The most current attempt to improve police service and community interaction, community-oriented policing, is also explored.

The key to a good police department is its personnel. Issues surrounding recruitment such as the importance of quality personnel, who becomes a police officer, requirements, competition with other agencies, and discrimination constitute the major portion of the discussion in Chapter 9, Recruitment: Quality of Personnel. Of particular interest in this chapter is the examination of the role of women in policing.

What type of person becomes a police officer? Why does a person become a police officer? What happens to that person after becoming a police officer? Chapter 10, The Personality of Police Officers, attempts to answer these questions, focusing on the individual police officer. This includes personality traits, personal relationships, job stress, the police subculture, styles of policing, and management versus rank-and-file personalities.

For a police officer to be able to cope successfully, do the job effectively, and survive in today's world, he or she must be aware of a variety of issues. Chapter 11, Issues: Today and Tomorrow, focuses on such important issues as the use of force, AIDS, and technology. Furthermore, this chapter examines professionalization of policing, a movement that started in the early 1900s and has remained a source of debate. Since the first professionalism movement, policing has prodded, provoked, and sometimes condemned the concept of professionalism. A detailed view of professionalism as it relates to policing is offered and includes such topics as education, training, lateral movement, and accreditation. Finally, this chapter looks at three major issues of the future of policing: personnel, administration, and police–community relations.

Overall, you should find *Understanding Today's Police* (2nd ed.) an innovative and informative textbook. Once you have completed reading this book, it is hoped that you will have gained much greater insight into policing and its function, and will want to continue to broaden your knowledge of this fascinating component of our criminal justice system.

In addition, any suggestions or comments you have that could improve future editions are welcome. Suggestions, comments, or questions may be addressed to the author at

University of Texas Pan American
Department of Criminal Justice
1201 W. University Dr.
Edinburg, TX 78539
mldantz@panam.edu

Acknowledgments

Writing the first edition of this text was one of the most interesting, time-consuming, enlightening, and frustrating things I have done since becoming a full-time academician. I thought that the revision would have been much simpler, but in many ways it was more interesting and much more frustrating than the first writing. Fortunately, I did not have to endure this process alone and would like to thank those who helped bring both editions of this text to fruition. For the first edition, my acquisitions editor was Robin Baliszewski, who supported me regardless of the abuse she received (of course she could dish it out just as well), and there was Adele Kupchik, production editor, whose hard work and good humor helped put the manuscript into a final quality worthy of publishing.

This revision brought together many new supporters from Prentice Hall: acquisitions editor, Neil Marquardt took the chance to authorize and support this second edition; editorial assistant Jean Auman and development editor Cheryl Adam provided continuous assistance; and Kim Davies, the policing/law enforcement acquisitions editor, although brought in toward the end of this project, maintained a strong and steady presence and offered unending support to bring this project to production.

Once again, I would also like to thank those individuals who took the time from their busy schedules to review the manuscript and whose suggestions and commentary assisted me in the completion of the first edition of this text. They were Wayne L. Wolf, South Suburban College; Lois A. Wims, Salve Regina University; Richard R. Becker, North Harris College; Donald J. Melisi, Middlesex Community College; James D. Stinchcomb, Miami–Dade Community College; Thomas Dempsey, Thomas Nelson Community College; Ronald G. Iacovetta, Wichita State University; Robert E. Bagby, Eastern Kentucky University; Thomas McAninch, Scott Community College; and Leslie W. Parks, University of Texas–Brownsville. I especially want to thank those individuals who reviewed the first edition and provided me with commentary and suggestions for this revision. They were Dr. Ellen G. Cohn, Florida International University; Ron Walker, Trinity Valley Community College; and Dr. Lois Wims, Salve Regina University.

In addition, as with the first edition, there were several others who provided assistance and support through their contributions to the text. My gratitude goes to the police departments in Chicago, Illinois; Denver, Colorado; Los Angeles, California; Indianapolis, Indiana; Wilmette, Illinois; and Scottsdale, Arizona. In particular I owe a special debt of thanks to Michael J. Heidingsfield (chief emeritus) and Mrs. Lynn Parsons (senior volunteer) of the Scottsdale Police Department for the time and effort they put into gathering, sorting, and offering a myriad of photos. Furthermore, for allowing me to share them with the world, I am indebted to Chief Beverly Harvard, Atlanta Police Department; Chief Penny Harrington (ret.), Portland Police Department; and Maritza Vega-Gentry (ret.), Los Angeles Police Department.

Finally, I would like to thank all my colleagues who have supported me through the years by adopting, criticizing, and praising the first edition, especially Vernon Farris (ret., Fort Worth Police Department) who has been a longtime friend, mentor, and colleague; but most of all, I want to thank my wife and extremely significant other, Dr. Gail Dantzker, without whose patience, love, cajoling, and support, this revision may never have been completed. I am extremely grateful to one and all.

UNDERSTANDING TODAY'S POLICE

THE POLICE ROLE IN OUR SOCIETY

Since the creation of the first modern police department, the role of the police officer has undergone a variety of identifiable changes. Although numerous definitions of policing exist, policing may be best viewed as an entity created by government to be used to oversee and maintain specific elements of public safety and social order. Police agencies are not to be confused with law enforcement agencies. Law enforcement agencies tend to have a singular purpose: investigation and enforcement of criminally defined activities. The specific elements of police agencies include the prevention and investigation of criminal activity, making arrests, maintaining order, and protecting the public, much of which is accomplished through the act of patrolling.

As noted in the Police Task Force Report of the 1973 National Advisory Commission on Criminal Justice Standards and Goals, "The police are the instrument of the people to achieve and maintain order; their efforts are founded on principles of public service and ultimate responsibility to the public" (p. 9). Retired Police Chief Anthony Bouza offers the following definition of the police mission, "to preserve the peace; protect life and property; detect and arrest offenders; prevent crime; and most important, to accomplish the task that gives the profession its name: enforce the law" (1990, p. 1). This mission is carried out by individuals society has labeled "police officers." Despite a fairly clear-cut multidimensional definition, which requires enforcing laws, maintaining order, and protecting constitutional rights, perceptually, the police role remains one-dimensional to many observers, practitioners and academicians alike.

To test whether perceptions of police officers are unidimensional, the author begins his police courses by posing this question: What do you perceive the roles of today's police officer to be? Most students state that the main role is to enforce the law; thus, describing the police officer as a "crime fighter." This same response is quite common among younger police officers when asked what they perceive as their role in society as police officers. This response has been documented by others as well. In their study of police roles, Hunt et al. (1983) surveyed more than 1200 police officers who, when asked to choose whether they perceived their police officer role as crime fighter or armed social worker,

(Bizarro © 1996 by Dan Piraro. Reprinted with permission of Universal Press Syndicate. All rights reserved.)

71 percent chose crime fighter. Despite the fact that this study was conducted more than 15 years ago, the author suggests that a similar result would be found if the same study were conducted today. However, responses may begin to change should the latest trend in policing, community-oriented policing, continue to take hold and remain a constant. Officers who practice community policing may lean toward the "armed social worker" response, but chances are still good that the "crime fighter" response would prevail.

The image of crime fighter projects enforcing laws, apprehending felonious criminals, stopping all crime and saving the world in a single bound, mightier than . . ., faster than . . ., kind of a superhero. However, the reality is that crime fighting is often a very small part of the police officer's role. For example, the 1997 activity report for the Wilmette, Illinois, Police Department showed that 87.5% percent of the calls for police were service oriented and not criminally related. Recent studies of larger police departments found that crime-related calls account, at most, for half of all calls for police service. However, these studies and figures can be misleading because each police agency has its own definitions and categories for calls for service. Therefore, it is difficult to determine the actual percentage of time police officers spend being crime fighters. Yet, there does appear to be a consensus among criminologists that crime fighting is only a small part of the police role (Cordner, 1989). Whether crime fighting is as much a part of being a police officer as providing service or assistance, the image of the police officer as a crime fighter thrives and dominates perceptions. Why is this image so pervasive?

THE PROBLEM: IMAGE VERSUS REAL LIFE

One of the most difficult aspects of policing to understand is the prevailing image of crime fighter that many people have about police officers.

> The general public knows the police, or feels that it knows the police, from the media and various news reports on policing nationwide. There are also the perceptive friends who have had experiences, or who have friends who have had experiences, with some policeman, somewhere, at some time. This series of generalizations provides the basis for the American public's image of the police (Hernandez, 1989, p.85).

To try to understand why such an image continues to exist it is necessary to understand the problem. The problem, simply put, is one of image versus real life.

According to *Webster's Collegiate Dictionary,* "image," with respect to policing, may best be defined as "a popular conception projected especially through the mass media." An image is a creation of what one might want or wish something to be. With policing, the image perpetuated is that of a crime fighter. "Real life" is best defined as "existing or occuring in reality." If a police officer spends a majority of his or her time providing service-oriented assistance to the community, then reality dictates that the role not be that of a crime fighter but of a social servant, a role that may gain greater recognition as community-oriented policing continues to develop. Community-oriented policing may change the realistic role of policing, but as long as there are sources that continue to perpetuate the crime-fighter image, this image will continue to be acceptable to community members.

The image of policing as crime fighting has generally been accepted because of the constant display of media that perpetuates this image. This media blitz is generated primarily through two broad sources: entertainment and news. However, it should also be acknowledged that there is a third source guilty of perpetuating the crime-fighter image: the police themselves (Walker, 1999).

Throughout the years the entertainment media has offered a variety of image-provoking movies and their sequels, including *Dirty Harry, Beverly Hills Cop, Robocop, Die Hard,* and *Lethal Weapon.* These movies and others like them promote a crime-fighter image of police officers. In this promoted image, police officers solve crimes using a variety of methods that, in real life, would find the officer disciplined, fired, or dead. However, movies are not the sole culprit.

The television media has also played a big part in promoting this crime-fighter image. Fantasy police shows such as *NYPD Blue, Nash Bridges, Pacific Blue,* and *Homicide* have all sparked a certain degree of expectancy in the viewing audience—this is how our police should be. The reality is our police are

(Queen of the Universe reprinted by permission of Sam Hurt)

nowhere near equivalent to their media counterparts. Even considering shows that rely on real footage or reenactments of police situations, such as *COPS, Real Stories of the Highway Patrol*, and *LAPD: Life on the Beat*, the public is being introduced to specific aspects of policing that selectively emphasize the crime-fighter image rather than depict the complete picture of policing, or at least the more human side of policing.

■ CASE IN POINT

In an attempt to show the human side of policing, a television show about the Louisville, Kentucky, Police Department was introduced to the public in February 1997. The first few episodes of this show, called *Inside Look*, focused on a variety of units, a ride-along, and the public.

The news media also provides support for the crime-fighter image because of its interest in the dramatic news story. The news sometimes inaccurately depicts a given situation or exposes only those activities that are directly linked to criminality. For example, during the two-week period after the Rodney King–LAPD verdict was reached (May 1992), a study of the two major newspapers in Chicago, Illinois, found that an average of four police and crime articles appeared daily that depicted the crime-fighting imagery of policing. Stories included police-involved shootings, the growing number of homicides, and police activities against gangs and drugs. During that period, a total of four articles on general police activity could not be found. Those that were found dealt with the appointment of Chicago Police Department's new superintendent and his ideas for improving police sensitivity and other training needs. Also, since the Rodney King incident it is fairly common to see similar types of recorded events on local and national newscasts.

The truth is that the news media, both electronic and print, seldom presents the less-than-glamorous, service side of policing. The primary reason for this is that reality is often boring and mundane—seldom exciting or glamorous; it is just not very interesting. Interesting is what draws attention; it is what sells papers and attracts viewers and listeners. The crime-fighter image attracts attention. We must face facts. No one really wants to see just how boring or tedious a police officer's job can really be.

■ CASE IN POINT

Two of the earliest police shows that attempted to depict a more realistic police setting were *Dragnet* and *Adam-12*. Although both shows enjoyed initial success, their long-term appeal was limited, which lead to their eventual cancellation. However, both shows are syndicated and reruns can still occasionally be seen on some cable channels specializing in early 1960s and 1970s television shows. A more recent example was a show called *High Incident* (1996–1997), which emphasized a more realistic look at police work from the patrol officers' perspective. Although it had its share of crime-fighting excitement, it tended to lean more toward the human side of policing. Despite critical praise, ratings were low and eventually the show was canceled.

Finally, the police themselves can be partially blamed for perpetuating an unrealistic image. Why would they do that? In one word—funding. The effectiveness of a police agency depends in large part upon the adequacy of its budget; funding is usually based on needs. Although budgetary needs frequently exceed availability of finances, a good case must nevertheless be made for receiving as much funding as possible. More often than not, the threat of crime, escalating crime rates, public fear of crime, and crime fighting receive more financial attention than anything else because the other tasks that police are required to perform are seldom perceived to be as important as crime fighting. Therefore, from a purely financial standpoint, the crime-fighter image is important to policing. This could also be said of the entertainment and news media because the crime-fighter image draws attention, and attention translates into money.

IMAGE AND REAL LIFE: THE NEED TO DIFFERENTIATE

Although policing in real life is not nearly as glamorous or as productive as its popular image, reality must prevail; otherwise, society and policing face unfortunate consequences as a result of misperceptions about policing. Two major consequences that need to be recognized are **unrealistic public expectations** of police performance and the **role conflicts** police officers face in their daily attempt to fit an image and meet reality head on (Broderick, 1988; Walker, 1999).

When a police officer is called to the scene of a crime, that officer is expected to recognize and collect all the evidence, apprehend the criminal, and complete the report for the prosecutor quickly. It is generally supposed that this is all accomplished with little or no problem. However, this is seldom the case. In many situations, the case cannot ever be solved. There may be little evidence and no witnesses; or the criminal cannot be identified. Yet, because of the perceived image, if the officer does not accomplish the task as expected he or she is viewed as incompetent. In most cases, incompetence is not the problem; it is the public's perception of policing that creates the problem. Because of the way the police are portrayed in the media, the public expects near-miraculous solutions of crimes that do not often occur in reality.

■ CASE IN POINT

In the movie *Beverly Hills Cop II*, the hero, Axel Foley, was able to retrieve a perfectly iden-tifiable fingerprint off a matchbook cover using superglue and the fluorescent light from a fishtank. Then he took the fingerprint down to the police computer, and, presto, his suspect is identified. Now, after seeing this, many people are convinced that finding fingerprints and matching them is relatively easy. Similar capabilities are demonstrated time and time again in almost all the police shows where in an hour's time (or less when you account for com-mercials!), the show's lead cop is able to uncover remote evidence and with the aid of computers or other technological advances, identify, locate, and arrest a suspect. This is almost always accomplished without warrants or having to write a report. In fact, many police shows routinely have heroes ignoring report writing, apparently regarding it as not "real police work" (even in the face of a supervisor's direct orders to finish reports), while going off to run down esoteric clues.

The reality is that being a crime fighter is just not that easy. Although it is known that heated superglue gives off a fume that will attach to skin oils on certain objects, this process is nowhere near as effective as depicted in *Beverly Hills Cop II*. As for the computer to which Detective Foley had access, it does exist; however, only since the late 1990s have police agencies had access to such a system, let alone own one. A limited number of police agencies have the luxury of possessing the high-tech tools that are depicted on television shows or in movies; yet, the public receives the impression that all police agencies have these capabilities for solving crimes. Ultimately, these depictions create an ill-informed public with unrealistic expectations.

It is difficult for police officers to be successful when expectations and per-ceptions are beyond reality. This clashing of expectations and reality creates an additional problem for police officers, role conflict, which is becoming especially evident with the adoption of community-oriented policing.

As previously noted, crime fighting tends to be a small part of the officer's role, and as will be demonstrated later in the chapter, will continue to become even smaller under community-oriented policing. Despite this fact, a tremendous amount of emphasis is placed on the crime-fighter role. This can cause much conflict for the police officer, especially when the officer discovers the existence of a variety of roles not associated with crime fighting that demand more of the officer's time. Therefore, a solution is required; however, before one can be reached, a greater understanding of the police role is needed.

● THE CONCEPT OF "ROLE"

Clearly the image of policing versus reality creates problems; however, this has not created nearly as many problems as the real-life role itself. The role of today's police officer is extremely complex, ambiguous, and at times, ambivalent.

Although published more than 25 years ago, the following statement from the 1973 Police Task Force Report still aptly describes the dilemma of today's police officers:

> The role the police officer plays in society is a difficult one; he must clearly understand complex social relationships to be effective. He is not only a part of the community he serves, and a part of the government that provides his formal base of authority, he is also a part of the criminal justice system that determines what course society will pursue to deter lawbreakers or rehabilitate offenders in the interest of public order (p. 9).

Before continuing to examine the police role, it is helpful to clarify what is meant by the term "role." From a sociological perspective, a role generally refers to the position or place an individual holds within the communal social structure. Psychologically, a role refers to those attitudes and beliefs attributed to the position held in the social structure. Although the police role can be examined as a combination of both perspectives, it is probably best viewed as expectation of behaviors and attitudes that society has for its police officers and that officers hold for themselves.

Every day every one of us plays several roles. These roles may include spouse, sibling, student, and employee. When we look at the police role, it is found to be a multitude of roles. In addition to crime fighter, following are examples of the different roles the author recalls having to fulfill on an almost daily basis as a police officer.

Investigator. This generally was the role when a suspected crime was in progress or had taken place. It is in this role that the officer collects information and evidence in hopes of solving the crime.

Order Maintainer. This role often came about as a result of disturbances such as loud parties or unruly juveniles, or when simply having to direct traffic at the scene of an accident.

Social Worker. More times than not, this was the author's main role. On numerous occasions he was called on to check the well-being of an individual, to give a stranded person a ride, to sort out problems at a domestic disturbance, or simply to console a victim of a crime. Although this was a difficult role to accept early in his career, he eventually realized that this was a chief part of a police officer's job.

Medic. This role was assumed when person(s) medical assistance was required and an ambulance had yet to arrive. Although the author never had the experience, several of his colleagues had to deliver or assist in the delivery of a baby.

Legal Adviser. On more than one occasion victims and suspects sought legal advice from the author, such as whether a victim should prosecute or whether a suspect should plead guilty or get a lawyer. A police officer should not offer legal advice, but that never stops people from asking.

Psychologist. Obviously, most police officers are not trained psychologists. Yet, much of what an officer does relies on being psychologically savvy. From calming down a crime victim to talking down a potential jumper, or relieving the fear of individuals who report of voices and people only they can hear and see, the role of psychologist is one of the leading police roles.

Traffic Director. A malfunctioning traffic light, a fire, or an accident all require the police officer to make sure traffic is directed or rerouted in a manner to avoid further problems.

Other roles include report taker, confidant, teacher, student, babysitter, and mechanic—none of which involves crime fighting, per se.

Needless to say, with the variety of roles a police officer must fill there will be conflicts. Understanding these conflicts and why they exist is extremely important to understanding policing.

POLICE-ROLE CONFLICTS

When examining the police role from a conflict standpoint, it is easiest to examine the conflict as a result of police actions. Three primary actions are probably responsible for most conflicts. These actions have been described as **prescribed, preferred,** and **enacted** (Walker, 1999). The conflict arising from the *prescribed* action is a result of what the state's statutes say police *must* do. The *preferred* action arises from what the officer *thinks* should be done. What the officer ultimately does is the *enacted* action. In any given situation, the police officer must respond appropriately. How he or she responds often results in some type of conflict between prescribed, preferred, and enacted behaviors.

■ CASE IN POINT

An officer is dispatched to a local convenience store on a "theft" call. When the officer arrives, the store manager comes out and advises that he has caught a shoplifter. It turns out the shoplifter is a thirteen-year-old child who appears to the officer to be severely undernourished. The items the child attempted to steal: five dollars worth of lunch meat. The owner wants an arrest and prosecution as *prescribed*. The officer would *prefer* to pay for the meat and then release the child to social welfare. What is the *enacted* action? Does the officer face role conflict?

Undoubtedly, the police role is complex and conflict filled. Explanations for why the complexity and conflict of the police role occur and remain include that the police officer must deal with a wide variety of tasks. Although apparently similar tasks continuously arise, each must be handled differently because not every person involved has similar characteristics. Furthermore, with the wide variety of tasks a police officer is asked to perform, a constant conflict occurs as the result of the differences among actions taken for similar as well as for differing tasks. Finally, an overabundance of ambiguity exists for each task because of such factors as the discretionary powers of the police, the ambiguity of the law, differing perceptions and perspectives among cultural and ethnic groups, the involvement (or lack thereof) of social welfare components, and social hypocrisy toward the carrying out of the tasks by police officers. For example, it is common for the public to applaud the handling of a certain task by a police officer when carried out against anyone but themselves.

■ CASE IN POINT

Although going as fast as the rest of traffic, you are stopped for speeding. You ask the officer why you were stopped instead of anyone else. When the officer explains that everyone cannot be stopped, you question why it had to be you. Because you were the one he could catch at the time. It doesn't seem to faze you that you were speeding, only that you got caught instead of someone else.

It can be said that the variety of tasks police are required and requested to perform, along with the ambiguity of the law, policies, and public attitudes, are the main elements of role conflict. However, the conflicts and ambiguity of the police role are not a recent development, which leads to the following questions: Has role conflict always been a problem, or have developments in policing caused this conflict? What should the police role be?

THE DEVELOPMENT OF THE AMERICAN POLICE ROLE

Explanations of the role development of police in the United States have been attempted through a variety of methods. Many authors expend tremendous efforts to provide broad, in-depth, historical analyses by decade, whereas others' strategies include explorations into eras. For example, Kelling and Moore (1991) chose to divide the history of police development into three broad eras: (1) political (1840s to early 1900s, when there were very close ties to politics); (2) reform (1930s to late 1970s, when there was a reaction to politics and increased emphasis was placed on professionalism and crime control); and (3) community (early 1980s to present, when professionalism, providing services, and quality of life direct the police role). Such efforts often provide a wealth of information. However, it is not always easy to understand or follow the police role's development as it pertains to today's role and accompanying problems.

Perhaps today's police role and the causes of the role conflict in the development of American policing are better examined along a police-role/timeline (Figure 1-1). This timeline covers six basic phases or periods of development generalizable across police agencies in America: colonial times, preindustrial America, industrial America, Modern America, crisis America, and community policing. It should be noted that although these periods appear definitive in the timeline, an inherent overlapping should be acknowledged. Remember that change has occurred in slightly different ways and at slightly different times in each of the oldest agencies, whereas others were not formed until relatively far along the timeline. Still, this will serve as a general explanation of the historical development of policing in the United States.

Colonial Times

American policing began with ideas brought over by early European colonists. In examining today's police role, there is no doubt that the influence of this country's English heritage is evident in the structure, function and role of its

FIGURE 1-1 Police-Role Timeline

1700s to 1820s	1820s to 1850s	1850s to 1920s	1920s to 1960s	1960s to 1980s	1980s to Present
Colonial Times	Preindustrial America	Industrial America	Modern America	Crisis America	Community Policing
Reactive Crime Fighter	Reactive Crime Fighter	Proactive Crime Fighter	Mobile Proactive Crime Fighter	Proactive Social Servant	Multi-faceted Problem Solver

Key Highlights

Colonial Times: Results of English heritage; adoption of limited authority and local control; primary law enforcement institutions included the sheriff, constable, and the watch

Preindustrial America: London Metro Police Department created in 1829 and used as a model for Boston, New York, and Philadelphia—homes of America's first "modern" police agencies

Industrial America: Industrial revolution, World War I, the need for a stable police role

Modern America: Technology; Wickersham Commission, O.W. Wilson, and the Federal Bureau of Investigation

Crisis America: Landmark Supreme Court cases, civil unrest, rise in crime, Law Enforcement Assistance Administration; the need for order maintenance, crime fighting, social service

Community Policing: Multifaceted mobile individual expected to be everything to everyone; community policing includes problem solving and community interaction

Note: This timeline was initially designed by the author of this text as a teaching aid for his introductory police course. It is offered to students as one possible explanation for the role conflict in policing as well as a quick, historical reference for the development of policing in the United States.

10

WHAT DO YOU THINK?

The Police Officer: Crime Fighter or Social Worker?

The overwhelming perception of police officers is that they exist to prevent and control criminal behavior. Yet, many studies on the types of calls for police service have found that a majority are unrelated to criminal activities. Instead, most calls for police service can be categorized as service or order maintenance oriented. Examples include the request to quiet a party, remove an improperly parked vehicle, calm a domestic disturbance, or remove an unwanted animal from a residence. Furthermore, a criminally-related call often may require the police officer to be more social service than law enforcement oriented. For example, a police officer is dispatched to a housing complex in response to a neighbor's call that there are several children in an apartment whose parents have not been seen for days. On arrival the officer finds that five children ranging from ages two to seven have spent several days alone with little food and no adult supervision. Is this a criminal situation or a social service situation? In most states it is probably both, but what is the responsibility of the police officer? Despite the fact that police officers handle a variety of calls that are more social service oriented than criminally oriented, citizens and police officers alike refuse to surrender the idea that police officers are primarily crime fighters.

1. Is there a difference between the perceived and real roles of police officers in today's society?
2. If police officers spend more time being "socially" responsive, should their training include more social-service oriented subjects, such as counseling or social psychology? Why or why not?
3. Does the police officer have greater responsibility to find and arrest the parents or to take care of the children?
4. Should police departments attempt to limit or improve their social role?
5. Should police officers be whatever society defines them to be? Why or why not?

police.[1] Although there are a variety of minor observable features, two features of our nation's English heritage dominate today's police, **limited authority** and **local control** (Alpert & Dunham, 1998; Bopp & Schultz, 1972; Walker, 1999).

Limited authority pertains to the fact that each police agency may exercise its police power only within its physical and legal jurisdictions. Both are established

---

[1] At this point in many texts authors would provide an extremely in-depth, historical presentation of policing. It is this author's belief that the majority of *introductory criminal justice* texts provide ample history and it isn't particularly necessary to be repetitious. However, for those students who have never taken an introductory criminal justice course or for those who wish to broaden their historical knowledge, several good sources are noted within and at the end of the chapter.

by federal and state constitutions and statutes. For example, a city police officer has authority to exercise police power within the physical jurisdiction for which the officer is employed or within other jurisdictions where special permission has been granted (i.e., a member of a multijurisdictional task force). Regardless of where, the officer must exercise this power by the laws of the state and the U.S. Constitution.

Limited authority supports local control. The administration and management of a police agency are carried out under the guidance and direction of its governing body—be it a city, county, state, or federal agency. Unless there is a court-mandated reason, interference from an outside authority is seldom, if ever, welcomed by a police agency. In other words, someone from the San Diego, California, Police Department could not tell the Los Angeles Police Department how to operate, nor could the San Diego Police Department legally operate as a police agent outside the confines of San Diego's jurisdiction unless granted special permission by a task force or another police agency with jurisdiction.

These two features have caused the fragmentation of American policing. There are currently more than 15,000 police agencies in America. Each has its own jurisdictional authority and control. This is unlike many centralized European police agencies, which have one authority center for the country and whose officers have much broader police power.

During the colonial period of U.S. development, there were primarily three types of police institutions, all of which were adopted from England: **sheriff, constable,** and **the watch.** The *sheriff,* a position that still exists today, emerged as the most powerful police agent of the time. Although the sheriff's role included countywide jurisdiction for all criminal and civil disturbances, his primary role was that of tax collector for the government. As for his police role, the sheriff was, and is still, considered a **reactive** police agent, responding when summoned.

The *constable,* often referred to as a "little sheriff," was limited to the jurisdiction of a particular town or city. The role of the constable included both criminal and civil matters. Yet, like the sheriff, the constable was mainly used to collect taxes. He, too, was a **reactive** police agent.

The only early police institution from which the role of today's police officer could truly be said to be derived was *the watch.* The watch was a local level police entity whose main concern was criminal activity. The watch was initially a voluntary organization of concerned citizens who would stand guard on selected corners where they could be available if needed. The initial role of the watch was to stop crime before it happened, to provide **proactive** protection. Yet, its function, too, was more nearly reactive than proactive.

Regardless of what was expected from these early police institutions, little was received. One of the greatest problems was reaction versus proaction. As noted, only the watch could have been considered proactive in policing even though, in reality, it was often merely reactive. Unfortunately, this really did not make much difference then as these early police institutions were never very effective anyway. They were ill equipped, received no training, were corrupt, and were simply unable to provide adequately what was really expected—order maintenance

(Bopp & Schultz, 1972). All this led to an unwillingness to serve and citizen disrespect. It also created major confusion with regard to the police role: reactive crime fighters, proactive crime fighters, order maintainers, or civil servants.

Preindustrial America

The modernization of policing and the development of the police role in the United States did not really begin until 1833. From 1833 through 1854, the United States began to see the birth of its first real police departments in Boston, New York, and Philadelphia. Considering the general lack of knowledge in the United States about policing at this time, the development of policing required copying an existing model. The model chosen was found in England in the form of the **London Metropolitan Police Department.**

The recognition that the existing police structure could no longer be counted on lead to increased social disorder and crime in England in the early 1800s. Change was necessary, and it was up to English legislators to provide a solution. One legislator believed he had. Sir Robert Peel offered legislation, that if passed, would establish a new police force in England. In 1829 the legislation was passed, and the London Metropolitan Police Department (LMPD) was created. Its main objective was **crime prevention,** using a strategy referred to as **preventive patrol.** The following are the fundamental principles that Sir Peel promoted for the organization and development of the LMPD:

1. The police must be stable, efficient, and militarily organized under government control.
2. The absence of crime will best prove the efficiency of the police.
3. Crime news must be widely distributed.
4. Territorial distribution of the force by hours and shifts must be accomplished.
5. No quality is more indispensable to an officer than a perfect command of temper; a quiet, determined manner has more effect than violent action.
6. Good appearance commands respect.
7. Proper securing and training of personnel lies at the root of police efficiency.
8. Public safety requires that every policeman be given a number.
9. Police headquarters should be centrally located and easily accessible to all the people.
10. Policemen should be appointed on the probation basis.
11. Police records are necessary for the correct distribution of police strength.
12. The best way to select men is to "size them up" and then find out what their neighbors think of them (Bopp & Schultz, 1972, pp. 30–31).

More than 170 years later, Peel's principles are still valid and considered an integral part of today's policing and the police role. Furthermore, it has been suggested that at least one of Peel's principles "could be considered the seed of community policing" (*Understanding Community Policing,* 1994, p. 7).

With the existence of the LMPD, the birth of what would become modern American policing began to occur. It would not be easy; corruption, poor training, and politics would make the birth of policing difficult. Yet, considering the problems of earlier attempts at American policing, America had begun to develop a policing entity that was expected to be proactive.

Industrial America

During the 1850s to 1920s American policing was in its infancy. In general, the reception to police development was good. However, this period produced an extremely politically active climate in this country, particularly in policing.

Every major aspect of policing—personnel standards, recruitment, policy priorities, and corruption—was tremendously influenced by politics. In some cases, this is still true today, particularly in the area of personnel.

During this phase of police development, personnel standards were virtually nonexistent. Jobs were often obtained through political contacts, or **patronage.** There was no official training; a man was handed a gun and a badge and was sent out to work. Job stability and security depended upon the political regime in power at the time. Every time the political scene changed, so did a large portion of the police personnel. Therefore, the politics in policing provided very little positive reinforcement to individuals who thought about becoming a police officer unless they were associated with the political party in control. Yet, there was one broadly applicable positive note. In comparison to other types of unskilled jobs available at the time, the pay for policing was generally high. So, when an opportunity arose for an individual to become a police officer, regardless of how short a period the job might be held, it was often considered worthwhile.

The work itself in those days was severely limited.

> At first, the police had only a fuzzy idea of what it was they were supposed to do. The maintenance of order was probably the most important task of the policeman, and he did it by physically walking his beat and keep[ing] a watchful eye (McDowell, 1985, p. 169).

Yet, irresponsibility, public disrespect, a lack of professionalism, and corruption made it difficult to establish any clear-cut role for the police officer. One of the biggest problems was **corruption,** which was considered a direct product of political interference and influence (Bopp & Schultz, 1972; Walker, 1999).

Although corruption was fairly widespread, it was primarily found in two broad areas: **nonenforcement of the law** and **internal personnel practices.** It was not unusual for a police officer to avoid enforcing certain laws for a tavern because of the owner's political affiliations or the payoffs he made. Neither was it unusual for an officer to buy a promotion.

Needless to say, the 1850s to 1920s was not a simple period for the development of policing. Role development was severely hampered simply because what was expected of the police or who would be around long enough to fulfill the role was uncertain. Serious changes were needed if police officers were going to become useful to the whole community and not just to politicians.

Early 1900s Police Department. (Courtesy of the Denver, Colorado, Police Department)

Modern America

It was not until the late 1920s, up through the 1960s, that the United States began to see a tremendous change in policing as well as role development. Several factors deserve recognition for assisting or making the changes that occurred. The following are examples of the factors that are believed to have been among the most influential.

Technology

Some of the greatest changes in policing occurred through technological innovations. The common usage of the telephone, patrol cars, and the two-way radio aided a transformation that would forever change policing. These changes allowed the "foot officer," whose response and duties were limited, to provide quicker response and cover a larger area by vehicle. The ability for the public to contact the police was enhanced. Unfortunately, human relations skills, which are a very important part of policing, would suffer (Alpert & Dunham, 1998; Bopp & Schultz, 1972; Walker, 1999). Before all the technological innovations, there was greater interaction between the public and the police on an everyday basis on terms that did not necessarily require police action. Technology removed the police from daily nonrequisite interaction with the community and created an "only when needed" contact, which hampered the development of strong human relations skills (Bouza, 1990; Walker, 1999).

Denver, Colorado, Police Department's first motorized police wagon (1909). (Courtesy of the Denver, Colorado, Police Department)

The Wickersham Commission

By the late 1920s there were a variety of problems prevalent in policing. Two of the greatest problems were brutality and corruption. To study the current situation and possibly to provide a remedy, a national commission was formed. Named after its chairman, former U.S. Attorney General George Wickersham, the Wickersham Commission (1929) examined the numerous policing problems, in particular brutality and corruption. Although the commission would provide numerous recommendations, its overall conclusions were that better educated police personnel were required. The findings and recommendations of this commission would bring a national focus to improving the quality of police personnel.

O.W. Wilson

If there is one person who could be identified as a major contributing influence to police changes in the United States that person would have to be Orlando Winfield Wilson. O.W. Wilson was and is still considered, both nationally and internationally, a leading expert on police administration. Wilson's career began in 1921 as a police officer in Berkeley, California, and lasted close to fifty years. During Wilson's career, he was a police chief in Wichita, Kansas (1928–1939), a professor and dean of the school of criminology at Berkeley (1939–1960), and he finished his career as the superintendent of the Chicago Police Department (1961–1970). Wilson's experience and knowledge made a powerful impact on policing. As an author of one of the first textbooks on police administration, which is still used today in some college police administration classes, Wilson offered a variety of innovative organizational and administrative concepts. Although many of these concepts were initially controversial, some even radical, many are widely used today. For example, the one-man patrol car concept began with Wilson. However, it should be noted that Wilson might not have been as influential if August Vollmer had not been his mentor.

Vollmer was the first police chief to initiate and require actual training courses for police officers. He was also the first chief to push for and hire individuals with some college experience. Vollmer was one of the driving forces for professionalization of policing (Dantzker, 1997). His leadership and ideas inspired Wilson to become a key police motivator and innovator. (Further discussion of Vollmer is provided later in the text in the section on professionalism.)

The Federal Bureau of Investigation

Technology, commissions, and individuals would all have impact on police change. An unexpected source of change for local policing came as a result of changes in a federal police agency. The Federal Bureau of Investigation (FBI) became the first law enforcement agency, at any level, to require all of its recruits to possess a minimum of a bachelor's degree. By adopting this new requirement, the FBI became a strong advocate for police change. The requirement of a college degree was designed to bring a professionalism to law enforcement that did not exist at any level. Furthermore, extensive training and technological developments, particularly for investigations, became an FBI trademark. These have had, and continue to have, impact on municipal and state agencies who request FBI assistance in training and investigations.

Despite the training and technological advances occurring in policing, it appears that an overall catalyst for change in policing has been education. While the FBI was the first police agency to emphasize the need of a college degree, California became the first state to emphasize education for police. In 1931 San Jose State University created the first full-fledged undergraduate program in law enforcement. However, education would not be the only element to promote change.

Through the 1940s and 1950s, a slow change in the police role continued to occur. Education was emphasized. "Professionalism" was a new buzzword. The Los Angeles Police Department, under Chief William Parker, became a national model for "professional" police departments. The professionalism of this agency was first introduced to the national public through the television series *Dragnet,* which attempted to accurately depict how Los Angeles police officers operated. Furthermore, recruitment standards were raised and training was upgraded. Policing and the roles of the police officer were beginning to take shape. The role of a well-trained, educated crime fighter was becoming recognizable.

Crisis America

"Drugs, sex, and rock–roll!"; "Hell no, we won't go!"; and "Make love, not war!" were slogans from a period that would introduce various changes. In the 1960s a variety of events affected society and created a need for change. In particular, these events affected policing and the police role.

The major events of this period that directly influenced policing included civil unrest caused by political and social issues such as the Vietnam War and the civil rights movement as well as a series of Supreme Court cases such as *Mapp* v. *Ohio* and *Miranda* v. *Arizona*. All of these events, including rapidly increasing crime rates, eventually required changes in police behavior and performance. The police role had to become more proactive and community minded.

Society was changing. Police officers were required to react to a "new public" that refused to accept the police role, which was viewed as a reactive agent of the government. Although the societal changes were providing enough problems for policing, it was the decisions of the U.S. Supreme Court that served as guidelines for behavior and prompted new expectations of policing and of police officers.

Often referred to as the **"due process"** revolution, the U.S. Supreme Court handed down a series of decisions that were believed to change the police role forever: *Mapp* v. *Ohio* (1961) required police officers to have a search warrant, based on probable cause, before they could execute a search of a private home or business; *Escobedo* v. *Illinois* (1964) required police officers to permit individuals access to legal counsel when questioning went from informative to accusatory, and *Miranda* v. *Arizona* (1966) required police to advise suspected criminals of their constitutional rights, in particular, the right against self-incrimination.

The belief at that time was that the Supreme Court had limited the ability of the police to do their job and was siding with the criminal. This debate continues today. Although it does not appear that policing was negatively affected, these decisions had a tremendous impact on how the police approached their crime-fighter or law-enforcer role. The changes in criminal law and procedures were not the only changes to impact police behavior.

Civil strife also affected the police role. The 1960s were a time of civil unrest. Riots in New York, Los Angeles, Detroit, and Chicago demonstrated the inability of police to handle civil disorder. (This inability arose again in 1992 after four Los Angeles police officers were found not guilty of the use of excessive force against a black motorist. The Rodney King–LAPD verdict sparked several days of rioting in Los Angeles, San Francisco, and Las Vegas against which the police appeared ill prepared.) The need and ability for order maintenance became an imperative part of the police role.

Along with the civil unrest came the question of discrimination. As with the handling of civil unrest, racial discrimination by police officers was an area in which the public demanded change. To address these two problems, several commissions were created, the most prominent were the **President's Commission on Law Enforcement and Administration of Justice** (1965–1967) and the **National Advisory Commission on Civil Disorders** (1967–1968).

In response to commission reports, Congress created the **Law Enforcement Assistance Administration** (LEAA) in 1968 to provide funding for improvements to policing in several areas. The area that received the most attention was education. Out of LEAA came the **Law Enforcement Education Program** (LEEP). LEEP encouraged criminal justice personnel, particularly police officers, to obtain college degrees by providing funds to individuals and academic institutions.

Next to education, one of the most important outcomes of LEAA was assistance to police-related research. There were, and remain, several areas in policing about which little is known for which research was, and still is, the best way to obtain knowledge and insight. Early research included projects such as **The Kansas City Preventive Patrol Experiment,** which was touted as one of the first field experiments on the use of randomized patrol. Its findings indicated that random patrol had little influence or impact on crime or public attitudes (Kelling, Pate, Dieckman, & Brown, 1974). The **Kansas City Police Department Response Time Analysis** examined the utility and value of rapid response by police to calls for service. Its findings suggested that in a majority of cases it made no difference how quickly the police arrived (no author, 1980) **Differential Police Response Strategies** focused on a variety of response strategies by the Birmingham, Alabama, Police Department and found that certain alternatives were successful (Farmer, 1981). **The Criminal Investigation Process** studied methods to improve investigative techniques and processes (Greenwood & Peterselia, 1975). Other research projects made possible because of LEAA funding include the San Diego Police Department one officer versus two officers study; the Newark, New Jersey, and Flint, Michigan, foot patrol experiments; and the policewomen on patrol experiment, which was the first attempt at having women police officers on patrol.

Overall, LEAA was well intentioned and provided building blocks for future police change. Unfortunately, lack of government funds led to its demise. There is still need for funding of items that assist police change, such as research and education. Although some funding sources still exist, such as the Department of Justice, the Police Foundation, the Police Executive Research Forum, and the National Institute of Justice, they are generally limited and usually geared toward specific problems such as the money currently being allocated throughout the country, at all levels of policing, to battle the growing drug problem and to implement community policing.

Policing made it through the 1960s and 1970s with a relatively new and more stable idea of its role. During the remainder of the 1970s, policing saw the growth of police unionism, higher educational requirements, and affirmative action in hiring. In addition, a number of police organizations arose in an effort to assist in improving policing. These groups include the Police Foundation, the Police Executive Research Forum, the National Organization of Black Law Enforcement Executives, and the International Association of Chiefs of Police (*Understanding Community Policing,* 1994).

Along with all the other changes, policing also saw a transition in the police role. Crime fighting was often no longer the primary activity simply because society required more from its police than being crime fighters. The growing need for the police to be social service- and order maintenance oriented was imperative to society and the police role.

From the 1970s through the 1980s police development was somewhat smoother. The 1980s should be noted for technological advances such as mobile data computers, fingerprint computers, and lasers and for changes in the law that slightly loosened the behavioral expectations set during the due process revolution, such as *U.S.* v. *Leon* (1984), in which the court allowed the admittance of evidence obtained by a warrant believed to be valid (this has become known as the good faith exception). Furthermore, during the 1980s policing began to accept community policing, a concept that some argue is reminiscent of the early days of policing (*Understanding Community Policing*, 1994), whereas others look at it as a new and wondrous idea.

Community Policing

"Regardless of how one experiences it, something is happening, and this 'something' is an attempt to rethink and restructure the role of police in society" (Rosenbaum, 1998, p. 3). This statement refers to moving away from the traditional, reactive police officer to a proactive, problem-solving police officer who works closely with the public to improve the quality of life in a community. This movement is most often referred to as community policing.

Although the modern concept of community policing began in the early 1980s, the most prolific movement began in September 1994 when President Clinton gave approval to the Violent Crime Control and Law Enforcement Act (Maguire, Snipes, Uchida, & Townsend, 1998). More than nine billion dollars would be allocated to the "Cops on the Beat" program to assist in placing 100,000 new officers on the street throughout the United States by the year 2000. This started a rush by many police agencies to submit grant proposals to a newly created community-policing office in an effort to receive a piece of the financial pie under the banner of implementing community policing.

The basic premise behind community policing is to place police officers in a position to better interact with the public in a cooperative effort to improve the community and services provided by the police organization. It requires the police role to become more of a problem solver. Despite the fact that it was originally touted as a philosophical concept that would require serious changes in police organization, structure, and approach (Trojanowicz, Kappeler, Gaines, & Bucqueroux, 1998), it currently appears to be more project driven than concept driven. The result has been the inability to provide a commonly accepted definition and process of community policing. However, this has not impeded many police agencies from attaining funding to create and implement some form of community policing. Because the position taken in this text is that a majority of today's community policing practices are more approach or program oriented than concept oriented, additional discussion is provided in Chapter 8.

Crime fighter, social servant, or problem solver? Considering the number of changes policing has seen since its modern-day inception, obviously the police role has changed as well. This role has gone from being a simple, one-dimensional political appointee to a multifaceted, educated, complex individual. Today, the police role continues to expand. As the role expansion continues, the role conflict grows. Because role conflict adds to the ambiguity and ambivalence of police officers, controlling the police role becomes imperative to policing and society, especially in light of community policing.

It can be said that the police role is shaped through a variety of **social, political, legal,** and **administrative** factors (Alpert & Dunham, 1998; Broderick, 1987). Control of these factors is difficult. One possible reason so much conflict

Today's police officers must be everything from law enforcers to public relations specialists. (Courtesy of the Scottsdale, Arizona, Police Department)

exists and control is so difficult stems from the fact that police are expected to be society's number one means of human control, whereas in earlier times other entities such as the church, school, and the family were expected to take an equal part in controlling human behavior. Despite the ideals of community policing and its effort to reinstate other entities of human control, the reality remains that the police are relied on as the first line of control. Unfortunately, policing is limited in its capacity to control others' behavior. Policing is just one part of a complex societal behavior system. Other components of the criminal justice system, our political system, the educational system, and the social welfare system should be held just as responsible for public behavior as policing (Walker, 1999). Yet, policing is expected to shoulder the burden, to be everything to everyone. The reality is that such a thing is just not possible. Therefore, a solution is required.

CONTROLLING THE POLICE ROLE

The most obvious solution to controlling the police role is simply to define it. Through legislative mandate and agency policies, a clarification as to what is expected and required from policing can be made. Then, police officers need to understand their role. This point is well supported. The 1973 Police Task Force Report stated, "Every police agency immediately should take steps to insure that every officer has an understanding of his role, and an awareness of the culture of the community where he works" (p. 34). To meet this need, the task force recommended the following:

1. The procedure for developing policy regarding the police role should involve officers of the basic rank, first-line officers, and middle managers. Every police employee should receive written policy defining the police role.

2. Explicit instruction in the police role and community culture should be provided in all recruit and in-service training.

3. The philosophy behind the defined police role should be a part of all instruction and direction given to officers.

4. Middle managers and first-line supervisors should receive training in the police role and thereafter continually reinforce those principles by example and by direction of those they supervise.

5. Methods of routinely evaluating individual officer performance should take into account all activities performed within the context of the defined role. Promotion and other incentives should be based on total performance within the defined role rather than on any isolated aspect of that role (p. 34).

Although the commission's recommendations are more than twenty-five years old, they are still quite applicable to many of today's police agencies. These appear particularly relevant and applicable to community policing. Whether through traditional or community-oriented policing, it seems that once expectations and the role are defined, and the police understand them, public education is required.

Again relying upon statements from the 1973 Police Task Force Report that are applicable today, "Every police agency immediately should establish programs to inform the public of the agency's defined role" (p. 38). The task force suggested using such programs as classroom presentations in public and private schools, participation in classes at the collegiate level, officer participation in youth programs, speaking engagements to civic and business groups, and writing and distributing an annual report indicating the agencies' objectives and priorities. Today, many of these programs do exist as part of the community-policing effort. Whether any of these programs are specifically police-role oriented or successful, however, still remains unclear.

A lack of police-role clarification for both the police and the public will continue to cause problems. Public misunderstanding, role conflict, and problems in police management will continue. Therefore, it is important to clarify and establish the police role. Yet, role definition is just one possible solution for controlling role conflict.

A variety of solutions have been offered to assist in eliminating the police-role conflict. As previously noted, formal policy statements from police agencies in the form of standard operating procedures (SOPs) or general orders (GOs), which describe how an officer should handle the many tasks encountered, would help place limitations on role conflict.

▮ CASE IN POINT

Domestic violence in this country is on the rise and police agencies are expected to do more today than in previous years. In the past, a solution to the problem was often left to the discretion of the individual police officer. This is changing. Several police agencies have adopted policies, in conjunction with state laws, that require a specific action by the police officer in given situations, such as an arrest of the spouse who assaults the other spouse—even when the victim does not want to press charges. This type of policy leaves little room for discretion and limits the role conflict the officer might face—the question of which role should prevail, law enforcement or social worker, is eliminated.

Role specialization has also been offered as a means to eliminate role conflict. Assigning officers to handle only tasks falling within their area of specialization (like narcotics or vice) could alleviate several role problems simply because the number of tasks the officer would need to perform are limited, thus limiting the number of roles the officer must fill. Educating the public as to what police officers can and cannot do, along with improved officer training, could have a positive effect on the police-role conflict. When the public is well informed as to what the police officer can and cannot do, their expectations are reasonable and they require less from a police officer. Additionally, a well-trained officer may deal better with the diversity of roles because he or she possesses more tools and skills for solving the numerous problems and tasks the officer faces on a daily basis. Finally, a complete acceptance and implementation of community policing may assist in alleviating many role problems; however, it may just increase the role conflict. Overall, eliminating the role conflict for police officers will not be easy, nor does it appear to be simple. Changes in the law, better trained and educated police officers, and a well-informed and cooperative public will go a long

"I know what you think, Marmaduke, but there's more to being a policeman than eating donuts."

(Marmaduke reprinted by permission of United Feature Syndicate, Inc.)

way toward limiting the role conflict. Otherwise, policing will continue to be perceived as society's first line of defense against chaos, something other than it truly is.

SUMMARY

The perception of many citizens and police officers is that the role of the police officer is that of a crime fighter. Although, in reality, crime fighting is often a small part of the police officer's role, this image is difficult to eliminate. Television shows, movies, news sources, and the police themselves can be blamed for enhancing this image. However, this image must be revised so that public expectations become more realistic and that role conflicts for officers become less prevalent.

A better understanding of the role problem in policing can be gained by examining police growth in this country through a timeline that shows how the police role began as reactive crime fighting and is develop into a multifaceted, complex role despite the overwhelming perception that police officers are primarily crime fighters. Controlling this role is important in alleviating conflict. Role definition, clear departmental policies, and role specialization have been suggested as possible methods for controlling role conflict.

In conclusion, policing has undergone numerous changes since its modern-day inception. These changes have undoubtedly affected the police role. It is still not completely clear whether the police officer's role is that of crime fighter or agent of social control. In most cases, police officers are both and more. The fact is that the police role has become one of complexity, ambiguity, and ambivalence, especially with regard to community policing. One point is certain: further changes are imminent; as society changes so will the police role.

DO YOU KNOW . . .

1. How to solve the image versus real life problem? Do we really want to solve it? Why?
2. Why policing as practiced in Europe is not practiced in the United States? What problems would arise if this method was implemented here?
3. How it is that the insight of an English legislator, more than 170 years ago, is still applicable today? Or, is it? How well have these principles been followed?
4. What additional roles, from those listed in the chapter, a police officer fulfills?
5. Whether the community-policing era appears to provide a clearer chance at rectifying the role problem of police officers?
6. Whether the role conflict of policing can ever be eliminated? What would it take to accomplish this task?

REFERENCES

Alpert, G.P., & Dunham, R.G. (1998). *Policing in urban America* (3rd ed.). Prospect Heights, IL: Waveland Press.

Bopp, W.J., & Schultz, D.O. (1972). *A short history of American law enforcement*. Springfield, IL: Charles C. Thomas, Publishers.

Bouza, A.V. (1990). *The police mystique*. New York: Plenum Press.

Broderick, J.J. (1987). *Police in a time of change*. Prospect Heights, IL: Waveland Press.

Cordner, G.W. (1989). The police on patrol. In D.J. Kenney (Ed.), *Police and policing* (pp.60–71). New York: Praeger Publishers.

Dantzker, M.L. (1997). Being a police officer: Part of a profession? In M.L. Dantzker (Ed.), *Contemporary policing: personnel, issues and trends* (pp. 75–98). Newton, MA: Butterworth-Heinemann.

Farmer, M.T. (Ed.). (1981). *Differential Police Response Strategies*. Washington, D.C.: Police Executive Research Forum.

Greene, R.R., & Mastrofski, S.D. (Eds.). (1991). *Community policing, rhetoric or reality*. New York: Praeger Publishers.

Greenwood, P.W., & Petersilia, J. (1975). *The Criminal Investigation Process—Volume I: Summary and policy implications*. Santa Monica, CA: Rand Corporation.

Hernandez, J., Jr. (1989). *The Custer syndrome*. Salem, WI: Sheffield Publishing Company.

Hunt, R.G., McCadden, K.S., & Mordaunt, T.J. (1983). Police roles: Context and conflict. *Journal of Police Science and Administration, 11*(2), 175–184.

Kansas City Police Department Response Time Analysis—Volume II, Part I: Crime analysis. (1980). Washington, D.C.: U.S. Government Printing Office.

Kelling, G.L., & Moore, M.H. (1991). From political to reform to community: The evolving strategy of police. In J.R. Greene & S.D. Mastrofski (Eds.), *Community policing, rhetoric or reality* (pp. 3–25). New York: Praeger Publishers.

Kelling, G.L., Pate, A., Dieckman, D., & Brown, C.E. (1974). *The Kansas City Preventive Patrol Experiment: A technical report*. Washington, D.C.: Police Foundation.

Kenney, D.J. (Ed.). (1989). *Police and policing*. New York: Praeger Publishers.

Maguire, E.R., Snipes, J.B., Uchida, C.D., & Townsend, M. (1998). Counting cops: Estimating the number of police departments and police officers in the U.S.A. *Policing: An International Journal of Police Strategies & Management, 21*(1), pp. 97–120.

McDowell, C.P. (1984). *Criminal justice: A community relations approach*. Cincinnati, OH: Anderson Publishing Company.

Police Task Force Report. (1973). Washington, D.C.: National Advisory Commission on Criminal Justice Standards and Goals.

Rosenbaum, D.P. (1998). The changing role of the police. In Jean-Paul Brodeur (Ed.), *How to recognize good policing: Problems and issues* (pp. 3–29). Thousand Oaks, CA: Sage Publications.

Trojanowicz, R., Kappeler, V.E., Gaines, L.K., & Bucqueroux, B. (1998). *Community policing: A contemporary perspective*, (2nd ed.). Cincinnati, OH: Anderson Publishing Company.

Understanding community policing: A framework for action. (1994). Washington, D.C.: Bureau of Justice Assistance.

Walker, J.T. (1997). Re-blueing the police: Technological changes and law enforcement practices. In M.L. Dantzker (Ed.), *Contemporary policing: personnel, issues and trends* (pp. 257–276). Newton, MA: Butterworth-Heinemann.

Walker, S. (1999). *The police in America* (3rd ed.). New York: McGraw-Hill.

FROM A SYSTEMS
PERSPECTIVE

When a student ventures into the study of criminal justice, one of the first concepts introduced is the criminal justice system. This system is generally described as a threecomponent system: courts, corrections, and police. Yet, seldom is the concept of a **system** discussed. To be able to understand fully any system, especially one as complex as the criminal justice system, familiarity with systems is useful.

WHAT IS A SYSTEM?

Although there are a variety of formal definitions of system, the underlying basis of each remains consistent and can simply be stated as *a set of interrelated components working separately or together toward a specific goal, usually within a complex setting* (Gannon, 1979; Luthans, 1985). Examples of systems are the electrical system of a motorized vehicle, the respiratory system of the human body, and the criminal justice system of the United States.

In examining criminal justice from a systems approach, one becomes aware of the complexity when introduced to the concept of **subsystems.** A subsystem is often a system, too. The police are a subsystem of the criminal justice system. Yet, when the focus is directed on the police subsystem, it may be viewed as a complex system of its own, composed of subsystems (Figure 2-1). In the police system, the subsystems are often referred to as **levels of policing.** The levels of policing, or subsystems, are labeled "federal," "state," and "local." Each of these subsystems can be viewed as an independent system, too, or in other words, "cogs within cogs."

Examination of the criminal justice system reveals that the police subsystem is its largest subsystem, employing close to one million full-time personnel in 1996 (Reaves, 1997; Reaves & Goldberg, 1998). Among the police subsystems, the local level is statistically the largest, based on personnel, employing more than 600,000 sworn officers compared to approximately 55,000 sworn state officers and the 43,000+ federal personnel with police/investigatory power (Reaves, 1997; Reaves & Goldberg, 1998) (see Table 2-1).

FIGURE 2-1 The Police System

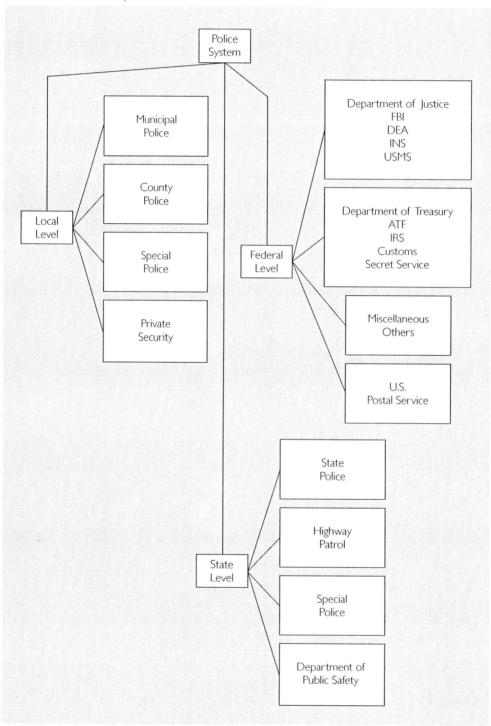

TABLE 2-1

Personnel Employed in the Police System, by Level, 1996

Level	Total	Full-Time Sworn	Full-Time Nonsworn
Local	838,236	608,948	231,276
State	83,742	54,587	29,155
Federal	74,908	43,908	30,585

*Sources: Reaves, B.A., & Goldberg, A.L. (1998). *Census of State and Local Law Enforcement Agencies, 1996*. Washington, D.C.: U.S. Department of Justice. Reaves, B.A. (1997). *Federal Law Enforcement Officers, 1996*. Washington, D.C.: U.S. Department of Justice.

WHY STUDY POLICING FROM A SYSTEMS PERSPECTIVE?

Some students may wonder why policing should be studied from a systems perspective. Depending on the source,[1] there are approximately 14,000 to 18,000 police agencies in the United States, including federal agencies, with policing/law enforcement powers. Each is an autonomous entity with a jurisdictional responsibility that often may overlap into another agency's jurisdiction. Trying to study each agency is impossible, and despite the autonomy, there are enough similarities among many agencies to categorize them. Fortunately, a natural categorization is available by government type, or as suggested earlier, by levels. Placing these levels into a systems perspective allows for better comparisons and a clearer understanding of policing in the United States today. Furthermore, because it has been observed that the average criminal justice student often appears to view policing as a single-dimensional component of the criminal justice system, a systems perspective helps clarify the multidimensional nature of the police in the United States.

THE LOCAL SYSTEM

As previously noted, based on the statistics and its complex role within the police system, as well as in society, the local-level subsystem is, statistically, by far the dominant police subsystem. Viewed as a system, the local level of policing is composed of four subsystems, or types of agencies: municipal (often referred to as local), county (or sheriff's department), special police (or districts), and private security. Of the four, the municipal and county systems usually receive the most attention in textbooks and from the media. Statistically, the municipal system is far superior in scope and size compared with the others.

---

[1]Several sources contain information about police agencies in the United States. Three primary sources identified by Maguire et al. (1998) are the Uniform Crime Reports, the Directory Survey of Law Enforcement Agencies, and the Justice Expenditure and Employment series (p. 104). A fourth possible source is the National Directory of Law Enforcement Administrators.

Municipal Systems

What exactly is a municipal police system? A municipal police system is a police unit established by a city, town, or municipality, commonly referred to as a "police department." It can be urban, suburban, or rural, depending on its location and surroundings. Urban police departments often provide services to extremely populated but geographically contained areas. Probably the best known and largest urban police department in the United States is the New York City Police Department, which in 1996 employed more than 36,000 sworn officers (Reaves & Goldberg, 1998). The remaining top five urban police departments, by number of officers employed, serve Chicago, Illinois; Los Angeles, California; Philadelphia, Pennsylvania; and Houston, Texas.

A suburban police department generally serves communities located directly outside the jurisdiction of an urban police department. In many cases, the suburban police agency provides services to what may be considered a "mini city" compared with bigger urban areas.

■ CASE IN POINT

The Chicago, Illinois, Police Department is the second largest urban police department in the country. It anchors Cook County, which has approximately 128 police agencies. Many of these agencies are referred to as suburban departments because they are located outside the Chicago city limits, yet they have attributes similar to Chicago but on a lesser scale. Palatine, Cicero, Skokie, Oak Park, and La Grange are a few of Chicago's suburban cities that have urban traits, in that they support both business and residential activities. They also tend to have many of the same problems as Chicago, such as gangs, burglaries, robberies, drugs, and domestic disturbance, only in less volume.

Finally, a rural municipal police agency serves a jurisdiction geographically removed from both the urban and suburban settings, often perceived as "the country." In most cases, these are very small departments (fewer than 10 sworn officers) that serve a population that is primarily residential in nature.

Regardless of whether the agency is urban, suburban, or rural, the basic municipal agency typically delivers four primary types of services: law enforcement, crime prevention, order maintenance, and social services (each of which is discussed in greater detail in Chapter 3).

Although not usually viewed in this manner, the divisional breakdown of a municipal agency is, in reality, a variety of subsystems often called "divisions." Each has its own identity and function. These divisions may include, but are not limited to, patrol, investigations, traffic, and communications.

■ CASE IN POINT

The Tempe, Arizona, Police Department is organized into four divisions: patrol, investigations, support, and technical. The patrol division includes four geographically oriented patrol bureaus, special services (mounted and K-9), the crime prevention unit, and the jail. The investigations division houses criminal investigations, traffic, and special enforcement (e.g., narcotics). Support services include professional development, communications, internal affairs, and VIPs (volunteers in policing). Finally, the technical division is comprised of records and information management.

Each division is expected to exist on its own yet work cooperatively with other divisions. For example, the traffic division is assigned tasks associated with traffic enforcement; traffic officers, rather than patrol officers, will be assigned to work an accident. This relieves patrol officers to do tasks related to their specific duties. If traffic officers need assistance, patrol officers often assist. However, this cooperative effort does not always work as well as one might expect. Sometimes cooperation is almost impossible to find, even within the same division.

■ CASE IN POINT

Both the patrol and criminal investigations divisions of the municipal agency have distinct duties. The patrol officer is generally the first responder to a call for police. If an offense has been committed, the patrol officer makes a report and submits it to the appropriate investigator. Once this has been accomplished, the patrol officer seldom gets any feedback as to how the investigation is proceeding. In general, once an investigator gets that report, the case is now his or hers and he or she does not ask for further input from the patrol officer who was the first responder. One would think the investigator would want all the help he or she could get to solve the crime; however, this is rarely the case.

Although the types of services often separate municipal agencies from county agencies, this in itself does not dictate the attention that municipal agencies receive or their domination of the local level of the police system. In 1996, municipal agencies employed more than 385,000 full-time sworn officers (among 13,000+ agencies), compared with approximately 152,000 sworn officers among 3000+ county or sheriff's departments (Reaves & Goldberg, 1998). Overall, statistically and service related, municipal systems are the dominant portion of the local level subsystem. However, county agencies cannot be ignored.

County Systems

The second largest subsystem in the local level police system is composed of the county systems, or what are often referred to as "sheriffs' departments." It should be noted that some areas actually have agencies referred to as "county agencies" that are not sheriffs' departments but municipal-like police agencies that serve a county jurisdiction. These may be independent entities or fall under the jurisdiction of a sheriff's department.

■ CASE IN POINT

The Chatham County, Georgia, Police Department provides full police services to unincorporated areas of the county, whereas the Chatham County Sheriff's Department primarily provides correctional, judicial, and civil services. The Cook County, Illinois, Police Department provides general patrol services to unincorporated areas of the county and is under the administrative jurisdiction of the sheriff's department.

In 1996, 3097 "county-equivalent entities" (Reaves & Goldberg, 1998, p. 10) were served by a sheriff. "One sheriff serves the five counties that make up New York City" (Reaves & Goldberg, 1998, p. 10). Areas not served by a sheriff's department include Alaska (27 boroughs), the District of Columbia, Hawaii's five counties, and one county in Kansas (Reaves & Goldberg, 1998). Although many county agencies may offer services similar to those of a municipal agency, they frequently differ dramatically from municipal agencies in several areas.

The first major difference is that of the top administrator. In municipal systems the agency head is usually called the chief, superintendent, or commissioner. Regardless of the title, this individual is generally appointed by some member(s) of the governing body of the jurisdictional area of the agency. How long the top police administrator stays in that position depends heavily upon how impressed the appointing personnel remains with this individual and his or her operation of the police agency.

Conversely, the top administrator of a county agency is often the sheriff. Except for a few sheriffs who are appointed, the majority are elected by general, popular vote. A sheriff's tenure in office is generally four years and he or she usually can only be removed by a recall vote. The fact that most sheriffs must be politicians, court a political party's nomination, and win popular elections may have influence on their role as police administrators. The sheriff's position also differs from the status of a municipal top administrator's in that it is a position mandated by many states' constitutions.

A second major difference between municipal and county agencies reflects the scope of services provided. A municipal agency is relied upon to deliver in a well-rounded manner the four basic services previously noted, whereas the services of the county agency are sometimes much more limited.

A research study from the 1970s identified four models of sheriffs' departments (Brown, 1978), in terms of services offered, that still appear appropriate today. The rarest type of sheriff's department is the **full-service** model. This model provides all the same basic services as the municipal agency as well as judicial, civil, and correctional services. An example of this model is the Los Angeles County, California, Sheriff's Department in which services are divided among patrol, investigations, jail operations, and court operations. Using data from 1996, among the 25 largest sheriffs' departments (by number of sworn personnel), 16 could be classified as full-service agencies because some percentage of their officers' areas of duty include patrol, investigations, jail operations, and court operations (see Table 2-2). In most cases, the patrol and investigatory services are only provided to unincorporated parts of the county or to cities that have no municipal agency.

■ CASE IN POINT

In May 1998 the Clay County, Missouri, Sheriff's Department began supplying services to the city of Avondale after its town board disbanded the city's police force (two full-time and eleven part-time employees). Additional assistance would be received from the North Kansas City Police Department.

The second type of sheriff's department is the **law enforcement** model. The services of this model are devoted primarily to the responsibilities associated with enforcement of the law. For example, the primary duty of the officers of the Hillsborough County, Florida, Sheriff's Department is patrol (law enforcement). The **civil-judicial** model is the third type. Its primary duties revolve around all aspects of civil law enforcement and the requirements of the courts, including

TABLE 2-2

Top Full-Service Sheriff's Departments, by Percentage of Full-Time Personnel, 1996

Agency/County	Full-Time Sworn Personnel	Patrol/ Response (%)	Investigations (%)	Jail Operations (%)	Court Operations (%)
Los Angeles (CA)	8014	41	13	28	19
Cook (IL)	5309	4	3	58	32
Harris (TX)	2484	19	9	60	6
Palm Beach (FL)	1620	33	12	40	7
Riverside (CA)	1357	35	8	19	8
Bexar (TX)	1169	28	5	65	7
Sacramento (CA)	1155	35	12	32	9
San Bernardino (CA)	1149	36	13	30	1
Nassau (NY)	1004	1	1	94	4
Orleans (LA)	800	4	5	80	15
Wayne (MI)	800	19	6	25	25
Alameda (CA)	771	26	28	53	18
Hamilton (OH)	764	26	7	62	5
Jefferson (LA)	722	60	17	29	9
Ventura (CA)	706	44	11	29	10
East Baton Rouge (LA)	625	16	9	46	3

Source: Reaves, B.A., & Goldberg, A.L. (1998). *Census of State and Local Law Enforcement Agencies, 1996.* Washington, D.C.: U.S. Department of Justice.

Note: According to the authors, some figures add up to more than 100 percent because of methodological issues from the original data collection.

courtroom security and the serving of summons, subpoenas, and eviction notices.

The type of county agency that is probably the most prevalent model today is the **correctional-judicial** model. The agency established under this model is responsible for the care and custody of persons arrested and awaiting arraignment or trial, those who have been sentenced and are awaiting transfer to a prison facility, or those who must serve out the sentence within the county jail. The agency following this model is also responsible for all the functions associated with assisting the courts (i.e., prisoner transport and security, bailiffs, etc.).

■ CASE IN POINT

The sheriffs' departments in Fulton County, Georgia, and Maricopa County, Arizona, are examples of agencies whose primary duties fit under the correctional-judicial model. In 1996, the primary function for sworn personnel in both agencies was in jail operations (Reaves & Goldberg, 1998).

A few other differences between county and municipal agencies should be noted. These include jurisdiction, tax base (for budgeting), and personnel selection criteria. Jurisdiction of county police officers includes cities and municipalities within a county as well as any unincorporated county areas. Municipal police officers generally only have jurisdiction within their given municipality. The budget for a county system includes taxes raised from citizens living in cities within the county as well as from those who live in unincorporated county areas. Municipal budgets do not usually receive county tax assistance. Although it varies

from state to state, personnel selection for county systems is still politically motivated in many agencies, whereas municipal systems more frequently fall under
some type of civil service or merit system (Doerner, 1998; Purpura, 1997; Territo,
Halsted, & Bromley, 1998).

In counties in which budget constraints have forced changes, some municipal
and county agencies have consolidated into **metropolitan** police agencies (e.g.,
Miami–Dade County, Florida; Charlotte–Mecklenburg County, North Carolina;
and Las Vegas–Clark County, Nevada). These consolidated agencies provide the
full gamut of services. Additionally, a more current movement appears to be the
consolidation of county police agencies into sheriffs' departments.

■ CASE IN POINT

In 1997 the state of New Jersey experienced a trend in which county agencies merged
with sheriffs' departments. The Hudson County Police Department was dismantled in
favor of the county corrections department and the Essex County Police Department
joined the ranks of the consolidated when in February 1997 County Executive James Treff-
inger proposed such a merger.

Regardless of whether they are sheriffs' departments, county police agencies,
or metropolitan police, their services will be compared and contrasted with municipal agencies in a manner that provides each a separate and unique identity.
The same is true for the other parts of the local police system.

Other Local Systems

Even though the municipal and county subsystems make up the largest proportion of the local-level system, there are other agencies that deserve to be acknowledged. The most prominent are the **special district** or **special police**
agencies. The most often recognized special district systems include the university, transit, housing, park, hospital, school, and water district police agencies.
Table 2-3 shows selected special police agencies and the number of full-time
sworn personnel employed in 1996.

TABLE 2-3

Selected Special Police Agencies, by Type and Personnel, 1996

Type of Special Police	Number of Agencies	Full-Time Sworn Personnel
College/university	699	10,496
Public school district	117	5247
Transportation	28	4274
Parks/recreation	68	2595
Airport	84	2407
Water/harbor	38	1291
Public housing	13	1245

Source: Reaves, B.A., & Goldberg, A.L. (1998). Census of State and Local Law Enforcement Agencies, 1996. Washington, D.C.: U.S. Department of Justice.

For years, many of these agencies were viewed by the municipal and county subsystems as a hindrance. Despite lack of acceptance by municipal and county officers, an increasing number of these agencies have been created with the initial purpose of assisting the municipal and county agencies by providing extra police service. However, these agencies sometimes provide a variety of problems because of less well-trained officers, jurisdictional disputes, and communications problems.

■ CASE IN POINT

Several years ago in New York City, a New York transit police officer was killed while pursuing a robbery suspect. A major contributing factor to this officer's death was the officer's inability to communicate with New York City police officers called in to assist in the pursuit. As a result, many of today's special district agencies now have access to a police radio channel monitored by municipal and county officers. Additionally, to prevent a similar situation from occurring again, in April 1995, both the New York City transit and housing policing agencies were consolidated into the New York City Police Department.

Communications are not the only problem. A second problem involves the question of jurisdiction. Who should have priority in investigations that occur within the special district? It has been frequently observed that the county or municipality, or both, will claim priority jurisdiction over the special district police in investigations that develop tremendous positive publicity. Yet, when county or municipal agencies are asked for assistance by the special districts in minor investigations, the special district agency may be ignored. Special district police agencies can provide a very positive impact on police services; however, communication and jurisdictional problems have tended to detract from their positive contribution to policing.

A fourth component within the local-level system, which until recently has received little recognition in criminal justice textbooks, is **private security.** According to a National Institute of Justice report (Cunningham, Strauchs, & Van Meter, 1991), "Private security is now clearly the nation's primary protective resource, outspending public law enforcement by 73 percent and employing two and one-half times the workforce" (p. 1). More than $52 billion was spent for private security, compared with $37 billion spent on local public law enforcement in 1990. It has been projected that by the year 2000, approximately $100 billion will be spent on private security, compared with slightly more than $40 billion for law enforcement (U.S. News & World Report, 1993). In addition, private security employed more than 1.5 million people in 1990, almost as many as all three components of the criminal justice system employed in the same year.

Despite their increased presence in many cities and the assistance they provide to public police officers, such as checking business alarms first and being an extra pair of eyes and ears, private security officers are still not readily accepted by public policing. This has been due primarily to issues such as poor personnel selection criteria for security officers and inadequate training. For example, although many states mandate training for armed guards, only 14 states require training for unarmed guards. The estimated amount of training a uniformed guard currently receives is 4 to 6 hours (Cunningham et al., 1991).

Comparatively, the average amount of training a public police officer, in agencies that employed more than 100 officers, received in 1993 was more than 1000 hours (combination of class and field) (Reaves & Smith, 1995).

Considering that several private security functions overlap public policing, the lack of acceptance by police officers is understandable. However, the attitude of police officers is slowly changing as improvements are made in private security recruitment and training, such as higher standards for selection and more rigorous and extensive training. Furthermore, police agencies are beginning to recognize just how much private security can assist the municipal police department.

■ CASE IN POINT

In March 1997 the Dallas, Texas, Police Department launched its "Spring Enforcement Initiative." This effort made use of the city's 15,000 private security officers to assist in fighting gang problems, curfew and parole violations, traffic problems, and truancies. The private security officers were asked to serve as additional eyes and ears and to report any related criminal or suspicious activity. Obviously, an additional 15,000 "watchers" certainly couldn't hurt the efforts of the 2800 police officers.

Regardless of their respective roles, municipal, county, special district police, and private security constitute the largest of the three police subsystems, which because of its size and diversity of components, as well as its extensive participation in policing when compared with state and federal levels, it attracts more attention from the media and academicians. Furthermore, its participation stimulates and is the focus of a majority of police research, especially with regard to grant awards.

■ CASE IN POINT

In April 1996 it was announced that 15 communities across the country would receive approximately $11 million in grants to fight youth violence. Individual awards would range from $500,000 to $1 million. The communities slated to receive those awards included municipal police agencies in Austin and Dallas, Texas; Boston, Massachusetts; Chicago, Illinois; Detroit, Michigan; Indianapolis, Indiana; Jersey City, New Jersey; Kansas City and St. Louis, Missouri; Miami, Florida; Oakland, California; Phoenix, Arizona; and Salt Lake City, Utah. County consortiums, including Los Angeles and Orange County, California, would also receive funds. In another announcement that same year, more than $14.6 million was to be awarded to 288 law enforcement agencies in 36 states to fund a community-oriented policing effort to redeploy officers.

This level of policing is also the target of most of the criticism related to policing and police practices. One of the many complaints periodically arising about the local-level system among academicians is the fragmented nature of this level. Examples of problems that may be currently observed within this system are the lack of coordination and cooperation, jurisdictional disputes, duplication of duties and services, and general lack of uniformity in standards, policies, and procedures among the variety of agencies competing to provide similar services to the public. Therefore, a solution is required.

The most obvious solution appears to be **consolidation,** which is similar to the concept of metropolitan police agencies at the county level. Although

WHAT DO YOU THINK?

Separation or Consolidation?

In October 1993 a merger began between the Charlotte, North Carolina, Police Department and the Mecklenburg County, North Carolina, Sheriff's Department, which today is known as the Charlotte–Mecklenburg Police Department. The individual brought in to oversee the functional completion of the merger was a police chief from Illinois, Dennis Nowicki. This merger required him to eliminate disputes over programs that had been available in one agency but not the other, such as the take-home car program sheriffs' deputies had participated in but Charlotte officers had not. Unfortunately, because funding was not available to provide take-home vehicles to all members of the newly consolidated agency, the program ended. Despite such problems, Chief Nowicki has pointed out that the advantages of consolidation outweigh disadvantages. In particular, consolidation helped eliminate the jurisdictional squabbles that arose in the past. Increases in funding and personnel resources are an obvious improvement, too.

1. Regardless of the advantages, should a municipal and county agency consolidate? Why or why not?
2. Despite being shown how advantageous consolidation could be, why haven't more agencies made such an effort?
3. How much do politics influence the consolidation effort?
4. Other than those discussed above, what are some advantages and disadvantages of consolidation?
5. If your city and county police agencies wanted to consolidate, and it required a vote by the citizens, how would you vote? Why?

relatively new, this approach appears to be doing quite well in such places as Miami, Florida; Nashville and Knoxville, Tennessee; Las Vegas, Nevada; Indianapolis, Indiana; Honolulu, Hawaii; and Charlotte, North Carolina. In consolidation, county and municipal agencies combine their resources into one unified system. This provides solutions to several of the problems associated with fragmentation, such as jurisdictional disputes and lack of personnel. Although consolidation has not totally eliminated all problems associated with fragmentation, it appears to limit the number of problems and to be an acceptable solution to police agencies and their communities simply because it seems to improve the quality of and ability to provide services.

THE STATE SYSTEM

The second largest component of the police system is the **state-level** subsystem. Initially, this country did not have statewide police agencies simply because municipal and county police were able to handle all police needs. An interesting debate revolves around which organization is considered the first state police agency. Most sources contend that the Texas Rangers, initially formed in 1835 but not commissioned as police officers until 1874, were the first state-formed police entity. However, their duties were and are still fairly limited to investigating and tracking down violent felony offenders (Schmalleger, 1997; Territo, Halsted, & Bromley, 1998). In 1865 the state of Massachusetts created a police force whose primary focus was to enforce vice laws in the state. Although they too eventually received full police powers, the first truly modern statewide police agency was not created until 1905, the Pennsylvania State Constabulary, which today is called the Pennsylvania State Police. Its original powers and duties included providing a variety of policing services throughout the state.

Today there is some type of statewide police agency in every state, except Hawaii, whose department of public safety primarily supports court services. Originally, these agencies were formed to carry out the same basic law enforcement functions as municipal and county agencies in rural and unincorporated areas that don't receive any other police services. However, a division of role and mission evolved leading to two broad categories of statewide police agencies: the highway patrol and the state police.

The primary role and functions of the highway patrol are traffic enforcement—investigating accidents, issuing citations, and traffic control. The organizational structure of the highway patrol contains such divisions as administration, safety and training, special services, and weights and truck inspection.

■ CASE IN POINT

The Ohio State Highway Patrol provides traffic, emergency response, and support services to the public on a statewide basis. It also investigates criminal activities on state-owned and leased property and provides security for the governor. The primary functions of the Kansas Highway Patrol are the enforcement of vehicular laws, including licensure and registration, and traffic regulations. Both agencies can be accessed through the Internet. Ohio's web address is www.odn.ohio.gov/ohp/, and Kansas is located at www.tyrell.net/~khp/.

Today 12 states have a highway patrol. The largest state highway patrol is the California Highway Patrol (CHiP), which employed more than 9000 full-time personnel in 1996, more than 6000 of which were full-time sworn officers (Reaves & Goldberg, 1998).

Although the highway patrol focuses primarily on traffic enforcement, the state police have developed into a uniformed field patrol force whose responsibilities include the general police services found in municipal agencies in addition to highway patrol. This style of agency is currently found in 31 states (see Figure 2-2). Its organizational structure includes bureaus or divisions such as criminal investigations, personnel and training, administrative services, and highway patrol. The largest state police agency is the Pennsylvania State Police, which employs more than 4000 full-time sworn officers.

In keeping up with today's demands for broader services, many of the state agencies that were originally primarily traffic-enforcement oriented have

FIGURE 2-2   State Agencies

Alabama Department of Public Safety	Nebraska State Patrol
Alaska State Troopers	Nevada Highway Patrol
Arizona Department of Public Safety	New Hampshire State Police
Arkansas State Police	New Jersey Division of State Police
California Highway Patrol	New Mexico State Police
Colorado State Patrol	New York State Police
Connecticut State Police	North Carolina State Highway Patrol
Delaware State Police	North Dakota State Highway Patrol
Florida Highway Patrol	Ohio State Highway Patrol
Georgia Department of Public Safety	Oklahoma Highway Patrol
Idaho State Police	Oregon State Police
Illinois State Police	Pennsylvania State Police
Indiana State Police	Rhode Island State Police
Iowa State Police	South Carolina State Highway Patrol
Kansas Highway Patrol	South Dakota Highway Patrol
Kentucky State Police	Tennessee Department of Public Safety
Louisiana State Police	Texas Department of Public Safety
Maine State Police	Utah Highway Patrol
Maryland State Police	Vermont Department of Public Safety
Massachusetts State Police	Virginia Department of State Police
Michigan State Police	Washington State Police
Minnesota State Police	West Virginia State Police
Mississippi Highway Safety Patrol	Wisconsin State Patrol
Missouri State Highway Patrol	Wyoming Highway Patrol
Montana Highway Patrol	

Source: 1998 National directory of law enforcement administrators, correctional institutions, and related agencies (Vol. 34). National Public Safety Information Bureau.

reorganized and are now recognized as **departments of public safety.** Although their administrative structures may vary from that of a state police agency, the services available are similar. These services include law enforcement, general patrol, traffic enforcement, criminal investigations, criminalistics (crime lab and forensics), and training of municipal and county officers. Organizational divisions can include service, administration, driver's license, criminal investigations, telecommunications, and highway patrol. There are currently six states with a department of public safety. Texas has the largest department, which employed approximately 7000 full-time personnel in 1996, but less than half were full-time sworn officers.

Overall, the state police system employed more than 83,000 full-time personnel in 1996, 54,000 of which were sworn officers. Despite its relatively small size, the state police system plays an important part in the police system because of its ability to provide services unavailable from municipal and county agencies.

Although these two divisions of the state level—the highway patrol and the state police (or departments of public safety)—are the most often mentioned, there is a third division of the state system. This might best be referred to as the **special police.** Today many states have established other agencies that perform law enforcement functions, and their personnel are considered police officers. Examples of these agencies include an alcohol beverage commission that supervises and

enforces state liquor laws, a parks and wildlife department for the protection and
enforcement of hunting and recreation laws, the investigation division of the state
attorney's office, a bureau of narcotics enforcement, and state capitol and gaming
police. Descriptions of state officers with police power are usually found in the
state's Code of Criminal Procedure.

State police agencies continue to grow in strength and popularity, and at one
time they represented the second largest police subsystem. Recently, however,
this system has been overtaken by the federal level.

THE FEDERAL SYSTEM

The third component of the police system is the federal level. For many years this
level was, statistically, the smallest of the three components. Today, because it
employs more officers with arrest powers than the state system (74,000 in 1996),
it is the second largest subsystem. Also, it is probably the most complex level in
the police system in terms of subsystems and agencies.

Established by federal statutes, the role and mission of each agency are much
more specific and defined than those of the state and local police agencies. In
particular, the largest number of federal officers (approximately 32,000, or 43%,
in 1996) are charged with enforcing laws, through criminal investigations,
whereas their state and local counterparts are charged with "policing," which includes enforcing laws as well as providing the other services previously noted.
However, other functions of federal officers can include corrections, patrol and
response, noncriminal investigations, court operations, and security and protection (Reaves, 1997).

Originally, federal agencies were established to concentrate on the enforcement of federal criminal laws in the United States and its territories. Today the
scope of federal agencies has broadened not only in the United States, but in
other countries as well. As a result, the role of federal agents has expanded and
includes a variety of tasks.

■ CASE IN POINT

The following is a description of the criminal investigator's role for the Department of Treasury:

Agents employed by the Treasury Department investigate a variety of criminal violations of
federal laws within the enforcement jurisdiction of the Department of Treasury. They also
investigate certain noncriminal violations related to the functions of the department. Investigations may involve surveillance, participation in raids, interviewing witnesses, interrogation, search and seizure of contraband, equipment, and vehicles, and securing and
executing search and arrest warrants. (Application for Department of Treasury, special
agent.)

There are more than 71 agencies in the federal system with some type of
police power or a police division. In 1996 these agencies employed more than
74,000 individuals with arrest and firearm-carrying powers. This system is best
viewed as a four-subsystem component: Department of Justice, Department of
Treasury, U.S. Postal Service, and other federal systems. Each subsystem and its

respective agencies deal primarily with a particular aspect of federal law as designated by the Constitution and statutes.

Department of Justice

The largest federal subsystem, in terms of personnel and expenditures, is the Department of Justice. As of June 1996 this subsystem employed approximately 28,000 full-time officers with authority to carry firearms and make arrests (Reaves, 1997). The four agencies[2] that compose this subsystem, listed according to number of officers (most to least), are the Immigration and Naturalization Service, the Federal Bureau of Investigation, the Drug Enforcement Administration, and the U.S. marshals.

Immigration and Naturalization Service

The **INS** is the oldest bureau in the Justice Department. Created in 1891, the INS is charged with enforcing immigration and naturalization laws. These laws deal with admission, deportation, and the naturalization of individuals without U.S. citizenship. The responsibilities of INS agents include

> enforcing the laws regulating the admission of foreign born persons (i.e., aliens) to the United States and administering various immigration benefits, including the naturalization of resident aliens. The INS also works with the Department of State, the United Nations, and the Department of Health and Human Services in the admission and resettlement of refugees (1998 National Directory of Law Enforcement Administrators, Correctional Institutions, and Related Agencies, p. 697).

The most recent employment figures show that the INS employed more than 12,000 fully authorized officers (Reaves, 1997), 44 percent of which were part of the Border Patrol, the main enforcement tool of the INS. Border Patrol agents "interdict undocumented aliens and contraband, including narcotics" (Reaves, 1997, p. 2), and are most widely active in areas where aliens illegally attempt to cross into the United States (i.e., Texas, New Mexico, California, New York, and the Canadian border). Illegal aliens and drug smugglers have become the two main concerns of the INS and the Border Patrol.

■ CASE IN POINT

In August 1996 Border Patrol agents in El Paso, Texas, recovered 873 pounds of marijuana after exchanging gunfire with suspected drug smugglers. In February 1997 Border Patrol agents in California detained more than 10,000 illegal immigrants (a record number.)

More information about the INS can be accessed on the Internet at www.ins.usdoj.gov/index.html.

---

[2]The question may be raised about a fifth component of the Department of Justice, the Federal Bureau of Prisons. Although it employs the Justice Department's second largest number of federal officers authorized to carry firearms and make arrests, the primary function of these individuals is corrections and not law enforcement/investigations; therefore, the Federal Bureau of Prisons is not viewed as part of the federal police system.

Federal Bureau of Investigation

Until 1996 the **FBI** was the largest agency in this subsystem as well as in the federal police system, employing more than 10,000 agents. However, it became the second largest agency when the INS grew to more than 12,000 agents. Created in 1908, the FBI's responsibilities focus primarily on the enforcement of more than 250 federal criminal law violations. Such violations include bank robberies, embezzlement, civil rights violations, and interstate crimes such as kidnapping or transporting stolen goods. Furthermore, FBI agents are not limited with regard to where they enforce the laws or how.

■ CASE IN POINT

In 1996 the FBI closed down a fake fencing operation they had set up in Garfield, New Jersey. After 19 months the FBI netted more than $38 million in stolen goods (a bureau record). Along with the New Jersey State Police, the FBI arrested 62 suspects. In 1997 the FBI ended a sting operation at New York's Kennedy Airport. After three years the FBI netted more than $13 million in stolen goods.

In addition to its law enforcement functions, the FBI offers extensive investigatory services to other police agencies, such as access to its crime lab or psychological unit.

For many years the FBI basked in the glow of a strong, professional reputation. However, in recent years it has suffered setbacks as a result of various unfortunate incidents such as the 1993 assault on a Branch Davidian compound in Waco, Texas; the 1994 sexual harassment lawsuit filed by two female agents; questions of poor judgment by agents investigating the 1996 bombing in Atlanta's Centennial Park; and most recently, allegations of poor or improper lab work.

More information about the FBI can be found on the Internet at www.fbi.gov.

Drug Enforcement Administration

The **DEA** was established in 1973 as an U.S. narcotics enforcement agency. Today the DEA, which employs approximately 3000 full-time agents, shares investigative functions with police agencies in other countries that retain sovereign jurisdiction. The responsibilities of DEA agents include

enforcing the federal drug laws as outlined in the Controlled Substances Act of 1970, and its subsequent amendments, as well as developing a National Drug Intelligence System and by cooperating with federal, state and local law enforcement agencies curbing drug abuse nationally (1998 National Directory of Law Enforcement Administrators, Correctional Institutions, and Related Agencies, p. 706).

In view of the increasing number of drug-related crimes, this agency has received a tremendous amount of attention in recent years. However, because so many other federal agencies are also dealing with drug-related offenses and drug smuggling, a current debate concerns combining the DEA with the FBI. Additional facts about the DEA can be discovered at www.usdoj.gov/dea/index.html.

U.S. Marshals

Although the first U.S. marshal was appointed in 1789, the bureau was not established as a bureau of the Justice Department until 1973. In 1996 the bureau employed 2650 full-time agents (Reaves, 1997). The duties of a U.S. marshal include custody of federal prisoners (which includes transportation to and from court), apprehension of federal fugitives, and protection of federal judiciary; U.S. marshals have the broadest jurisdiction within modern U.S. law enforcement.

The selection process for U.S. marshals is unlike that of any other law enforcement agency in the United States, at least at the federal level.

> [U.S. marshals are] not selected by the director of the service or the U.S. attorney general, but are chosen either by the senior senator of the president's political party or other political sponsors, and are appointed by the president with the advice and consent of the senate (Gonzalez, 1998, p. 8).

This practice began in the eighteenth century and continues today. However, professionalization via reforms appears to be on the horizon (Gonzalez, 1998). Piqued your interest? Go to www.usdoj.gov/marshals on the Internet for more.

Department of Treasury

The second largest subsystem in the federal system is the Department of Treasury. According to June 1996 figures, this subsystem employed more than 18,000 individuals authorized to carry weapons and make arrests (Reaves, 1997). Although there are seven divisions within the Department of Treasury, personnel are distributed among the four most closely linked to law enforcement practices.

U.S. Customs Service

The U.S. Customs Service, initially created in the late 1800s, did not become a federal bureau until 1927. Based on the number of authorized employees (9749 in 1996), this is the largest agency in the Department of Treasury and the third largest in the federal system. This agency enforces the laws of import and export. In particular, its main enforcement tool, the Office of Investigations, is responsible for "conducting investigations of all violations of customs and related laws and regulations pertaining to the illegal entry, or exportation of contraband, or merchandise" (1998 National Directory of Law Enforcement Administrators, Correctional Institutions, and Related Agencies, p.719).

Among the primary duties of U.S. Customs agents are conducting investigations relative to the prevention and detection of fraud involving the illegal entry of any type of merchandise into the United States, the smuggling of illegal or clandestine merchandise, cargo theft of merchandise in Customs custody, currency of more than $10,000 dollars transported into or out of the country, neutrality (violations of the Arms Export Control Act), violations of navigation laws, organized crime, and child pornography. Furthermore, U.S. Customs has recently joined forces with the DEA to attack the flow of illegal drugs into the United States.

■ **CASE IN POINT**

The summer of 1996 was a busy and productive time for U.S. Customs agents. In Atlanta, Georgia, Customs agents confiscated more than 900 pounds of cocaine. Hidden in a box that allegedly contained women's lingerie, the cocaine was discovered by workers at the company to which the box was delivered. At the Mariopsa, New Mexico, port of entry, Customs agents found 301 pounds of cocaine that had been hidden in the rear door of a commercial trailer. At this same location, with the assistance of drug-sniffing dogs, agents seized 489 packages of cocaine hidden in a shipment of electrical transformers. At the port of Houston Texas, agents seized a ton of cocaine concealed inside two steel cylinders.

Internal Revenue Service

The **IRS** is one federal agency with which most Americans are familiar. It is the second largest agency in the Department of Treasury, employing approximately 3800 authorized investigators in 1996. This agency is charged with enforcing all federal tax laws, particularly those related to income and wagering or gaming devices. From a practical perspective this agency could be considered one of the most powerful federal agencies in existence; for instance, no one else can walk into a bank and seize a citizen's accounts simply by identifying himself or herself as a federal agent. This agency is often called on to assist in the investigations of suspected organized crime bosses or white-collar criminals to find connections between the suspect's assets and how they were obtained. For example, the efforts of the IRS eventually led to the downfall of Al Capone (who was accused and found guilty of tax evasion).

Secret Service

Along with the IRS, the Secret Service is one of the oldest Treasury Department agencies, having been in existence since 1862. It employs the third largest number of agents (more than 3000). Among the 3000 employees, 2034 are investigators, and the remaining 1000 are part of the Uniformed Division. Although the agency was originally established to enforce counterfeiting laws, today's Secret Service agents could very well be considered professional bodyguards. It is their duty to protect political candidates, visiting dignitaries, and current political leaders, such as the president and former presidents and their families. However, the Secret Service still investigates violations of laws relating to counterfeiting or forgery of currency, obligations and securities of the United States, and foreign governments. They also investigate credit card and computer fraud.

Alcohol, Tobacco, and Firearms

The **ATF,** created in 1972, is charged with enforcement of all federal laws dealing with illicit liquor (manufacturing and distribution), tobacco (primarily taxation requirements), and explosives and firearms (in particular, automatic weapons, licensing, and registration). In recent years, the ATF has become more involved in drug-related enforcement primarily because of the increased use of automatic weapons and explosives by drug dealers as well as street gangs. Despite being the smallest (by number of employees) agency in the Department of Treasury, it has certainly managed to receive its share of attention. Unfortunately, much of which has been negative.

◼ CASE IN POINT

During the 1990s the ATF became a better known entity to the public primarily because of its role in the 1993 assault on the Branch Davidian compound in Waco, Texas. Although the results of that event have brought about reforms in the ATF, it is still a very touchy subject. If agency actions against citizens weren't enough, in July 1996 the ATF settled a discrimination lawsuit brought by African-American agents. The agreement was for $5.9 million in damages and legal fees to be divided among 240 current and former agents.

In all, the Department of Treasury is comprised of agencies created to provide a myriad of law enforcement services, many of which are related to financial issues. More on each agency can be found through the Internet at the following addresses:

U.S. Customs Service http://www.customs.ustrea.gov
IRS http://www.irs.ustreas.gov/prod
Secret Service http://www.treas.gov/usss
ATF http://www.atf.treas.gov

U.S. Postal Service

Created in 1829, the U.S. Postal Service is probably the oldest federal subsystem. Often overlooked and underrated, the U.S. Postal Service plays an important role in federal law enforcement. In 1996 the U.S. Postal Service employed more than 3500 individuals authorized to carry firearms and make arrests, the majority of whom were assigned to criminal investigations with the remaining officers providing the physical security. The responsibilities of these individuals include

jurisdiction in criminal matters affecting the integrity and security of the mail. Postal inspectors enforce more than 100 federal statutes involving mail fraud, mail bombs, child pornography, illegal drugs, mail theft and other postal crimes as well as being responsible for the protection of all postal employees (1998 National Directory of Law Enforcement Administrators, Correctional Institutions, and Related Agencies, p. 726)

Probably the worst events for postal inspectors in the 1990s have been the investigations of shootings by disgruntled and former postal employees. To learn more about the U.S. Postal Service, log on to http://www.usps.gov/websites/depart/inspect.

Other Federal Systems

This section incorporates all other federal agencies that employ criminal investigators and/or have a police division but are not necessarily viewed as a federal police agency. Examples of these agencies include the Departments of

Agriculture, Education, Commerce, Energy, Transportation, Health and Human Services, as well as the Environmental Protection Agency and the Federal Deposit Insurance Commission. Other agencies include the National Park Service, U.S. Capitol Police, U.S. Fish and Wildlife Service, and the U.S. Forest Service. Officers and investigators from these agencies conduct investigations involving violations of regulations and contractual commitments, criminal and civil fraud, uniformed patrol, and other activities as they relate to programs and operations of each department.

Needless to say, the Federal level of policing is much more complex and diverse than it would initially appear. Furthermore, it has often been suggested by practitioners and academicians that federal officers tend to project an elitist attitude toward their state and local colleagues. Why has this perception occurred? Some observers might suggest that it is a result of the higher selection criteria required for employment in a federal agency. Currently the federal system is the only system, as a whole, that requires recruits to possess a four-year college degree. The FBI, which has always been the strictest in this regard, for many years would accept only individuals with a law or accounting degree. Only about 1 percent of all other law enforcement and police agencies, among both the state and local systems, require recruits to possess such a level of education (Reaves & Smith, 1995).

Another possible reason for the elitist perception is that federal officers do not generally play a visible role in society's everyday policing functions as do state and local police officers. Federal officers are not as well known by citizens and often tend to receive more glory (or are glamorized in the news and entertainment media more than local or state police officers). Therefore, when a federal officer appears on the scene of a crime, citizens may perceive that the situation is extremely important, thus promoting that elitist perception.

Regardless of the reason(s) for the elitist perception, the truth is that federal agents generally are not much different from any other law enforcement agents. They are subjected to similar problems and stresses with enforcing laws as their state and local counterparts, including the violent confrontations.

■ CASE IN POINT

In April 1997 two U.S. Customs inspectors were wounded when an individual began shooting inside a border crossing station in Calexico, California. Although the subject was shot by federal officers and died at the scene, neither inspector received life-threatening injuries. Unfortunately, the results were not as positive for two Border Patrol agents shot and killed in July 1998 when they went to the assistance of local police officers attempting to apprehend an individual who had allegedly shot several people earlier in the day. This assailant was also killed in the shootout. From 1991 through 1995 there were 3886 assaults on federal law enforcement officers (Reaves, 1997).

A better understanding of policing in the United States requires taking an appropriate approach. A systems approach not only applies to understanding policing externally but internally as well.

INTERNAL SYSTEMS

No discussion of policing from a systems perspective would be complete without at least acknowledging the existence of **internal systems.** The internal systems of a police agency exist in a formal and informal state. The formal internal system refers to the structure of the agency—how it is organized into its units or divisions. As previously noted, every unit or division in an agency has a specific purpose or role in the system and must follow particular guidelines or rules.

■ CASE IN POINT

Practically every police agency has a uniformed patrol division. This division is assigned a number of officers who are allocated among different shifts and have specific days off. There are a specific number of supervisors and special equipment designated only for this unit. It is the duty of the officers in this unit to follow the mandates set down for patrol officers as well as those mandates all officers in the agency must follow. Other units have elements similar to those of the patrol unit.

The informal aspect of the internal systems perspective deals primarily with communication. Although there are formal lines of communication, it is the informal lines, whether vertical or horizontal (unit to unit or supervisor to subordinate; grapevine and rumor mill), that play an important role in the overall operation of the agency. Officers often rely upon the informal lines of communication to find out what is transpiring elsewhere in the agency.

Overall, the internal systems perspective relates to the formal division of services among the different units and the informal communications. Although the internal systems are important to the systems perspective of policing, they are not as easily recognized as the external aspect of the systems perspective.

It is important not to lose sight of the fact that each of these police subsystems is also a subsystem of the entire criminal justice system. What is sometimes not clear is how the police interact with the rest of this system. The remainder of this chapter focuses on this aspect of the systems perspective.

INTERACTING WITH THE REST OF THE CRIMINAL JUSTICE SYSTEM

Police agencies have a responsibility to participate fully in the system and cooperate actively with the courts, prosecutors, prisons, parole boards, and noncriminal elements—mental health clinics, drug rehabilitation centers, social service agencies, youth programs, mental hospitals, and educational institutions (Police Task Force Report, 1973, p. 70).

As the remainder of the criminal justice system relies upon the police to be the impetus for activity and often requires police assistance, one would expect that the police would be extremely respected and well accepted. Yet, this is not necessarily the case.

The Police and the Prosecutor

The relationship between police and prosecutors, which should be the closest and most successfully cooperative relationship for police, is often the worst. Although considered teammates in the battle against crime, there is more often an adversarial relationship than the bond of teammates. The prosecutor is usually the top law enforcement official for the county or state, and a part of the prosecutor's role should be building a working link between the police and the prosecutor's Office. Yet, this link is frequently extremely weak. One reason for the difficult relationship lies within the prosecutor's role as an adviser to the police.

Although police officers receive some training and schooling with regard to the legal issues of their work and in conducting investigations, they seldom have the in-depth legal background that prosecutors have or access to resources, such as law updates and reports of court decisions, which keep prosecutors up to date on changes in the law. As a result, police officers sometimes suffer dismissal of cases or plea bargaining because the officer has not provided the prosecutor with the evidence necessary to make a case in court. This is where the prosecutor should be acting as a legal adviser. However, it should also be noted that police officers do not always accept or listen to what the prosecutor has to say.

The police and the prosecutor have or should have similar goals—deterring and preventing crime—and each must rely on the other to meet their goals. Why, then, is their relationship frequently so negative? Three possible reasons exist: **lack of communication, perceptions and perspectives on the application of law,** and **individual characteristics.**

Lack of Communication

One might suppose that the prosecutor would insist that there be constant communication between the prosecutor's office and the police; however, except in extremely noteworthy cases, this is seldom true. As a rule, the only time the police and prosecutor communicate is after an officer has completed (or believes to have completed) an investigation and files charges with the prosecutor or when an officer is scheduled to testify at a hearing or trial.

If the case is not complete or is poorly put together, there will be communication between the prosecutor and the officer. Unfortunately, it usually is not a pleasant conversation. The prosecutor sometimes does nothing more than criticize the officer's work, or adequacy thereof, in gathering the information that will be needed in court. In response, the officer complains that the prosecutor is not familiar with conducting an investigation "on the street" and only wants to prosecute "smoking gun" cases—cases in which the suspect is apprehended at the scene by officers and there is substantial, supportive evidence (witness, physical evidence) that would guarantee a conviction. There may be validity in each side's criticisms of the other.

Although communication during initial case preparation is extremely important, it is even more crucial when it is time for the case to go to court. Frequently, the prosecutor has not spoken to any of the officers involved in the case before the day of the court appearance. This means that the officer is requested to arrive several hours before the trial begins to discuss the case with the prosecutor.

Often, an officer, usually the preliminary investigator or the patrol officer, is required to be standing by when the trial begins and throughout its duration in case testimony from this officer becomes necessary. What this leads to is the "hurry up and wait" syndrome, an element that appears to be a leading cause in poor police–prosecutor relations.

▊ CASE IN POINT

The patrol officer was working the dayshift. At approximately 11:00, the officer was advised by the dispatcher to "report immediately to district court, see the prosecutor reference a case that needs your testimony." About fifteen minutes later the officer arrived at the courtroom and requested the bailiff to let the prosecutor know he was here. A few minutes later the bailiff returned and told the officer that the prosecutor wanted him to wait in the witness room. Twenty minutes later the prosecutor came into the witness room and advised the officer that a recess for lunch had been called and that the officer would probably not be needed before 3 P.M. Needless to say, the officer was slightly irritated that the urgent radio dispatch to report to the courtroom led only to the discovery that not only would it be several hours before he would testify, but also that it would be after the end of his shift. This situation becomes even more frustrating if the officer is off duty and sleeping when summoned to court.

Another one of the most frustrating communication problems of the police–prosecutor relationship arises when the police officer is subpoenaed to court, arrives at the time requested (often 8:00 A.M.), and then must wait until the prosecutor decides to speak with the officer.

▊ CASE IN POINT

A crime scene officer was subpoenaed to testify in a murder trial. The subpoena requested that the officer arrive at 8:00 A.M. On the day of the trial the officer arrived at the courtroom as ordered and proceeded to the prosecutor's room where he was supposed to be briefed by the prosecutor. The officer arrived before the prosecutor, so he sat down and waited. At approximately 8:30 A.M. the prosecutor walked in, said "hello" to the officer, then proceeded to sit and read the newspaper and drink coffee. Forty-five minutes later he finally got around to speaking with the officer who, by this time, was moderately upset and frustrated with the prosecutor.

Although the prosecutor tends to receive the brunt of the blame for poor communications, police officers cannot be excused as totally blameless. It is common practice for a police officer to withhold critical information from a prosecutor, thinking that the case won't go to trial if the information is known. However, if the case does go to trial and the information then comes out, it could cause the prosecutor to have to change his or her approach to the case or maybe even dismiss the case. No matter whose fault it is, good communication is an important part of a successful police officer–prosecutor relationship.

Perceptions and Perspectives of the Application of the Law
An aspect of the police–prosecutor relationship seldom examined from a practical perspective is differences in the application of law. Regardless of theory,

there are two distinct differences; one can be viewed as "pure applied," and the other might best be labeled "street functional."

In the world of the prosecutor, crime is represented by facts on a piece of paper that must meet strict, written guidelines that have been learned by the prosecutor during several years of specific schooling and practice. The application of these guidelines must fit neatly into the arena that is responsible for their existence, the courtroom.

Conversely, crime to police is applied—a function of the street—therefore, the requisite, neat guidelines of the courtroom do not always fit. Sometimes this leads officers to behaviors that are not readily acceptable by the courts but because of other circumstances become admissable.

■ CASE IN POINT

In *Murray* v. *United States,* 487 U.S. 533 (1988) officers had illegally entered a warehouse and observed what appeared to be several burlap bags of marijuana. The officers left the warehouse, obtained a warrant, returned to seize the drugs, and arrested the defendant. On appeal of his conviction, the defendant claimed the warrant was invalid because the illegal entry. The officers claimed that the warrant was based on previously obtained information and not on the observations during the illegal entry. The court ruled in favor of the officers, advising that evidence initially discovered during an illegal search may be admissible in court if the same evidence is discovered during a legal search that came about because of information unrelated to the illegal search.

When the circumstances of a police arrest, search, or seizure do not meet the criteria of the courts, this upsets prosecutors and sets off criticism of the police. It also leads to plea bargains and dismissal of legal proceedings, which upset the police. The major problem is the failure of both sides to truly understand the other's world. Without doubt, the big difference between the worldview of police and that of the prosecutor causes serious problems and strains their relationship.

The fact is that the prosecutor relies upon the police to obtain evidence, following legal procedures, so that the prosecutor can be assured of obtaining a conviction. Although the prosecutor is extremely well versed in the laws of procedures—arrest, search and seizure, evidence collection—the legal knowledge of police officers is often more limited and more street applicable than court applicable. The result is sometimes a lack of evidence or tainted evidence that leads to no charges, plea bargains, and dismissals. Is either side to blame?

In fact, both sides may be to blame. The prosecutor may need to take greater interest in making sure that local law enforcement officers are up to date and as knowledgeable as possible in the law and legal procedures. At the same time, police agencies need to be sure that their training is current in respect to the law, and, when necessary, they must provide in-service training to keep officers aware of changes in law. It may take a concerted effort on both parts if the police and prosecutor are going to sustain a positive working relationship.

Individual Characteristics

Communication and application of the law are very important parts of the police–prosecutor relationship and are the more obvious parts. There are, however, some less obvious factors that appear to have an impact on the relationship. These factors may be attributed to the individual characteristics that separate police and prosecutors. They include differences in background and socialization, education, and career.

Background and Socialization.   When one compares the background of the average prosecutor to that of the average police officer, several differences appear to exist. For example, the average police officer has often been identified as a "blue-collar" person whose position in policing is often the result of family tradition or because it is a better job than the officer's parents had. The average prosecutor appears to come from a more middle- or upper-class background where prestigious employment (e.g., law or medicine) is a family tradition. This difference, in itself, can create problems in the police and prosecutor relationship. The fact is that the police officer may be more in tune with the streets and their activity, whereas the prosecutor has less experience with them. While this may be a favorable factor for the officer on the street, it becomes a negative aspect when the officer gets into the prosecutor's arena—the court—which is established and run from a perspective more similar to the prosecutor's than the officer's.

Another problem may be lack of socializing between the police and prosecutors. The reality is that the police often stick with their own socially, and the same is true of prosecutors. The result, however, is a limited ability on both sides to communicate or understand the other's perspectives, attitudes, and values.

Education.   The average educational level of police officers is often only that of a high school graduate. Prosecutors are required to have several years of college, including a law degree. Because the prosecutor has more education and, more specifically, a legal education, there may be animosity on the part of the prosecutor toward the police officer who wishes to argue over points of law. Although the general level of education among police is rising, there is still a distinct difference in educational levels between most police officers and prosecutors; when police officers have equivalent levels of education to those of prosecutors, seldom is their degree in law. Simply put, the prosecutor is well educated in law; the police officer seldom is well educated in law. Therefore, what the prosecutor says should be the correct interpretation of the law. This situation may not please all police officers; however, until a time comes when both the police and prosecutors share similar legal backgrounds, the police will have to defer to the prosecutor's judgment and decisions.

Career Commitments.   Although it can be argued that both prosecutors and police officers have the same job-oriented goals—deterrence and prevention of crime—individual goals often differ dramatically. Barring a situation or incident beyond the officer's control, it is generally the plan of the officer to make policing a lifetime career with the department initially employing him or her. The same can seldom be said for prosecutors; in many cases, the young prosecutor has higher goals and aspirations. Many prosecutors plan to start as an assistant prosecutor and work up the ladder to chief prosecutor, or even judge. Seldom can this climb be made in the individual's first place of employment. Therefore, although the prosecutor may only be in a particular job and community for a short time, the police officer sees the same job and community as his or hers forever. This difference in career commitment may be a cause for problems between the police and prosecutor simply because the police appear to have long-range goals and visions for their community, whereas prosecutors frequently have short-range goals and are interested in immediate problem solving rather than long-term solutions.

Considering the importance of the relationship between the police and prosecutor, it seems imperative that they develop a strong relationship. Historically, this has not been the situation, however, that may be changing. In view of recent rises in crime, the need for the police and prosecutor to get along has risen to new heights. To stimulate and promote the growth of positive relationships, many jurisdictions have implemented an innovative idea: **police–prosecutor teams.**

According to a 1989 report from the National Institute of Justice, higher arrest and conviction rates for crimes related to drugs, homicide, and gangs were experienced in jurisdictions that have formed the police–prosecutor teams. As previously noted, lack of communication between the two can cause severe problems and frustrations on both sides. These teams have helped eliminate the frustrations and solidify the relationship, which in turn has improved performance of both the police and prosecution (Buchanon, 1989).

■ CASE IN POINT

Maine's forty-agent and eight-prosecutor team, the Bureau of Intergovernmental Drug Enforcement, whose focus is primarily on drug-related crimes, has been so successful that the legislature has agreed to continue its funding. Multnomah County, Oregon's, Organized Crime/Narcotics Task Force, consisting of twelve area investigators and two prosecutors, aids area narcotics units in fighting the increase of drug-related crimes while promoting a positive relationship between police and prosecutors. New York City's Homicide Investigation Unit and Oriental Gang Unit each have prosecutors assigned specifically to them. These prosecutors are available through every step of an investigation, providing officers with the legal input necessary to ensure conviction.

The underlying element of these teams and their success is cooperation, which in turn reduces conflict. As noted by Buchanon, "The removal of barriers to close working relationships has made possible a blend of police and prosecution skills in the pursuit of the same goals—making strong cases and convicting criminals" (1989, p. 8).

In conclusion, several challenges face the police and prosecutors. The need for improved cooperation is imperative. The police–prosecutor team is an innovative method for improving the relationship.

The Police and the Courts

Police relationships with other parts of the criminal justice system are also important. The relationship with the courts has often come under scrutiny. Like the prosecution, the courts must often "ride roughshod" over police officers because of improper behavior or action. Issues relating to the admissibility of evidence, interrogations, confessions, or the use of force can cause problems between police and the courts. Furthermore, the court can call on police power in addition to its own judicial power; this lack of reciprocity puts the police at a disadvantage.

Historically, the relationship between the police and the court has been strained. This strain has primarily been the result of U.S. Supreme Court decisions that have been viewed as limitations on police performance. Since the early 1960s when the Warren Court began handing down rulings requiring officers to safeguard the constitutional rights of an individual, police and many of their supporters have viewed the courts as guardians of the criminal. In the late 1980s to early 1990s the Rehnquist Court tended to lean more toward the police than the accused; however, this does not mean that the courts are abandoning the accused. Although U.S. Supreme Court decisions from this period may seem to favor the police—such as the acceptance of *Miranda* warnings that had not been read exactly as printed, broadening the scope of a vehicle search to all sealed containers without the need of a warrant, and allowing the officer to have all occupants of a vehicle submit to a "frisk"—some decisions still seem to limit the police. For example, a Court ruling has increased the number of situations in which *Miranda* warnings must be given and access to a lawyer allowed.

Another area of strain and tension is the result of interpretation of the law. The police, like the courts, are in a position where they must interpret and apply the law equitably. The problem is that the police officer often must make a split-second interpretation and application while the courts are provided a longer period for study before making a considered ruling of law. In addition, the individuals who staff the courts—judges—are usually trained and educated specifically for this role, whereas police officers receive only the amount of training that will make them functionally acceptable by their police agency. Thus, the courts may criticize an officer's application and interpretation of the law without giving much thought to the limitations under which the officer's decision was made. Although these functions of courts are important safeguards to justice, they may sometimes be a source of frustration to police officers. It is also rare that a police officer is given an opportunity to explain his or her decision outside the limits of specific questions asked by the attorneys or judge.

■ CASE IN POINT

The officer was testifying in a murder trial. After having responded to several questions from the prosecutor, the officer thought that he had not been able to clarify his actions. When the officer requested that he be allowed to expand on his answers, the judge ordered him to be quiet and only speak when spoken to. Not only was the incident embarrassing to the officer and did little to improve his opinion of the judiciary, but also prevented him from testifying fully.

Broderick (1987) offers reasons for the strained relationship between the police and the courts. He suggests that the police are critical of the courts because of poor management and administration of the court process. Furthermore, police officers often reflect the values and attitudes of those they serve, which often conflicts with the values and attitudes of judges. Finally, the role-status reversal (now the judge is the higher-ranking authoritarian) that tends to occur when the officer testifies, delays in testifying, and the lack of respect shown when officers are given last-minute notification to appear in court tends to create ill will toward the court and its officers (pp. 172–173).

Realistically, the court's role and extended legal knowledge often supersedes that of police officers. The result has been a strained relationship between the courts and police. This strain will continue until both sides realize and accept the role of the other and the limitations and guidelines each must work within. The relationship will also improve as police departments take responsibility for increasing the educational level, training, and abilities of their police officers so that interpretation and understanding of legal applications improves.

The Police and Corrections

One of the least-examined relationships is that of the police and correctional entities. Although there is often very little direct interaction between these two entities or their representatives, there exists a strained relationship. This is primarily the result of the differing roles of policing and corrections.

The apprehension of alleged offenders is an integral part of policing. Corrections is charged with maintaining, supervising, and rehabilitating the convicted offender and ultimately placing the individual back into society. Simply, the two roles are at opposite ends of the justice process. This in itself can cause conflict and tension.

However, the strain increases when the individual is released from the correctional institution, returns to society, and violates the law again. When this occurs, the police often characterize correctional efforts as lax and useless. The correctional response is usually one of indignation based on a belief that limited resources prevent optimal efforts to rehabilitate or resocialize individuals who have been convicted of lawbreaking. In fact, policing as a whole, both nationally and locally, receives more funding than corrections; yet, the police expect corrections to work miracles. This is particularly true of probation and parole.

Although more often considered an element of the courts, probation and parole are major parts of the correctional aspect of the system. They are also the most visible elements of it to police officers. Because of the increasing number of arrests and convictions, probation and parole officers find themselves with larger and larger caseloads. Their difficulty in effectively monitoring all cases leads to offenders who continue to violate the law while on probation or parole. When these individuals are apprehended and the police are advised of the parole probation situation, the first person blamed by police officers for the law violation is not the offender, but the parole or probation officer who is charged with monitoring the individual's behavior. In addition, police officers think they are doing the parole or probation officer's job. This complaint is not well received by probation and parole officers.

■ CASE IN POINT

A robbery detective and a parole officer almost came to blows when the discussion between the two became extremely heated after the detective accused the parole officer of failing to do his job. Apparently, one of the parole officer's parolees was suspected of several robberies of convenience stores. The detective was attempting to obtain a current address for the suspect, which the parole officer should have had; however, the parolee had moved without reporting the change to the parole officer. The detective believed that if the parole officer was doing his job in monitoring the parolee, he would have had the address—thus, the heated discussion and a near physical confrontation between the detective and parole officer.

Parole and probation officers are better educated as a group than police officers because of employment requirements for higher educational attainment and frequently view their job as assisting the offender to "fit in" with other citizens or return to society. Parole and probation officers frequently possess a social work orientation, whereas police officers would rather simply remove the individual from society. These differing attitudes and backgrounds add fuel to an already flammable relationship. The result is a strained and tumultuous relationship. As with the courts, this relationship will not improve until a complete, mutual understanding of roles and limitations is achieved.

The Police and the Defense Attorney

No discussion of police relationships would be complete without a brief look at the relationship of police and defense attorneys. Police officers and defense attorneys often appear to be on different sides of the law. Police officers sometimes view defense lawyers as peers of the people they represent. Defense lawyers often view police officers as uneducated and ignorant with no regard for the law. Although neither perception is accurate, both seem common.

Police officers want to see the accused go to jail, whereas the defense attorney wants to avoid that scenario whenever possible. Ultimately, there is little love lost between police and defense attorneys. The result of this relationship is sometimes an attempt, by either or both sides, during a trial to discredit the other in any manner possible.

■ CASE IN POINT

The patrol officer was testifying at a trial of a drunk driver he had arrested after the driver had been involved in a traffic accident. In an effort to frustrate, upset, and discredit the patrol officer, the defense attorney proceeded to ask the officer several questions to test the officer's knowledge of alcoholic beverages, such as their odor and what "proof" meant, as well as the officer's knowledge of the slope of the street on which the accident occurred and the sidewalk on which the field sobriety tests had been conducted. In this case, the officer was up to the task, correctly answering all the questions in a professional manner. Eventually, it was the defense attorney who ultimately became frustrated and ended up looking less than competent to the officer, prosecutor, and jurors. However, this is not always the case.

The fact is both sides have their respective roles to fill. Although their tasks tend to be in conflict, both are necessary components of the criminal justice system. Like the relationship with the courts and corrections, the relationship between the defense attorney and the police officer will improve when both sides resign themselves to the reality of the other's job and accept it for what it is, a necessity of the system.

Noncriminal Components

The relationship of the police to the other criminal justice components is important; yet, their relationship to noncriminal components of American society cannot be ignored. It has been noted in many introductory criminal justice textbooks that the police are just one portion of the societal control system and cannot be expected to control human behavior alone. Other components such as schools, churches, and social service agencies need to be involved too. Often it takes the cooperation of police agencies and these other societal elements to maintain order and discipline; yet, it has sometimes been difficult to establish this cooperation simply because of the closed nature of the police agency. This has long been a key factor in failed intergroup relationships. As a result, situations or incidents occur that could be avoided or easily remedied.

■ CASE IN POINT

Reports of child abuse have been on the rise in this country. It should be a concern of all social agencies—schools, child welfare, medical facilities, and the police. Yet, it is not unusual for school personnel or social welfare workers to ignore signs of child abuse, despite laws requiring reporting suspected child abuse, because they do not wish to get involved with the police. Unfortunately, this failure to report sometimes leads to severe injury or even death to a child, when police involvement is obviously too late for the child.

There can be little doubt that there is room for improvement in the interaction between police and other social agencies. One area generating increased concern is violence in schools. Since 1985 the number of shootings and other violent activity has been on a yearly increase (*Sourcebook of Criminal Justice Statistics*, 1997; *Trends and Issues '91: Education and Criminal Justice in Illinois*, 1991). To combat this problem, police and schools are beginning to attempt cooperative efforts aimed at eliminating these problems.

■ CASE IN POINT

Prince George County, Maryland, in an effort to reduce school violence, launched a program in spring 1992 that included roving teams of police and security officers in selected schools. This joint effort gives police authority to use hand-held metal detectors when there is reason to believe a weapon has been hidden in a locker or a tote bag. That same spring in Madison, Wisconsin, a committee composed of police, city, and school officials was studying proposals that would increase police presence in schools in an effort to limit violence. In 1998 the Seattle, Washington, Police Department announced similar plans to get police officers back in the schools in an effort to deter violence.

The relationship between the police and other social agents is extremely important. Control of social behavior is a joint venture; lack of cooperation and failure to interact positively only leads to more problems.

Finally, although it is not considered a systemic component, the relationship between the police and crime victims is very important to the success of the system as a whole. For many years, the police have not received much praise for the manner in which they deal with victims. The reputation and perceptions have often been negative. It was fairly common to hear complaints of how police officers responded to victims in ways reminiscent of the "Joe Friday" syndrome, in which officers showed no emotion and simply sought the facts.

Although perhaps a reasonable perception, it is unfair because in many cases the best way for an officer to deal with a crime victim is to detach himself or herself from the personal aspect and simply focus on solving the problem. If an officer shows emotion or becomes "personally involved" it can cloud judgment. It may even lead to actions of impropriety or charges against an officer.

■ CASE IN POINT

A police officer concerned with the safety and emotional state of female burglary victims had a habit of "checking back with the victim" later in the shift and sometimes after the shift ended. This prompted some of the victims to file complaints about the officer.

Fortunately, there is a middle ground. Officers can show concern and support without "becoming too familiar." However, this is a function of good training and interpersonal skills that police agencies do not often provide or enhance. Nevertheless, an effective and efficient system begins with positive interactions between the police and victims.

SUMMARY

From a systems perspective, policing is not a simple component of the criminal justice system; it is a complex variety of systems and subsystems. Each system—federal, state, and local—is composed of agencies that have a particular, relevant function and role within the overall system. The local level includes municipal and county agencies, special district or special police, and private security. The state level includes highway patrol, state police, departments of public safety, and special police. The federal level includes several agencies, falling into four subsystems: the Department of Justice, the Department of Treasury, the U.S. Postal Service, and other federal systems. In addition to the external systems and subsystems, an internal system exists in policing.

The police are only one part of a three-part system that requires cooperation and communication among the parts to be effective. Yet, the relationship between the police and other parts of the system is often strained. One of the most important relationships is between the police and the prosecutor. As the top law enforcement officer of a given jurisdiction, the prosecutor essentially has the last word on arrests and charges. The police are necessary to the prosecutor because of their ability to investigate and obtain evidence. Therefore, it is important that a good relationship is established. Historically, however, this has not occurred. A recent innovative attempt to improve this relationship has been the police–prosecutor teams.

The strain between the police and the courts is primarily the result of court decisions viewed by police as a hindrance to their performance. This strain will lessen as officers become better educated on the legalities and implications of the Constitution. The courts must also realize that police knowledge of the law is not as deep as that of those who have been schooled specifically in the application and interpretation of the law. However, it is ultimately the responsibility of the police to become "better schooled."

Although not as important as the relationship with the prosecutor or the courts, an amicable relationship between the police and corrections personnel is necessary. Their roles may be nearly at opposite ends of the spectrum, however, their goals are interrelated and involve the protection of society. Therefore, it is beneficial for each side to understand and accept the other's role.

The least amicable relationship is that of the police and the defense attorney. There is often little respect between the two simply because their goals are completely opposite: one wants conviction and incarceration; the other does not. Yet, this relationship must also improve or at least find a neutral ground.

Finally, the interaction between the police and other components of social control, including victims, occurs regularly. The importance of a positive relationship between these components and police is obvious. Effective control of social behavior requires a cooperative effort by the police and other social agents.

DO YOU KNOW . . .

1. How many individuals are employed by the police system in your state? How are they distributed among the subsystems? How much is spent in your state on policing?
2. Why there is a lack of cooperation between divisions? Is it jealousy or a power struggle?
3. What serious problems would occur if a county and municipal agency in your state attempted to consolidate? Is consolidation a feasible solution to the fragmentation problem?
4. How many state agencies have some type of police power in your state? Can you name them?
5. Why there are such a large number of federal agencies with some type of police power? Why is this system so diverse yet so small? Has there been any change in its growth over the past ten years? If so, what has contributed to the change? Should consolidation of some agencies be considered?
6. Why the majority of federal police agencies require recruits to have a four-year college degree, although state and local agencies do not? Are different educational standards enough to create federal elitism?
7. Why police–prosecutor relationships continue to be strained?
8. Whether your local jurisdiction has a police–prosecutor team?
9. What other methods could be employed to improve the police–prosecutor relationship?
10. Why prosecutors and the courts do not afford the police greater courtesy with respect to their work schedules and court dates? How can this be improved?
11. Whether the relationship between police officers and probation and parole officers would improve if probation and parole officers had the same power of arrest as police officers?

12. Whether there can ever be a good relationship between police officers and defense attorneys?
13. The best way for police officers to interact with crime victims?

REFERENCES

Broderick, J.J. (1987). *Police in a time of change* (2nd ed.). Glencoe, IL: Waveland Press.

Brown, L.P. (1978). The role of the sheriff. In A.V. Cohn (Ed.), *The future of policing* (pp. 227–247). Beverly Hills, CA: Sage Publications.

Buchanon, J. (1989). Police–prosecutor teams: Innovations in several jurisdictions. *NIJ Reports, 214,* 2–8.

Coffey, A.R. (1974). *Administration of criminal justice: A management systems approach.* Englewood Cliffs, NJ: Prentice Hall.

Cohn, A.V. (Ed.). (1978). *The future of policing.* Beverly Hills, CA: Sage Publications.

Cunningham, W.C., Strauchs, J.J., & Van Meter, C.W. (1991). *Private security: Patterns and trends* (National Institute of Justice—Research in brief). Washington, D.C.: U.S. Department of Justice.

Doerner, W.G. (1998). *Introduction to law enforcement: An insider's view.* Newton, MA: Butterworth-Heinemann.

Gannon, M.J. (1979). *Organizational behavior.* Boston: Little, Brown and Company.

Gonzalez, E. (1998). A new way to choose U.S. marshals. *Police Chief, 65,* 4.

Luthans, F. (1985). *Organizational behavior* (4th ed.). New York: McGraw-Hill.

Maguire, E.R., Snipes, J.B., Uchida, C.D., & Townsend, M. (1998). Counting cops: Estimating the number of police departments and police officers in the USA. *Policing: An International Journal of Police Strategies & Management, 21,* 97–120.

Murray v. United States 487 U.S. 533 (1988).

1998 National directory of law enforcement administrators, correctional institutions, and related agencies (Vol. 34). Stevens Point, WI: National Public Safety Information Bureau.

Police Task Force. (1973). Washington D.C.: National Advisory Commission on Criminal Justice Standards and Goals.

Purpura, P.P. (1997). *Criminal justice: An introduction.* Newton, MA: Butterworth-Heinemann.

Reaves, B.A. (1997). *Federal law enforcement officers, 1996.* Washington, D.C.: U.S. Government Printing Office.

Reaves, B.A., & Goldberg, A.L. (1998). *Census of state and local police departments, 1996.* Washington, D.C.: U.S. Government Printing Office.

Reaves, B.A., & Smith, P.Z. (1995). *Law enforcement management and administrative statistics, 1993: Data for individual state and local agencies with 100 or more officers.* Washington, D.C.: U.S. Government Printing Office.

Schmalleger, F. (1997). *Criminal justice today* (4th ed.). Upper Saddle River, NJ: Prentice Hall.

Sourcebook of criminal justice statistics, 1997. Washington, D.C.: U.S. Government Printing Office.

Territo, L., Halsted, J.B., & Bromley, M.L. (1998). *Crime and justice in America* (5th ed.). Newton, MA: Butterworth-Heinemann.

Trends and issues '91: Education and criminal justice in Illinois. Chicago: Illinois Criminal Justice Information Authority.

3 PATROL

If someone were to ask you what the most important element of policing was, how would you respond? You might suggest that management, personnel, communication, community support, or training was the most important. All of these are essential elements of police agencies, but the most visible and critical element is **patrol.** Patrol is a particularly interesting aspect of policing because it can be viewed as both an integral division of the police agency and as a function.

AS A DIVISION

Depending on the size of the police agency, patrol, as a division, might be found under uniformed services, operational services, or simply designated the patrol division. Where it is located is often a reflection of the police agency's command structure.

CASE IN POINT

The patrol section of the Chicago, Illinois, Police Department is located under the command of the first deputy superintendent for the Bureau of Operational Services. Within this same bureau are Special Functions, Operations Command, Special Operations, Special Events and Liaison, and Detached Services. For the Chicago Police Department, traffic enforcement is part of the Patrol Division. In contrast, the patrol division of the Fort Worth, Texas, Police Department is found under the deputy chief of the Uniform Services Bureau, which includes Traffic and Reserves, Tactical Unit, Foot Patrol, K-9, and Mounted Patrol.

Regardless of where patrol is located in the command structure, patrol is considered the backbone of a police agency. It is the most visible element of policing; readily identifiable police vehicles operated by uniformed officers often act as the first line of contact between the police agency and the community, lending to an atmosphere of safety. Police agencies are created to serve the community, and the patrol division is that first line of communication between the community and the police agency. If this division did not exist, there would be little need for the rest of the police agency, as nearly everything a police agency handles begins with the patrol officer.

The patrol division is important to the police agency itself for yet another reason. From a personnel perspective, patrol is the starting point for most rookie police officers. It is from patrol that officers receive many of their formative experiences.

Given the importance of patrol as a division and the fact that it is the most expensive part of the police service, one would assume that patrol receives the attention and respect it deserves. In reality, patrol officers are the lowest paid police officers and are the least consulted, even though they are more involved in answering citizens' calls for service than any other member of the agency (Broderick, 1987; Doerner, 1998; Police Task Force, 1973). They are often taken for granted. In addition, the rank of "patrol officer" receives low marks in status (Alpert & Dunham, 1998).

Patrol, as a division and as a position, is commonly underrated and unnecessarily criticized. Yet, the importance of this entity is supported statistically. Among agencies that employ more than 100 sworn officers, approximately 95 percent indicate that patrol and first response are their primary responsibilities. Furthermore, 89 percent of these sworn police personnel are assigned to field operations, largely to patrol (Reaves & Smith, 1995). In addition to the "traditional" patrol approach—uniformed officers in marked patrol units responding to calls for service—the patrol division employs a variety of other useful approaches.

Other Units in the Patrol Division

As noted in the previous Case in Point, organizationally, the unit referred to as "patrol" may have other types of units assigned to it. Although not all agencies may have these other types of patrol units (the size of the agency usually dictates the number and type of units), "specialized" patrol units may be found in many police agencies.

Traffic Units

The traffic unit is often assigned to the patrol division but also may exist as a separate division of a police agency. Traffic units provide two major services: (1) relieve the regular (general service) patrol officers of duties associated with traffic-related services and (2) generate revenue for the agency. Because the number of drivers is increasing, patrol officers continue to be severely burdened with traffic-related duties (i.e., working accidents and issuing citations). The creation of traffic units allows patrol officers to perform more patrol-related duties (delivery of services). Traffic officers work accidents, issue citations, direct traffic, work crowd control for special events, and are utilized for special details such as sobriety checkpoints. As a source of revenue, traffic units can be major contributors; their focus on traffic enforcement allows traffic officers to generate a substantial number of citations, which in turn generate revenues.

Traffic officer working a sobriety checkpoint. (Courtesy of the Scottsdale, Arizona, Police Department)

Tactical Response Teams

The tactical response team is a specially trained group of officers who respond to such situations as hostage taking or barricaded suspects, sniper attacks, major raids, and "sting" or surveillance setups. **TACT** or **SWAT** officers are specially trained in such areas as building entry, firearms, and the handling of hostage situations. In small agencies, TACT or SWAT officers may be assigned to general patrol duties when tactical services are not required. In large agencies, officers are assigned specifically to this unit because constant training and immediate availability for action are imperative.

Canine Units

In this popular unit, **K-9** officers work with specially trained dogs. These dogs are used for building searches, suspect searches (open field), and drug sniffing. In recent years, K-9 units have increased the discovery of drugs, particularly at border crossings and airports. K-9 units are becoming so popular that some police agencies are using them as traditional, general service patrol units (assigned to a specific beat like one- and two-officer patrol units). However, most agencies employ K-9 units for more specific purposes.

■ CASE IN POINT

In August 1996 the Omaha, Nebraska, Police Department's six new K-9 officers graduated from an eight-week training session. The primary functions of these officers are to help locate missing persons, track down felony or serious misdemeanor suspects, and search for contraband and evidence.

Tactical officers making an entry. (Courtesy of the Scottsdale, Arizona, Police Department)

K-9 officer and his trusty partner. (Courtesy of the Scottsdale, Arizona, Police Department)

Police Reserves

One of the more underrated and excessively criticized yet extremely valuable resources to the patrol division are the police reserves (auxiliary or part-time officers). Reserves provide additional police officers for a very limited amount of funding (some work as volunteers) and are quite useful for departments, large or small, whose budgets do not allow for increased numbers of paid officers.

■ CASE IN POINT

The Harrison County, Texas, Sheriff Reserve Unit has been in existence since 1975. It is composed of 43 men and women, all certified Texas peace officers. This contingent serves in all areas of the department from patrol through administration (http://www.arpolice.com/texas.html). The city of Richmond, California, has 18 level-1 reserve officers (unpaid volunteers with full police powers while on duty) to assist its 200 regular officers (http://www.arpolice.com/calif.html). New York City has an auxiliary police force of approximately 4000 officers. However, unlike reserves in other areas, NYPD auxiliary officers never carry firearms or engage in law enforcement activities (http://www.arpolice.com/newyork.html).

Reserve officers are particularly useful to police agencies that require more patrol officers during seasonal times such as holidays or spring break (Weinblatt, 1995).

■ CASE IN POINT

Two popular spots for college students during spring break are Daytona Beach, Florida and South Padre Island, Texas. On a daily basis throughout the spring break period (approximately February through April), both locations experience transient population swells several times their normal residential populations (Daytona is typically about 65,000, and South Padre is about 3000). Obviously the police agencies for these two cities could not adequately meet demands and needs with their regular complement of sworn, full-time officers (Daytona has about 220, and South Padre has about 30). Therefore, both agencies rely heavily on reserve officers.

Despite how useful reserve officers can be in supplementing the standard compliment of full-time officers, the reputation of police reserves has long tainted their usefulness. With a general reputation as John Wayne wannabes who like to play "policeman" but could not make it as "real" (full-time) police officers, police reserves have long suffered from an unfair perception and are often not very popular among (full-time) police officers.

In the early years of policing, many reserve police officers were volunteers who were often poorly trained and probably deserved the poor reputation they had. Today many reserve officers do not deserve this reputation. Yet, because of the existing perception among some "real" police officers, reserves do not receive the respect or proper recognition for the service they provide. This perception can be blamed in part on the fact that most reserves are full-time employees of other professions; many full-time officers do not understand why these individuals want to be part-time police officers, especially in instances in which no pay is involved.

Conversely, many individuals see the police reserves as a means of contributing to society or as a civic duty. In some cases, a position as a reserve police officer can supplement or enhance an individual's full-time occupation. For example, a full-time criminal justice professor became a police reserve to observe the "real world" and hopefully to intertwine his experience with classroom theory. Also, for some it is a good way to make a few extra dollars.

Regardless of why a person becomes a reserve, in many states reserve candidates must undergo training just like the full-time officers.

■ CASE IN POINT

The state of Texas requires that every police reserve be state certified as police officers before performing certain functions and duties. This means that the individual wanting to become a reserve must complete a 640-hour basic peace officer certification course. To be a Los Angeles County, California, reserve deputy, individuals must complete 200 hours of field training and 200 hours of observed training. This qualifies them to ride with a fully certified officer. For reserve deputies to ride alone, they must pass the same academy training as regular full-time deputies (approximately 460+ hours). To be an Allen County, Indiana, police reserve, individuals must complete approximately 350 hours of academy training.

Police agencies are beginning to see reserve officers as a support unit that deserves funding. For example, the reserve officers in Camden County, New Jersey, ably assist the 70 full-time officers "who file 40,000 calls for police service a year" ("Gloucester Township's Specials," 1995, p. 7), all within a 25-square-mile area. Full-time officers are appearing to begin to accept the reserve as a "regular" police officer, realizing that this individual is doing the same job and risking his or her life just like "real" officers do. Police agencies see reserves as a recruitment pool for full-time, paid positions. An example of this is the Josephine County, Oregon, Sheriff's Department, in which 90 percent of the department's regular officers were once reserves, including the current sheriff (*Reserve Law Officer News*, 1993). Undoubtedly, training and demonstrating their abilities to be patrol officers have assisted in improving the perception and position of police reserves. Still, maybe the best boost given to reserves is police agency accreditation, which requires that there be written standards or guidelines for the reserves and that the reserves be treated the same as full-time officers. Failure to meet these standards could present a problem for the agency.

■ CASE IN POINT

In early spring 1998 the Fort Lauderdale, Florida, Police Department had to suspend the use of its 13 reserve officers because it lacked the written guidelines and directives required by Florida's Law Enforcement Accreditation Commission. Although the reserves' duties generally included guarding the police memorial, transporting prisoners, and working security details, it was common for them to work the streets just like the full-time officers. However, until the guidelines and directives are written, no reserves are to be employed in Fort Lauderdale.

Overall, no matter who it is that makes up the patrol unit, the major function of the patrol element is the same. Therefore, the act of patrolling requires further attention.

⚬ AS A FUNCTION

Patrolling, as a function, is one of the few areas of policing that has seen little change since the early 1850s. Patrolling is an action involving constant movement within a given area or, in policing, within a given beat. As noted in 1973 and still quite applicable today, "In its simplest terms, patrol is the deployment of police officers in a given community to prevent and deter criminal activity and to provide day-to-day police services to the community" (Police Task Force, 1973, p. 189).

Although the adoption of and/or adaptation to community policing may cast a slightly new spin to the manner in which patrol is accomplished, the general reasons for patrolling have remained relatively the same since the formation of the London Metropolitan Police Department—to deter criminal activity and to provide security to the community. Theoretically, the function of patrol has been to eliminate the opportunity for crime. By creating a proactive presence, patrolling gives the impression of constant awareness by the police of community activities. This awareness purportedly leads to a limitation of criminal activity. In reality, patrolling has been primarily a reactive function (Cordner, 1989), addressing the symptom rather than the root of the problem. However, the patrol function under community policing is geared toward dealing with the root of the problem.

The patrol function is intended to create a belief that the police are doing their job and to allow citizens to enjoy a sense of security in their homes and businesses. Yet, for most of the 1980s and early 1990s, with few exceptions, there were consistent increases in crime rates (Sourcebook of Criminal Justice Statistics, 1996). In response to the perception of increasing threats of crime, citizens have resorted to barred windows and doors, alarm systems, private security, and firearms to enhance their sense of security (Alpert & Dunham, 1998) and appear to believe that patrolling is ineffective (Sourcebook of Criminal Justice Statistics, 1996). Although community policing is attempting to change perceptions, lower crime rates, and make the act of patrolling more effective, the traditional reasons for patrolling still exist.

Historically, deterrence and security were mainstays of the patrol function. Today, although community policing efforts are redirecting the focus of patrol and attempting to improve police–nonpolice cooperation, the primary function of patrolling is to provide four basic services to the community: **crime prevention (proactive deterrence), law enforcement (reactive deterrence), order maintenance (security),** and **social services (community welfare).**

Crime Prevention

Every year newspaper headlines remind citizens that crime is increasing in one area or another. When this occurs, it appears that police are not doing their jobs. In fact, crime prevention, a goal of policing since its earliest days, is one of the most difficult services for the police agency to provide effectively. Funding, personnel, reporting, and citizen involvement (or the lack thereof) all relate to how well the police can prevent crime.

The service of crime deterrence, more commonly referred to as crime prevention, has been the subject of debate for years. Crime prevention is the police agency's ability to prevent criminal activity before it occurs. As previously noted, crime prevention is actually a proactive function of patrolling. However, the oft-heard complaint, "There's never a cop around when you need one," seems to summarize a longstanding attitude of the general public toward the police's ability to prevent crime. Although it is unrealistic to expect patrol officers to be everywhere a crime is committed, public opinion polls tend to indicate that is exactly what the public expects. This failure to prevent crime as readily as the public perceives it should be done creates the impression that the service of crime prevention is extremely limited.

Meeting the objective of crime prevention through the act of patrolling has existed since the days of the London Metropolitan Police Department. Today a major objective of policing remains crime prevention through the act of patrol. Yet, it would appear that the act of patrolling is not a very effective crime prevention tool. Conversely, what might the levels of crime be if police agencies quit using patrol? What if patrol officers remained at substations until called? What might happen to crime levels then? Partial answers to these questions were provided by way of an experiment conducted in the early 1970s in Kansas City, formally known as the Kansas City Preventive Patrol Experiment (KCPPE).

For the KCPPE, fifteen geographical areas were chosen and divided into three experimental components. Each area was considered similar in terms of population and calls for police service. In one area, the number of patrol officers was cut from normal levels; one area remained status quo; and the last area was saturated. When the experiment ended and the results analyzed, "The overwhelming evidence is that decreasing or increasing routine preventive patrol within the range tested in this experiment had no effect on crime" (Kelling et al., 1989, p. 59). In other words, it was believed that the number of officers on patrol did not have much impact on crime. Despite some of the methodological problems, it was the first scientific attempt to truly examine the effectiveness of the patrol function.

Besides the act of patrolling, police officers provide crime prevention through special services such as neighborhood watch, business and residence security checks, and through crime prevention units. Yet, the patrol function is ultimately held responsible for any failure to prevent crime consistently.

Furthermore, crime prevention is often confused with crime suppression. Crime prevention is eliminating the factors that could lead to criminal activity in the first place. For example, adding extra patrol to an industrial complex that has been suffering an increase in burglaries or meeting with business owners to discuss enhanced security measures—these are crime prevention activities. Crime suppression is really stopping the crime before it gets started or is completed. Staking out a building and waiting for someone to break in and then making an arrest is crime suppression.

In sum, police agencies constantly look for ways to improve their ability to provide crime prevention and crime suppression services. Yet, not all crimes can be prevented or suppressed—a reality both society and the police have to accept. However, community policing is an attempt to increase the chances of eliminating and preventing crime.

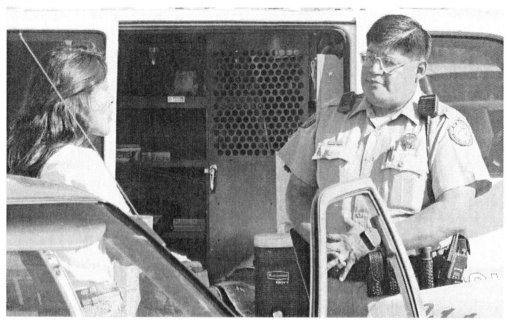

Patrol officer interacting with a citizen. (Courtesy of the Scottsdale, Arizona, Police Department)

Law Enforcement

The service of crime prevention is considered the proactive service of the patrol function; the service of law enforcement can be viewed as the reactive service. The service of law enforcement occurs after a criminal violation has occurred. As part of the patrol function, patrol officers provide this service when they respond to calls for assistance, such as a domestic disturbance, burglary, or theft. Often these calls are related to crimes that have already occurred.

The public expects the patrol officer to solve the situation immediately, preferably by arresting the offender. If making an arrest is not an immediate possibility, the public demands that the patrol officer do everything possible to enhance a quick arrest, such as collecting evidence, matching fingerprints, or making an arrest or search without a warrant. Often, a quick arrest is impossible because of the lack of evidence or information as to who the offender is and where the offender may be located. However, the public's lack of understanding as to why immediate apprehension is often impossible leads to conflict between the police and the public, and criticism of law enforcement as a service. In addition, lack of citizen cooperation, reporting of crime long after it has occurred, and apathy among both the police and citizens leaves the law enforcement service under constant scrutiny by citizens.

Finally, the reason every person wants to be a police officer is to apprehend the "bad guys." The cornerstone of policing is enforcing laws. This is accomplished on a daily basis through issuing traffic citations, enforcing city ordinances, and making arrests. The possibilities for enforcement are extremely broad; yet, the ultimate experience for most patrol officers is the apprehension of an individual committing a felony. Although these are rare, when the opportunity arises the officer must be prepared to deal with the circumstances.

■ CASE IN POINT

About 4:00 A.M. the patrol officer decided to cruise through the local park on his beat. The officer had barely entered the park when suddenly a completely naked woman appeared in front of the patrol car screaming, "He was trying to rape me, and he is still in the car." Needless to say, the officer's adrenaline kicked into high gear, his thoughts and pulse racing faster than normal—a rape in progress! The woman got into the police vehicle, where she covered herself with the officer's raincoat, while the officer requested immediate backup. The woman quickly told the officer that the suspect should still be in her car, which was parked only a short distance from the patrol car. Shining the spotlight on the car, hoping backup would arrive soon, the officer yelled for the suspect to get out of the car and walk toward the patrol car with his hands in the air. The suspect, who was still in the car, got out and began to approach the officer. Backup soon arrived, and the suspect was taken into custody. Obviously, the immediacy of the situation required the officer to think and respond quickly to the victim, suspect, and overall circumstances without placing the victim or himself in further danger as well as apprehend the suspect.

Order Maintenance

Ensuring public safety and security is no easy task. The ability to do so is best referred to as "order maintenance." According to Moore, Trojanowicz, and Kelling (1988), the core mission of the police in the United States is to control crime. Although this may be the core mission, police spend a great deal of time simply keeping order. Quieting the loud party, directing traffic at an accident scene, and providing crowd control during events such as parades, road races, and political rallies are all examples of order maintenance tasks performed by police officers on a daily basis.

Order maintenance by the police is expected by the community, and circumstances arise frequently for which police presence is requested. These occurrences may not need any police action other than a request for quiet or movement of an inappropriately parked vehicle (e.g., a neighbor's car blocking your driveway). Although these calls for service may be perceived by officers as "a waste of time" or "not crime related," it is to their advantage to remedy the situation so that it does not escalate into something more than a minor disturbance. Although order maintenance calls are not popular among police officers, they tend to constitute many calls for police service. For example, in 1997, 87.5 percent of the calls to the Wilmette, Illinois, police department were service related (Wilmette Police Department Annual Report).

Order maintenance remains an extremely important part of the patrol function. Citizens have come to expect the police to maintain peace and order in our society regardless of what that requires.

One form of order maintenance is working traffic accidents. (Courtesy of the Scottsdale, Arizona, Police Department)

Social Services

Accepting the role of social service provider by a patrol officer is difficult. Patrol officers are usually willing to accept their responsibility for delivery of the other services, but when it comes to social services, the willingness to serve frequently seems to disappear. Yet, studies of calls for police have indicated that a large proportion can be classified as a social service (Cordner, 1989; Kessler, 1985).

Assisting an individual in entering a house or vehicle after the keys have been locked in or lost, transporting persons to medical facilities or other helping agencies, offering conversation to a lonely elderly person, or simply changing a tire on a vehicle are all considered a social service. Patrol officers are the first source of assistance in a variety of circumstances when there is no one else to call, even though the problem is not a crime- or order-related matter.

However, like order maintenance calls, social service calls are not usually enthusiastically responded to by police officers. Many officers voice a belief that it is not their job to provide social services. Yet, it would appear that society

(Jump Start reprinted by permission of United Feature Syndicate, Inc.)

expects this service of their police. Although it is understandable why police officers do not readily accept their social service role, it is apparent that if they did not fulfill this role, who would?

It is the function of patrol to provide effectively and efficiently four services: crime prevention, law enforcement, order maintenance, and social services. Although these services can be viewed as distinctively different categories, it should be noted that these services often overlap. For example, a request to quiet a boisterous party (order maintenance) could lead to arrests (e.g., alcohol consumption by minors or drug usage), a law enforcement task. Yet, although they may overlap, the way these services are provided and how effectively is primarily the result of how patrol, the division, is organized and patrol, the function, is used.

ORGANIZATION AND DELIVERY

The effectiveness and efficiency of the delivery of services in any organization are primarily the result of the delivery system's organizational structure. This is a particularly relevant point when examining patrol as a division.

As noted earlier, in the larger metropolitan police agency patrol is often located in a bureau or division led by a deputy chief. Under the deputy chief there are a variety of middle-line managers, such as captains, lieutenants, and sergeants. The patrol area is then usually divided into geographical sectors, regions, or districts. This breakdown is related to such factors as crime rate, population, and type of activity (e.g., residential, business, or combination). Within each of these, there is a further geographical breakdown into what is commonly referred to as the patrol "beat." Similar factors as those used to make the initial geographical divisions are used to establish the beats.

▮ CASE IN POINT

In January 1998 the Manchester, New Hampshire, Police Department began a new patrol plan built around remapping the city. The new plan divided the city into three geographic areas: West Side, Northeast and North End, and South Manchester. Each sector has four patrol routes, or beats. These routes were established based on calls for service.

Along with the assignment to specific patrol areas, patrol officers are often divided among three work shifts, or "watches." While the times of these shifts may differ from agency to agency, the common practice is to have a day, evening, and night (sometimes referred to as "graveyard" or "hoot owl") shift. Some departments use a fourth shift, often referred to as a "swing" or "power" shift, which overlaps the evening and night shifts. This shift is used in cities that experience a higher call demand during certain hours. For example, a power shift might start at 7:00 P.M. and last until 3:00 A.M.

Patrol officers are assigned to their beats and shifts in ways that sometimes cause debate among officers and criticism of administrators by officers. There are several factors taken into account when distributing officers within the patrol division. The first factors to be considered are geographic and economic conditions. A patrol sector that is geographically too large to be patrolled by the number of officers assigned to it leads to inability to provide services equitably. High-crime areas frequently require more patrol officers than relatively crime-free neighborhoods; however, taking officers away from stabler areas and placing them in the more crime-infested areas is often unpopular with those who reside in the more crime-free neighborhoods. Of course, this is one of the problems supposedly being addressed by community policing, in which officers are assigned to all areas on a more permanent basis and hopefully are given the means to maintain the status quo in low-crime areas and turn high-crime areas into low-crime areas.

Another factor considered is the time of day or shift requiring the most officers. Customarily, the evening shift is the busiest patrol shift. People coming home from work in heavy traffic having accidents, discovery of home burglaries committed while people were away at work, and family disputes add to demands for a greater provision of patrol services. Thus, more officers need to be available.

Similarly, days of the week are an important factor. The days of the week traditionally requiring the greatest availability of patrol services have been the weekend—Friday, Saturday, and Sunday. The increase in calls for police service occur because weekends tend to include partying (and its related alcoholic consumption) and family get-togethers. This combination frequently leads to requests for police services (loud music, arguments, and fights).

A final factor affecting distribution of officers and services is the type of patrol employed by a police agency. With several types from which to choose, a police agency has to decide what is the best way to patrol a given area.

TYPES OF PATROL

The predominant means for conducting patrol in the United States is still by automobile. However, the effectiveness of other means and the requirement to use other means (such as foot patrol for community policing) is bringing about additional methods of patrol.

Foot Patrol. Officers patrol on foot, walking the beat in both a proactive and reactive mode. Until community policing brought foot patrol back to residential neighborhoods, it was mainly used in business or downtown areas.

Horse/Mounted Patrol.   Officers patrol their assigned areas on horseback. This form of patrol is extremely popular in cities with lots of city park area to cover. Chicago, Illinois, makes use of mounted patrol along its lakeshore areas, which stretch for more than 30 miles.

Motorcycle Patrol.   Although more often linked with traffic enforcement, motorcycles of all sizes have a place in patrol.

Helicopter Patrol.   Perhaps one of the more versatile types of patrol is by helicopter. Because of the ability to cover large areas, track suspects and vehicles, and have a more oppulent view of the city, helicopter patrol can add to the general abilities of patrol. One agency that recently took to the sky was the Omaha, Nebraska, Police Department, which began its helicopter patrols the summer of 1997. At the same time, the Los Angeles, California, Police Department added three new state-of-the-art helicopters to its longstanding helicopter patrol program.

Boat/Water Patrol.   If the city has a body of water to patrol, obviously boats are the best means of patrol. However, in an age of changing technology, boats may become passé.

■ CASE IN POINT

In 1996 the Massachusetts State Police Marine Unit added a new tool: jet skis. Troopers patrol waterways, in particular recreational areas, on these new devices.

Bicycle Patrol.   The most recently reemployed method of patrol is by bicycle, especially as part of the move toward community policing, either as a special unit or part of uniform patrol. Bicycle patrol brings a dimension of fleetness and accessibility many other forms of patrol cannot. Early reports indicate that using a bicycle changes, and sometimes betters, the traditional mode of patrolling.

Because bicycle patrol is becoming so popular, especially as a part of community policing, some changes in "traditional" bicycle patrol techniques are occurring. For example, in 1997 the Dallas, Texas, Police Department added a new twist to its bicycle patrol abilities by using the ZAP Police Powerbike—a motorized bicycle that can reach a speed of 20 miles per hour—in the central business district.

■ CASE IN POINT

In July 1996 it was reported that the Mount Sterling, Kentucky, Police Department's bicycle unit had 10 times as many interactions with the public, per hour, than the marked patrol units. That same year, from June through mid-August, bike patrols in Anchorage, Alaska, were credited with making 36 felony and 315 misdemeanor arrests.

Although there is more than one way to provide the function of patrol, marked vehicles are still the most dominant form of patrol. As such, they continue to be a subject of debate with regard to whether this form of patrol should be occupied by one officer or two. Recall from Chapter 1 that in the 1970s the San Diego Police Department conducted landmark research that focused on one-versus two-officer patrol units. The results from that study indicated that although two-officer units were safer, one-person units were more productive. Although productivity is important to the police agency, safety should also be an issue.

Motorcycle patrol. (Courtesy of the Scottsdale, Arizona, Police Department)

This is particularly true in state police agencies where the practice is one-person units. Research continues to show that one-person patrol units are riskier ("One-Officer State Police Cars Raise the Risk to Cops' Lives," 1997).

Realistically, whether in a marked car, with either one person or two, or on horse, foot, or bicycle, the form(s) of patrol employed by a police agency will depend on its needs and the type of environment in which it must provide patrol services. Geography, population, crime rate, calls for services, day of week, and time of day all are important to the effectiveness of patrol as a function, but they are not the only factors.

In addition to the factors noted, the effective function of patrol relies upon professionalism, attitude, supervision, and in-service training. To begin with, professionalism and attitude play important roles in the effectiveness of patrolling because they assist in determining the type of tactic employed by the patrol officer when patrolling. It is believed that a positive attitude and a professional demeanor tend to create a proactive, aggressive patrol officer who fervently attempts to meet the demand of the public for the services patrolling is intended to provide (Broderick, 1987). A poor attitude or an unprofessional demeanor detracts from effectiveness (Alpert & Dunham, 1998).

Mounted patrol. (Courtesy of the Scottsdale, Arizona, Police Department)

Well-trained patrol supervisors are a commodity all police agencies like to develop. Supervisors play an important role in the delivery of services, for it is these individuals who must oversee delivery of service and ensure the public and the police agency that the patrol services are being provided in the best manner possible under agency conditions and policies. Police administration literature identifies the existence of three types of patrol supervisor. First, there is the **"hands-on"** supervisor. This individual has a tendency to get involved in situations, whether as an assisting officer or the lead officer. Second, there is the **"command"** supervisor. This individual shows up at crime scenes whether requested or not and simply gives orders. The third type of supervisor is the **"counsel"** supervisor, who, by request, arrives at crime scenes to offer advice. All three types have a time and place; however, on the whole, the most effective supervisors appear to be those who choose and use appropriate characteristics of each type as situations require. It is this type of supervisor that most

Bicycle patrol. (Courtesy of the Scottsdale, Arizona, Police Department)

police agencies should want to develop and retain (Swanson, Territo, & Taylor, 1998).

Finally, an element sometimes neglected after completion of the basic police academy is ongoing in-service training for patrol officers. In recent years, the number of changes occurring having a direct impact on policing is increasing. Changes in the law, technological advances, weaponry, drugs, and general societal changes affect the delivery of services. The basic police academy is no longer enough to fully prepare patrol officers for a lifetime of service, and additional in-service training is becoming important to keeping patrol officers up to date. In an effort to ensure that such in-service training does occur, some states requiring police officer certification (licensure) are also mandating that officers receive a specified number of in-service hours each year. For example, Nevada and Texas require police officers to receive a minimum of forty hours of in-service training every year to retain their licenses; Georgia requires its officers to have at least twenty hours of in-service training yearly.

The delivery of services plays an important part of the patrol function. However, the recognition these services receive is frequently overshadowed because attention is more often focused on the individual tasks, situations, incidents, or crimes a police officer faces during a patrol shift or "in the line of duty."

IN THE LINE OF DUTY

Every day thousands of police officers patrol our streets. While carrying out this function, they deal with a myriad of issues, situations, and problems. They must also cope with periods in which little is occurring, and constant movement and attentiveness are the rule in responding to a call for help that may have life and death implications. This is true whether the officer is patrolling large rural spaces or a small urban beat. As previously suggested, it is more the exception than the rule for many patrol officers to have to deal with truly crime-related incidents, especially crimes in progress. Still, officers must always be vigilant and ready because they never know when that "big call" will come that will require every ounce of knowledge and courage to survive.

■ CASE IN POINT

On February 28, 1997, Los Angeles, California, Police Department officers Loren Farrell and Martin Perello, while on uniformed patrol, observed what they believed to be a bank robbery in progress. Not only was the observation correct but the suspects would turn out to be heavily armed, protected by Kevlar ("bullet-proof" material), and not afraid of confronting the police. By the time the confrontation was over, literally hundreds of rounds had been fired by both police and the suspects. Although several officers and a few citizens were injured, fortunately, the only individuals who died that day were the two suspects. Being shot at, let alone hit, is probably every police officer's worse nightmare and, unfortunately, one does not have to be a "big city patrol officer" to see those fears realized. Also in 1997, a West Virginia State Police trooper, Paul Burton, was shot in the leg by a robbery suspect while the trooper was making a traffic stop on the suspect. Even with the wounded leg, Trooper Burton managed to chase down and apprehend the suspect. Finally, in January 1998, a Jefferson County, Missouri, sheriff's deputy, Ray Edler, pulled Corporal D. Cummings to safety after Cummings had been shot in the head by an individual at a mobile home. The kicker to this event was that Edler had also been shot, in the face and hand, during his effort. Both officers are recovering, and Edler was nominated for his department's Medal of Valor.

The myriad of situations or activities a patrol officer may engage in can be divided into three categories: dangerous, routine, and frustrating.

Dangerous Situations

As participants in a very hazardous occupation, police officers have the potential for encountering life-threatening conditions or the actual loss of life on a daily basis, as indicated in the previous Case in Point. Fortunately, such situations do not occur as frequently as believed by individuals with little knowledge or experience with policing (as do criminal justice students or family members of would-be police officers). Still, no situation should be taken lightly, because even the most common activities could end tragically.

■ CASE IN POINT

In May 1998 two veteran Tampa, Florida, homicide detectives, Randy Bell and Rick Childers, were shot and killed by a murder suspect wanted for questioning in the death of his girlfriend's four-year-old son. The suspect, who had been handcuffed and believed to have had a key hidden on his person, got free of his cuffs, took one of the detective's guns, and killed both detectives. Eventually, the suspect took his own life, but not before killing another police officer, Florida Highway Patrol trooper James Crook.

Although every situation has the potential to become dangerous, two particular situations during which a police officer could lose his or her life, or the life of another could become threatened, deserve special attention: pursuits and felonies in progress.

Pursuits

One of the more controversial activities for a patrol officer is engaging in a pursuit. Pursuits have garnered tremendous attention from the media and the courts. The police pursuit may either be "on foot" or "vehicular." A pursuit occurs when an officer either attempts to stop a vehicle or make an arrest, and the suspect flees. Although the hazards of a foot pursuit should not be ignored, the vehicular or "high-speed" pursuit receives more attention primarily because it poses a danger to the pursuing officers, suspects, and innocent bystanders.

■ CASE IN POINT

In 1996 a Shelby County, Indiana deputy sheriff, Stacia Alyea, died after her patrol car flipped over during a high-speed chase. She was believed to have been chasing a suspected drunk driver when the accident occurred. In 1997 a West Memphis, Arkansas, police sergeant, Stan Burch, was seriously injured when his vehicle crashed head on with another vehicle while he was pursuing a suspected stolen vehicle. Two people in the car that Burch collided with died. In 1998 an innocent driver was killed when a stolen vehicle fleeing Tulsa, Oklahoma, police ran a red light and struck the driver's side of the victim's car. The pursuit, which lasted less than two minutes, finally ended in a four-car crash.

The magnitude of injury or loss of life from a high-speed vehicular pursuit has become well documented. Injuries to and deaths of officers, suspects, and innocent bystanders have forced state legislatures and police departments to reevaluate and write or rewrite pursuit policies.

■ CASE IN POINT

In 1998 a Connecticut legislative committee approved and sent to the senate a proposal that would establish a statewide policy for police pursuits. This policy is similar to a growing number of pursuit policies that require the officer to notify a supervisor prior to engaging in a pursuit. However, the officer would not have to wait for permission to start the pursuit.

Of particular interest are pursuit policies that try to regulate the type of pursuit in which an officer can engage.

■ CASE IN POINT

Fairfax County, Virginia, allows its police officers to engage in high-speed pursuits of serious offenders. In Virginia Beach, Virginia, until June 1998 when the policy changed, officers could pursue intoxicated drivers, car thieves, and other nonviolent offenders. In Hackensack, New Jersey, police officers are to avoid pursuits whenever possible, but the decision is ultimately left to the officer's discretion.

The issue of high-speed pursuits has reached the point where the courts have become involved. The issue the courts are examining is liability. Who is liable when someone not involved in the pursuit is injured? The courts have been somewhat ambivalent in these cases. In some instances the courts have placed liability on the police for injury occurring from a pursuit when the police apparently should have recognized the obvious potential for danger and continued the pursuit anyway. In other instances the courts have found that the police are not liable and are not violating an individual's rights when injury or death results from the pursuit.

■ CASE IN POINT

In 1997 a Virginia state trooper was convicted of reckless endangerment after causing an accident during the pursuit of a speeder. The trooper lost control of his vehicle and struck another, killing a minister and seriously injuring his wife. The same year, a circuit court judge held a Millington, Tennessee, police officer partially responsible for the accidental death of a person who was killed when a car being chased by the officer struck the victim's vehicle. In what appears to be the biggest case to date affecting pursuits, the U.S. Supreme Court ruled in favor of police officers in the case of *County of Sacramento* v. *Lewis* 98 F.3d 434 (1998). The Court held that a police officer does not violate the Fourteenth Amendment guarantee of substantive due process if death is caused through deliberate or reckless indifference to life during a high-speed pursuit. The Court further ruled that only an intentional action to cause harm unrelated to the legitimate object of effecting an arrest would be cause for the officer to be held liable.

Court decisions, whether in favor of or against the police, have forced police agencies to establish appropriate guidelines and policies for high-speed pursuits. The effects of these changes on police pursuits is yet to be confirmed. There is some concern that curtailing police pursuits may cause more people to flee from the police; however, unnecessary injury or death stemming from pursuits is not acceptable. Therefore, policies are necessary, and it has been suggested that policies address these factors: violation or offense, environment or area in which chase occurs, and traffic and weather conditions (Alpert, 1998).

■ CASE IN POINT

The following are excerpts from a November 1991 revision of the Wilmette, Illinois, Police Department's pursuit policy:

Policy: The Wilmette Police Department carefully regulates vehicular pursuits and closely supervises personnel who may be engaged in such action to reduce the likelihood of injuries to officers and civilians.

Procedure: The purpose of pursuit is the apprehension of a suspect who refuses to voluntarily comply with the law requiring drivers to stop upon command. (1) The primary goal
of the Department is the protection of life and property. (2) To the extent that a pursuit
exposes any officer, suspect, or member of the general public to an unnecessary risk of
harm or injury, then pursuit is inconsistent with that goal. (Wilmette, Illinois, Police Department).

*The remaining part of the policy includes definitions of motor vehicle pursuit, routine traffic
stops, and roadblock; notification and termination of pursuit procedures; supervisory responsibilities; a detailed explanation of the roles and responsibilities of everyone who will be involved in
the pursuit; emergency vehicle operation and tactics; and interjurisdictional pursuits.*

Reality dictates that police officers cannot simply ignore a suspected criminal offender because the individual does not want to yield to a police officer. Pursuits
are part of the patrol experience, therefore, officers and departments have to be
prepared for these events. Pursuits, however, are not the only type of dangerous
situation for which officers need to be prepared.

Felonies in Progress

The definition of a felony may differ from one state to another, but what constitutes a felony is fairly uniform among state legal codes. Murder, rape (sexual
assault), robbery, and burglary are examples of felonies commonly found in
every state. When one of these is reported as "in progress," the response of the
police officer dispatched may well save life, limb, and property. Policies covering
response to these types of calls are important and often include similar issues,
such as authorization to respond "code" (lights and siren), approaching the
scene, and coordinating with backup.

Running code is a particularly interesting issue. Being able to respond quickly
to an in-progress call has been believed to improve the chances of apprehending
the suspect(s), and, it is hoped, to preserve life or property. However, the question has arisen through the years as to what types of in-progress calls should
allow code response. Some police agencies allow code responses to all domestic
disturbances, whereas others only permit such a response to apparent "life-or-
death" calls and "alarm" calls (burglary and robbery). The factors used to determine "response" policy differ from agency to agency.

Regardless of types of calls to which officers respond code, the safety of
others and officers is imperative. A police sergeant once told his platoon after an
officer was injured in an accident running code, "Remember, you are no good to
the person needing assistance or the department if you hurt yourself or someone
else while in route to a call running code."

While felonies in progress can be quite dangerous, the danger involved in
felony traffic stops must also be recognized. A felony traffic stop is when an
officer has reason to believe the individual(s) inside the vehicle have committed
or are about to commit a serious offense. Although officers should use caution on
all traffic stops, greater precautions should be taken for the felony stop. A patrol
officer should never attempt to make a felony traffic stop on his or her own.
Once the vehicle has stopped, the officer needs to gain control of the occupants

WHAT DO YOU THINK?

To Pursue or Not to Pursue?

At approximately 2:00 A.M. a female San Antonio, Texas, patrol officer disappeared during a foot pursuit. The officer had responded to a possible burglary in progress at an apartment complex. On her arrival, an individual was observed fleeing from the alleged burglary location. With another officer, she pursued the individual on foot. The individual led the officers to the back of the complex, where they split up, with the female officer still pursuing the suspect. The chase continued through a small creek that ran behind the complex. Later that morning the officer's body was found floating in the creek. Speculation was that the suspect observed that he was being pursued only by the female officer, turned and attacked her.

1. What do you think actually happened?
2. Should the female officer have continued to pursue on her own, or watched the suspect and requested assistance?
3. Did the officers make a wise decision by splitting up or should they have stayed together?
4. Although the worse possible outcome occurred, what were some possible less catastrophic outcomes?
5. Unless an officer definitely knows a crime has occurred, should he or she pursue a fleeing subject?
6. When should an officer pursue? Why should he or she pursue?

immediately by having them disembark from the vehicle, one at a time, in a manner that affords the officer all possible chances of control or escape should the person have a weapon and try to attack the officer.

Whether engaging in a pursuit, responding to a felony in progress, or making a felony traffic stop, the potential for danger exists and must be recognized. Policies covering these events, as well as other potentially dangerous situations, must exist and be understood by all officers because it is a major function of policing to preserve life, not to lose it.

"Routine" Situations

During an officer's career, the officer will deal with a variety of situations, some occurring on a daily basis; such situations have been referred to as "routine." The viewpoint offered here is that there is no such thing as a routine situation—only routine responses to situations.

The application of the term *routine* to patrol work is misleading. Its application can create a perception of patrol work as mundane and boring and that there is no variety among similar events. Reference is frequently made to the "routine call." Yet, to refer to any event that occurs while on patrol as routine can

A felony traffic stop. (Courtesy of the Scottsdale, Arizona, Police Department)

only lead to trouble. Nothing a police officer must respond to is routine; yet, the practice of referring to certain calls as "routine" continues because the definition of the term *routine*, whether as an adjective or noun, is lost when used to describe police work.

As a noun, routine can be defined as, "a regular course of procedure; habitual or mechanical performance of an established procedure." The adjective form of routine is defined as, "in accordance with established procedure" *(Webster's Collegiate Dictionary)*. Labeling a specific event or situation in policing as routine can be deceiving and, potentially, very dangerous.

For example, traffic stops are most often referred to as "routine." It is not that traffic stops, in themselves, are routine, but the procedure used to stop and approach the vehicle may be routine. The training and policies for making such a stop are shared with all officers; therefore, there is an established routine. However, the reason for the stop differs, thus making the tag, "routine," misleading. Speeding, disregarding a red light or stop sign, an expired license plate, suspected drunk driving, or the vehicle matches a suspect vehicle from an offense are a few of the reasons for stopping a vehicle. Some may happen every day, some every now and then. None is routine, no matter how many times the situation may occur.

In addition to the differing reasons for stopping the vehicle, every driver is different. Age, gender, race, socioeconomic status, and attitude are different with every motorist. For traffic stops to be truly "routine," everyone stopped under similar circumstances would have to possess similar characteristics. Furthermore, every traffic stop would have the same outcome. Yet, not every one does. Some drivers may be issued a ticket, whereas others receive a warning, and a few may even be arrested. Therefore, to label traffic stops or any other police service or activity as "routine" is inappropriate and could be fatal.

■ CASE IN POINT

A five-year veteran patrol officer who enjoyed making traffic stops was assigned to a special traffic enforcement unit. The primary purpose of this unit was to issue citations. Having located a stop sign that was often disregarded by motorists, this officer wrote an average of fifteen citations every day. After several weeks of this, the officer began to approach every stop the same way, giving little regard to the type of vehicle or who was occupying the vehicle. It even got to a point where the officer did not even bother to radio his position. One day, while approaching a vehicle he had just stopped, the officer was shot. Fortunately, he was not killed. Obviously, the "routine" mentality could be detrimental to a police officer.

A patrol officer may issue a citation; work an accident; take a burglary, assault, or theft report; settle a disturbance; or make an arrest almost every day. The fact that an officer may do this every day, or several times a day, has lead to the descriptor "routine" for many of these activities. In the truest sense, everyday activities are far from routine. The procedure(s) used to handle or perform daily activities may be routine, but the event itself will differ somewhat event to event, day to day. Thus, for a police officer to view every activity as "routine" almost guarantees that he or she will eventually walk into a situation without being prepared for the potential danger that could exist.

■ CASE IN POINT

For several months the burglar alarm at a local warehouse went off on a weekly basis. Initially it was responded to in an appropriately cautious manner. However, after weeks and weeks of false alarms, responding officers began to approach the call as a "routine false alarm." One day it turned out to be a legitimate alarm. However, the approach of the responding officer was one of indifference, assuming it was just another false alarm. On his initial arrival at the scene, not noticing anything unusual, the officer advised his backup to disregard the call and casually drove into the parking lot at the rear of the building with his vehicle lights on and was shot at by two subjects who were busy loading a pickup truck with merchandise. Although the suspects were apprehended by other units responding to the officer's call for assistance, the officer had to explain why he disregarded an assist in the first place and was reprimanded for the damage done to the police vehicle by the gunshots.

Frustrating Situations

Although police officers on patrol face a variety of frustrating situations on a daily basis, some areas are often particularly frustrating. Whether because of laws, role conflicts, or attitudes, the following are examples of areas that appear to provide

WHAT DO YOU THINK?

Working Patrol: Routine Occurrences or Routine Procedures?

As a patrol officer the situations one encounters and the calls to which one responds vary on a daily basis. No two days are ever alike, and no two calls are ever alike, although many are similar. For example, an officer might respond to a domestic disturbance every day for two weeks straight and, although the reason for the disturbances and how they are approached may be relatively similar, the people involved, the conditions in which they occur, and the outcomes may differ. Yet, because officers answer so many calls in a similar manner, they begin to think of them as routine. Soon, officers are not as careful or alert when responding to certain types of calls; caution is thrown out the window. Then one day an officer responds to another "routine" call; only this time it isn't so routine and the officer gets injured or, worse yet, killed.

1. Based on your beliefs, is police work "routine"? Why or why not?
2. Why do officers often refer to some types of calls as "routine" (e.g., "routine" traffic stop)?
3. What can police departments do to ensure that officers do not fall into the trap of viewing calls as "routine"?
4. How much impact does the "routine" mentality have on officer safety?
5. Is the "routine" mentality a product of the types of encounters or the procedures used to respond to the encounters?
6. Do you think it's possible that police training assists in creating the "routine" label? How?

police officers with a variety of problems, which make them particularly frustrating to handle, especially when the patrol service required is often more social service or order maintenance related.

Domestic Violence

For years, society tended to turn a "blind eye" to domestic incidents even when they turned violent. No where was this better illustrated than with how the police approached domestic disputes. It was common for the police to do nothing more than intercede for the moment, make threats that next time someone is going to jail, and leave. However, domestic disputes, domestic violence in particular, have recently received more attention from the public and the police, especially because the number of incidents reported to police seems to be rising. For example, figures for the state of Maine showed that police in that state handled more than 4400 domestic violence cases in 1995. It appears that Maine is not an exception to the rule in that domestic violence in the United States has been on the rise during the past ten years (*Sourcebook of Criminal Justice Statistics*, 1997).

(Jump Start reprinted by permission of United Feature Syndicate, Inc.)

It has long been believed that domestic violence calls are the most dangerous calls to which an officer could respond. Although domestic violence calls can be unpredictable, there is little statistical support for this belief. This does not mean that officers have nothing to worry about when responding to such calls because they are one of the most unpredictable types of calls for an officer—a factor that could lead to an officer's death.

■ CASE IN POINT

In January 1997 two Cabazon, California, sheriff's deputies responding to a domestic violence call were shot and killed by a sniper armed with an M-1 military rifle. Several shots were fired at other officers before the suspect was apprehended several hours later.

Other than the inherent unpredictability and possible danger, one might wonder why police officers find responding to this type of call frustrating. The truth is that police officers often resent being forced to intervene in what they believe to be a family matter. Some officers believe that it is not the business of the police—it is neither their job nor their place—to interfere in family quarrels unless a criminal act has been committed. In the past, even when a criminal act was committed, police officers often did little more than separate the quarreling parties (Black, 1980; Oppenlander, 1982).

Before police agencies recently began to change their policies on how a domestic situation, particularly a violent one, would be handled, a range of police intervention styles were identified. The four most common forms of intervention are penal, conciliatory, therapeutic, and compensatory (Black, 1980).

The first and least used method is **penal,** or arrest. The fact is that police officers do not like to make an arrest in these disputes. Many police officers believe that an arrest is only a short-term solution that often escalates the problem when the offender is released (Smith, Spradlin, & Cerrato, 1989; Williams, 1992), particularly if the courts do not require any type of follow-up counseling or treatment (Sherman & Berk, 1985).

A second style is the **conciliatory,** or "making-up," style. Probably the most often used method of dealing with domestic disputes, it consists of separating the disputants and talking to each one alone. The idea is to show them the senselessness of the disturbance and to advise them of the possible outcome if more drastic measures are needed, leading to at least a temporary cessation of the dispute.

The third style, counseling, or **therapeutic** intervention, is not a method most officers are prepared to implement. In this intervention mode officers try to determine the problem and provide solutions. The problem with this approach is that police officers are seldom trained counselors.

Finally, police officers might insist on restitution, or make use of a **compensatory** style. With this method the officer tries to persuade the offender to pay for damages. However, the application of this style is usually limited to disturbances between nonmarried combatants, such as roommates.

Which method a police officer used in these situations was left to his or her discretion and was often influenced by a variety of factors, which can be divided into two broad categories: general and mitigating. General factors include the socioeconomic class of the disputants, their race or ethnicity, age, and type of relationship (spouses, parent/child, roommates). Mitigating factors include use of a weapon, injuries, intoxication, and the presence of children.

In an effort to determine what type of intervention worked best, an experiment was conducted in Minnesota, referred to as the Minneapolis Domestic Violence Experiment (Sherman & Beck, 1985). This experiment required police officers to give up their discretion and to take whatever action had been randomly dictated to them. Before going out on patrol, participating officers were given unmarked, sealed envelopes they could only open prior to responding to a domestic violence call. Dictated actions included mandating arrest, separation, or mediation. The findings indicated that only 10 percent of those arrested were repeat offenders. Although the researchers advised that the findings should not be generalized, several police agencies changed their policies to reflect arrest in many instances (Williams, 1992).

Despite the research findings, albeit their limitations, it would take more to get most police agencies to change their policies on handling domestic disputes. A main reason for this change appears to be a concern of the state over the welfare of its citizens. In addition, the growing concern over civil liability lawsuits against governmental bodies, police agencies, and individual officers has assisted in promoting changes in the law. The issue within these lawsuits has been that of equal protection (Smith et al., 1989).

Since 1988, several court cases have been heard in which a police agency was found to be liable for failing to protect individuals who requested protection from violent spouses or ex-spouses. Such cases include *Balistreri* v. *Pacifica Police Department and Al Olsen, Police Chief* 855 F2d 1421 (9th Cir., 1988) in which, over a three-year-period, the plaintiff suffered through a variety of incidents including beatings and a fire bombing by her husband (eventually ex-husband) and *Watson* v. *Kansas City, KS* 57 LW 2183 (CA 19th, 1988), in which the court ruled in favor of the plaintiff that the police agency failed to provide equal protection. In this case, the police failed to enforce several restraining orders against Mrs. Watson's husband. Although multiple incidents of violence occurred against Mrs. Watson by Mr. Watson, no arrests were ever made. The final incident, which ultimately led to the lawsuit, was Mr. Watson's breaking into Mrs. Watson's house and raping, beating, and stabbing her. There have been several other cases like *Balistreri* and *Watson* in which the police have failed to provide equal protection or have not taken seriously the threats of one spouse (or ex-spouse) against another. Cases such as these and those in the following Case in Point are forcing changes in police policy on the handling of domestic disturbances, especially those in which violence has occurred.

■ CASE IN POINT

Within a few months at the end of 1991 and the beginning of 1992 in two different Cook County, Illinois, cities, women were killed by their ex-spouses in public settings. In both cases there was a history of violence that had required police intervention. The first woman was stabbed several times in the hall of a courthouse while trying to obtain a restraining order against her assailant ex-husband. The other woman was shot several times at her place of employment by her ex-spouse, who had recently been released from jail after a judge lowered his bond for charges related to harassing and threatening the victim. The judge had not been informed by either the police or the prosecutor that the suspect had threatened to harm his ex-wife when he got out of jail.

To avoid lawsuits and to protect victims, police agencies, with a boost from changes in state laws, are implementing new domestic dispute policies. Among local-level police agencies employing more than 100 officers, 95 percent have established policies directly related to domestic disputes (Reaves & Smith, 1995). Many of these policies require officers to make an arrest any time violence has occurred.

■ CASE IN POINT

Police departments in San Diego, California, Phoenix, Arizona, and Mesa, Arizona are among the many that are taking a new, holistic approach to handling domestic violence. This approach involves social workers and prosecutors right from the beginning. It also includes an edict that if a person assaults another in these situations, the assaulter will be arrested.

In addition to policy changes, some agencies are creating special units that focus on domestic violence. For example, the Nashville, Tennessee Police Department created a domestic violence division that in its short existence appears to be making a difference and serving as a model for other police agencies.

State and local policy changes are definitely a step in the right direction. Yet, perhaps the passage of the federal domestic violence law, known as the Domestic Violence Offender Gun Ban, may have some of the greatest impact on domestic violence in this country. The concern, however, is the impact it may have on policing, because the heart of this law is that anyone convicted of a misdemeanor domestic violence offense is prohibited from possessing a firearm. The passage of this law has lead to court battles over constitutionality and has placed some officers in precarious positions.

■ CASE IN POINT

In 1997 a Minneapolis, Minnesota, police sergeant was in a position to lose his job if convicted of domestic assault. The provisions of the federal domestic violence law would prohibit him from carrying a weapon. In 1997 an Eliot, Maine, police officer resigned from the force after being charged with assaulting his wife. A conviction in this case would have forced the town's board to take disciplinary action. In 1998 a New York City police captain faced dismissal for failing to properly investigate a complaint filed against a police officer by a former girlfriend who was eventually stalked and killed by the officer.

The solution to the dilemma arising from the federal law is not to change the law, but to address the issue of police officers assaulting family members, a position supported by the International Association of Chiefs of Police. The fact is that police officers who assault their loved ones are no better than nonpolice officers who do the same thing and should be punished accordingly.

Overall, domestic disputes, especially those involving violence, are a type of activity that police officers generally prefer to avoid. However, with incidences of domestic violence on the rise, officers should be fully prepared to handle such situations.

Juvenile Offenders

An article that appeared in the May 22, 1998, edition of the *Savannah Morning News* is indicative of what the police are facing today. "Searching for Answers behind School Violence" gave an account of the eight shootings that had occurred on school grounds across the nation from October 1997 through May 1998. The ages of the shooters ranged from 11 to 17. One such incident occurred in Arkansas where an 11 year old and a 13 year old were arrested after killing four fellow female students and a teacher.

For many years, police interaction with juveniles usually stemmed from violations such as truancy, theft, or possession of alcohol. Today the types of juvenile offenses the police are called on to deal with involve a wide range of more serious crimes, including murder. Furthermore, it appears that those involved in these types of crimes are getting younger and younger, and gender shows no barrier.

■ CASE IN POINT

In 1996 a 16-year-old from Michigan was arrested and charged with bludgeoning to death and beheading a man he followed along the railroad tracks. In 1996 five teenage boys from California were tried for kidnapping and gang raping a 13-year-old girl. Stemming from this incident, an 82-year-old man was shot to death by a 12-year-old. In 1996 a 15-year-old female gang leader from Ohio was indicted on charges of attempted murder, aggravated riot, and complicity to rape. Her victim was a fellow 18-year-old gang member who had been forced to perform oral sex with 15 men, was beaten with a board, and had a cement-filled bucket dropped on her. In 1997 a 12-year-old Texas girl faced up to 40 years in prison after she was convicted of beating to death a 2-year-old girl. In 1997 an 11-year-old Michigan boy was charged as an adult for the murder of an 18-year-old. In Delaware in 1998 two brothers, ages 8 and 9, and an 8-year-old girl were charged with the rape of a 9-year-old girl. In 1998 four boys from Ohio, ages 8 to 10, were charged with sexually assaulting a 7-year-old girl.

The fact that these types of incidents occur at all is enough to frustrate police officers. Add drugs and gangs[1] to the mix, which in themselves create tremendous frustration for police officers, and policing juveniles becomes even tougher.

◼ CASE IN POINT

In late 1990, Billings, Montana, was plagued with a series of gun shop burglaries and drive-by shootings. The police department suspected that members of two well-known Los Angeles-based gangs, the Crips and the Bloods, were responsible. The beating of an off-duty sheriff's deputy and an increase in the reports of fights were blamed on gang activity. Officials voiced their concern that this activity began occurring about the time crack cocaine appeared in Billings. The police department has been frustrated because it has been difficult to directly link these growing criminal activities with any specific gang or members of a gang. This is a relatively new problem for Billings, Montana, Police Department; however, Billings is not alone. The Las Vegas, Nevada, Police Department reported having a dramatically increased variety of problems with juveniles in 1991. Many of the problems were gang related, including fights over drugs, territorial disputes, and revenge.

Adding to the frustration caused by the offenses, drugs, and gangs are police role conflict and criminal laws. The role conflict arises from the officer's need to enforce the law and the desire to deter juvenile criminality. Although it is the police officer's role to apprehend and detain law violators, it is also natural for many officers to prefer to see juveniles stay out of the justice system. The conflict of these two roles adds to the frustration. Furthermore, although the influx of drugs and gang activity (particularly graffiti, or "tagging") has changed the nature of many police–juvenile contacts, a large portion of these contacts still do not involve major law violations. Often the contact is the result of an incident or situation that, if committed by an adult, would not be a violation of law. These include possession of alcohol, alcohol consumption, curfew violations, and truancy. However, juveniles are becoming more aggressive and violent, causing the police to react in a more forceful yet careful manner.

The method of handling juveniles who have violated the law further complicates the situation. The juvenile justice system commonly puts the juvenile offenders back on the street with little or no punishment, leading to officers' frustration. When a police officer comes into contact with a juvenile offender any one of five methods of juvenile disposition could be used: referral to juvenile courts, handled within the department and released, referred to criminal or adult court, referred to another police agency, or referred to a welfare agency *(Sourcebook of Criminal Justice Statistics, 1996).*

When the situation warrants it, simply releasing a juvenile at the scene is the preferred method of disposition. It is not unusual for an officer to give a stern lecture or a warning to a juvenile, advising of the possible consequences if arrested. Forcing a juvenile to destroy or dispose of items that led to the contact,

---

[1] Gangs are increasingly becoming a major problem for police officers. Their discussion deserves an extensive amount of space. This text does not allow for that type of depth. Several texts on gangs are available, therefore, it is suggested that students wishing to pursue further knowledge of gangs read any of the existing texts.

Gang graffiti. (Courtesy of the Scottsdale, Arizona, Police Department)

such as alcohol or drugs, is a method used by many officers before release. The release of the juvenile may be with or without parental knowledge. Occasionally, the best punishment an officer can provide is to take the juvenile home and release him or her into the custody of the parents. If the officer wishes to emphasize the situation, the juvenile is taken to police headquarters and, when it exists, to the juvenile unit where the release is handled by a juvenile officer and requires no further action.

Sometimes the situation requires an arrest be made. Several factors have been identified that influence an arrest of a juvenile (Roberts, 1989; Walker, 1999). These factors include the seriousness of the offense, the juvenile's attitude or demeanor, the wishes of the complaining party or victim, and the ethnicity and socioeconomic status of the juvenile. Being a felonious actor, demonstrating a "bad attitude," and being poor and a member of a minority group often cause a juvenile to be arrested instead of released. Once arrested, these factors contribute to further disposition.

In 1972, 50.8 percent of the juveniles arrested were referred to juvenile court, whereas 1.3 percent were referred to criminal or adult court. By 1995, 65.7 percent were being referred to juvenile court, and 3.3 percent were referred to criminal court or adult court. The percentage of cases being handled within the police agency dropped from 45 percent (1972) to 28.4 percent (1995) (*Sourcebook of Criminal Justice Statistics, 1996*). These statistics might indicate that juvenile crime is getting worse or that the police are becoming so frustrated that release is less used as an option for dealing with juveniles. Whatever the reason,

(Jump Start reprinted by permission of United Feature Syndicate, Inc.)

the methods police agencies use to handle juvenile contacts has had to change over the years.

To help combat the rising crime among juveniles, police agencies are creating special units devoted to the handling of juvenile offenders and gang activity. Such units have experienced some success. For example, both Denver, Colorado, and Houston, Texas, reported decreases in gang activity and juvenile crimes in 1995. In Houston, the decline was credited to the city's gang task force. City governments are also assisting in alleviating the juvenile crime problem through law changes, especially curfew laws. According to information in a December 1997 report by the U.S. Conference of Mayors, more and more cities are using curfew laws to help curb gang violence, vandalism, and other lesser crimes. For example, in Daytona Beach, Florida, on September 1, 1998, a curfew law went into effect in which adolescents under 18 are not allowed on the streets between midnight and 6:00 A.M. Violators of the law can be warned to leave, taken into protective custody, issued a warning for trespassing, or placed under arrest.

Overall, it appears that special units, programs, and curfew laws do not necessarily relieve the frustration of the officer on the street. Furthermore, it seems the continuing lack of adequate and appropriate facilities, the "revolving door" of the juvenile justice system, lenient laws, the limitations on punishment, and even how parents respond continue to fuel the frustration of police officers in dealing with juvenile offenders. Regardless of the frustrations, the police will have to continue to deal with juveniles in the best available manner.

Homeless People

Although it has not received nearly as much attention as it did during the 1988 presidential election, homelessness is still considered one of the worst problems facing the United States. A major concern in many cities is the growing number of homeless people. Because of a sluggish economy, high unemployment, the lack of affordable housing, and "personal liberty" releases for people who previously would have been confined in mental hospitals, many individuals (a 1990 estimate was more than 2 million) are living on the street. More recently, the number of homeless people in this country has increased because of illegal immigrants, whose overall estimated population is 5 million (McDonald, 1997). Often referred to as "transients" or "street people," these individuals present a growing concern for society and, in turn, the police, who are expected to monitor and control the behavior of these individuals.

The increasing number of homeless people has forced many cities to delegate certain areas of the city to these people by default. These areas have been given such names as "Tin Pan Alley," "Skid Row," "Transient Alley," and "The Bottoms." To ease the strains and pressures in these areas, night shelters, Red Cross or soup kitchens, job outlets, and a detoxification center are often located there to provide needed services. Yet, there is not enough assistance. The result is a need for police intervention.

In general, the police are expected to accomplish two primary tasks when dealing with homeless people: contain the area in which they are living and maintain order. Both are difficult and frustrating. Lack of facilities, the nature of the justice system, and the inability to control and investigate criminal activity add to the frustration and difficulty. The lack of permanent residence, limited or no identification, and high mobility increase the difficulty police have in controlling and dealing with homeless people. However, some of the frustrations the police have with the homeless are being alleviated because of changes in the law.

Historically, it was not an uncommon practice for police officers to arrest the homeless for such crimes as vagrancy, disorderly conduct, loitering, and public intoxication. In recent times such arrests have declined because of the development of alcohol programs, detoxification centers and night shelters, and changes in the law. Many cities no longer recognize vagrancy or being homeless as a crime. These changes have tended to lessen the need for police involvement with homeless people from a criminal perspective and, instead, caused an increase in a more social service approach, which tends to frustrate many officers.

Some police officers believe that dealing with the homeless is not their problem; welfare and other social agencies should handle it. However, because of lack of such assistance from other agencies, police officers often find themselves dealing with homeless people, sometimes poorly or inappropriately.

■ CASE IN POINT

In June 1990 the mayor of Fargo, North Dakota, was faced with having to deal with increasing friction between the city's police officers and homeless people because a number of homeless people were reporting incidents of harassment from officers. In Gastonia, North Carolina, a city council member requested an independent investigation of the city's police department after three homeless people complained that officers had tossed oil on them.

Whether they empathize with homeless people or not, police officers will be called on to deal with them and all that goes with them, such as the loitering, the public drunkeness, and the assaults. Like domestic disturbances, dealing with homeless people may not be the officer's concern or number one priority until a criminal offense occurs, but it is the officer's duty to assist when called on to deal with homeless people.

Drugs

Among the most difficult and frustrating offenses for police officers to handle are those related to drugs. The increase in drug arrests since the 1980s is staggering. In 1986 more than 600,000 individuals 18 years of age and older were arrested for drug-related violations. Among 7587 agencies reporting figures in 1995, there were more than one million drug-related arrests of adults 18 years of age and older *(Sourcebook of Criminal Justice Statistics, 1996)*. Despite the billions of dollars spent to combat the drug problems in this country, they continue to plague the police and society.

■ CASE IN POINT

In June 1996, in a series of raids in northern New Jersey, the police seized more than 1000 pounds of cocaine with a street value of approximately $50 million. In 1998 Tennessee police uncovered $2.8 million buried by known marijuana dealers. In the same state, officials said that methamphetamine was being produced in growing numbers in rural areas. Agents are said to be seizing, on average, two "meth" labs a month. (Also, recall from Chapter 2 the drug seizures made by federal agents.)

Since the 1960s the police have had to deal with a variety of drug crazes. First, it was marijuana. Then came LSD (lysergic acid diethlamide), a hallucinogenic drug that could lead to psychotic episodes, and PCP (phencylidine), which has anesthetic, analgesic, and hallucinogenic effects. Eventually these drugs were replaced by heroin, cocaine, crack, and ice, a concentrated form of methamphetimine that is less expensive and reportedly a "better" high than crack. However, the use of heroin as well as LSD is again on the rise. The effects of these drugs upon people who take them is to make users' behavior extremely unpredictable. Officers have had to try to talk individuals down from building roofs because the individuals thought they could fly; several officers have been needed to restrain an individual whose strength was believed to be several times greater than normal because of the drugs; and, the worst scenario, the individual who is so high on drugs that, even after being shot a number of times by police officers, continues to attack others.

Putting the effects of drugs aside, the public's hypocritical stance on drugs also creates problems for the police. In some instances, society has been tolerant of some drug usage. For example, in the early 1980s, California decriminalized marijuana for medicinal purposes (walking down the street smoking a joint was still considered illegal). In subsequent years, public opinion has not been as accepting. Incidents such as the drug-related deaths of actors John Belushi, River Phoenix, and Chris Farley; use by major sports stars like Lawrence Taylor, Dexter Manley, Roy Tarpley, and Steve Howe; as well as the rising number of deaths from drug–gang-related activities have caused some segments of society to demand more be done by the police to increase the "war against drugs."

The effects of drugs on behavior and the changing public opinion toward drugs influence the frustration of police officers when dealing with drug-related situations. The impact of drugs on criminality also adds to the frustration, particularly the number of homicides attributed to drug-related activities.

In 1990, cities such as Washington, D.C., and San Antonio, Texas, set new records for the number of homicides. Many of these homicides were attributed to fights over control of territory for drug distribution and sales and bad drug deals. Many of these homicides have been difficult to solve; there were few or no willing witnesses and little evidence. They are even more difficult to prevent. The reason for the increase in the number of homicides is simple: money!

The drug business is a multibillion dollar per year business. There is probably more money in drugs than all of this nation's agencies combined spend on all law enforcement, let alone on drug enforcement. For example, an Office of National Drug Control Policy report estimated that in 1990 Americans spent close to $40 billion on illegal drugs. The highest amount spent, almost $18 billion, was on cocaine. The large sums of money available through the sale of drugs attracts many individuals, some of whom otherwise might work for minimum wages. The amount of money available from drugs may also create temptation on the part of police officers to become corrupt. When a drug seizure includes several million dollars in cash and an officer makes $20,000 a year, it can be difficult for some officers to resist "skimming" some of the money, confiscating the drugs for themselves, or accepting a bribe.

■ CASE IN POINT

In October 1991 a Pennsylvania State Police narcotics investigator was sentenced to seventeen and a half years in prison after being convicted for conspiracy to sell 25 kilograms of cocaine. In April 1992 a sixteen-year police veteran of the Chicago Police Department was convicted for her involvement with a drug ring run by her son.

As long as there is demand for drugs, the battle will continue. The police may confiscate large quantities of drugs, seize millions of dollars, and make a number of arrests; however, the reality is that, as long as there are consumers, there will be sellers. The police simply cannot arrest every individual who uses drugs. Unless society puts a stop to illegal demand, the police are stuck fighting what is probably an unwinnable battle and, thus, continuing to be frustrated.

In all, the calls for services to which patrol officers respond can be dangerous, frustrating, or viewed as routine. Despite how they are labeled, the provision of services (responding to requests from citizens) is an important part of the patrol function. However, delivery of services is only one aspect of the patrol function worthy of discussion. Other aspects of the patrol function that some may describe as dominant features require some discussion.

DOMINANT FEATURES

Many features of the patrol function have serious implications with regard to effectiveness and efficiency. This section focuses on two aspects that appear to have tremendous implications on the effectiveness and efficiency of patrolling: **communication** and **patrol time.**

Communication

The act of communication can be said to be one of the most vital aspects of patrol. In discussing communication, there appear to be three important elements: (1) how the patrol officer initially comes into contact with a citizen (community contact), (2) who communicates information to and from the patrol officer (communication operators), and (3) the reason for communication between a citizen and a patrol officer (nature of calls).

There are three primary means through which police–citizen contact occurs: (1) telephone calls for assistance or service by an individual seeking it for himself or herself, (2) reports from third parties, and (3) direct observation by the patrol officer (often referred to as "on view"). Of the three methods, calls for assistance or service through a 911 emergency telephone system account for the largest percentage of police–citizen contacts. It should be noted that approximately 95 percent of all local-level police agencies serving a population of more than 2500 participate in a 911 emergency telephone system, with almost 75 percent using an enhanced system[2] (Reaves & Smith, 1995). As a result, patrol officers depend greatly on citizen discretion in making calls and communication operators in screening the calls.

Communication operators in larger agencies are often divided into two roles: call takers and dispatchers. Patrol officers depend on these individuals to screen incoming requests for police service, and to obtain and relay relevant and important information so the responding officer is prepared to contact and communicate with the citizen needing assistance and service.

The call taker is usually the starting point for police–citizen contact initiated by the citizen. It is this individual's responsibility to ascertain as many details as possible about the request for assistance before passing the request on to the dispatcher unless the call taker believes the call to be a matter of "life or death," such as a shooting or a felony in progress. If so, only the most basic information—incident, caller's name, location where the assistance is needed, and whether medical attention is required—is initially obtained and forwarded to the dispatcher with additional information to follow. It is then the dispatcher's duty to assign the nearest available unit(s) to respond to the request and to provide all the information obtained by the call taker to responding officers. The failure either to obtain pertinent information or to pass on this information could be fatal for the officer or citizens involved in the incident.

■ CASE IN POINT

A woman calls the police for assistance after her boyfriend assaults her. In obtaining the information, the call taker inquires as to whether the suspect is still on the scene, and if so, whether he has a weapon. A positive response is obtained from the woman to both questions. The call taker never asks what type of weapon the suspect has. The information is then routed to a dispatcher who assigns a unit to take an assault report. Although the

---

[2]The enhanced 911 system identifies the phone number and address from where the call is being placed.

patrol officer is told the suspect is still on the scene, no mention of a weapon is made. The officer arrives on the scene, knocks on the door, and is met by a man with a shotgun who threatens to kill the officer, anyone inside the house, or himself. He could simply have shot and killed the officer without warning.

The importance of the call taker and dispatcher is so great that it mandates good recruitment, training, and supervision. An issue raised among police personnel and criminal justice students is: who should be a call taker and dispatcher? Some agree that sworn police officers make the best call takers and dispatchers because they have a better working knowledge of the situations and circumstances an officer can confront. Several police agencies use police officers in this capacity. However, opponents of this view complain that this is very expensive compared to employing nonsworn personnel in such positions and is not a good use of trained police officers, carefully selected and trained nonsworn personnel can be just as effective and efficient, in their opinion. Tightening budgets have forced many police agencies to examine this issue.

Regardless of who fills the call-taker and dispatcher roles, the need to screen calls is extremely important. Even though many citizens call the police for what they believe to be criminal incidents, when investigated, a large portion of calls do not involve a criminally defined matter. Is this the result of poor communicators and how they screen calls? More often than not, the answer is no. Then why the difference?

Why a noticeable difference exists between the calls perceived by citizens to be criminally related, yet, turn out not to be crime related has three basic reasons. First, citizens often lack the knowledge to differentiate between criminal events and civil matters; what a citizen believes to be a criminal offense may, in reality, be a civil matter.

■ CASE IN POINT

A woman arrives home from work to find that her apartment has been broken into. The only thing missing is a stereo. She calls the police to report a burglary. When the officer arrives, the complainant explains what has occurred and what is missing, adding that she is convinced that her ex-boyfriend is the culprit because he bought it while they were living together. The officer discovers that the complainant and "suspect" had lived together for more than a year and that he had just moved out even though his name was still on the lease. The officer advised the complainant that this was a civil matter, not criminal, because legally, the "suspect" still had a right to enter the apartment and take what belonged to him, and if the complainant thought that whatever was taken did not belong to the "suspect," then she would have to sue him to get it back.

The second problem arises from the tremendous discretion granted police officers. What might well be a criminal matter may be turned into a civil matter or dismissed simply because of the officer's power of discretion, such as two individuals who get into a fight over an alleged debt one person owes the other. One or both individuals could be charged with assault; yet, based on the information the officer discovers during the investigation, the officer suggests that the person owed money take the other person to court.

Communications center of a police department. (Courtesy of the Scottsdale, Arizona, Police Department)

Finally, the broadness and ambiguity of criminal law help create misperceptions. What might be perceived as an assault to one person may not legally be a criminal assault (e.g., spraying a neighbor with water from a hose). In addition, some offenses, such as assault, trespassing, and criminal mischief, are both criminal and civil. The result is confusion among citizens when reporting to or requesting assistance from the police.

There is no doubt of the importance of communication for the patrol officer. Whether it is directly with a citizen or through communication operators, the act of communication itself is a vital part of officer survival and departmental image. A poor communication system or poor communications between the agency and the public, the communicators and callers, the dispatchers and the officers, or the officers and citizens sometimes adversely affects the outcome of the contact between the two parties. The outcome could be, in some instances, life or death.

Patrol Time

An examination of the FBI Uniform Crime Reports for the past decade shows that crime rates for certain offenses have continuously risen. When any crime rate rises, citizens ask why. Police departments often blame lack of personnel for adequate patrol; there simply are not enough patrol officers to do the job. However, this is not necessarily the case. Sometimes it is a matter of how the patrol officers make use of their time on patrol. As noted by Cordner (1989), "The biggest portion of patrol officers' time is uncommitted, and officers vary greatly in how they utilize this time" (p. 69).

Patrol officers have been criticized for their use of patrol time. However, use of patrol time often depends on the shift and assigned section of the community. If an officer is working the afternoon shift in one of the busiest parts of town, there is seldom time to patrol. Most time is spent simply responding to calls, one right after another. In some cities, on certain nights, it is not unusual for an officer to respond to as many as 25 or 30 calls during the shift. Therefore, if the average time for each call were only 10 minutes (not counting travel time), 300 minutes of a 480-minute shift are gone. Then, when you add in travel time from call to call and the time it takes to write reports, clearly the officer does not have time to patrol.

Conversely, some officers do not work an action-packed shift or area, making their patrol time extremely tedious. Although a slow beat or shift provides plenty of time to patrol, the slowness and the boredom that arises often lead a police officer to look for action in someone else's area or simply to do nothing. Regardless of the area or shift, some portion of patrol time must be spent on activities unrelated to patrolling. Vehicle maintenance, service-oriented calls, order-maintenance situations, or running errands for supervisors are all examples of activities that subtract from patrol time.

The greatest criticism of patrol officers with respect to patrol time is evading duty. Evasion of duty occurs when the patrol officer ignores the responsibilities entrusted to the officer. There are a variety of ways an officer can evade duty. One of the most common methods of evading duty is referred to as "milking a call." The officer, to avoid additional duties, takes much longer on a call than is required. This tactic is often used toward the end of a shift so as not to get stuck with another call that will mean working overtime or, conversely, to work a call into overtime and extra pay. Another method of evading duty is "failing to acknowledge a call." If an officer is dispatched to a call that he or she does not want to handle, the officer simply ignores the call. When the dispatcher inquires as to the officer's "estimated time of arrival" at the scene, the officer responds as if the call was never received. If the officer is lucky, another unit will be close to the scene and will have already responded, thus allowing the officer to disregard the call. Additional methods of evasion of duty include sleeping, taking care of personal business, parking in a secluded area to read, or stopping at the houses of friends or family.

Regardless of the method used, evasion of duty can critically damage the patrol function. Use of patrol time is a critical element of the patrol function. Inappropriate use of patrol time limits the effectiveness of the patrol function. Then again, the effectiveness of the patrol function has been questioned for many years.

PATROL EFFECTIVENESS

Increases in crime cause the effectiveness of patrol to be questioned. At the beginning of modern-day policing, the overall effectiveness of the patrol function as a deterrent to crime went unchallenged; it was assumed to be effective.

Research in the late 1960s and early 1970s led to studies challenging this assumption.

Before 1970, there were a few attempts to research patrol effectiveness, such as the New York Police Department's Operation 25, 20th Precinct, and Subway Experiment. The results of each had shown that increasing the number of patrol officers decreased crime in specific areas. However, methodological errors in the way the study was conducted and manipulation of the data collected detracted from the reliability of the results. Therefore, little was still known about the effectiveness of patrolling.

As noted earlier, the results of the Kansas City Preventive Patrol Experiment gave policing its first "scientific" look at the effectiveness of patrol. Although the data from that experiment showed that there was little difference in crime rate among the three levels employed, thus not supporting the assumption that patrolling was an effective crime deterrent, the experiment provided a starting point for future research. It also added fuel to the long-standing question of patrolling: **proactivity** versus **reactivity.**

As noted in Chapter 1, policing—particularly patrolling—has principally been reactive in nature, not responding until after an incident occurs. The results of the Kansas City experiment demonstrated that there was little difference in the effectiveness of patrol regardless of whether it was extremely proactive or reactive. This has left researchers, academicians, and police administrators in a quandary. Apparently the traditional methods of patrolling are not, overall, a very effective crime deterrent. Therefore, solutions for improving the effectiveness of patrolling have been sought for several years.

Improving the Effectiveness of Patrol

Through the years, police agencies have attempted to respond to concerns about effectiveness by fielding as many patrol officers as fiscally possible. The data from the Kansas City experiment indicated that maximum coverage is not the answer. What is? Recently, several approaches have been used to attempt to improve the effectiveness of patrol, such as categorizing calls for assistance or service in a "need to respond" priority and the use of units specifically designated to handle low priority, or, "report calls."

■ CASE IN POINT

Many police agencies use a priority call system for dispatching calls. As calls are received they are categorized by a "need to respond." High-priority calls such as a shooting, fight in progress, or other life-threatening incidents receive immediate attention and are dispatched first. Level-two priority calls that might include a burglary or robbery where the suspects have just fled the scene are the next calls dispatched. Finally, a priority-three call (where taking a report is the only thing the police officer can do) is the last call to be dispatched. However, because of the large number of priority-three calls, a police officer may spend his or her whole shift taking reports and, thus, not being able to patrol. To alleviate this problem, some police departments have created the police report car. This unit is assigned to a particular area and is responsible for taking as many of the report calls as possible. This helps free up the primary patrol unit to respond to higher-priority calls and to patrol. Other police agencies have created the community-service officer in a response to such problems. This individual is assigned activities that do not require a sworn police officer such as report taking, traffic direction, or other service-related activities.

Another approach to improving patrol effectiveness is through directed patrol. In this approach, the patrol unit or units are designated to look only for specific types of crimes such as burglaries or auto thefts. These units are often assisted, where it exists, by a crime analysis division that examines data regularly, identifies locations or types of crime, and provides specific information, such as descriptions of suspects or suspect vehicles and modus operandi.

A current approach to improving patrol effectiveness is through community-oriented policing. Community-oriented policing is similar to directed patrol. With this approach, officers are provided with a profile of the beat through crime analysis and citizen input, and are able to prevent crimes or other related problems before they occur. (Further details of community-oriented policing will be discussed in Chapter 8.)

To date, there is little empirical evidence to support or reject assertions about the utility of any of these methods. Although the reported rise in crime rates keep alive the question of the effectiveness of patrol as a crime deterrent, other components of policing such as criminal and special investigatory units, as well as government's and community's roles, should be examined. Patrolling should not necessarily "take all the heat."

● SUMMARY

Patrol can be viewed as both a division and function of policing. It is the backbone of a police agency in either respect. It is the first line of contact for citizens, and it is how the majority of police officers begin their careers. How well the patrol element functions and its delivery of services depend on its organization, including geographical and economic divisions, deployment of officers by shift, and types of patrol used.

Provision of services—law enforcement, crime prevention, order maintenance, and social services—are often viewed as activities, incidents, or events that may be dangerous, routine, or frustrating. Such events include pursuing suspects, responding to felonies in progress, making traffic stops and dealing with accidents, taking reports, controlling domestic violence, limiting juvenile offenders, coping with homeless people, and investigating drug-related activities. The provision of services and handling of such events remain a cornerstone of the patrol function.

Communication and use of patrol time are vital to the function of patrol; poor communications and inappropriate use of patrol time are two reasons often cited to account for patrol ineffectiveness. Research has created doubts about the effectiveness of patrol as a crime deterrent. However, solutions such as call prioritization, report cars, community-service officers, and community-oriented policing have been offered as attempts to improve patrol effectiveness.

DO YOU KNOW . . .

1. What the major function of patrol should be? Why?
2. How many officers should be assigned to patrol? When crime rates rise should "special units" be converted back into patrol units?
3. What type of patrol police agencies use most often? Why?
4. What activities performed by patrol officers are considered order maintenance? law enforcement? crime prevention? social services?
5. Whether your city or county police department has a policy for high-speed pursuits?
6. What types of calls should be responded to as a "felony in progress"?
7. If viewing certain activities as "routine" has any effect on how an officer performs the duties associated with handling these activities?
8. What can be done to alleviate police officer frustration with domestic violence, juveniles, homeless people, and drug-related crime?
9. Whether communication operators in your city's police agency are citizens or sworn officers? In your opinion, which should they be?
10. How patrol can be made more effective?

REFERENCES

Alpert, G.P. (1998). A factorial analysis of police pursuit driving decisions: A research note. *Justice Quarterly, 15,* 347–59.

Alpert, G.P., & Dunham, R.G. (1998). *Policing urban America* (3rd ed.). Prospect Heights, IL: Waveland Press.

Black, D. (1980). *The manners and customs of the police.* New York: Academic Press.

Broderick, J.J. (1987). *Police in a time of change.* Prospect Heights, IL: Waveland Press.

Cordner, G.W. (1989). The police on patrol. In D.J. Kenney (Ed.), *Police and policing* (pp. 60–71). New York: Praeger.

Doerner, W.G. (1998). *Introduction to law enforcement.* Newton, MA: Butterworth-Heinemann.

Gloucester Township's specials: Earning a spot on the map. (1995). *The Shield, 4,* 7–9.

Kelling, G.L., Pate, A.M., Dieckman, D., & Brown, C. (1989). The Kansas City Preventive Patrol Experiment. In D.J. Kenney (Ed.), *Police and policing,* (pp. 45–59). New York: Praeger Publishers.

Kessler, D.A. (1985). One- or two-officer cars? A perspective from Kansas City. *Journal of Criminal Justice, 13,* 49–64.

McDonald, W.F. (1997). Criminal and illegal immigration. *National Institute of Justice Journal, 232,* 2–10.

Moore, M.H., Trojanowicz, R.C., & Kelling, G.L. (1988, June). Crime and policing. *Perspectives on Policing.* Washington, D.C.: National Institute of Justice.

One-officer state police cars raise the risk to cops' lives. (1997, February 14). *Law Enforcement News, 4,* 11.

Oppenlander, N. (1982). Coping or copping out. *Criminology, 20,* 49–65.

Police Task Force. (1973). Washington, D.C.: National Advisory Commission on Criminal Justice Standards and Goals.

Reaves, B.A., & Smith, P.H. (1995). *Law enforcement management and administrative statistics, 1993: Data for individual state and local agencies with 100 or more officers.* Washington, D.C.: U.S. Government Printing Office.

Roberts, A.R. (1989). *Juvenile justice: Policies, programs, and services.* Chicago: Dorsey Press.

Sherman, L.W., & Berk, R.A. (1985). The Minneapolis Domestic Violence Experiment. In J.J. Fyfe (Ed.), *Police management today*. Washington, D.C.: International City Management Association.

Smith, G.W., Spradlin, L.W., & Cerrato, J. (1989, January). Domestic violence and police response, a growing field of liability. *Texas Police Journal*, 10–13.

Sourcebook of Criminal Justice Statistics, 1996. (1997). Washington, D.C.: U.S. Government Printing Office.

Swanson, C.R., Territo, L., & Taylor, R.W. (1998). *Police administration* (4th ed.). New York: MacMillan Publishing Company.

Walker, S. (1999). *Police in America* (3rd ed.). New York: McGraw-Hill.

Weinblatt, R.B. (1995). Seasonal reserves: Part-time paid personnel fill in the gaps. *The Shield, 4*, 12–13.

Williams, H. (1992, October). *Spouse abuse research raises new questions about police response to domestic violence* (Police Foundation Reports). Washington, D.C.: Police Foundation.

Wilmette Police Department Annual Report, 1997. (1998). Wilmette, IL: Wilmette Police Department.

CRIMINAL
INVESTIGATIONS AND
OTHER SUPPORT UNITS

4

If patrol is the backbone of policing, what makes up the rest of the police agency? Although a variety of elements may make up the composition of a police agency (depending upon the size of the agency), one element found in most police agencies is criminal investigations (Reaves & Smith, 1995). However, in all but the smallest of police agencies, there are additional units that lend support to patrol and criminal investigations. For example, according to available data, among municipal police departments employing more than 100 officers 98 percent have a community crime prevention unit, 74 percent have a missing children unit, 80 percent have a child abuse unit, and 53 percent have a domestic violence unit (Reaves & Smith 1995). This chapter examines criminal investigations and several support units possibly found in police agencies.

CRIMINAL INVESTIGATIONS AS A DIVISION

As a division, criminal investigations is important to the police agency because of its investigative support to patrol, which eliminates a burden from patrol officers. In addition, it provides avenues of change or advancement for those officers who do not want to remain patrol officers their whole career. Finally, it allows the police agency alternatives to the patrol function. Approximately 20 percent of sworn personnel in state and local police agencies are assigned to investigations (Reaves & Goldberg, 1998).

From a structural perspective, criminal investigations may be located in the police organization as the detective division (e.g., Chicago, Illinois, Police Department), investigations (e.g., Walnut Creek, California, Police Department), or the criminal investigations division of the investigative services bureau (e.g., Fort Worth, Texas, Police Department). Additionally, criminal investigations can be composed of a variety of specialized areas such as homicide, burglary, robbery, theft, and sexual assault. Some police agencies simply divide criminal investigations into property crimes and violent crimes (e.g, Washington, D.C., Metropolitan Police Department). Other agencies divide criminal investigations into a second division often referred to as special investigations. This division often includes areas such as vice, narcotics, gangs, and juveniles (youth).

It is seldom difficult to locate the criminal investigations division regardless of the agency size. Although how criminal investigations is structured or located within the police organization may differ from agency to agency, the function and activities are similar.

CRIMINAL INVESTIGATIONS AS A FUNCTION

The criminal investigations function appears to be a very popular element of policing. The media—television, movies, and news—tend to emphasize the investigative function of policing. The glamorizing of this facet often goes beyond reality. Some major misconceptions created by this glamorization include the notions that this is where "real" police work occurs, all crimes can be solved with relative ease, and detectives possess certain special skills patrol officers do not have (Walker, 1999; Weston & Wells, 1990). Reality provides a different perspective. The criminal investigative function is often anything but glamorous. It is usually tedious and demanding work. Unlike their television or movie counterparts, such as the detectives in *Homicide, Law and Order, Nash Bridges,* and *NYPD Blue,* who spend much of their time tracking down leads, rousting informants, or simply "working the streets," many criminal investigators spend a great deal of time doing paperwork. In the real world, criminal investigations are often carried out from behind a desk by telephone. This is far from the methods depicted in the media.

■ CASE IN POINT

A shooting had occurred outside a house. The victim was a twenty-four year-old male. The suspect, identified by witnesses as a male over fifty years old and allegedly a friend of the victim's family, had fled the scene in his vehicle. On television or in the movies it is almost certain that the criminal investigators would conduct a license plate check, which would give the suspect's address, then they would proceed to that address, force their way in, and arrest the suspect. All done rather flamboyantly, glamorously, entertainingly, and probably illegally from "real-world" standards. In this real-life scenario, the homicide detective actually called the suspect, advised him that his vehicle was observed at the scene of the shooting, and requested he come in for questioning, which the suspect did. During questioning (not the heavy-duty browbeating you see on television), the suspect admitted he shot the victim. He was arrested and charged with murder. No glamour or rock and sock 'em action, just straightforward, methodical work. This is often the way of the real-world criminal investigative function.

The idea that all crimes can be solved with relative ease is far from reality; a large percentage of crimes actually go unsolved. For example, in 1997 the number of rapes in Los Angeles, California, was 1413, however, there were only 352 (24 percent) arrests for rape *(1997 Los Angeles Police Department Annual Report).*

In the real world, criminal investigators spend a lot of time working from their desks. (Courtesy of the Scottsdale, Arizona, Police Department)

Finally, the skills of an investigator or detective are acquired with experience starting in patrol. All patrol officers learn to be investigators. However, after an officer becomes a criminal investigator, those skills attained through patrol are honed. Thus, it is not that criminal investigators have special talents, just more time and opportunities to better their investigative talents.

A brief look at the development of the detective assists in understanding that today's detective is far from being like the detectives depicted on television or in the movies. The title "detective" was first used in the 1840s, when the three phases of the detectives' development began (Kuykendall, 1986). The first phase, the **secretive rogue** (1850s to 1920s), was the result of a transition of private detectives to public. (Until this transition, Pinkerton's, a private detective firm, had been used by many police agencies to investigate crimes that needed "detective" work.) Frequently a somewhat corrupt individual, the secretive rogue never wanted to be identified (even to patrol officers) and believed in clandestine work.

The second phase gave policing the **inquisitor** (1890s to 1960s). It was with this phase of detecting that systematic uses of evidence and upgrading of investigative techniques began. It was also during this phase the "third degree" received its notoriety. That is, until a variety of Supreme Court cases (i.e., *Mapp, Escobedo,* and *Miranda*) all but totally eliminated the "inquisition" style of questioning.

Today the detective is seen as a **bureaucrat** who is primarily a "paper pusher," expending a tremendous amount of time and energy simply going over information with limited success in solving crimes or following up leads through telephone contacts or computer searches. Paperwork is the mainstay of today's detective. Yet, even with this knowledge, many police officers still want to become criminal investigators.

In reality, the criminal investigations function does not provide a very exciting picture; yet, there are several reasons why it is so popular among police officers. First, criminal investigators often receive higher pay than patrol officers and are allowed to wear "street" clothes. This in itself is often enough motivation to become a detective. Second, criminal investigators have freedom of movement (usually not restricted to doing their work in only one part of the city) and are able to use more initiative in solving crimes. They have few boundaries. Finally, criminal investigations is one of the few areas that supports the image of being a crime fighter. The handling of minor traffic accidents, disputes, or provision of social services are no longer a detective's responsibility; it is simply the application of police skills and knowledge to the solving of crimes. In addition, although only a small percentage of crimes are solved, when a crime is solved it can be extremely satisfying to the detective. These are often reasons enough for most individuals to pursue being a criminal investigator.

The major function of the criminal investigator is to identify and explore information that assists in the solving of crimes or in the clearing of cases. Generally, a case is considered solved or cleared when an arrest is made. The easiest case for a detective to solve is one in which the patrol officer has obtained all the relevant information and apprehended the suspect at or in the immediate vicinity of the crime scene. When this occurs, all the detective usually needs to do is obtain a signed confession and file appropriate papers and reports with the prosecutor. Unfortunately, immediate apprehension by the patrol officer does not always occur, therefore, additional investigation is frequently required. This creates the need for a two-stage investigative process. The two basic stages are referred to as **preliminary** and **follow-up.**

The Preliminary Investigation

Although this stage is often conducted by a patrol officer and could be viewed as part of the patrol function, it is discussed here for two reasons: (1) to establish the continuity of the criminal investigative function and (2) in some cases the patrol officer may be the sole investigator, or a criminal investigator may arrive on the scene before a patrol officer and conduct the investigation from start to finish. In either case, the process begins the same way.

Regardless of the size of a police agency, the preliminary stage of an investigation begins with the officer initially assigned to respond to the crime scene, most often a patrol officer. Although the patrol officer is seldom given the credit deserved, the positive results of the investigation rely primarily on the actions of the preliminary investigator. What the preliminary investigator does can have a crucial impact on the eventual conclusion of the investigation. Therefore, it is important that a consistent method or procedure be used in conducting the preliminary investigation.

Although the various textbooks on criminal investigations offer differing sets of procedures, the underlying fundamentals are similar. (For a more modern means of examining criminal investigations procedures, visit http://police2.ucr.

edu on the Internet.) First, when the preliminary investigator arrives at a crime scene it must be determined if any medical assistance is required for the victim (or suspect). In some cities medical personnel are often on the scene before the police arrive.

Next, if the suspect is still on the scene the officer must effect an arrest (based on probable cause). If the suspect has fled the scene, the officer must ascertain all available information about the suspect as quickly as possible and then broadcast this information so that other police units in the area can "be on the lookout." After the broadcast has been given, or the suspect arrested, several concurrent procedures should occur. These include identifying, maintaining, and protecting the crime scene (this includes any and all possible evidence); identifying and interviewing the victim(s) and witness(es); and noting all the conditions of the scene, the events, and the facts observed and discovered.

Final procedures include interrogation of the suspect (if in custody); arranging for the collection and preservation of evidence; reporting the incident fully and as accurately as possible in the proper (departmentally required) format; and finally, when appropriate, yielding the crime scene and remaining responsibilities to the follow-up investigator. The efficient and accurate following of these procedures will usually improve the chances of solving the crime. Solving the crime depends on the case's solvability factors (Brown, 1998).

Solvability is an important aspect of the criminal investigation that begins with the preliminary investigation. Solvability or solvability factors pertain to the quality and quantity of evidence discovered during the preliminary investigation. These factors include such evidence as witnesses, suspect identifiers (i.e., name, description, and vehicle), physical evidence, and identification of a significant modus operandi (MO) (method of operation). The failure of the preliminary investigator to identify solvability factors and report them appropriately will make solving the case more difficult for the follow-up investigator.

The Follow-up Investigation

In police agencies where size permits, on completion of the preliminary investigation by the patrol officer, the second stage of the investigation, the follow-up, is turned over to a criminal investigator. (In smaller police agencies both the preliminary phase and the follow-up are usually completed by the patrol officer first assigned to the call.)

The tasks of the follow-up investigator are best summed up as follows:

1. Verify the completeness and accuracy of the preliminary investigation.
2. When appropriate or required, examine the crime scene.
3. If there is no apprehension, continue working on leads or solvability factors to identify and apprehend the suspect.
4. When the arrest is made, prepare the necessary reports for the prosecutor.
5. Testify at preliminary hearings, grand jury inquiries, and trials.

Although the success of the investigation is often contingent on the preliminary investigation, a poor follow-up can limit the chances of solving the case. The ultimate goal of the investigative function is to solve the crime. This is not always a simple task. Therefore, it is important that all investigators be well trained in search and seizure, evidence collection and preservation, arrest, and report writing.

The follow-up function of criminal investigations has received criticism for its ineffectiveness for solving crimes; yet, for the most part, the criticism is unwarranted. The information obtained during the preliminary stage is critical to solvability, and when the preliminary investigation is not complete it hampers the follow-up stage and solvability.

■ CASE IN POINT

A veteran patrol officer was dispatched to investigate a burglary of a business. The report this officer turned in to the burglary detectives read like this: "Officer was dispatched to scene reference a burglary report. Upon arrival on the scene officer met with complainant who advised that during the night unknown suspect(s) gained entry through a rear window and took unknown quantity of items. No other information was available at the time of this report." Now it's up to the detective to solve the crime. However, there is little information with which to proceed—important information is missing such as which window, how entry was gained (pried, broken, unlocked), whether there is an alarm, a brief description of types of items taken, or whether there was any physical evidence (e.g., fingerprints, blood). The lack of such information requires the follow-up investigator to return to the scene, often a day or two after the offense, to examine a scene that has probably already been cleaned up and repaired. Information that could have been obtained by the preliminary investigator is no longer available. Failure to solve the case is blamed on the follow-up investigator when it was really a result of the inadequate preliminary investigation. Yet, it should be noted that even when a preliminary investigator does a thorough investigation, there is sometimes very little evidence or information to help the follow-up investigator.

As a result of the differing levels of preliminary investigations, investigators are required to use a process referred to as **case screening.** Case screening is a process by which crime reports are grouped in order of solvability. The most solvable crime is one in which a suspect is in custody or has been identified. These crimes get priority attention. They are followed by those crimes in which a suspect is not identified, but there is evidence and information that make identification and apprehension of a suspect easier. The reports that receive limited attention, yet are the most abundant, are those in which there is little or nothing from which to identify a suspect. Considering that this type of case is prevalent, it is no wonder that often only a small percentage is solved. Those who have criticized the ineffectiveness of police agencies in solving crime place the blame on the way in which the criminal investigation function is managed. However, some of the blame should actually be placed elsewhere: one factor that appears to contribute to the low solvability of cases is the general lack of cooperation between criminal investigations, patrol, and the public.

A key element of the investigative function is cooperation; cooperation of the citizen, and cooperation between patrol officers and detectives. Over the years, through discussions with criminal investigators and personal observations, it appears that a decline of citizen cooperation in criminal investigations has occurred. Many citizens apparently do not want to get involved in the investigative process. When citizens are questioned as to why, responses researchers and poll takers receive include that they feel that it is none of their business, they are afraid of repercussions, or they do not trust the police (Friedman, 1992; Weston & Wells, 1990).

■ CASE IN POINT

The setting was a downtown street of Dallas, Texas, where a crowd of onlookers watched, and some allegedly cheered, when a street person shot and killed a Dallas police officer with the officer's own weapon. Few people came forward to cooperate in the investigation. In early 1992 on a Chicago, Illinois, street, a female bank teller was attacked near the bank where she worked. Witnesses say at least two people drove right by, failing to stop and assist or even to report the incident to the police. Two nearby mechanics eventually heard the woman screaming and went to her aid. In Savannah, Georgia, in 1997 approximately 300 people witnessed the shooting of an individual. It took three months before one person would come forward and talk to investigators.

In some respects it is easier to understand the lack of citizen cooperation than the lack of cooperation between patrol and criminal investigations. One would think that both are on the same side and are interested in similar results. Yet, it has been observed by ex-police officers, as well as individuals who currently work as police officers, that cooperation between patrol and criminal investigations is often limited.

Although there may be a number of underlying reasons that cause a lack of cooperation between patrol and criminal investigations, a reason often observed is territorial jealousy. Criminal investigators want the "glory" of solving the case. Patrol officers recognize this and, therefore, occasionally refuse to cooperate past the preliminary investigation. This attitude is perpetuated by the perceived status of criminal investigators as being "better" and "more important" than patrol officers. This perception severely hampers the amount of cooperation from either side. The ultimate goal of both is the same, putting the "bad guy" behind bars. However, egos and attitudes often prevent this from occurring as quickly as it might if patrol officers and investigators cooperated. It should also be noted that cooperation between criminal investigators is often strained.

■ CASE IN POINT

Both homicide and robbery investigators were working on cases in which the respective suspect(s) were the same. Yet, rather than share their information, it was a race to see who would actually apprehend the suspect(s) first. In addition, patrol officers could have been used to obtain additional information but instead were completely ignored. The failure to cooperate caused both homicide and robbery to spend more time on the investigation than would have been needed if they had worked together.

There needs to be an improvement in the cooperative efforts of criminal investigators, patrol officers, and citizens. How this is accomplished will require

---

WHAT DO YOU THINK?

Who Should Get the Credit?

For several years detective Holmes has worked out of the robbery division. During his tenure in robbery detective Holmes has been fairly successful at clearing cases, often with relatively little assistance from anyone else, particularly patrol officers. Holmes has gained a reputation as a good investigator, but every now and then a tough case occurs in which even Holmes needs some assistance. However, he seldom gives any credit to those who helped. This has resulted in a lack of cooperation between Holmes and many patrol officers. During the past few weeks several robberies of convenience stores have occurred, and Holmes has been assigned the cases. Because of the nature of the offenses (when, where, and how they are occurring), Holmes realizes he will need some assistance from patrol. Therefore, he distributes a bulletin containing all the information he has gathered about the robbery suspects. Holmes requests patrol officers to "be on the lookout" but not to apprehend without contacting him first. Two days later two patrol officers responding to a silent hold-up alarm at a convenience store confront and apprehend the suspects. The next day Holmes obtains signed statements from the suspects, and closes the cases. Holmes receives accolades from the mayor, police chief, and a business group for a job well done.

1. Does detective Holmes deserve the credit for clearing these cases?
2. What about the patrol officers? What, if any, recognition should they receive?
3. Why is cooperation between patrol officers and detectives important?
4. What could a police department do to improve cooperation between patrol officers and detectives?
5. Do you think detectives are really necessary? What if patrol officers handled all cases from start to finish?

---

changes in how a police department recognizes and awards productivity, as well as creating an air of equality between career patrol officers and criminal investigators. The communication structure between investigations and patrol will need improvement too. With respect to citizens, it is initially up to police agencies to change how officers respond to citizens. Treating citizens as if they are a source of useful information as opposed to treating them as nuisances is a beginning. Replacing the traditional Joe Friday approach of "Just the facts, ma'am" with a more open, interested approach is a start. (Community policing is an attempt to implement this type of approach.)

Cooperation between citizens, patrol officers, and investigators is considered a major tool to solving a criminal offense. There are, however, a variety of other tools available to the criminal investigator that could assist in solving cases.

Investigative Tools

One of the most important investigative tools is the crime lab and physical evidence. The locating, recognizing, identifying, and preserving of physical evidence is extremely important to the criminal investigator. The strength of this evidence is often the difference between a conviction and a lost case. Physical evidence includes such items as weapons, fibers, fingerprints, tool marks, and body fluids. The crime lab assists in the identification of and matching of the physical evidence to the crime scene, victim, and suspect.

A second valuable investigative tool is records and files. The criminal investigator has a variety of such sources available to help identify victims and suspects. These sources include the files and records of the officer's agency as well as crime files from other police agencies, such as the state or FBI, utility companies, schools, employers, tax and voting records, and driver's license files. Each file or source may contain or provide valuable information relevant to the investigation.

■ CASE IN POINT

Serial rapes and murders, although fortunately not common occurrences, do occur in this country. These types of cases are among the most difficult cases to solve for local police authorities. An investigative tool of considerable worth in these types of cases has been the resources of the FBI's Human Behaviors Unit. This unit has developed "profiles" of serial rapists and murderers that have assisted in the apprehension of such individuals as David Berkowitz ("Son of Sam"), Richard Ramirez ("The Night Stalker"), John Wayne Gacy, and Ted Bundy.

Surveillance has become a popular investigative tool. Although more often used for covert (undercover) investigations, such as vice or narcotics, than for property crimes, such as burglaries or auto thefts, or personal crimes, such as assaults, surveillance is also used to keep tabs on a suspect whom the police believe may commit another crime or simply lead the investigator to evidence of previously committed crimes.

Finally, investigators must be aware of the usefulness of witnesses and informants. Witnesses can give the investigator the luxury of firsthand observations. The informant generally supplies information that is "hearsay" and more difficult to support in court. However, this information can lead the investigator to other evidence that supports the case without having to use the informant in court. Overall, investigators have a variety of investigative tools at their disposal that, when appropriately employed, can dramatically improve the chances of solving a case.

Although investigatory tools are extremely important to the investigative function, so are the individuals who conduct the investigation. For years, criminal investigations (with the exception of rape and child-related crimes) had been primarily handled by men. However, changes occurring in society, particularly with respect to women's roles, are being reflected in policing. For instance, the number of women in policing continues to increase, which, in turn, increases the number of female investigators. The abilities female officers demonstrate as patrol officers and investigators have assisted in their expansion from investigating only crimes involving women and children to other investigative areas, such as homicide, robbery, gangs, vice, and narcotics.

Female Investigators

Women have fought a long, difficult battle in policing (a more in-depth look at this struggle is provided in Chapter 9). The first female officers were investigators; their scope was limited to juveniles and to some crimes against women. Today female investigators are used in every area of investigation and have proved themselves to be as able investigators as their male counterparts. However, despite their accomplishments as officers and investigators, female investigators are still often viewed more as "investigative tools," used in roles that assist in solving or preventing crime, rather than the able-bodied investigators they have proven to be. The following sections highlight a few of the needs and roles fulfilled by women as investigators.

Interviewing/Interrogation. In many instances victims and suspects seem to relate better to a female officer than to a man, it is not unusual for a male suspect to be more open with a female detective than her male counterpart. Therefore, women are sometimes more successful in obtaining statements than their male counterparts.

Arrest/Search. Because of the male investigator's fear of sexual harassment complaints or accusations of sexual improprieties, female detectives have assisted by being available for the search and arrest of female suspects. Transportation of female suspects by female officers also tends to lessen complaints against and problems for male officers (although this is obviously not the reason why women become police officers). However, in a changing society, female investigators are no longer totally free from sexual complaints from men or women. In addition, the presence of female investigators in many circumstances has been found to help diffuse potentially explosive situations.

Decoy/Undercover. No area of criminal investigations has improved more from the presence of female investigators than decoy and undercover operations. Female detectives add a whole new dimension to covert operations. The use of such officers in vice and narcotics operations is popular in police agencies. Posing as a prostitute, a drug dealer, a junkie, or the girlfriend of a "criminal" are just a few possible roles that the female officer may fill in an undercover operation.

■ CASE IN POINT

As a method to arrest several drug suspects at one time, criminal investigators in a Michigan city invited the suspects to a "wedding" for an alleged drug dealer. All the members of the wedding party and the band were police officers. In this operation, the "bride" was a female investigator who had spent several months helping set up this sting operation by posing as a drug dealer and girlfriend of a drug dealer (who was a fellow investigator).

Simply, women have had a tremendous positive impact in the investigative aspects of policing. Their abilities to carry out a successful investigation have proven equal to that of their male colleagues. In sum, female investigators bring an added dimension to policing, the ability to fulfill a variety of undercover roles, solicit statements and confessions, and provide a calming affect in an otherwise hostile environment, all of which improve the investigative function.

Task Force

A more recent investigative aid used to improve criminal investigations has been the investigative task force. These are members from various police agencies assigned to investigate a specific crime or series of crimes. Members have joint power and jurisdiction within the task force's target area. The federal government has used task forces for years to investigate organized crime and drug trafficking. On a local level, task forces have been popular for use in solving homicides, such as those committed by Ted Bundy and Henry Lee Lucas. However, it doesn't take a serial murderer before a task force is created.

■ CASE IN POINT

In fall 1991, a fifteen-year-old Skokie, Illinois, youth was found dead in the Cook County, Illinois, Forest Preserve located in Morton Grove, Illinois. Because of the nature of the death (strangulation) by unknown assailant(s), the location, and limited local resources, a task force was created using members of the Skokie, Morton Grove, Cook County Forest Preserve, and Illinois State police departments. Unfortunately, as of this writing the task force has had little success finding the murderer(s). In spring 1992, Illinois officials approved the formation of a task force to assist with the crime problem in East St. Louis, Illinois. This task force included five state police detectives, two assistant attorneys general, an attorney general inspector, and two clerical workers. The task force was charged with investigating violent crimes and crimes that have remained unsolved.

Technological Aids

Some of the best investigative tools available today are those of a technological nature. High-speed cameras, intricate recording devices, and high-power lenses assist in the surveillance arena. From a more investigative aspect, lasers and computers are rapidly improving the odds of solving cases (a more in-depth technological discussion is featured in Chapter 11.)

Overall, the criminal investigative function assists patrol in preventing crimes, apprehending criminals, recovering stolen property, and solving crimes. It is often viewed as a glamourous function, but in reality, it frequently involves tedious and sometimes mundane tasks. Nonetheless, its existence is extremely beneficial and supportive to patrol and the police function as a whole. It is not, however, the only support unit for patrol worthy of discussion.

Crimes may be easier to solve when several agencies work together (Courtesty of the Scottsdale, Arizona, Police Department)

SUPPORT UNITS

Although patrol and criminal investigations constitute a large portion of police agency activities, they both require assistance from other areas. These other areas are known as **support units** or **support services.** A support unit can simply be defined as a unit of the police agency that lends technical or investigative support to the patrol and criminal investigation divisions. Support services are critical to the efficient operation of any police line function, such as identifying a criminal suspect, searching a building, or effecting an arrest. As noted by the Police Task Force (1973), "The failure of a vital support service can severely impair the effectiveness of an operational police unit" (p. 292). The number of support units established is largely dictated by the size of the police agency. The units discussed in the remainder of this chapter are those units that are among the most prevalent among modern urban midsized and large agencies. They include communications, training, research and analysis, and specialized units.

Communications

You should recall from Chapter 3 the discussion of the importance of communications as a feature of patrol. It is also a dominant support unit for the entire agency. In many respects, the communications division can be compared to the central nervous system of a human being—if anything goes wrong, it can affect the entire operation. This unit not only must be the link between patrol and the community but also between all parts of the agency. It is through this unit that other units can be in contact with the agency or other parts of the agency. It is also where information, such as outstanding warrants and license checks, is obtained or confirmed. If the communications unit is poorly operated or should falter for uncontrollable reasons, like the malfunctioning central nervous system of the human body, it can cripple a police agency or worse yet, perhaps delay aid to someone in need.

■ CASE IN POINT

One night in November 1994, it took police officers approximately 45 minutes to reach a dying young man despite more than 20 calls to 911. Ultimately, it was determined that the system was overburdened, there were not enough officers on patrol, and communications personnel needed more and better training.

Training

If the communications unit is the "central nervous system" of the police agency, the training unit could be viewed as the "heart and soul." After years of experience with and observation of police agencies, this author believes that the training unit is one of the most valuable support units in the police agency. The quality and efficiency of the police agency are primarily the result of training. Inefficient training, poor training, or a lack of training have an adverse effect on the manner in which the police agency will be able to provide services.

Although every new officer receives basic training, it is also the role of the training unit to provide up-to-date training and retraining. For example, in-service training on Supreme Court decisions, use of nondeadly force, or firearms updates are all relevant training issues that not only improve police officer performance but assist in limiting the liability situations that could arise. If this unit is underused or improperly used police officers may find themselves in situations they cannot handle because they are unaware of changes in procedure or the development of new solutions. In addition, police agencies are being held more accountable by the courts for incidents that arise from actions of poorly or undertrained officers. The importance of this unit to the police agency is becoming increasingly obvious with the growing number of lawsuits against police agencies (further discussion is offered in Chapter 6). Therefore, training has become an extremely valuable support unit for the police agency.

Defensive tactics are just one part of police training. (Courtesy of the Scottsdale, Arizona, Police Department)

Research and Analysis

Police agencies with a research and analysis (R & A)—or research and development or criminal analysis—support unit have a very valuable "crime-fighting" tool. When used correctly, the R & A unit provides such data as areas of concentrated criminal activity, modus operandi, and gang activity. These data, when distributed and used properly, can assist patrol officers to target specific crime areas or problems, and criminal investigators to be able to link a series of crimes or criminal activity (Peterson, 1997).

■ CASE IN POINT

There had been a rash of auto thefts in a particular part of a city. Both patrol officers and auto theft detectives were becoming frustrated with the inability to solve the problem. It was an officer in the police agency's R & A unit who provided a key to the solution. For several weeks, the R & A officer had been analyzing auto theft reports in an attempt to provide some data that could assist investigators. Finally, this officer was able to provide information, such as the hours of theft, a possible MO, and a possible description of the suspect(s). This information was used by investigators to set up a surveillance using the type of vehicle being stolen by this group. The same night that the surveillance was set up, the suspects were apprehended and later led officers to a "chop shop," a place where the vehicles were being stripped and the parts sold. The key to this bust was the information from R & A.

Other Support and Specialized Units

Many more support units and specialized units exist in today's police agencies. An attempt to discuss them all would be a book in itself. However, the student of policing should be aware that a variety of these units do exist and can play valuable support roles.

1. The *Bomb Squad* is a group of specifically trained officers who must deal with locating, defusing, and destroying all types of explosives.

2. Members of the *repeat offenders unit* are charged with identifying, tracking, and, when necessary, apprehending felons with a history of repetitive criminal activity.

3. *Crime prevention* is a community-oriented unit that employs a variety of methods to prevent crime, such as establishing neighborhood watches and conducting building security inspections.

4. The *records division* maintains all reports filed with the agency and all criminal records.

5. A *public information officer* is responsible for delivering relevant and pertinent information to the public and to the news media.

6. A *crime lab* can be one of the most useful special support units to a police agency. A police agency without such a unit must rely on other agencies for investigative assistance, which can create delays that can severely hamper an investigation. Having access to its own crime lab may hasten the investigative process for a police agency.

A discussion of support units would not be complete without noting some issues associated with units. Such issues include how many of these units should exist, personnel selection (officer versus civilian), and liabilities.

The number of support units an agency has is limited by its size. It could be argued that in smaller agencies too many support units burden the agency by depleting resources from the more crucial units (e.g., patrol). However, some may argue the same thing is true for larger agencies.

◼ CASE IN POINT

The new chief of a midsize police agency (approximately 900 sworn officers) was very fond of specialty units. In less than two years of his tenure as chief, several new units were created. The personnel for these units were taken primarily from patrol. Since the number of officers in patrol was already below necessary staffing levels, and was decreasing because of the new units' demand for personnel, it became increasingly difficult to staff patrol beats adequately. This, in turn, lead to a decrease in the provision of services to some segments of the community.

Personnel selection (civilian or officers) for these units often depends on the type of unit being formed. For example, units like the bomb squad, repeat offenders, or plainclothes patrol will obviously require their personnel to be sworn police officers. However, units like the crime lab, R & A, or communications do not necessarily require their staff to be sworn officers. Therefore, many agencies who want to staff these units and yet not deplete their sworn ranks hire civilians. The hiring of civilians for some support units has also been found to be cost effective.

■ CASE IN POINT

After an organizational evaluation was completed by an outside research firm, a midsize police agency's communication division went through a complete transition. Instead of being run by the police agency any longer, communications are now being run by a private business. There is no involvement of police officers in the communications division. This switch allowed the police agency to reassign officers previously assigned to communications to areas of greater need, such as patrol. This move is expected to save the agency money because it is cheaper to have the privatized communication center (civilian costs per hour are less than that of sworn officers) and to reassign the officers, lowering the number of new officers required in other units.

Finally, the use of civilians in some units may save the agency money in personnel costs. Yet, when civilians begin to replace officers a question of liability is raised. The courts are holding police agencies liable for the their shortcomings (e.g., improper or poor training of officers) and their officers' activities. Therefore, because the agency is responsible for all its employees, the question of liability is moot as long as the civilians' acts are governed by agency policies, agency policies do not violate any constitutional rights, and the civilian is properly trained.

Obviously, the patrol and criminal investigative divisions and their respective functions do not, nor can they, exist on their own without support. This support comes from a variety of units charged with specific duties integral to the complete functioning of a police agency.

● SUMMARY

While the patrol division is the mainstay of the police agency, it must have support. This support can be found in the criminal investigations division, the second largest part of the police agency and usually a follow-up function to the patrol function. As a division it can be located under various headings and composed of several investigatory specialities.

As a function, the goal of criminal investigations is to solve crimes. To be successful, both preliminary and follow-up investigations need to be conducted. Who conducts them and how well depends on the size of the agency and the quality of training. Regardless, certain procedures should be followed in both phases of the investigation. Furthermore, criminal investigators have a variety of tools at their disposal, with technological advances such as computers among the most beneficial.

Both patrol and criminal investigations require support from a variety of other areas or support units. These units may include communications and training or other specialized units such a bomb squad and the crime lab. Each has a particular purpose and role in the scheme of policing and the structure of the police agency.

DO YOU KNOW . . .

1. Why criminal investigations receive more attention than patrol?
2. How your local police agency selects its criminal investigators?
3. What a police agency can do to improve the cooperation between detectives and patrol officers?
4. Some of the current investigative techniques available to criminal investigators?
5. How the police agency can improve cooperation between investigators and citizens?
6. What other types of support units can be found in police agencies?
7. What special units are in your local police department?

REFERENCES

Brown, M.F. (1998). *Criminal investigation: Law and practice*. Newton, MA: Butterworth-Heinemann.

Kuykendall, J. (1986). The municipal police detective: A historical analysis. *Criminology, 24*, 175–211.

1997 Los Angeles Police Department Annual Report. (1998). Los Angeles: Los Angeles Police Department.

Peterson, M.B. (1997). Criminal analysis. In M.L. Dantzker (Ed.), *Contemporary policing: Personnel, issues and trends* (pp. 167–194). Newton, MA: Butterworth-Heinemann.

Police Task Force. (1973). Washington, D.C.: National Advisory Commission on Criminal Justice Standards and Goals.

Reaves, B.A, & Goldberg, A.L.(1998). *Census of state and local law enforcement agencies, 1996*. Washington, D.C.: U.S. Government Printing Office.

Reaves, B.A., & Smith, P.Z. (1995). *Law enforcement management and administrative statistics, 1993: Data for individual state and local agencies with 100 or more officers*. Washington, D.C.: U.S. Government Printing Office.

Walker, S. (1999). *The police in America* (3rd ed.). New York: McGraw-Hill.

Weston, P.B., & Wells, K.M. (1990). *Criminal investigations*. Englewood Cliffs, NJ: Prentice Hall.

5 ORGANIZATION AND MANAGEMENT

Regardless of the nature of services offered, one of the most important aspects of any people-oriented institution is its organizational structure and managerial practices or style. For years, the police agency has been the target of severe criticisms for its ineffective organization and management, particularly the paramilitary structure and lack of management training. Although whole courses can be devoted to this broad and complex area, this chapter offers an introduction to the various problems associated with police organization and management.

ORGANIZATIONAL THEORY

In the police administration literature at least one chapter of modern-day textbooks is devoted to the discussion of organizational theories. The following discussion is a survey of some of the particularly salient portions of organizational theory provided for the purpose of giving students some initial insight into the concept of organizations.

The broadest view of an organization is the *closed* versus *open* organization. The basis of many police agencies is found in the theories of a closed organization, one that attempts to be self-sufficient and allows very little input from or access to members outside the organization. The theories associated with the closed organization are often referred to as traditional organizational theories (Dantzker, 1999). There are basically three theories: **scientific management, bureaucratic,** and **administrative.**

Scientific management theory is anchored by efficiency. Introduced by Frederick Taylor, scientific management theory is the view that employees' actions are guided by their economic self-interest. It was Taylor's belief that organizations should be run scientifically, using a mechanical approach emphasizing clearly defined laws, rules, and principles. The employee satisfies economic self-interest by successfully fulfilling goals of the organization while at work. In scientific management there is no concern about meeting other human needs in the workplace lest the organization's efficiency will suffer. As it might relate to the police organization, "there is no overwhelming recognition of scientific management theory in police departments. However, the idea that the organization comes first and the employees second was not an uncommon theme among early police agencies and is far from uncommon today" (Dantzker, 1999, p. 22).

The *bureaucratic* theory of organization was offered by Max Weber. Weber considered the bureaucracy as the most efficient form of organization (Gerth & Mills, 1946). However, the bureaucracy tends to constitute a threat to employees simply because of its impersonal and oppressive methodology. The key to a bureaucratic organization is the rational legal authority it bestows, which, according to Weber, is the identifying and examining of problems, and determining the most suitable means to solve them within the scope of the organization (see Gerth & Mills, 1946; Shafritz & Whitbeck, 1978). With respect to police agencies, a majority began as and continue to operate under bureaucratic theory (Dantzker, 1999; Reiss, 1992).

The last of the three closed organization theories is the *administrative* theory. Unlike the others, no one person can be credited with its development.[1] The basis of this theory is the emphasis of "how to." In practice this theory attempts to operationalize and reinforce the many features of the bureaucratic model (Dantzker, 1999).

These three theories have received their share of criticism. In particular, the application of these theories is said to cause man to be viewed as a machine, enforce inflexibility, cause lack of innovation and a stagnancy within the organization, and emphasize production and efficiency. All of these are not conducive to the operation of the public-service–oriented organization, such as a police department. This is especially true for agencies that are serious about adopting community policing, which requires an organizational approach not based on traditional organizational theories (Dantzker, 1999).

The counterpart to the closed organizational theories are the open organizational theories that emphasize flexibility and adaptation. These theories include **human relations, behavioral,** and **open systems.**

The *human relations* theory emphasizes the recognition of human values and needs as a mainstay for the effective organization. Based on the results of a series of experiments, often referred to as the Hawthorne studies (see Gannon, 1979; Luthans, 1985), it was noted that interpersonal relations and the spirit of cooperation are very important to production and, therefore, are important to the organization. This concept completely opposes to the closed theories. Yet, the examination of today's police agencies finds that this theory is not readily accepted. However, if community policing is to be fully adapted, the more humanistic approach will be required.

The *behavioral* theory is a compilation of several ideas. The basic concept offers that organizations are composed of interrelated behaviors which must be acknowledged. The key to this theory is the attempt to make an organization more democratic and participatory (see the works of Argyris, Homans, Lewin,

---

[1]For the student interested in pursuing further knowledge of this theory, see the writings of Fayol, Gulick & Urwick, Mooney, and Reiley. A good source is Shafritz and Whitbeck (1978).

McGregor in Shafritz & Hyde, 1978). The police organization truly interested in the community approach to policing might do well to explore this theory (Dantzker, 1999).

The last theory, the *open systems* theory (often referred to as the "bridging theory"), offers a view of the organization from a combination of traditional and open theories concepts. Several theories actually fall somewhere between the traditional and open theories, thus the "bridging" effect. The key concepts of these theories are cooperation and rationality. An organization needs to be efficient yet aware of the humanistic element. "Today's police organizations should focus their energies in trying to reform their agencies" (Dantzker, 1999, p. 28); perhaps the ideas and concepts of this theory are the means to such reformation.

In all, none of the theories is singularly represented in current police organizations. They do, however, provide some insight into why some police organizations may be more efficient than others. They also provide some possible means to improving the police organization through the adoption of a theory most befitting policing. The key is for the police administrator to be willing to review and examine the agency, seek out knowledge of organizational theories, and then apply that which best works for the community, the agency, and its employees. However, theory is just one element to better understanding how the police organization functions.

ORGANIZATION: CONCEPT AND DESIGN

The previous discussion offered a brief introduction into organizational theory. Before continuing the examination of organization and management as it applies to policing, a general understanding of the terms *organization* and *management* is appropriate. The term *organization* is often confusing, particularly when its application has two meanings. The first meaning deals with a process or act of being organized. The second application pertains to that of being a functioning structure characterized by a conformity to particular standards and requirements. In respect to policing, both meanings are applicable.

Although the organizational theory and structure literature are replete with definitions and characteristics of an organization, an organization can be viewed as a purposely structured social entity focused on a singular goal or set of specific goals (Dantzker, 1999; Gannon, 1979; Luthans, 1985; Shafritz & Whitbeck, 1978). Recognition of police agencies as this type of entity is enhanced by the presence of the following characteristics:

1. *Specific goals.* The overall goals of the police organization could be viewed as crime control (law enforcement and crime prevention) and maintaining social order. Within these overall goals several subgoals can be found that have been established by politicians, police administrators, and the public. What these goals are and how these goals are achieved often depends on the size of the police agency and its service population.

2. *Rational division of responsibilities.* Labor, authority, power, and communication are important elements of any organization. To policing, the strategically or rationally planned manner of these elements is extremely important. Who is responsible is often very clear in the police organization's hierarchical structure.

3. *Rules and norms.* All police organizations must function within the guidelines established by federal and state constitutions, court decisions, and federal and state statutes. In turn, each police organization establishes its own policies and procedures to which every member must adhere.

4. *Identifiable authority center.* In general, the chief, commissioner, or superintendent is the main authority center of the police organization. Additional authority centers may be created by the top administrator to provide what is often perceived as a stronger managerial chain (deputy administrators, assistants, commanders, etc.) (Alpert & Dunham, 1992; Blau & Scott, 1962; Brown, 1986; Dantzker, 1999; Luthans, 1985).

A distinction that should be made when discussing organizations is the difference of informal versus formal. Police agencies are formal organizations, a type most often referred to as a bureaucracy.

As with organizations, bureaucracies have been described by many authors. They are best recognized as a formal social organization possessing certain characteristics, such as a complex organizational structure, specialized sections, policies and procedures, a defined hierarchical structure, and career movement (Blau & Marshall, 1982; Dantzker, 1999; Gerth & Mills, 1946; March & Simon, 1958; Wilson, 1961). Using these characteristics, a police agency is easily recognized as a bureaucracy (Alpert & Dunham, 1998; Dantzker, 1999; Walker, 1999; Wilson, 1961).

1. *Complex organizational structure.* There are four basic types of structural designs that a police organization could employ. The simplest is the *line structure.* With this type of design authority flows from the top to the bottom in a clear and undisturbed pattern or line creating a set of superior–subordinate relations.

A second design is the *line and staff* structure which adds support functions to the line elements. Some advantages of this design include the providing of expert advice to line units (e.g., a legal adviser or forensics lab) and achieving organizational conformity in specific activities that could affect the entire police department (e.g., an internal affairs unit to investigate misconduct allegations).

The third type of structural design is referred to as the functional design. This structure calls for the modification of the line and staff design by delegating managerial authority to personnel outside their normal spans of control (e.g., assigning the SWAT commander to oversee a special patrol force designated to work burglaries during Christmas). Finally, the last structure is called the *matrix* design. In this structure members of functional areas (e.g., patrol) are assigned to specific projects (e.g., a plainclothes street crimes task force).

Which structural design is employed will depend on the size of the police agency. The fact is police bureaucracies can be complex organizational structures. Examine the organizational examples provided. Note how clear-cut and simple a small agency's organizational structure is compared with that of a larger police agency. The structure of a police organization is extremely important in how effectively and efficiently it will function. The police bureaucracy can be very complex, and not always as efficient and effective as desired, although complexity does not necessarily lead to inefficiency or ineffectiveness.

2. *Specialized sections.* The police bureaucracy is well known for its diversity. Although often criticized for its degree of differentiation, today's police role requires specialization. The organizational charts provide a very good example of how specialized the police bureaucracy can be, even in smaller police agencies (see Figures 5-1, 5-2, and 5-3).

3. *Policies and procedures.* Little is more important to the police bureaucracy then a set of clearly written and established policies and procedures. All police bureaucracies have what are most often referred to as general orders (GOs) or standard operating procedures (SOPs). These rules and regulations define everything from organizational responsibilities to uniform specifications and dress codes to how to handle different tasks.

■ CASE IN POINT

Following are excerpts from the procedures and general orders manuals of two police departments (Chicago, Illinois, and Fort Worth, Texas):

Chicago PD General Order 90-8: Organization and Function of the Bureau of Investigative Services

II. Organization
 A. The Bureau of Investigative Services is commanded by a deputy superintendent who reports directly to the superintendent of police.
 B. The Bureau consists of the following:
  1. Detective Division
  2. Organized Crime Division
  3. Youth Division
III. Bureau Responsibilities
 The Bureau of Investigative Services coordinates and directs the efforts of its divisions toward completing thorough and unified investigations. Responsibilities include the apprehension of offenders, assisting in the preparation of court cases, providing information and liaison with department personnel in matters of criminal, organized crime and youth related offenses. Cooperation is extended to outside agencies with similar responsibilities. [The complete GO is four pages long.]

Fort Worth GO 356.01 Critical Police Incidents—Defined

 A. Category I Critical Police Incidents—Defined
  1. Any discharge of a firearm by a department employee, whether the discharge is determined to be intentional or accidental, that results in a gunshot wound to any person.

FIGURE 5-1   Wilmette, Illinois, Police Department Organization Chart (February 13, 1997)

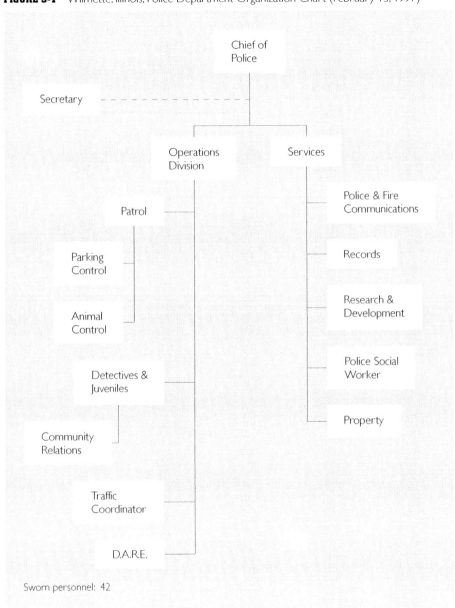

Sworn personnel: 42

FIGURE 5-2 Indianapolis, Indiana, Police Department Organization Chart (March 23, 1998)

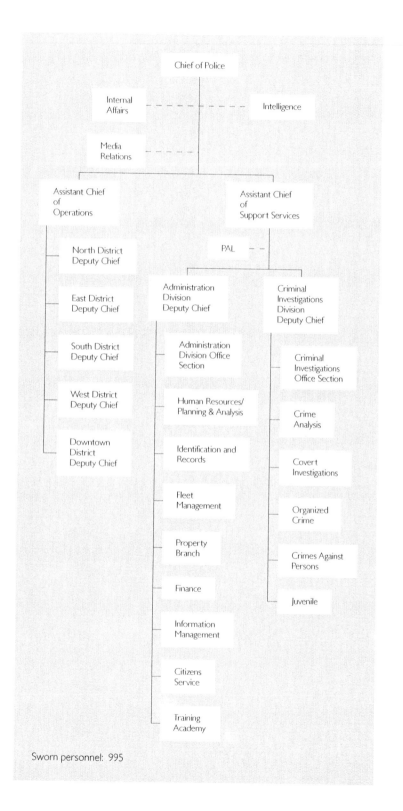

FIGURE 5-3 Chicago, Illinois, Police Department Organization Chart (April 1, 1998)

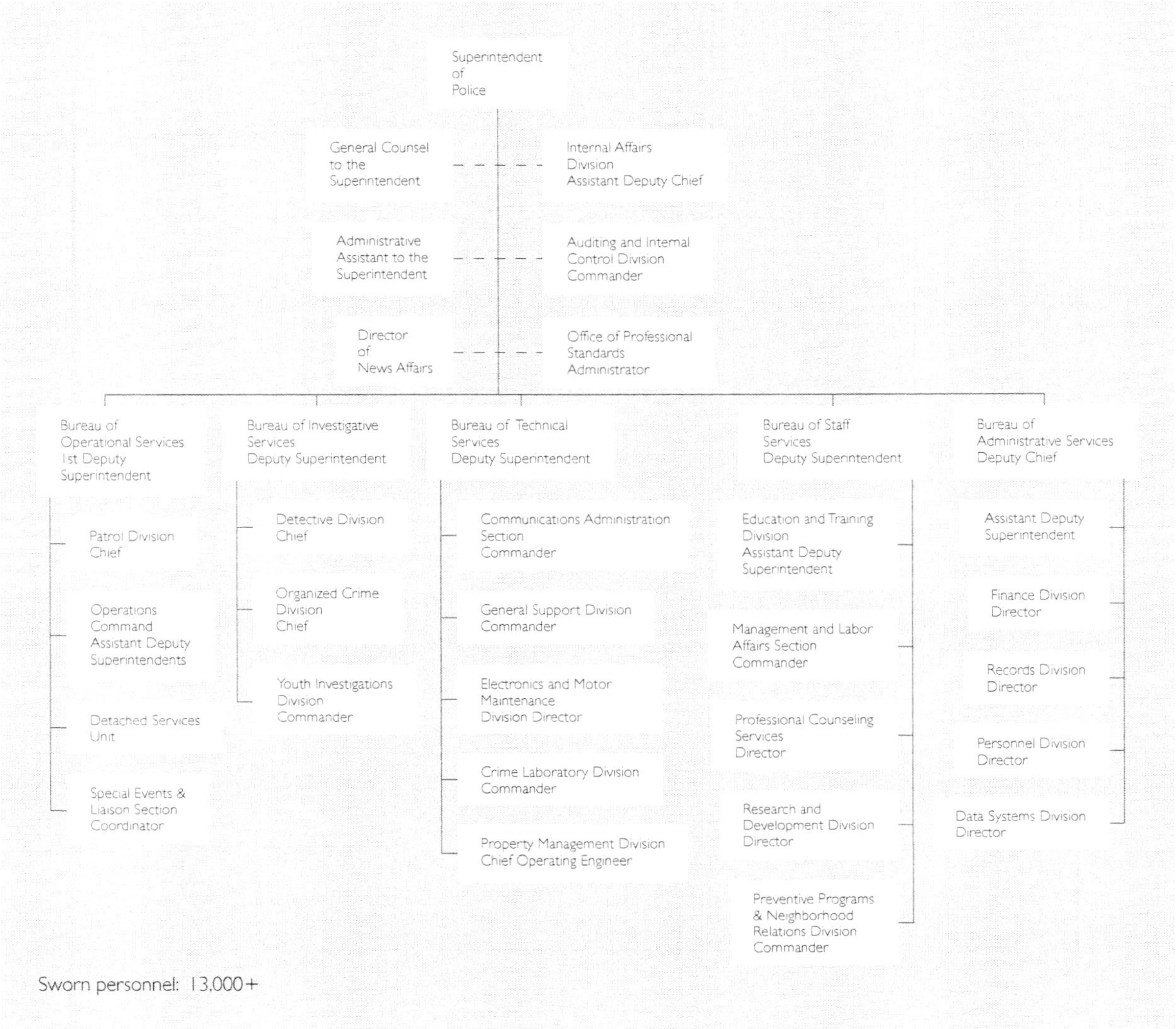

Superintendent of Police

General Counsel to the Superintendent

Administrative Assistant to the Superintendent

Director of News Affairs

Internal Affairs Division
Assistant Deputy Chief

Auditing and Internal Control Division
Commander

Office of Professional Standards
Administrator

Bureau of Operational Services
1st Deputy Superintendent

- Patrol Division Chief
- Operations Command Assistant Deputy Superintendents
- Detached Services Unit
- Special Events & Liaison Section Coordinator

Bureau of Investigative Services
Deputy Superintendent

- Detective Division Chief
- Organized Crime Division Chief
- Youth Investigations Division Commander

Bureau of Technical Services
Deputy Superintendent

- Communications Administration Section Commander
- General Support Division Commander
- Electronics and Motor Maintenance Division Director
- Crime Laboratory Division Commander
- Property Management Division Chief Operating Engineer

Bureau of Staff Services
Deputy Superintendent

- Education and Training Division Assistant Deputy Superintendent
- Management and Labor Affairs Section Commander
- Professional Counseling Services Director
- Research and Development Division Director
- Preventive Programs & Neighborhood Relations Division Commander

Bureau of Administrative Services
Deputy Chief

- Assistant Deputy Superintendent
- Finance Division Director
- Records Division Director
- Personnel Division Director
- Data Systems Division Director

Sworn personnel: 13,000+

      2. An employee involved in non-traffic incidents resulting in death or serious injury to any person, including employees, wherein the involved employee's status as a member of the department is relevant to the incident. Serious injury is defined as being when any person is hospitalized as a result of injuries sustained in a police-related incident.

      3. The death of any person in department custody or in the custody of the Tarrant County Sheriff's Department as a result of a police department arrest.

   B. Category II Critical Police Incident—Defined

      1. Any discharge of a firearm by a department employee whether the discharge is determined to be intentional or accidental where a gunshot wound does not occur to any person. [The complete GO is four pages long.]

4. *Defined hierarchical structure.* The police bureaucracy, like the military, has a strict, clearly recognizable "chain of command." Whenever a problem arises in a police agency, whether internal or external, it goes through the chain of command, usually with a goal of solving the problem at the lowest possible level. Most police bureaucracies use a hierarchical command designation by ranks that usually begins with the patrol officer, followed by the corporal, sergeant, lieutenant, captain, deputy chief, and chief. Each rank most often must reports to the rank immediately above.

5. *Career movement.* By simply examining the organizational structure and specialization of the police bureaucracy, it is easy to see the variety of career possibilities. Officers can be promoted along the chain of command, seek assignment to a specialized unit, or both.

Bureaucracies, particularly the police bureaucracies, have received a tremendous amount of criticism from citizens, academicians, and practitioners (see Alpert & Dunham, 1998; Dantzker, 1999; Franz & Jones, 1987; Harrison & Pelletier, 1987; Kuykendall & Roberg, 1982; Walker, 1999). This is primarily the result of bureaucracies being viewed as inflexible, ineffective, and uncreative. Furthermore, police bureaucracies are accused by these critics of limiting the spontaneity and self-realization of their employees. Do the police bureaucracies deserve these criticisms?

When one examines the quasi-military structure of policing, the uniforms, the rigid chain of command, training, and policies, it is easy to understand why the police bureaucracies receive the criticisms they do. With the exception of the discretion police officers have in certain situations, police organizations dictate many of the officers' actions. This includes enhancement of skills, educational attainment, and career mobility. In that respect, police bureaucracies, in the past, have done little to deter the criticism they receive. However, by adapting to the true nature of community policing, police bureaucracies will have to change how they operate. Nonetheless, the bureaucratic structure is not the only element influencing the criticism; management practices have also added fuel to the fire.

POLICE MANAGEMENT

One of the most important elements of an organization is its management or leadership. Management is that element that leads, directs, or manages the organization toward its goals. Leadership has been defined to include the process by which organizational members are influenced to facilitate the meeting of the organization's goals and objectives. Managing or leading any bureaucratic organization can be an extremely difficult task, even for the most experienced manager or administrator. This is especially true for the police manager, particularly when the majority of management experience most top police managers bring with them to this position is limited to that gained while climbing the police ranks. Police agencies have been criticized for many years for their lack of managerial preparation (Dantzker, 1999; Fyfe, 1985; Gaines, Southerland, & Angell, 1991; Kuykendall & Roberg, 1988; Steinman, 1984).

There has been a long-standing debate among academicians and some police practitioners as to the managerial quality of police bureaucracies. More often than not, the top police manager is a career officer. Although having climbed the police ladder and served in a variety of quasi-managerial roles, the average police manager typically has had little formal preparation for the tasks at hand.

O.W. Wilson, an expert in the field of police administration, identified eleven tasks for which the police manager must be qualified. These tasks include (1) organization, (2) leadership, (3) planning, (4) communications, (5) controlling, (6) decision making, (7) budgeting, (8) productivity, (9) associations and unions, (10) discipline, and (11) job enrichment (Wilson & McLaren, 1977). An additional item of importance today is politics (Dantzker, 1995, 1996, 1999).

Many organizational and management theorists offer an alternative to Wilson that would be appropriate to apply to police management. One such alternative has become recognized by the acronym POSDCORB (Dantzker, 1999; Gulick, 1978; Gulick & Urwick, 1937): (1) planning, (2) organizing, (3) staffing, (4) directing, (5) coordinating, (6) reporting, and (7) budgeting. Finally, Swanson, Territo, and Taylor (1998) suggest that a police leader's responsibilities include fulfilling the mission of the police department, making work productive, ensuring that subordinates are achieving, and producing impacts. Probably the most interesting aspect related to the police management skills issues is that there is no consensus on what skills a police manager should possess (Dantzker, 1996, 1999).

Regardless of which list of tasks is considered, the truth is that police managers should possess the skills necessary to handle the variety of problems and issues associated with the job; in reality, very few police managers have had the opportunity to obtain these skills simply because the police bureaucratic management structures have not provided ample opportunity to acquire the necessary skills (Dantzker, 1999). However, changes are gradually coming about with the creation of schools and programs geared specifically toward educating the police executive in the ways of management.

■ CASE IN POINT

In an effort to improve management skills, the New York Police Department sends selected captains, deputy inspectors, and civilian managers through an advanced training program primarily taught by the faculty of the Graduate School of Business, Columbia University. It is the teaching of this program by these faculty members that separates this training from other police management programs. A goal of this program is to provide participants with a broad range of management techniques and theories in an application to policing. Other such programs can be found through the FBI, the International Association of Chiefs of Police, and other university-related training institutions such as California's Law Enforcement Command College and the Southern Police Institute in Dallas. The result is a more management-oriented individual.

Teaching someone the skills to become a manager is one thing, how that person actually goes about managing is another. A person's management style can influence how well the organization and its members operate.

Management Style

Knowledge or skills to perform the various tasks or functions is just one area in which police managers have been criticized; these can be taught. An area of police management that provides a greater problem than the lack of skills is management style. Generally, management style cannot be taught. It is instinct, training, experience, and—sometimes—just plain common sense. Every individual has a distinct management style. Throughout the management and organizational theory literature, a variety of management styles are identified (see Alpert & Dunham, 1998; Dantzker, 1999; Fayol, 1949; Gaines et al., 1991; Lane, 1982; Luthans, 1985; Shafritz & Whitbeck, 1978; Taylor, 1916; Territo et al., 1993; Walker, 1999; Wilson & McLaren, 1977). This text will discuss three primary styles: **classical, human relations,** and **humanist.**

The primary emphasis of the **classical** style of management is on efficiency (see the writings of Fayol, Gulick & Urwick, Taylor, Weber in Shafritz & Whitbeck, 1978; Shafritz & Hyde, 1978). The workers of the organization are simply viewed as tools; there is little concern by management as to the personal aspirations and goals of the workers. All concern focuses on the success of the organization. The police executive who practices the classical style is an authoritarian who believes that everything he or she says is right, and no one should challenge his or her authority. The bottom line is the attitude: "I run this organization. You do it my way or go somewhere else."

Police agencies, for years, have been viewed as strict, quasi-military organizations; therefore, their top executives have often been classical style managers. Classical management style does little to promote personal growth of the employees or humanitarianism among the organization's employees. As a leadership style the classical manager could be described as an authoritarian leader who makes all decisions without consulting anyone else. With regard to community policing, this style of management has no chance for success.

A second style of management is the *human relations* style (found in the writings of Barnard, Mayo, Parsons, Selznick, Simon, in Shafritz & Whitbeck,

WHAT DO YOU THINK?

The New Police Chief

It has been ten long years for the officer who has climbed the ranks to reach police captain. During this promotional climb the officer has worked in several different areas of the police department, has witnessed and participated in many managerial decisions (many of which the officer has had doubts about), and has attained a bachelor's degree in criminal justice and a master's degree in public administration. The captain feels as prepared as possible for that ultimate promotion, to police chief, and the opportunity has finally come: the department's chief of fifteen years is retiring. Although several other ranking officers have their sights set on the position, the captain thinks the position should be given to the most qualified individual, in terms of college education and managerial experience. Morale is low. There have been a corruption scandal and a questionable shooting, and the crime rate in the city has increased over last year. Citizens have started complaining, and the politicians are listening. Rumor has it that next year's budget may be cut, and there will be no raises. The new chief will have his or her hands full. The captain is interviewed for the chief's position. You are that captain.

1. For many years the management style of the retiring chief has been described as classical; what is your management philosophy and style? (If necessary refer back to the management style discussion.)
2. What would you do as chief to improve department morale? department effectiveness?
3. How difficult do you think it will be to incorporate your management and organizational education into practice within the police department?
4. Even though you think you are well qualified, progressive, and an open minded, what are the chances that the police bureaucracy will lure you into a more traditional stance on issues and procedures?

1978; Shafritz and Hyde, 1978). The human relations–style manager realizes and recognizes the importance of and need for human input into the organization. Employees are not mere laborers, as viewed by the classical manager. Known for a consultative approach to management, the human relations–style manager is more receptive to ideas and concerns from those under his or her leadership than the classical manager. The human relations leader can be viewed as democratic: a police executive who holds monthly roundtable discussions with middle managers, allows input in decision making, and does not hold to the premise that "all I say is gospel." It is assumed that this style of manager will often get more effort from the rest of the organization than the classical manager. This may be particularly true today with a greater number of better-educated individuals moving up the police management ladder (Brown, 1985; Kuykendall & Roberg,

1988). Furthermore, this style of manager should be fairly successful in a community-policing environment.

The last type of management style may best be described as the *humanist* style (found in the works of Bennis, Drucker, Maslow, McGregor, Ostrom, Rogers in Shafritz & Whitbeck, 1978; Shafritz & Hyde, 1978). The police executive who employs this style of management allows and welcomes—almost requires—participation and input into organizational decisions and goals from all levels of the organization. Under this management style, decision making is no longer left up to the chief or the immediate upper echelon of management only; all levels of rank are allowed some type of input into the goals of the organization and are involved in decisions that affect the organization. The humanistic leader takes a more passive approach to dealing with subordinates. The most successful community-policing manager will have to be a humanist.

Some questions that arise at this point are, which management style or what kind of leader belongs in the police bureaucracy? Are police bureaucracies capable of establishing a consistent management style that allows extensive participation by those not specifically identified as management? Although the answers to these questions may not be relatively obvious, they can be found. Of course, it also depends on whether the police agency employs a traditional approach or the community-policing approach to service.

The police manager or leader is a major component in the successfulness of the police agency. Although there are different approaches to leading or managing, successful leaders must possess certain skills and then be able to translate those skills into action.

A failed leadership will often lead to a failing organization. Understanding of how or why the agency is failing is not always obvious. Therefore, a mechanism is required that assists in the recognition of failure and success. As with most organizations, a key mechanism for identifying effectiveness, efficiency, or failure, is through accountability.

ACCOUNTABILITY

As an individual goes from childhood to adulthood his or her accountability for conduct or behavior increases. As policing has matured, it, too, has been held increasingly accountable. Accountability, with respect to policing, refers to the department or individual officer being held answerable, responsible, and capable of explaining actions, objectives and goals, and, in particular, productivity (or lack thereof). Accountability is an extremely important issue in policing at both the agency and individual levels.

> The accountability of individual police officers is a fundamental issue for police executives. This is fitting: Police officers are the public officials society has authorized, even obliged, to use force (Kelling et al., 1990, p. 15).

Moore (1990) adds, "The accountability of police officers for their activities and actions is more vital than in other professions simply because of the authority granted to police officers as a part of their duties" (p. 11). Therefore, accountability is a necessity in policing.

ACCOUNTABILITY AND POLICING

Accountability of the police should be viewed from two dimensions: accountable for something and accountable to someone. The police can be held accountable for the role they portray in society, their behavior and actions, and the services they provide (Dantzker, 1999; Pisani, 1993; Walker, 1999).

Role

In Chapter 1, the complexity, ambiguity, and multifaceted nature of the police role was discussed. Although there are a variety of perceptions of what the police role could be, it is difficult to pinpoint what, exactly, the police role is. As noted, police officers are viewed as crime fighters, enforcers, servants, and jacks-of-all-trades. This complexity presents problems for police accountability, and increases with regard to community policing. Society holds the police accountable for their role without either police or society having a complete understanding of what that role is.

Currently, the police are responsible for fulfilling whatever immediate role their community requires. When they are unable to fulfill that role, society asks, "Why not?" The reason usually includes the inability to live up to everyone's expectations and to meet everyone's demands. Thus, although society holds the police accountable for their role, society has not provided a definitive direction to that role. Therefore, role accountability will continually change with changes in society's needs and demands of the police. The conclusion is that although the police are held accountable for fulfilling society's expectations of the police role, society is responsible for defining that role, an issue of extreme importance when attached to community policing.

Behavior and Actions

Police are held most accountable for their actions or behavior. Regardless of the police role, how the officer behaves and the action taken while performing the duties of the job will be scrutinized most closely, especially if deemed unacceptable to societal or departmental expectations. Behavior that exhibits racism, brutality, discrimination, and corruption is not acceptable to society. The police are expected to be free from such behaviors and, therefore, are held accountable, with little exception, when inappropriate behaviors occur.

◼ CASE IN POINT

A circuit court in Jefferson County, Kentucky, found the city of Louisville and its police officials partially liable for the actions of an off-duty Louisville police officer who seriously wounded his girlfriend with his department-issued firearm in a 1986 shooting incident. The court held that the city and the police agency knew of the officer's history of alcoholism and abusive behavior toward women and were, therefore, partially liable for his actions toward his girlfriend.

Services

Policing involves the delivery of four basic services: law enforcement, crime prevention, order maintenance, and social services. Police departments are held accountable for the delivery of these services. Equality, efficiency, and effectiveness are key criteria in accountability. The equity of services refers to whether all the community receives similar services.

Equity of services has been an issue in policing for years. Even though the distribution of services is often as equitable as resources allow, sometimes citizens' perceptions interfere with recognition of this situation. If a citizen does not see a patrol car pass by his or her house at least once a day, the perception is, "My neighborhood doesn't receive equal treatment." It is unfortunate that there are not enough police to be everywhere all the time; because that may never occur, police agencies will remain fully accountable for the apparent lack of equity in services, regardless of the resource problems.

As well as being held accountable for something, there is always the element of being held accountable to someone. The police are accountable for how they fulfill their role, their behavior, and provision of services. Both the agency and the individual officers are accountable to the community, the legal system, and the specific agency.

Community

Considering that the police exist to meet community needs such as order maintenance or law enforcement, it is natural that they be accountable to their community. For this discussion, "community" refers to both citizens and government. Both entities deserve police accountability because of economics and concerns about personal safety of citizens. Local police agencies receive most of their funding from their community. Whenever increases in funding are required, the community is asked to provide. This relationship requires that the police be held accountable to the community. If a police agency cannot provide a reasonable explanation for its failure to meet objectives and goals, to provide equity in services, or to decrease crime (despite yearly budget increases), its relationship with the community will suffer. A lack of accountability results in a loss of community trust and desire to provide additional resources to the agency.

■ CASE IN POINT

Since the March 1991 beating of Rodney King by four Los Angeles, California, police officers the question of accountability has loomed large in Los Angeles. During a house subcommittee hearing shortly after the beating, Professor James Fyfe (American University) advised that a major problem in Los Angeles was the police department's lack of accountability. Fyfe stated, "Because its organization does not provide for accountability or checks on power, it has long been the outlaw among big American police departments" (*Criminal Justice Newsletter*, April 1, 1991, p. 2). In an effort to rebuild trust and accountability, police chief Daryl Gates was forced out of office and replaced by the former police commissioner of Philadelphia, Willie Williams. Although Chief Williams made strides toward improving accountability, it is currently up to Chief Bernard C. Parks, a longtime member of the LAPD, to complete the establishment of accountability.

The police are looked to for protection. Our society considers protection of its members the duty of the police. When they fail to do so, society wants to know why, especially when the adopted motto of many police agencies has been "to serve and protect." The adoption of such a creed requires the police agency to be accountable when the promise is not completely fulfilled.

The Legal System

Input and outcomes of the legal system, prosecution, and the courts are primarily linked to the police. Entry into the system begins with a police report and arrest. When the police fail to do their jobs adequately or correctly, it creates problems for the legal system. The filing of charges, case preparation, evidence, and, ultimately, the findings of the court are directly related to police performance. Because there is such dependence on police performance by this system, the police must be able to explain to the other parts of the criminal justice system why the actions taken occurred, whether it leads to failure of the case or not. Otherwise, the relationship between the police and the other components will be strained.

Furthermore, the police are accountable to the law itself. As police officers they are required to uphold and enforce criminal laws while recognizing the existence of civil rights and laws. Landmark Supreme Court cases have often been used to remind officers of their obligations. When they fail to follow the rules and guidelines the law has established, officers must be held accountable. In this setting accountability could range from the dismissal of a case to criminal or civil charges against the police officers and their employers.

The Agency Itself

Employees are always held accountable to their employers for their actions. Police officers are no different. An officer's activities and performance are monitored by the department. When the officer does not meet standards, fails to follow guidelines, policies, and procedures, or steps outside the realm of "authorized police behavior," such as becoming corrupt or engaging in brutality, the officer must answer to the department. Because an officer's actions can cause such detrimental results to the department as poor publicity or making it financially liable, the department must hold officers accountable for their behavior. Failure of police agencies to hold its officers accountable for their behavior may lead to chaotic situations and very unpleasant results.

■ CASE IN POINT

A San Antonio, Texas, police chief found himself in a rather awkward position when a rookie officer marched into his office and advised him that he would not continue to work with corrupt officers. After the officer explained, an investigation was launched and a small group of officers was discovered to be involved in illegal drug activities, such as confiscating drugs and reselling them from their patrol cars. Disciplinary action (firing and criminal charges) was taken against these officers. They were held accountable for their behavior. So was the chief. Even though the chief "cleaned up the mess," he was dismissed by the city manager on the grounds that he was responsible for the problem having occurred in the first place. The chief was held accountable by the city manager for his officers' actions.

A problem that arises is by what means should a police agency or its members be held accountable, and by what means should accountability be gauged?

MEASURING ACCOUNTABILITY

Accountability is a difficult element to deal with; particularly when in most cases accountability for policing translates to productivity; deciding what should be measured compounds the difficulty. Accountability refers to being answerable or responsible; although the police are accountable for a variety of areas, the most common concern is with police performance. Therefore, the problem arises of adequately measuring police performance so that it can meet requirements of accountability. To do this, accountability must be divided into departmental and individual accountability.

Department Accountability

Because accountability can be viewed as productivity, a problem that arises is the difficulty in measuring police agency productivity. With the focus of accountability on performance, the problem is what should be measured to determine departmental performance? For a business, accountability can be measured by profit and loss or production levels; policing is not as clear-cut. The performance measures of a police agency often focus on the delivery of the basic services. Although many of these services can be measured statistically, a variety of tasks performed by the agency's members are simply unmeasurable. Such tasks have often been referred to as the intangibles of policing—"intangible" being something that is not corporeal or material. Courtesy, goodwill, or ideas are intangibles. Despite the need to recognize the intrinsic existence and the value of intangibles, an increasing problem for the community policing agency, most agencies still remain solely devoted to measuring the tangible tasks.

The number of calls for service, reports taken, arrests made, and cases cleared are all examples of tangible items used to measure departmental performance. However, the most common measure of police agency accountability for performance is **crime rate.**

Crime Rate

It is difficult for the average citizen to know whether the local police agency is doing its job; however, crime rates are something that most citizens recognize and often stimulate public interest. When crime rates are low, citizens perceive that the police agency is doing its job; when rates climb, police performance is questioned. In either case, statistics become an imperative part of demonstrating accountability. Therefore, it is common for police agencies to prepare a yearly public report. In addition to addressing topics related to personnel and other departmental changes, this report provides a comparison of crime figures, which it is hoped will have positive implications for the agency.

■ CASE IN POINT

Despite the fact that a large proportion of crimes in this country are of minor stature, interest tends to focus more on the "Part I offenses" (homicide, rape, robbery, aggravated assault, burglary, larceny/theft, and vehicle theft). The numbers attached to these crimes generate the most concern and are more often supportive of accountability. Based on this belief, the police departments in Wilmette, Illinois, and Los Angeles, California, can claim to have been strongly accountable in 1997. Wilmette Police Department showed an overall decrease in Part I offenses (646 in 1996; 641 in 1997). LAPD was perhaps even more accountable in that the Part I crimes dropped 13.1 percent (235,228 in 1996; 204,555 in 1997). By simply using crime statistics, both agencies could claim that they were accountable.

A problem related to the use of crime rates as a measure for departmental accountability is that they are, on occasion, misleading. Police departments can only measure crimes that have been reported. It is a well-known fact, however, that not all crime is reported. Recognition of this fact has led to other measures such as victimization studies and self-report studies that attempt to fill the void believed to exist in police statistics. However, the combination of these statistics with police statistics can still be misleading. Therefore, the reporting of a low crime rate may not actually indicate that the police are doing a great job, only that crime reporting is low. The argument is sometimes made that citizens do not report crimes to police agencies that they do not trust or believe to be ineffective, whereas they do report crimes when they believe that the local police agency is honest, responsive, and effective. If this is true, crime rate reports may be an inverse measure in some cases. For example, with the change to a community-policing approach one of the pluses is that citizens become more comfortable with police officers and are more willing to talk with them and report crime. When this occurs routinely, crime statistics increase. This does not necessarily mean that the department is doing an inadequate job. It may mean that crime rates in previous years were actually higher but low reporting provided misleading data. Increased reporting may indicate that the agency is doing a better job.

Another problem is that crime rates are statistics. Statistics can be manipulated; there is no guarantee that the crime rate reported is in reality the true crime rate. Although crime rate is a current measure of department accountability, it is not a completely trustworthy measure. Therefore, it raises the question, "If crime rates are not completely reliable, what other measures can be used?"

It has been suggested that clearance rates and police–population ratio are possible alternatives. Like crime rates, both of these have an outstanding flaw. Clearance rates are computed on the basis of arrests, and they are a statistic that can also be manipulated, especially when bulk clearing (attributing several crimes to one arrestee) is considered. The police–population ratio is a statistic derived from the number of officers per 10,000 people in a given area. For example, in June 1996, national figures indicated that the number of sworn police officers was no less than 8 (West Virginia and Montana) per 10,000 people, and as high as 66 per 10,000 people (District of Columbia). The rationale behind this statistic is that the better the officer–citizen ratio, the better the agency's accountability. One of the problems with this measure is that this ratio includes all sworn police officers, and not all officers are directly involved in performing the law enforcement duties about which the community is most concerned.

The problem of measuring departmental accountability still exists. Improvement in this area in the near future will not be easy. Although it could include using several of the productivity statistics used for measuring the accountability of the individual officer, as well as measures currently applied to departments for accountability purposes, departments still need to find other means and measures that reflect all services and not just the crime-related service. This is especially true if agencies are to adopt a community-policing approach.

Individual Accountability

Measurement of departmental productivity for accountability purposes is a difficult task because of the lack of valid measures. Measuring individual officer productivity for accountability purposes can be almost as difficult. Many police agencies examine or rate officers primarily on productivity. Depending on the assignment, individual measures differ slightly. Measurement of patrol officers may include number of arrests by type (felony, misdemeanor, ordinances), number of traffic citations issued, and reports filed. Traffic officers may be evaluated by the number of citations issued by type (moving versus nonmoving), accidents worked, and DWI (driving while intoxicated) arrests. Finally, detectives' productivity can include cases cleared.

There is no doubt that the measuring of officers' productivity and holding them accountable for their actions are necessities; otherwise, discipline problems may occur, the department may require an excessive number of officers, or must promise more money and increased employee benefits to get the officers to do their jobs (Moore, 1990). Two main concerns associated with this issue are whether productivity measures are viewed as "quotas" and whether the measures employed are reasonable or fair assessments of officer performance.

For years the setting of productivity goals have been referred to as "quotas" (Van Meter, 1998), a familiar concept to both officers and citizens. Although quotas have often been linked to traffic enforcement, it is not uncommon for quotas to be linked to other types of activities. Police management has a right to expect and establish productivity standards. Unfortunately, quotas have long held a negative connotation despite their positive goals. Many police officers

A question of accountability? (75 Points by Jack Higgins reprinted with special permission, *The Chicago Sun-Times*, 1998; originally printed June 9, 1992)

have at least one story of how an individual after being issued a traffic citation complained that the officer must need to fill his or her quota. There is some truth to this allegation; if officers failed to meet these productivity levels, claims of failing to do his or her job would follow.

Setting productivity levels, whether as quotas or other standards, leads to the concern whether such a measurement forces officers to make arrests simply to maintain an acceptable performance rating to remain in their current assignments. The concern over quality and effectiveness often gets lost, and accountability becomes a numbers game. Officers failing to meet the target numbers are criticized, reprimanded, and even transferred from their preferred assignment. Does not reaching the set productivity levels really mean an officer is not doing his or her job? Not necessarily, but it certainly does raise that question.

Present accountability measures for both department and individual performances are mediocre at best. Yet, there is an obvious need for accountability. Current mechanisms are suspect. What is the answer? It has been suggested that, because of the shortfalls of current measures used to demonstrate both agency and individual accountability, other mechanisms of accountability must be established.

⬤ MECHANISMS OF ACCOUNTABILITY

Current methods of measuring police productivity for accountability, both departmental and individual, display faults and limitations. These limitations require that additional measures or processes be created. Other mechanisms of accountability have been offered as partners to current measures. These mechanisms can be divided into two categories: **external** and **internal.**

External Mechanisms

External mechanisms for police accountability are those found outside the police agency. These include the U.S. Supreme Court and civilian review boards, neither of which are very popular within police agencies nor have they had much success as mechanisms of police accountability.

Since the 1960s the U.S. Supreme Court has been viewed as a mechanism of police accountability because of decisions attempting to control police behavior. Although these decisions have consistently been viewed by many in policing as controversial, they nonetheless have placed some restrictions on police performance, making police more accountable for their actions. Many of these decisions have been viewed by some as "procriminal–antipolice." Critics of these decisions and similar decisions claim that they tend to handcuff the police and coddle the criminal. Yet, it has been difficult to prove or disprove that these decisions have had a negative impact on police performance. However, they have heightened public awareness and forced the police to remain within the constitutional guidelines they should be following. A question that arises at this point is, "How effective have the courts been as a mechanism of police accountability?"

Many would say that the courts have had limited impact or effect on police accountability. This is only true if the courts are viewed as purely a proactive mechanism. The courts, however, do not supervise the police on a daily basis and do not review actions until after they have occurred. When the courts are viewed as a reactive mechanism, it can be said that they are more effective.

Landmark Supreme Court decisions such as *Mapp, Escobedo,* and *Miranda* are just one way the courts can work as a mechanism for holding the police accountable for their actions. Decisions of this nature force the police to use prescribed methods because failure to do so results in the freeing of a criminal or the overturning of a decision. This forces the police to be accountable for their actions. Dismissal of a case or the overturning of a decision is only one mechanism of accountability from the courts. Others include civil suits, injunctions, and criminal sanctions.

In civil suits, the courts can hold the police accountable for their action by awarding monetary relief for damages under state or federal laws. When a police officer has violated an individual's constitutional rights (which includes commission of a crime by a police officer against an individual), that person can sue the police officer and the agency. If the court finds in the plaintiff's favor, the police department can be required to pay the plaintiff for damages. For example, a federal jury in Florida awarded $6 million to a woman who sued the Boynton Beach, Florida, Police Department. The lawsuit stemmed from an incident in which the plaintiff had been shot eight times by police. Cases do not always need to go completely through the court for an outcome unfavorable to the police.

CASE IN POINT

The West Virginia State Police settled a lawsuit, for the amount of $775,000, filed by the family of a woman killed during a police pursuit. The victim was killed when her vehicle was rear-ended by an individual trying to outrun the police. The suit accused a state trooper of employing excess speed (over 100 mph) during the chase, which was being filmed for television's *Real Stories of the Highway Patrol.*

An injunction is a court order that forces the police to discontinue specific activities until a determination can be made as to whether civil or constitutional rights are being violated. Injunctions are usually sought by groups or businesses that believe a particular police practice is being used in an unfair or discriminatory manner.

CASE IN POINT

In 1986 the Fort Worth Police Department's Street Crimes Unit was accused of harassment and racial discrimination as a result of continuous "bar checks" on certain bars and clubs frequented by blacks and Hispanics. Owners of these establishments requested that the courts put a halt to this action. Until an actual ruling could be made, a judge handed down an injunction that forced the unit to stop conducting the raids on these specific bars unless the same type of bar checks took place at all bars in surrounding areas.

An injunction gives all parties involved time to rectify the problems that lead to the action for which the injunction was needed.

Finally, the courts can impose criminal sanctions against the police officer. This mechanism is somewhat more difficult to impose than monetary awards or injunctions because it must be proven that criminal intent existed at the time of action. The Rodney King–LAPD incident is an excellent example. All four officers were indicted on criminal charges, yet a jury found them not guilty. However, because the actions of those officers came under civil rights protections, a retrial at the federal level occurred. The results here were somewhat different from those at the criminal trial. Two of the officers were found guilty of rights violations.

It can be said that the courts are a reactive, external mechanism for police accountability. Although not a very popular mechanism, it is not as unpopular with the police as another external mechanism, civilian review boards.

The civilian review board has existed since the mid-1950s with the formation of the New York Civilian Complaint Review Board. Review boards are composed of citizens, usually appointed by a top governmental official, charged with the review of alleged police misconduct. The purpose is to provide an unbiased, investigatory body outside police control.

■ CASE IN POINT

In October 1996 the Tucson, Arizona, City Council voted to create a citizens' committee to review complaints of police misconduct. This action came the same day a police officer was sentenced to three years' probation for molesting a fifteen-year-old girl while on duty. However, this panel would have no power to conduct investigations or subpoena witnesses. Later, in 1997, the council established a new ten-member Citizen Police Advisory Review Board in addition to an independent auditor. This new setup would give powers to the group that the committee the previous year did not have. The president of the Tucson Police Officers' Association voiced opposition to the board and questioned whether it was really needed, suggesting that recent police misconduct was an aberration.

Civilian review as a mechanism for police accountability has frequently met with adamant opposition from police officers for a variety of reasons.

First, citizen review boards are only empowered to make recommendations for disciplinary action. They have no power to impose sanctions. Second, these boards create an adversarial setting that places a citizen against a police officer. This does not help community relations. Finally, the composition of such boards seldom includes anyone with police or law enforcement knowledge. Some police and academic critics of citizen review boards believe that this lack of knowledge creates an automatic bias against the police. Yet, although the police officials are opposed to citizen review boards, citizens tend to favor their existence simply because they are seen as a mechanism for accountability to those whom the police serve. Citizens also tend to believe that the police do not always do a very effective or fair job of policing themselves and, therefore, see citizen review boards as a tool that forces objectivity into the process.

In conclusion, external mechanisms of police accountability are not very popular or effective. The courts are primarily reactive, and civilian review has been unwelcome and has very little power. Therefore, it is extremely important that solid internal mechanisms exist.

Internal Mechanisms

Internal mechanisms of police accountability are primarily linked to administrative factors. They include supervision, training, discipline, rewards, peer control, and audit mechanisms (Kelling et al., 1988, 1990; Moore, 1990). As with many other organizations, middle-line supervisors are held responsible for effectiveness and accountability in the workforce. Effective supervision is a valuable tool of accountability. Police supervisors who are knowledgeable about the policies and procedures of the department and enforce and support them, as well as fully comprehend the law and its applications, are valuable tools to any police department. When supervisors overlook or fail to enforce department regulations, productivity and officer performance suffer. Therefore, well-trained and effective supervisors are one way of maintaining internal accountability.

Training can have either a positive or negative effect on accountability. Inadequate training places police officers in a position in which behavior and performance may not meet acceptable standards (Doerner, 1997). Officers who are competently trained and educated are believed by many practitioners and academicians to be less likely to violate acceptable behaviors and maintain an acceptable level of productivity (Carter, Sapp, & Stephens, 1989; Shernock & Dantzker, 1997).

When officers know their responsibilities and perform as prescribed, little need for additional mechanisms of control may be required. Training is an important aspect of police performance, but it is no more a guarantee of perfect behavior than is the existence of qualified supervisors. Sometimes an officer knowingly violates acceptable or required behavior. When this occurs, the use of discipline is an effective mechanism.

Disciplinary action by police executives against officers who have violated policies or procedures demonstrates to other officers and the community that police officers who violate the law or department policies will be held accountable for their actions. It notifies other officers that they, too, will be held accountable if there is a violation.

■ CASE IN POINT

While attempting to apprehend a suspected auto thief, a police patrol sergeant somehow managed to allow his weapon to discharge accidentally at the suspect. Although a patrol officer witnessed the accidental discharge, the sergeant did not report the incident. It was not until the suspect filed a complaint against the sergeant that the department became aware of the incident. Disciplinary action was taken against both the officer and the sergeant, not only because of the gun being fired but also for failing to report the incident as required. The result was that the sergeant was demoted, and the officer was reassigned to the police auto pound.

Rewarding individuals for exemplary behavior is an effective internal mechanism for accountability. Police officers who perform over and beyond the call of duty should be recognized. This recognition, like discipline, informs other officers that all behaviors are monitored, and accountability is both positive and negative. Rewards include promotions, choices of assignments, and days off as well as monetary awards.

An interesting aspect of organizational theory is that peer pressure affects the production and behaviors of fellow workers. This phenomenon is particularly observable in policing. Peer control is an inherent mechanism for accountability to the police agency. Police officers are generally very vocal about the behavior and actions of fellow officers in the area of production, which has been identified as a major element of police accountability. It is not unusual for peer influence to affect an officer's behavior.

■ CASE IN POINT

Almost every veteran officer has a story of the rookie officer, who in an effort to prove his or her capabilities, goes out and writes numerous tickets, answers every call possible, or is constantly searching for "something to get into." There are very few stories of veterans who continue to perform as "rookies." However, on occasion, when a veteran officer finds himself or herself surrounded by young, eager officers who are constantly trying to be productive, it forces the veteran to be more productive so as not to be "shown up or outdone" by rookies and less veteran officers.

One form of reward is promotion. This officer has just been promoted to sergeant. (Courtesy of the Scottsdale, Arizona, Police Department)

The last of the administrative factors applicable to accountability are the audit mechanisms. These include officers' daily logs, worksheets, supervisor evaluations, and financial, supply, and equipment audits. To hold officers accountable for their activities, many police agencies require that officers keep a daily log or worksheet on which the officer lists all of his or her activities for the shift. These logs are then turned in to the immediate supervisor for review and are used at the end of the month for a statistical measure of accountability. Appropriate and honest use of these logs makes them a valuable tool for measuring or controlling behavior. Monthly evaluations of officers' performances by their immediate supervisors, when done fairly and diligently, provide an additional tool for accountability.

Administrative factors can be extremely useful internal controls of police accountability. However, even the faithful employment of these factors may not be adequate internal control. Therefore, a special unit within the police agency is often used as a mechanism of internal control, internal affairs (IA).

Historically viewed as a unit interested in "nailing police officers" and its officers referred to as "headhunters," IA units have suffered from unfair images. The general myth associated with this unit is that the officer is wrong until proven right and that once an officer is reported to this unit his or her career is in immediate jeopardy. In reality, these units tend to be one of the fairest and most thorough investigative bodies found in the police agency. Although this unit has only the power to investigate and recommend whether disciplinary action should be taken, it is a unit that is extremely feared within most police agencies.

Internal affairs serves three basic functions: investigation of citizen-generated complaints, review and investigation of reports and complaints generated by police officers against other officers, and self-initiated investigations of alleged misconduct. An IA unit is usually good for building police–community relations but is not positive for interdepartmental relations. The primary reason for this is that the unit sometimes fails to support an officer after clearing the officer from unfounded allegations.

■ CASE IN POINT

Two officers, a woman and a man, responding to a domestic disturbance found themselves having to arrest one of the male participants. While they attempted to effect the arrest, the other man intervened, allowing the first man to flee from the scene. The officers proceeded to arrest the second man while backups searched for and later apprehended the first man. A few weeks after the incident, the male officer was summoned to IA. Apparently the second man in the domestic disturbance filed a complaint with IA about the female officer, alleging that she forcefully entered the apartment of the complainant, and attacked the sleeping complainant and a companion before arresting them both. The complaint was far from the truth, as validated by statements from several other officers at the scene as well as a citizen witness. Although the investigation was dismissed, no charges were ever filed against the complainant for fabricating a police report. This did not make any of the officers involved, especially the officer who was the target of the complaint, very happy with IA.

Although IA has a negative image, it is usually one of the most effective means for holding officers accountable. However, what happens when IA officers are the ones being investigated? Who polices IA? In many police agencies the IA unit answers directly to the chief, which results in closer scrutiny. When the unit is not under the chief's immediate jurisdiction, wrongdoing in that unit can force the chief to change that situation.

■ CASE IN POINT

For years the IA unit of the New York Police Department was under the command of a deputy commissioner. In 1997 that unit came under fire because of allegations of poor investigations and corruption. To remedy the problem, all of the officers were reassigned and new officers were brought in. Furthermore, the unit was relocated, to fall directly under the control of the police commissioner.

Up to this point, several mechanisms for police accountability, external and internal, have been offered. The discussion would not be complete without at least mentioning one last suggested mechanism of police accountability that is both externally and internally oriented, the police–community relations (PCR) unit.

The PCR unit is a unique mechanism for police accountability because of its dual role. This unit serves two purposes: to provide a directly accessible source for citizens and to allow police officers an arena in which to focus directly on issues of community concern, such as crime prevention. The dual role allows this unit to be more accessible to the community and provides the department with an outlet for explaining certain behaviors and actions to citizens through neighborhood discussions, community meetings, and as guest speakers to local groups. Unlike many of the other measures and mechanisms of police accountability, the verdict on the success or failure of the PCR unit is not yet in. Furthermore, this unit is changing with the adaptation of community policing.

A review of police accountability finds that a variety of measures and mechanisms exist, each with its own pitfalls and shortcomings. Taken as a group, these measures and mechanisms still leave the police in a position in which actions and productivity cannot be satisfactorily measured, making accountability more difficult. Failure to be able to document department or individual productivity acceptably for accountability purposes can lead the police to appear extremely ineffective. This is a position in which no police agency wants to find itself. Therefore, regardless of the problems with the measures used for police accountability, their use must continue, until better means are found.

Although accountability is an important element of organization and management, there are other elements whose impact on the agency can be just as critical as well as difficult to comprehend. In particular, policy and change are relatively high-impact concepts that are often overlooked or underacknowledged when discussing police organization and management.

POLICY AND CHANGE

According to Williams and Wagoner (1992), "Because of the changing nature of society, as well as the changing nature and increased amount of crime, many have argued that change of the police is both desirable and/or eminent" (p. 2). Yet, if there is anything that is the most difficult to implement in police organizations it is change (Alpert & Dunham, 1998; Dantzker, 1999; Kuykendall & Roberg, 1982; Steinman, 1984; Williams and Wagoner, 1992). Changes in policing often occur in a fragmented manner, usually as a reaction to a given circumstance or situation.

■ CASE IN POINT

In the past, police officers were trained to use what was known as a "choke hold" to subdue violent or uncooperative individuals. However, after several deaths occurred from its inappropriate use, many police agencies reacted and changed their policy, banning the use of the "choke hold." Other uses of force have also come under question over the years. Today, 100% of all municipal police departments with 100 or more sworn personnel have policies related to all types of force (Reaves & Smith, 1995).

Regardless of why the change occurs there is always a question of the rationale behind the change. The rationale often escapes officers, especially the line officers. Because changes often must be carried out in practice by line officers, who seldom are allowed any input into the change, their understanding of the rationale is important. Unfortunately, experience and observations have found that there is a perception among line officers that policy changes are made by the chief executive with little thought of how the change will effect its target. To make matters more difficult, some policies seem to make absolutely no sense or appear to have no real uses in terms of assisting officers to do an efficient or effective job.

■ CASE IN POINT

The wearing of hats on patrol has been a traditional policy of most police agencies for many years. Many of today's officers cannot understand the need for a policy that requires the officer, before exiting the patrol car, to put on the uniform hat or face disciplinary action. Granted, a hat keeps the weather off the head, but what other value does it have? What is the reason for requiring uniform hats be worn? That it makes the officer look professional may be a satisfactory reason for this policy among supervisors; however, many patrol officers find it difficult to accept such reasoning.

Change and policy implementation in police agencies often create controversy; how or why the change has come about is often questioned. To understand better the intricacies of police policy change, one must understand what causes change to occur.

A variety of factors affect change of policy in police agencies. These factors can be either external or internal. External factors are primarily the community and politics. When changes occur within the community structure, the police agency must change to maintain community-acceptable services. If a community that has been fairly homogeneous begins to grow more heterogeneous, the police agency must develop policies that allow recruitment of officers that will reflect the composition of the community; recently, for example, many police agencies have implemented changes in selection that allow gays and lesbians to become police officers.

As noted in Chapter 1, politics have played a major role in policing since its inception: Who the mayor or city manager is or who is on the city council often affects policy. One particular policy area politics have always affected is the budget. Historically, if the political leaders are not happy with how the police agency is operating, one major way to force change is through budgetary limitations.

When a police executive is faced with making policy changes, the endorsement of political leaders often assists in the implementation of the policy changes. When political leaders are not pleased with the policy changes, chances are that the policy will not remain. Therefore, police chiefs must deal with political influence when deciding on policy changes. However, the lessening or removing of the influence of politics on policing has been attempted for years (Sparrow, Moore, & Kennedy, 1991). Unfortunately, it has not been completely successful.

Internal factors that cause policy change include administrative, managerial, and supervisory factors (Alpert & Dunham, 1998; Dantzker, 1999). Administrative factors include goals, mission, services, and relationships with external groups. Management factors include managerial structure and the daily operations of the agency. Supervisory factors include the quality, skills, and training of personnel. Each of these factors, in some way, affects policy and change in the police agency.

■ CASE IN POINT

Lee Brown, while commissioner of the New York Police Department, believed that community-oriented policing would improve the relationship between the department and the citizens of New York City. As commissioner he attempted to implement policies and procedures that would assist in this change. Educating middle management as to what community-oriented policing is all about and, thus, gaining support so that they will promote these changes among the line officers is crucial to the success of this policy change. Well-trained and educated supervisors are a major asset in readily implementing the changes required.

Considering the problems associated with policy change in policing and the lack of input from those it affects the most (the line officers), what can be done to improve the situation? One suggestion is **officer participation** (Alpert & Dunham, 1998). Advising officers during roll calls of current policy considerations and soliciting written input would allow a greater opportunity to participate in policy change. A second possibility is the selection or election of **squad representatives.** These representatives could attend monthly meetings with the police executive and designated staff where they could be apprised of upcoming changes and participate in discussions of how these changes might affect the organization and its employees. The representative could then disseminate this information to fellow squad members. A third possibility is the implementation of **midmanagement policy sessions** that would include line supervisors as well as the upper managerial staff. In these sessions patrol officers and specialized officers are represented by their immediate supervisors who pass along concerns and issues. A utopian viewpoint would suggest that a progressive, humanist-style police executive could even allow policies to be voted on by the representatives, middle managers, or the officers themselves. Finally, an agency could make use of **quality circles** (Dantzker, 1999; Territo et al., 1998). These are small work groups composed of individuals performing the same type of work as those the policy change would most affect. Although currently recognized for their identification, discussion, analysis, and solving of specifically identified work-related problems, quality circles can also be useful for studying and assisting in policy changes.

Regardless of how policy and change come about, there will always be controversy and criticism. Ultimately, it is the police executive who must answer to the community, politicians, and police personnel when policy changes occur, particularly if the changes are not popular.

● UNPOPULAR POLICY ISSUES

There are a variety of policy issues that are not popular yet need to be addressed. Although all of them cannot be covered in a single section, the few that have been chosen for discussion in this section are believed to deserve this special attention.

Promotion

Historically, promotional policies within police agencies were rather vague and often relied on the politics of the administration and city government. This sometimes led to inappropriate promotions (Alpert & Dunham, 1998; Greisinger, Slovak, & Molkup, 1979; Walker, 1999). The creation of civil service or the merit system and its adoption into policy has eliminated many of the criticisms but has also created a few of its own (Greisinger et al., 1979).

The adoption of civil service promotional policies has assisted in eliminating favoritism and political patronage promotions in many police agencies. The adoption of civil service into policy requires a referendum and approval by the citizenry. Once the policy change is approved, a civil service board or commission is created. The members of this commission are appointed by the top city government executive. The board is then charged with the power to develop promotional criteria, administer promotional examinations, certify that all promotional applicants meet requirements, and finalize the promotional list. In addition to input and control over promotions, civil service also covers recruitment and discipline.

■ CASE IN POINT

The state of Texas provides cities the option to adopt state civil service or establish their own civil service program through the electoral process. In adopting the state's policies, police agencies are required to follow promotional procedures that include

1. Creation of a local civil service board.
2. Posting of a notice announcing the time and date of the promotional examination and the material that will be covered.
3. A written examination given for each position (except deputy chief) with promotion based on score.
4. Officers seeking promotion must have served a minimum of two years at the immediate lower rank (i.e., promotion to sergeant requires a minimum of two years as a corporal).

One could assume that adopting promotional policy that conforms to civil service would be extremely popular. Although civil service eliminates discriminatory or political promotions, it receives criticism. First, members appointed to serve on the civil service board frequently have little or no working knowledge of law enforcement or police agencies. This may make it difficult for them to establish promotional examinations acceptable to the officers. Second, civil service promotional policies do not allow the chief to make promotions of qualified personnel. Under civil service the most qualified do not necessarily get promoted unless they are among the top scorers on the examination. This is probably one of the greatest criticisms of civil service; not everyone is a good test taker. As a result, some of the most capable individuals never get promoted. Yet another criticism may be of the test itself.

■ CASE IN POINT

The city of Chicago spent more than $5 million in 1994 for the creation of promotional exams for sergeants and lieutenants. However, after the exam for sergeants was given, charges of bias were leveled. Of the 4700 individuals who took the written exam, 56 percent were white. Of the 1937 top scorers who went on to the second phase, an oral exam, 75 percent were white. Finally, of the 114 officers who were promoted, 95 percent were white. The fact that so few minority group members were promoted influenced the complaints that perhaps the test and the process were biased against minority group members.

Finally, the general lack of flexibility of the civil service system makes it difficult, if not impossible, to skip a rank or to fill unexpected vacancies permanently. However, the system does allow for temporary, emergency promotions.

Regardless of the criticism, promotional policy that adopts civil service is still an improvement over the traditional way of politics and patronage. Future policies could include the requirement of a college degree for promotion to certain ranks.

■ CASE IN POINT

In June 1993 a new promotional policy was adopted by a major urban police department. Beginning in 1996 all individuals desiring to test for promotion from detective one (D1) to detective two (D2) and from D1 and D2 to sergeant must have 60 semester hours or a minimum of 45 hours college credit (and currently enrolled in 15 semester hours). By the year 2000 sergeants wishing to promote to lieutenants will be required to possess a bachelor's degree.

Equipment

A policy area that has sparked debate and will continue to cause criticism is policy dealing with equipment, in particular, officers' weapons. The traditional firearm policy limited the weapon an officer carried to a .38 caliber, six-shot revolver. In the earlier days of our country, this usually was more than enough firepower; in recent years, however, things have changed. Nowhere was this more evident than during a bank robbery shootout in which LAPD officers were severely outgunned and eventually had to borrow weapons from a gun shop in order to subdue the suspects. Furthermore, the growing number of drug- and gang-related shootings of both innocent citizens and police with high-powered, high-caliber, semiautomatic and fully automatic weapons demonstrates the need to change traditional policy for newer, improved weaponry. Many police agencies are adopting policies that change the standard .38 to a .357, 9mm, 10mm, or even a .45 (the size of which has been questioned as possibly being user discriminatory against women and small men). Some police agencies have left it up to the officer to carry what is most comfortable. Table 5-1 lists the duty-weapon policies (as of 1993) of selected municipal police agencies.

Other weaponry policy issues include the use of nightsticks, flashlights, tasers, stun guns, tear gas, and pepper spray. Although a few police agencies have experimented with the use of tasers and stun guns, there is no overwhelming consensus as to the appropriateness of their use as everyday weapons. Future policies will require extensive research not currently available. In addition, whether standard firearms will be enough firepower is yet to be seen. Keep in mind, weapons are just one area of equipment policy that could

Making lieutenant. (Courtesy of Scottsdale, Arizona, Police Department)

cause controversy. Other areas include vehicles (e.g., what types are really necessary) and uniforms (e.g., wearing of hats and types of uniform material such as wool or polyester).

Labor Relations

One of the most controversial policy areas has been labor relations, more specifically unionism. For decades, police officers have fought to establish police unions while management and government have fought just as hard to block unionism. Yet, during the last 15 years, police labor relations as a whole appear to have taken significant strides toward union affiliation.

TABLE 5-1

Firearm Type and Authorization

Agency	Supplied Weapon(s)	Authorized Weapon(s)
Birmingham (AL)	.38 revolver 9mm semiautomatic	.45 semiautomatic
Phoenix (AZ)		.38 revolver .357 revolver
Los Angeles (CA)	9mm semiautomatic	.38 revolver
Denver (CO)		.357 revolver .38 revolver .45 revolver .45 semiautomatic 9mm semiautomatic
Evanston (IL)	.357 revolver 9mm semi-automatic	
Hammond (IN)	.357 revolver	.38 revolver .45 semiautomatic 9mm semiautomatic
Lafourche Parish (LA)	.357 revolver .38 revolver .45 revolver 9mm semiautomatic 10mm semiautomatic Other	
Boston (MA)	9mm semiautomatic	
Minneapolis (MN)		.38 revolver .45 semiautomatic 9mm semiautomatic
Albany (NY)	.357 revolver .45 semiautomatic 9mm semiautomatic	

Source: Reaves, B.A., & Smith, P.Z. (1995). *Law enforcement management and administrative statistics, 1993: Data for individual state and local agencies with 100 or more officers.* Washington, D.C.: U.S. Government Printing Office.

With respect to policing, unionism has really taken a slightly different approach, unlike labor-intensive organizations. Although the term *union* is used, it is not completely appropriate for those organizations that represent police employees for the sole purpose of discussing such matters as salary and benefits. These types of organizations, which originated as "social" organizations, are generally referred to as police officer associations or fraternal associations. There are, however, some police officers who belong to union-affiliated chapters. This has not always been the case.

A brief historical examination of police labor relations finds that an attempt at organized labor first occurred in 1889 in Ithaca, New York, when the five officers in the department walked off the job over a pay decrease of $3 a week. (This meant their salary went from $12 a week to $9!)

During the next 20 years there were a few more, less than successful, attempts at police labor organization. It was not until 1919, in Boston, that the first recognizable attempt to unionize occurred. Current city policy forbade unionization. Yet, many officers became part a movement to create and support an

Firearms policies are important, but so are vehicular policies that dictate the types of vehicles available, such as a DUI enforcement van, and who is authorized to operate them. (Courtesy of Scottsdale, Arizona, Police Department)

American Federation of Labor chapter. Their concern was over the low wages and poor working conditions. To break this movement before it became too strong, the city dismissed 19 of the union's leaders. The dismissals lead 1117 of 1544 officers, to walk off the job. The public was outraged, particularly because of the looting and destruction that occurred after the walkout. All of the strikers were fired and replaced. These events cost time and money. Because no one wanted to see a similar occurrence happen again, the city granted three concessions: a raise of $300 per year, provision of uniforms, and the establishment of a pension plan. Although many officers considered their movement a success, in reality it would have little overall effect on labor relations for years to come.

From 1919 to 1964 there would be several unsuccessful attempts throughout the country to organize police unions. State laws, supported by court decisions, did not allow it to happen until 1965. During this year, as a result of a change in Michigan's laws that allowed public associations to form, the Detroit Police Officers' Association was formed. For the next 25 years police organizations and unions would grow quite rapidly.

Most sworn police officers belong to some type of police association or union (Swanson, Territo, & Taylor, 1998). What has not occurred yet is the establishment of a national union. Although there is national recognition of the Fraternal Order of Police, Police Benevolent Associations, and Police Officers' Associations, there is no one organization recognized as the leader in police labor associations.

However, the International Union of Police Associations, a segment of the AFL-CIO, celebrated its twentieth anniversary in 1997 with a membership of more than 13,000 officers (Stone, 1998).

A question that arises at this point is whether there is really a need for police officers to belong to a union–type organization. Some observers might say yes, primarily because of conflict between the police administration or city government and police officers over items such as salaries and benefits, contracts, shifts, or fitness standards.

■ CASE IN POINT

In 1996 police union officials in Memphis, Tennessee, were angered over a shift change implemented by the police director. The change would assign 25 percent more officers to the late afternoon and early evening hours. It would affect about 70 officers. This change did not require approval by the Memphis Police Association and was being implemented to cover times where statistics indicated an increase in criminality, particularly among juveniles. In 1997 a union representing Aurora, Colorado, police officers was able to delay the implementation of a new physical agility test until a resolution was found regarding disciplining those who failed to complete the test in just over one minute. After a grievance was filed by the Aurora Police Association, the police department agreed to give officers additional chances to pass before imposing discipline.

Union representation can provide officers with a very powerful tool for improving wages and other conditions of employment through **collective bargaining.**

The scope of collective bargaining, although not completely clear, is a result of the 1935 National Labor Relations Act. This act focused on such issues as wages, hours worked, and various other items regarding employment. The participants in collective bargaining are usually representatives of the association or union representing the police officers and representatives of the government entity. One reason police executives do not like collective bargaining is that they are not represented or present during negotiations. Yet, it is up to the chief executive to carry out and abide by the final contract.

■ CASE IN POINT

In 1998 the Massachusetts legislature overrode the governor's veto, the result of which would limit the power of police commissioners and public safety directors to override collective-bargaining agreements. A win for the officers, a defeat for top administrators.

Although wages and benefits can be improved through collective bargaining, so can various other job-related aspects such as shift assignments, promotional policies, or protection from possible civil rights intrusions.

■ CASE IN POINT

The police union, Local 1361 of the American Federation of State, County, and Municipal Employees, representing officers in Middletown, Connecticut, filed a complaint with the state labor board after street crime unit officers were tested for drug use. The president of the union advised that the testing was improper because there is no provision in the union contract for drug testing. The city claimed that because the contract does not expressly prohibit drug testing, the testing was proper.

In general, collective bargaining is very beneficial to the rank and file of a police agency. In 1993 collective bargaining was authorized by 73 percent of the nation's municipal agencies. However, the point to be made with collective bargaining is that it can have both positive and negative effects on the police department, the officers, and the community.

The availability of collective bargaining is only one problem for today's police executives in creating salary, work conditions, and benefits policies. The application of the **Fair Labors Standards Act** (FLSA) to municipal agencies, like the police, has also become a problem for police executives.

Enacted by Congress in 1938, the FLSA set minimum wages, overtime pay, equal pay, recordkeeping, and child labor standards. Initially, this act only applied to private employers directly engaged in commerce. In 1966 and 1974, this act was extended to a variety of government employees, including schools, hospitals, and transit employees. In 1985, as a result of the Supreme Court's 5-to-4 vote in *Garcia* v. *San Antonio Metropolitan Transit Authority*, it was decided that the FLSA should apply to state and local government employees. The result of this case was federal legislation that would require governmental entities to pay overtime or compensatory time to city workers, including police officers and firefighters, based on an established time frame. Primarily, anything over forty hours worked in a seven-day cycle would be considered overtime payable at time and one half. What this has meant for police agencies is a change in policy on many time usage issues, such as roll calls.

■ CASE IN POINT

Many police agencies held roll call fifteen minutes before the beginning of the shift. If the shift was 3 P.M. to 11 P.M., officers needed to report, ready to go to work, at 2:45 P.M. This meant that offers would be on the job eight hours and fifteen minutes but only get paid for the eight hours. Application of FLSA means that roll calls should be part of the eight-hour tour, or the department will have to pay for the roll-call time. New policies need to address this issue.

Although labor relations and its related policies have not always been popular, it has become an important aspect of policing. Unions have not enjoyed tremendous popularity; yet, their existence aids police officers in the areas of wages, benefits, and working conditions. It should also be noted that unions have assisted the drive for professionalism in policing by forcing city and department leaders to accept changes that promote its growth. For example, the requiring of higher education by a police agency has lead to requests for educational incentives. In 1993, 70 percent of large municipal police departments reportedly provided educational incentives to their officers (Reaves & Smith, 1995).

Finally, the two newest challenges for police departments with respect to labor relations policies are the **Americans with Disabilities Act** and the **Family and Medical Leave Act of 1993.** Effective since July 26, 1992, the Americans with Disabilities Act is federal legislation that requires the hiring of individuals with certain disabilities that would previously have barred the person from a law enforcement career. Examples of these disabilities include recovery from alcoholism and drug addiction, and some forms of psychological and physical impairments.

■ CASE IN POINT

> On January 12, 1998, the U.S. Supreme Court rejected an attempt by the city of Omaha, Nebraska, to avoid rehiring a police officer who was blind in one eye. The officer, who had worked as an Omaha police officer from 1973 to 1984, lost his vision in one eye in 1975 as a result of glaucoma. Despite the use of glasses, which made his vision 20/20, he was eventually fired from the department. In 1992 the officer sued the department under the Americans with Disabilities Act. The court ordered the officer be reinstated with nearly $51,000 in back pay and pension benefits in addition to $50,000 in punitive damages.

The Family and Medical Leave Act, which became effective August 8, 1993, entitles employees in organizations of fifty or more employees up to a total of twelve work weeks of unpaid leave during any twelve-month period. During this leave the employer is responsible for continuing all employee benefits. Furthermore, when the employee is ready to return he or she must be reinstated to his or her former position or a similar one.

How these acts will ultimately affect policing is still to be seen. However, they are changes that must be acknowledged by police departments. Therefore, a new policy or a policy change will be required.

Policy and change in policing are neither easy nor always acceptable. Yet, both are necessary so that police departments can maintain services that meet societal needs.

❋ SUMMARY

The discussion of policing from an organizational and managerial perspective includes recognition of organizational theories: closed versus open. Closed theories include scientific management, bureaucratic, and administrative. Open theories refer to human relations, behavioral, and open systems. These theories provide valuable insight into why a police organization operates the way it does.

The terms *organization* and *bureaucracy* are defined by means of characteristics identifiable with the police organization. Police management and leadership are also important concepts that, when defined and identified, help gain insight into the police organization. Furthermore, police organizations have been criticized for their bureaucratic operation and managerial structure. The influx of the better-educated police leader has begun to assist in the elimination of these criticisms, particularly those related to management.

Because of the nature of the job, police officers and agencies need to be held accountable. The police are held accountable for their prescribed role, the services they provide, and their behavior. They are accountable to the community, the courts, and the department itself. Measuring accountability has been a difficult task at both the departmental and individual levels. For the department, crime rates are the measure most often used. The accountability of individual officers depends on the area of assignment. The most common measures are arrests made, citations issued, reports written, and cases cleared.

Considering that none of the identified measures is 100 percent complete or accurate, other mechanisms of control are necessary. These mechanisms are either external or internal. External methods include the courts and civilian review boards; internal controls include factors such as supervision, training, discipline, rewards, peer control, and audit mechanisms as well as an IA unit. An additional mechanism is the PCR unit. Overall, police accountability suffers from inadequate measures and mechanisms; yet, being accountable is extremely important to the success of the police agency and its members in performing and providing services in a manner and at a level acceptable to society.

Police executives are faced with a variety of policy-making issues. Their decisions and policies are not always popular and receive criticisms from both inside and outside the agency. In addition, policy changes are often affected by external factors, such as the community and politics, and internal factors that include administrative, managerial, and supervisory elements. Some policy issues that receive more attention than others include promotion, equipment, and labor relations.

DO YOU KNOW . . .

1. Why most police organizations retain a paramilitary–type organizational structure?
2. What separates the police bureaucracy from other bureaucracies?
3. Which management task is the most important to a good police executive?
4. What type of management style belongs in a police organization?
5. What mechanisms are used by local police agencies to measure police performance? productivity?
6. Whether there are any equitable methods of police accountability?
7. Whether holding police officers accountable for a role they have little to do with developing is appropriate?
8. What happens if a police agency is not held answerable for its members' actions? (For instance, the Rodney King–LAPD incident.)
9. Whether a police executive should be held accountable for the actions of officers in his or her agency?
10. Why policy changes in policing often are implemented only after an incident occurs?
11. Which has more influence on policy, internal or external factors? Why?
12. Whether everyone in the police department who is affected by policy changes should be involved in developing such changes?

REFERENCES

Alpert, G.P., & Dunham, R.G. (1998). *Policing urban America* (3rd ed.). Prospect Heights, IL: Waveland Press.
Blau, P.M., & Marshall, W.M. (1982). The concept of bureaucracy. In F.S. Lane (Ed.), *Current issues in public administration* (pp. 234–238). New York: St. Martin's Press.
Blau, P.M., & Scott, W.R. (1978). The concept of formal organization. In J.M. Shafritz & P.H. Whitbeck (Eds.), *Classics of organization theory* (pp. 211–216). Oak Park, IL: Moore Publishing Company.

Brown, G.E. (1985). The metamorphosis of a police executive. In J.J. Fyfe (Ed.), *Police management today*. Washington, D.C.: International City Management Association.

Brown, W.J. (1986). Organization assessment: Determining the state of a police organization. *Journal of Police Science and Administration, 14,* 267–284.

Carter, D.L., Sapp, A.D., & Stephens, D.W. (1989). *The state of police education: Policy direction for the 21st century*. Washington, D.C.: Police Executive Research Forum.

Dantzker, M.L. (1994). Requirements for the position of municipal police chief: A content analysis. *Police Studies, 17,* 33–42.

Dantzker, M.L. (1996). The position of municipal police chief: An examination of selection criteria and requisite skills. *Police Studies, 19,* 1–18.

Dantzker, M.L. (1999). *Police organization and management: Yesterday, today, and tomorrow*. Newton, MA: Butterworth-Heinemann.

Doerner, W.G. (1997) Recruitment and retention. In M.L. Dantzker (Ed.), *Contemporary policing: personnel, issues and trends* (pp. 53–74). Newton, MA: Butterworth-Heinemann.

Fayol, H. (1978). General principles of management. In J.M. Shafritz & P.H. Whitbeck (Eds.), *Classics of organization theory* (pp. 23–37). Oak Park, IL: Moore Publishing Company.

Franz, V., & Jones, D.M. (1987). Perceptions of organizational performance in suburban police departments: A critique of the military model. *Journal of Police Science and Administration, 15,* 153–161.

Fyfe, J.J. (Ed.). (1985). *Police management today*. Washington, D.C.: International City Management Association.

Gaines, L.K., Southerland, M.D., & Angell, J.E. (1991). *Police administration*. New York: McGraw-Hill.

Gannon, M.J. (1979). *Organizational behavior*. Boston: Little, Brown and Company.

Gerth, H.H., & Mills, C.W. (1946). *From Max Weber: Essays in sociology*. New York: Oxford University Press.

Greisinger, G.W., Slovak, J.S., & Molkup, J.J. (1979). *Civil service systems: Their impact on police administration*. Washington, D.C.: U.S. Government Printing Office.

Gulick, L. (1978). Notes on the theory of organization. In J.M. Shafritz & P.H. Whitbeck (Eds.), *Classics of organization theory* (pp. 52–61). Oak Park, IL: Moore Publishing Company, Inc.

Harrison, G.F., & Pelletier, M.A. (1987). Perceptions of bureaucratization, role performance, and organizational effectiveness in a metropolitan police department. *Journal of Police Science and Administration, 15,* 262–270.

Kelling, G.L., Wasserman, R., & Williams, H. (1988). Police accountability and community policing. *Texas Police Journal, 38,* 13–19.

Kuykendall, J., & Roberg, R.R. (1982). Mapping police organizational change. *Criminology, 20,* 241–256.

Kuykendall, J., & Roberg, R.R. (1988). Police manager's perceptions of employee types: A conceptual model. *Journal of Criminal Justice, 16,* 131–137.

Lane, F.S. (Ed.). (1982). *Current issues in public administration*. New York: St. Martin's Press.

Luthans, F. (1985). *Organizational behavior*. New York: McGraw-Hill.

March, J.G., & Simon, H.A. (1978). Theories of bureaucracy. In J.M. Shafritz & P.H. Whitbeck (Eds.), *Classics of organization theory* (pp. 110–118). Oak Park, IL: Moore Publishing Company.

Moore, A. (1990). Mediocrity or accountability. *Texas Police Journal, 38,* 8–11.

Pisani, A.L., Jr. (1993, April). So this is what they call accountability? *Law Enforcement News, 19,* 12.

Police expert cites lack of accountability in Los Angeles. (1991). *Criminal Justice Newsletter, 22,* 2.

Police increasingly face public scrutiny through civilian review boards. (1991, April 15). *Law Enforcement News, 7,* 11.

Reaves, B.A., & Smith, P.Z. (1995). *Law enforcement management and administrative statistics, 1993: Data for individual state and local agencies with 100 or more officers.* Washington, D.C.: U.S. Government Printing Office.

Reiss, A.J., Jr. (1992). Police organization in the twentieth century. *Crime and Justice,* 51–97.

Shafritz, J.M., & Hyde, A.C. (Eds.). (1978). *Classics of public administration.* Oak Park, IL: Moore Publishing Company.

Shafritz, J.M., & Whitbeck, P.H. (Eds.). (1978). *Classics of organization theory.* Oak Park, IL: Moore Publishing Company.

Shernock, S., & Dantzker, G.D. (1997). Education and training: No longer just a badge and a gun. In M.L. Dantzker (Ed.), *Contemporary policing: Personnel, issues and trends* (pp. 75–98). Newton, MA: Butterworth-Heinemann.

Sparrow, M.K., Moore, M.H., & Kennedy, D.M. (1990). *Beyond 911: A new era for policing.* New York: Basic Books.

Steinman, M. (1984). Rationalizing police operations: Some explanatory factors. *Journal of Criminal Justice, 12,* 221–223.

Steinman, M. (1986). Managing and evaluating police behavior. *Journal of Police Science and Administration, 14,* 285–292.

Stone, R. (1998). Police union marks 20 years, adds members. *Police, 22,* 11.

Swanson, C.R., Territo, L., & Taylor, R.W. (1998). *Police administration* (4th ed.). New York: Macmillan Publishing Company.

Taylor, W.F. (1978). The principles of scientific management. In J.M. Shafritz & P.H. Whitbeck (Eds.), *Classics of organization theory* (pp. 9–23). Oak Park, IL: Moore Publishing Company.

Van Meter, D.J. (1998, February). Setting productivity standards, not quotas. *Law Enforcement News, 12,* 14.

Walker, S. (1999). *Police in America* (3rd ed.). New York: McGraw-Hill.

Weber, M. (1978). Bureaucracy. In J.M. Shafritz & P.H. Whitbeck (Eds.). (1978). *Classics of organization theory* (pp. 37–42). Oak Park, IL: Moore Publishing Company.

Williams F.P., III, & Wagoner, C.P. (1992). Making the police proactive: An impossible task for improbable reasons. *Police Forum, 2,* 1–5.

Wilson, O.W., & McLaren, R.C. (1977). *Police administration* (4th ed.). New York: MacMillian Publishing Company.

6 POLICE AND THE LAW

For a society to exist without chaos and anarchy, there must be laws. With the existence of laws comes a need for enforcers. The relationship between the police and the law is unique in that the existence, powers, duties, and behavior of the police stem directly from or are a result of the law. The application of the law to policing is provided through statutes created according to the constitutions of the United States and of the states themselves. This chapter examines the police and law relationship with respect to general enforcement, constitutionality, court decisions, liability, and corruption.

GENERAL ENFORCEMENT

During their daily duties the police are expected to enforce a variety of laws. Usually, the laws of most concern are those designated as criminal, traffic, and ordinances. Criminal laws are divided into misdemeanors and felonies; traffic laws include both moving and nonmoving violations; and ordinances may include a diverse array of wrongdoings, such as violations of specific permit/ licensure ordinances. Enforcement of each requires specific behavior by the police.

Criminal Laws

By the nature of policing, the area of enforcement often receiving greatest attention is criminal law. As previously noted, criminal law is generally divided into felonies and misdemeanors. The major differences between the two are punishment and enforcement. Felonies are crimes that carry a punishment of one year or more in a prison, and misdemeanors have a punishment of up to one year in jail. Although the difference in punishment is relatively clear, the enforcement difference often causes confusion.

Although felonious crimes such as murder, robbery, or sexual assault carry stiffer penalties than such misdemeanors as trespassing or public intoxication,

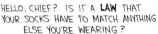

their enforcement offers the police great leeway. The acceptable behavior for enforcing felony violations rests on the burden of probable cause. A police officer does not have to witness a felony to make an arrest. The arrest can occur by warrant or through enough probable cause to permit the arrest.

■ CASE IN POINT

An officer is working the evening shift (3 P.M.–11 P.M.) and at roll call is provided with information in reference to a robbery of a local bank that occurred about an hour earlier. The information includes descriptions of the suspects and suspect vehicle. An hour later, while on patrol, the officer observes a vehicle that matches the description of the one used in the robbery. The vehicle's occupants appear to match the suspects' description. Legally, the officer can stop the vehicle and identify the occupants. During the investigatory stop, if the officer observes any evidence from the bank robbery or is convinced by the descriptions that these are the suspects, a warrantless arrest can be effected. This would not be the case if the offense committed had been a misdemeanor, traffic violation, or violation of a city ordinance.

The rule of thumb for the enforcement of misdemeanors is that the officer observes the offense or has a warrant. The exception is when there is overwhelming evidence that the suspect did commit the act.

■ CASE IN POINT

A woman sitting at a bus stop has reported that a man wearing only a raincoat walked up to her and exposed himself. While en route to meet the complainant the officer dispatched is advised that three more women have called in with the same complaint. A few blocks from the original complainant's location a man fitting the description given is observed by the officer. The officer stops and confronts the individual. His investigation finds that the man does not have any clothes on under his raincoat. The man is placed in the squad car, and other units bring the complainants one by one. All four women identify the man as the flasher. The burden of probable cause is enough to justify a warrantless arrest. If the man had not been located close to the scene or had been wearing clothes under the coat, but he had matched the description, no arrest could have been made until a report was filed and a warrant issued.

The enforcement of traffic and ordinance violations usually requires observation by the arresting officer. The exception is when one officer observes the offense but is unable to readily make an apprehension, and relays the information to other officers who then effect the arrest. A citizen's report of a violation is not enough for an arrest.

■ CASE IN POINT

During specific hours, school zones have reduced speed limits. One morning a teacher observes a vehicle drive through the zone much faster than the rest of the traffic. The teacher calls the police who advise that, unless an officer observed the vehicle, there is little that can be done. Conversely, if this same vehicle were observed by a patrol officer going in the opposite direction who could not readily pursue and stop the vehicle, the officer could advise other officers who may be in the area to stop the vehicle and issue a citation.

The enforcement of the law is rather simplistic and straightforward. Problems arise for the police when they fail to observe constitutional guarantees, more often referred to as **due process.** According to the Fourteenth Amendment of the U.S. Constitution,

No state shall make or enforce any law which shall abridge the privileges or immunities of citizens of the United States; nor shall any state deprive any person of life, liberty, or property without *due process* [emphasis added] of law; nor deny to any person within its jurisdiction the equal protection of the laws.

In our criminal justice system, due process is recognized as a safeguard of constitutional rights. Defining due process is rather difficult because the U.S. Supreme Court has not yet succeeded in giving it an exact definition. However, due process ensures that a person who is arrested, prosecuted, tried, and punished is done so according to criteria established by law.

Due process is of particular concern with respect to police activity. Areas such as arrest, search and seizure, and confessions are often scrutinized by the courts and have led to landmark Supreme Court cases governing police behavior and enforcing the recognition of due process (see Figure 6-1 and the following Case in Point).

■ CASE IN POINT

Knowles v. Iowa (1998): In March 1996 Knowles was stopped in Iowa for a speeding violation. Although a citation was issued, the officer requested to search Knowles' vehicle, informing him that he had the right to search. Marijuana and a pipe were found, and Knowles was eventually tried and found guilty of possession of drugs. Despite case law regarding searches of vehicles that should have made this search illegal, the law in Iowa gives officers the right to make "routine" searches of vehicles during a traffic offense. In this case, no other crime except speeding had occurred before the search, and the officer himself testified he had no reason to believe any other crime had been committed or was about to occur when he conducted the search. In December 1998 the U.S. Supreme Court handed down its decision in this case. The ruling was that the search was unreasonable and unconstitutional, a rare win for privacy rights (Asseo, 1998).

FIGURE 6-1 Examples of Landmark U.S. Supreme Court Cases That Affect Due Process

Search and Seizure

Mapp v. *Ohio* 367 U.S. 643 (1961): Applied to all state proceedings the exclusionary rule established in the 1914 case of *Weeks* v. *U.S.* Any evidence obtained in violation of the Fourth Amendment—unreasonable search and seizure—is not admissible in court.

Massachusetts v. *Sheppard* 468 U.S. 981 (1984): Allowed evidence obtained as a result of a warrant, later declared invalid by the Court, admissible and an exception to the exclusionary rule.

Wilson v. *Arkansas* 115 S. Ct. 1914 (1995): Unless exigent circumstances exist, under the reasonableness standard of the Fourth Amendment, police officers are required to knock and announce before entering a residence.

Stop and Frisk

Terry v. *Ohio* 392 U.S. (1968): An officer stopping an individual based on reasonable suspicion has the right to conduct an external "frisk" of the individual for possible possession of weapons. Reasonable suspicion is based on unusual conduct that gives an officer cause to believe a criminal activity has occurred or is about to occur.

Minnesota v. *Dickerson* 508 U.S. 366 (1993): If a frisk goes beyond that allowed under *Terry,* any evidence of a crime is inadmissible.

Arrest

Payton v. *New York* 445 U.S. 573 (1980): Entering a private residence to effect a felony arrest without a warrant is not acceptable unless exigent circumstances exist.

Interrogation

Miranda v. *Arizona* 384 U.S. 436 (1966): Unless an individual is advised of his or her constitutional rights against self-incrimination and right to counsel prior to a custodial interrogation, and those rights are waived, any evidence obtained is inadmissible in court.

Minnick v. *Mississippi* 498 U.S. 146 (1990): An individual who has not waived his or her *Miranda* rights may request a lawyer anytime during an interrogation. Once such a request is made, the interrogation must stop.

Right to Counsel

Escobedo v. *Illinois* 378 U.S. 478 (1964): An individual has a right to an attorney when questioning by police goes from informative to accusatory.

Source: del Carmen, R.V., & Walker, J.T. (1997). *Briefs of leading cases in law enforcement* (3rd ed.). Cincinnati, OH: Anderson Publishing Company.

When due process is overlooked or violated, the police are criticized and, when possible, sanctioned by the courts in some fashion, usually by a financial settlement to the plaintiff. For example, the cities of Los Angeles, California, and Philadelphia, Pennsylvania, have paid out millions of dollars in due process violation lawsuits. Perhaps the most noted monetary award was the more than $1 million Los Angeles had to pay Rodney King.

To avoid potential lawsuit situations, it is important that every police officer be knowledgeable of the Constitution and its guarantees as they apply to law enforcement, particularly due process. This can be done through preservice training, in-service workshops, and roll-call updates. Regardless of how it is accomplished, police officers must be familiar with the U.S. Constitution and its implications for policing.

CONSTITUTIONALITY, POLICING, AND THE SUPREME COURT

The relationship of the police to the Constitution is twofold in that the Constitution (1) grants a power to the states that allows for the existence of police and (2) places certain controls on police behavior. "Officers have the responsibility to enforce the law and are accorded certain privileges in carrying out their duties" (Ferrell, 1988, p. 93). The source of this responsibility is sometimes taken for granted and receives little acknowledgment; yet, it is an extremely important element of the existence of the police. This responsibility is a direct result of the Tenth Amendment of the U.S. Constitution. The amendment states: "The powers not delegated to the United States by the Constitution, nor prohibited by it to the States, are reserved to the States respectively, or to the people." With the power granted to the states by this amendment, they could enact statutes that would create, define, identify, and give power to individuals to enforce governmental wishes.

The existence of the Tenth Amendment explains why there is no national police in this country. Although Congress has granted the federal government powers to establish police for federal enforcement, the Constitution prevents federal formation of a national police. Therefore, the states must maintain their own enforcers of state laws. The result is a wide variety of law enforcers, police officers, peace officers, constables, marshals, and sheriffs. Regardless of what they are called, each has a responsibility to uphold the laws of their respective states.

It should be noted that although there is no direct constitutional limitation on the police with respect to their existence and duties, the Constitution does maintain certain controls over police behavior. These controls are primarily the result of the Fourth, Fifth, Sixth, and Fourteenth Amendments.

Fourth Amendment

State statutes grant certain powers and duties to police officers. These powers and duties cannot infringe on constitutional guarantees; nor, during the execution of their power and duties, can police officers violate the basic freedoms granted by the Constitution. The first of these rights specifically applicable to policing pertains to search and seizure. The Fourth Amendment states

> The right of the people to be secure in their persons, houses, papers, and effects, against unreasonable searches and seizures, shall not be violated, and no Warrants shall issue, but upon probable cause, supported by Oath or affirmation, and particularly describing the place to be searched, and the persons or things to be seized.

Thus, citizens are legally protected from police officers entering their homes or business, violating the individual's privacy, or seizing whatever items the police believe will lead to a conviction. Many issues have been raised regarding the Fourth Amendment and police behavior, such as arrests, searches incident to arrest, items or areas to be searched, and warrantless searches.

Arrest

The most notable task of the police when enforcing the law is the arrest. The Fourth Amendment refers to the phrase "probable cause." Probable cause is an accumulation of facts that allows any reasonable person to believe that a crime has been or is about to be committed. These facts must be proved by evidence. Instincts or "gut feelings" are not enough. Police officers must be able to demonstrate that enough probable cause existed to make an arrest. Failure to show probable cause negates the arrest.

■ CASE IN POINT

In *Dunaway* v. *New York* (1979), the U.S. Supreme Court upheld the requirement of probable cause for an arrest. In its decision, the Court decreed that the probable cause clause of the Fourth Amendment affords a citizen a certain amount of privacy that cannot be compromised in any manner. Simply put, the failure by police to establish probable cause disallows an arrest and any information obtained from the arrest. Yet, even an arrest based on probable cause is a violation of Fourth Amendment privileges if the arrest occurs in a house other than the suspect's if there was no search warrant for the place of arrest (*Minnesota* v. *Olson*, 1990).

Search and Seizure

An area of law enforcement that has stimulated criticism, concern, and debate is search and seizure. The issue has found a steady home in the Supreme Court since the case of *Weeks* v. *United States* (1914). The search and seizure clause of the Fourth Amendment has provided a variety of issues for both the Court and the police. The first of these issues has been the exclusion of evidence obtained from illegal searches and seizures. Although this issue had been around since at least 1791, it found little support at the state and local levels until the landmark decision of *Mapp* v. *Ohio* (1961). "The exclusionary rule," as defined by the Court, states that any evidence obtained as a result of an illegal search or seizure is not admissible in court. This meant that from that point onward the police would have to establish probable cause for their search and seizure, and, in many circumstances, obtain a warrant. What many police supporters had initially believed to be a strike against the police and their ability to perform effectively has really turned out to be a tool for ensuring that sound police work, within constitutional guidelines, has occurred. There are still some critics who believe the Court is too tough on the police. However, the Court's stance is changing slightly with decisions such as *United States* v. *Leon* (1984) and *Murray* v. *United States* (1988), in which the Court agreed to recognize "good faith" on the part of police officers executing what they believe to be a valid warrant. The Court has taken this one step further by voiding the exclusionary rule for evidence seized as a result of false information resulting from clerical errors.

■ CASE IN POINT

Arizona v. *Evans* (1995): A police officer stopped Evans for going the wrong way on a one-way street. A computer check of Evans found his license had been suspended and there was an outstanding warrant for his arrest. The officer arrested Evans and subsequently found him in possession of marijuana. After he was convicted, Evans appealed on grounds that the search was illegal because the arrest was illegal—Evans' arrest warrant had been dismissed two weeks before the traffic violation occurred. However, this information was never entered into the computer. The Court held that the exclusionary rule was not applicable in cases in which the arrest resulted from clerical errors by court employees.

The exclusionary rule is but one of several issues regarding search and seizure. Other issues include general searches, search incident to an arrest, the search of vehicles and containers in vehicles, consent, and plain view. A recent issue has been the searching of an individual's trash. In the decision of *California* v. *Greenwood* (1988) the Court ruled that any items such as trash placed outside the individual's curtilage (property lines) was open to search and seizure without a warrant and is not an invasion of privacy.

When an officer makes an arrest, it is permissible without a warrant to search the area within the immediate care, control, and access of the arrestee (*Chimel* v. *California,* 1969). In *Maryland* v. *Buie* (1990) the Court ruled that officers could make a limited protective search in a home during an arrest. With respect to the general searching of vehicles, the Court ruled in *Carroll* v. *U.S.* (1925) that a police officer without a warrant could search a vehicle, with probable cause, because of the mobility of a vehicle. Arising from this issue was the searching of closed or sealed containers. In *Colorado* v. *Bertine* (1987), *Florida* v. *Wells* (1990), and *Pennsylvania* v. *Labron* (1996) the Court upheld the search when probable cause existed or if the seizure was the result of a vehicle inventory according to established police department policy. In *Ohio* v. *Robinette* (1996) the Court ruled that a request to search a vehicle, after the issuance of a traffic citation but failing to advise the individual of his right to leave, was not a violation of Fourth Amendment rights. In *Maryland* v. *Wilson* (1997) the Court upheld the right of police officers to order all passengers out of a vehicle, pending completion of the stop, despite the lack of suspicion or threat. Officer safety was given as a prime reason for this decision.

Consent searches, a verbal or written agreement from an individual with a police officer allowing said officer to conduct a search without a warrant, almost always tend to raise suspicion in the Court. Issues that have been raised in the past with respect to consent include who can give consent to search or when consent to search is legally applicable in a given situation. For example, in the case of *Florida* v. *Royer* (1983) the Court ruled that evidence obtained through a consent to search after an arrest or detention is not admissible in court if the detention or arrest was made without probable cause. The leading issue has been who can grant consent for a search. In *Illinois* v. *Rodriguez* (1990) the Court specified that if the police officer is convinced that the person consenting to the search has authority over the area to be searched, a warrantless search is acceptable.

As with consent searches, the concept of plain view searches and seizures has required Court interpretation. An issue that has received attention is whether there is a need for probable cause or previous knowledge on behalf of the police that evidence seized under "plain view" was not the real reason for a warrant or the immediate cause of the search. In other words, did the police have knowledge of evidence and contraband, but not enough probable cause to search or obtain a warrant? Did they instead use "decoy" information to search or obtain a warrant, hoping that what they really wanted to seize would be seized under the "plain view" doctrine?

■ CASE IN POINT

Police officers in an unmarked unit were working an area known for drug trafficking. At one point they observed a pickup truck parked at a stop sign for a longer period than usual. Suddenly the truck turned without indicating the turn and proceeded at an "excessive speed." The vehicle was stopped for the traffic violations during which time the officers observed packets of drugs. Both occupants were arrested and eventually convicted. They appealed on the grounds that the traffic stop was used as a precursor for probable cause by the officers to make the drug arrest.

The facts and issue in the preceding Case in Point are from the case of *Whren and Brown* v. *United States* (1996) in which the Court found that if probable cause existed to make a traffic stop, evidence in plain view is admissible. This upholds the ruling in an earlier case, *Arizona* v. *Hicks* (1987), in which the Court advised that a plain view search and seizure, without probable cause or knowledge, of items believed to be contraband or evidence of criminal activity other than that for which the plain view search was initiated, is not a violation of the Fourth Amendment. Items not in plain view or that require movement to interpret their evidentiary status are inadmissible without a warrant. The Court has further supported the plain view search and seizure of evidence during a legal search even if there was some knowledge by the officer that the evidence would be found but was not listed in the warrant (*Horton* v. *California*, 1990).

■ CASE IN POINT

An officer is dispatched to a shooting in a residence. On arrival at the scene, the officer observes an individual, who appears to have been shot, lying on the floor. The officer has the legal right to make an initial search of the immediate area for a weapon or a suspect. If while conducting this search, the officer observes several packets of a white powdery substance, believed to be narcotics, lying on a table in plain view in a room other than the one in which the victim was found, the substance can be seized. Furthermore, if a police officer obtains a warrant to search a structure for evidence of one type of criminal activity, believing that there will be evidence of other types of criminal activity not specified in the warrant, a plain view seizure of this evidence is permissible.

The issues discussed pertaining to search and seizure have not been all-inclusive. They have, however, represented a majority of the issues that the police face every day when attempting to follow the guidelines of the Fourth Amendment as interpreted by the courts. One last issue deserving of recognition in this area is the use of an anonymous tip to conduct a search without a warrant.

In *Alabama* v. *White* (1990) the Court upheld a warrantless search initially stemming from an anonymous tip because the tip was sufficiently corroborated by police observations to establish a "totality of the circumstances" (*Gates* v. *Illinois*, 1983). If the police had failed to corroborate the tip, the search would have been held to be in violation of the Fourth Amendment.

Fifth Amendment

The freedoms from self-incrimination, double jeopardy, or arrest for capital or felonious crimes without just cause are guaranteed by the Fifth Amendment, which states:

> No person shall be held to answer for a capital, or otherwise infamous crime, unless on a presentment or indictment of a Grand Jury, except in cases arising in the land or naval forces, or in the militia, when in actual service in time of War or public danger; nor shall any person be subject for the same offense to be twice put in jeopardy of life or limb; nor shall be compelled in any criminal case to be a witness against himself, nor be deprived of life, liberty, or property, without due process of law; nor shall private property be taken for public use, without just compensation.

With respect to policing, the Fifth Amendment is most applicable to interrogations, obtaining of confessions, and arrest without just cause. Without a warrant, indictment, or probable cause, no person can be deprived of liberty.

Interrogation and Confessions

Early television police programs frequently showed the interrogation of a suspect and the attainment of a confession by means that are no longer acceptable. Although there may have been some slight exaggeration, in reality during the earlier years of policing it was not uncommon for such tactics to be employed (Bopp & Schultz, 1972). Today there is little or no tolerance for any such behavior regardless of how "harmless or unintentionally provoking" the behavior. The Fifth Amendment guarantees a right against self-incrimination. Therefore, any confession is suspect, particularly if it was given without advisement of this right.

The most noted case on this issue is *Miranda* v. *Arizona* (1966) in which the Court was forced to allow a murderer to go free because the arresting officers failed to advise the suspect of his right against self-incrimination. The result of this case is what everyone today recognizes as the *Miranda* warnings. This is one area in which the Court has been rather strict through the years. In the 1977 decision of *Brewer* v. *Williams* the Court ruled that any provoking or convincing of a suspect to confess without having been advised of the constitutional guarantees developed inadmissible evidence. The Court had further tightened the reins on the use of *Miranda* in the case of *Arizona* v. *Roberson* (1988) in which the Court ruled that continued questioning of a suspect after he had been granted a lawyer but was not within the lawyer's presence was a violation of the Fifth Amendment. However, in *McNeil* v. *U.S.* (1991) the Court provided some expanded power to police by ruling that police officers could question criminal suspects without their lawyers present. The Court ruled that a suspect could be questioned for crimes unrelated to one for which he is represented without an attorney, provided *Miranda* has been advised and willingly waived. This is not the first case in which some leeway has been provided to the police.

In *Illinois* v. *Perkins* (1990) the Court ruled that the obtaining of a confession by an undercover officer posing as an inmate was not a violation of *Miranda* because *Miranda* and the Fifth Amendment were protection from coercive interrogations, not strategic deceptions. Furthermore, the Court has accepted confessions when *Miranda* warnings were not given in the exact form as described by the Court in the *Miranda* decision. Again, the concern is with coercion. Warnings that counter the coercive aspects of the police interrogation may be used (Kalk, 1998).

Sixth Amendment

In some countries an individual suspected of criminal activities may be arrested and incarcerated for extended periods without a trial. When a trial is held, there is no jury or anyone to represent the accused. The evidence used against the accused may be the result of a confession the police have coerced or forced out of the accused. The Sixth Amendment provides protections to prevent this type of behavior from occurring in the United States. The Sixth Amendment says:

> In all criminal prosecutions, the accused shall enjoy the right to a speedy and public trial, by an impartial jury of the State and district wherein the crime shall have been committed, which district shall have been previously ascertained by law, and to be informed of the nature and cause of the accusation; to be confronted with the witnesses against him; to have compulsory process for obtaining witnesses in his favor, and to have the Assistance of Counsel for his defense.

The area of this amendment that most affects police behavior is the requirement of counsel for the accused before questioning. In recent years the courts have been quite supportive of this clause.

Counsel
The Sixth Amendment of the Constitution guarantees the right to counsel when an individual has been accused of a crime. The Court's first major address of this issue occurred in *Powell* v. *Alabama* (1932) when the Court ruled that an individual, regardless of wealth or intelligence, must be given the opportunity to be represented by counsel regardless of the lack of funds to pay an attorney. The right to counsel was upheld in *Gideon* v. *Wainwright* (1963). Here the Court ruled that the Constitution requires that a lawyer be appointed for an indigent person. Finally, the Court has ruled that when police questioning goes from investigatory to accusatory, the accused must be allowed access to counsel (*Escobedo* v. *Illinois,* 1964). This is one area in which there has been little leniency by the Court.

■ CASE IN POINT

U.S. v. *Henry* (1980): Henry had been indicted and jailed for armed robbery. A cellmate of Henry's was a government informant who was contacted by agents who advised him to be alert to any statements Henry might make about the robbery. However, he was warned not to initiate any conversations about it. After his release from jail, the informant contacted the government agents and relayed incriminating statements made by Henry. The informant was paid for this information. The testimony of this informant aided in the conviction of Henry for bank robbery. On appeal, the Court ruled that it is a violation of a defendant's right to counsel when government intentionally creates a situation likely to cause the defendant to make incriminating statements.

Fourteenth Amendment

According to Section 1 of the Fourteenth Amendment,

> All persons born or naturalized in the United States, and subject to the jurisdiction thereof, are citizens of the United States and of the State wherein they reside. No State shall make or enforce any law which shall abridge the privileges or immunities of citizens of the United States; nor shall any State deprive any person of life, liberty, or property, without due process of law; nor deny to any person within its jurisdiction the equal protection of the laws.

This requires that the police apply the law equitably to all persons. In recent years, the application of the Fourteenth Amendment to policing has been the most prominent in cases in which the police have failed to do their duty by not protecting an individual's rights. The failure to protect an individual's rights, or to provide an individual with equal protection under the law as described in the Fourteenth Amendment, has led to an increase in liability lawsuits against the police. This growing problem will be discussed in the following section.

The relationship between policing and the Constitution may be best viewed as a love–hate relationship. Without the Constitution there might not be any police; yet, it is also the Constitution that limits some police activities. Overall, the Constitution, with interpretation by the U.S. Supreme Court, has provided several behavioral guidelines for the police to follow when enforcing the law. Therefore, to abide by these guidelines, the police must be well schooled in procedural law.

Yet, even with this knowledge, there are times when police officers fail to remain within the guidelines and violate constitutional rights. In the past it was not unusual for the police to suffer only the throwing out of a case and a public reprimand by the Court. In recent years this has changed. Today when an officer violates an individual's constitutional guarantees (more commonly referred to as "civil rights"), not only the officer but the officer's agency and governing body could face the Court as the defendant(s). This has become known as **civil liability.**

CIVIL LIABILITY

Because of the uniqueness of the relationship of the police with the Constitution, they find themselves having unlimited rights of enforcement in some situations and limited rights in others. Violation of these rights could lead to the use of the law against the police. Of most concern is the violation of an individual's constitutional rights. Under Title 42, Section 1983, of the United States Code,

> Every person who, under color of any statute, ordinance, regulation, custom, or usage, of any State or Territory, subjects, or causes to be subjected, any citizen of the United States or other person within the jurisdiction thereof to the deprivation of any rights, privileges, or immunities secured by the Constitution and laws, shall be liable to the party injured in an action at law, suit in equity, or other proper proceeding for redress.

The recognition of this section's applicability to police has led to an increase in lawsuits. According to Stafford (1986), there had been more civil lawsuits filed against the police between 1975 and 1985 than at any other time in the history of the police. Reasons for this increase include the application of Title 42, Section 1983, to the police and several Supreme Court cases (del Carmen, 1991, 1993; del Carmen & Smith, 1997; Kappeler, 1997; Meadows & Trostle, 1988; Stafford, 1986).

The current status of civil liability is that police officers, agencies, and municipalities can be sued; however, it must be shown that a relationship existed between policy or custom and the specific act or that harm resulted from the officer's breach of duty.

■ CASE IN POINT

In June 1998 a federal jury in Tennessee awarded a rape victim $300,000 from the city of Memphis after finding her right to due process had been violated. In April 1996 the woman was attacked in her home while talking to a friend on the telephone. The friend called 911 but was unable to provide an address. Another friend offered to meet police near the house, but the police never arrived. According to transcripts, the dispatcher believed it was a domestic dispute.

As policing enters the twenty-first century, civil liability is rapidly becoming the number one concern for police management, agencies, and governmental entities. A growing trend appears to be litigation against the police officer, department, and city for police misconduct concerning the violation of rights. This is particularly the case if it can be shown that the officer acted under a policy or procedure of the agency or government entity. Civil lawsuits most often arise from false arrests, negligent acts, and the failure to protect an individual.

False Arrest

A false arrest is usually viewed as an unlawful restraint of an individual's personal liberty (del Carmen, 1991). When an officer is accused of false arrest it often means an arrest was made without probable cause. As previously noted, a police officer is required to have probable cause to make an arrest with or without a warrant. However, sometimes circumstances arise in which an arrest is made before the establishment of probable cause. When this occurs the arrestee can sue for both false arrest and false imprisonment.

■ CASE IN POINT

Delmar Dennis was arrested and jailed by a Mississippi deputy sheriff when a lawyer told the officer to go out and get the subject because there was an outstanding civil summons (child support issue). Dennis sued the sheriff and deputy sheriff for illegal arrest and detention. The court found in his favor. In its decision the court advised that the plaintiff's constitutional rights against unreasonable search and seizure were violated because the arrest was made without probable cause or a legal warrant (*Dennis* v. *Warren*, 1985). A civil lawsuit was filed in April 1996 by a diabetic who had been arrested by Lebanon, Missouri, police officers for suspicion of drunk driving. The subject was not intoxicated but rather had been suffering from insulin shock when arrested, and it was not recognized by any of the officers. In a similar 1996 case a Norwell, Massachusetts, man sued the state police for $30 million because of his arrest for drunk driving. At the time of the arrest the subject was having a stroke (not intoxicated) and claimed to have been held seven hours without medical care.

Negligent Acts

Negligence is not an acceptable defense to the commission of a crime nor are negligent acts acceptable behavior by police officers. Although a variety of situations or acts could be considered negligent, the negligent behavior that has been most recently recognized involves vehicle safety. A growing area of concern is high-speed pursuits. In recent years discussions have turned to whether safety of others is being overlooked to make an arrest. The argument includes the responsibility of the officer to consider safety more important than apprehension. If apprehension is not possible without jeopardizing the safety of innocent citizens, the apprehension should be foregone. In addition to pursuits, negligence claims have arisen from officers who, in responding to a call "red lights and siren," believe they have absolute right-of-way over other traffic, and end up in an accident. Another negligent act that has lead to lawsuits is the wrongful entering of a dwelling, particularly when it has lead to the injury or death of an occupant.

■ CASE IN POINT

In 1996 the city of Boston, Massachusetts, agreed to a $1 million settlement with the widow of a 75-year-old minister who suffered a fatal heart attack in 1994 after police officers broke into the apartment believing it was a drug den. The apartment had been wrongly identified. In 1998 a lawsuit was filed against the city of Houston, Texas, by the family of a man who had been shot and killed by police officers. It was alleged that the officers unlawfully entered the man's dwelling looking for drugs. The man was said to have been shot several times in the back. No drugs were found.

Failure to Provide Protection

One area of police liability that has received considerable attention in recent years involves cases of police failure to protect an individual. This has been the most notable in the area of domestic violence. For years the commonly used method for handling a domestic dispute was to separate the two parties with no arrest or report made. However, in view of the rising amount of family violence, the police have been called on to take more drastic steps. This became especially evident in the case of *Balistreri* v. *Pacifica Police Department and Al Olsen, Police Chief* (1988) in which the court held that the police violated the civil rights of Mrs. Balistreri by not providing her equal protection under the law as she suffered continuing violence and threats from her husband (eventually ex-husband). Yet, despite the growing concern in this area, police officers are still generally not held liable for their failure to protect (del Carmen, 1991). However, the circumstances of the case dictate whether liability is applicable.

■ CASE IN POINT

A New York State Supreme Court jury found the Nassau County police negligent for failure to protect a woman when they did not arrest the woman's husband for violating an order of protection. The husband later attacked the woman with a machete. The woman was awarded $1.55 million.

Claims of police misconduct have grown and should be a major concern for police management (Worrall & Marenin, 1998); yet, there has been no guarantee of judgments or settlements for plaintiffs. Still, this growth has caused police agencies to examine policies seriously in an effort to lower litigation (Meadows & Trostle, 1988; Worrell & Marenin, 1998). A question of concern is: What have been the results of such lawsuits? Answers to this include (1) increased procedural review, (2) improved recordkeeping, (3) increased disciplinary actions, (4) improved training, and (5) a greater exchange of information between city attorneys and the police (del Carmen, 1991; McCoy, 1985).

Although civil liability is not welcome by the police, it has assisted in improving enforcement by forcing police agencies to make changes that provide better service and protection of citizens and changing police behavior. It has also forced police agencies to examine policies and procedures more closely, primarily because a lawsuit against an individual officer often involves the agency as well. It is more common for plaintiffs to sue the agency than the officer simply because there is a better chance of achieving a cash settlement from the agency because the agency is wealthier than the officer. Blaming the police agency for the officer's actions has been referred to as **vicarious liability.** Although the police officer committed the violation, the agency may be held responsible and be penalized by the courts (*Monell* v. *Department of Social Services*, 1978). Furthermore, the courts have ruled that a city could be held liable, too.

■ CASE IN POINT

In October 1991 the city of Los Angeles was ordered by the California Supreme Court to pay $150,000 to a woman raped in October 1981 by an on-duty police officer. After stopping her for suspicion of drunk driving, the officer, Sergeant L. B. Schroyer, took the woman to her home and raped her. He was convicted of rape in 1982 and served eighteen months of a three-year sentence. In holding the city liable, the court reasoned that an officer acting as an official government representative with its inherent power and the potential for abuse makes that governing body liable.

Considering that police agencies have limited budgets and cannot afford lawsuits, many are beginning to purchase liability insurance. However, there are limitations to the amount of coverage. Therefore, to avoid lawsuits police agencies must keep up with the changing times by hiring qualified, competent individuals, and improving training and supervision.

■ CASE IN POINT

In 1988 rookie New York City police officer Edward Byrnes was killed while guarding the home of a witness in a drug case. In 1993 the parents of Officer Byrnes filed a $30 million lawsuit against the city claiming that their son's death was the result of improper training, poor positioning, and inadequate equipment for the task.

Individual officers need to be made more aware of the ramifications of civil liability. In a society in which litigation is rampant, police must proceed with great caution simply because of the nature of the job (e.g., the power to regulate behavior) and the duty of police officers to uphold the Constitution and enforce the laws. Civil liability may become even a greater issue with the emergence of community policing. Community policing is causing a variety of changes in how police deal with community members, and these changes could increase civil liability claims. According to Worrall and Marenin (1998), the means by which this increase may occur are "through state tort/negligence claims; through Section 1983 of the U.S. Code as the threshold of the 'color of law' becomes clouded; and through emerging ambiguities in the notion of 'legal duty'" (p. 125). State tort/negligence lawsuits may result from "officer error and/or citizen misunderstanding" and may involve "marginal/excluded communities" (p. 125). The "color of law" refers to the entire scope of policing, which leaves the potential for lawsuits almost unlimited. Finally, legal duty will become blurry as it begins to infringe on people's rights to privacy. The reality is that because community policing is still relatively new, what impact it will have on civil liability is yet to be seen. However, Worrall and Marenin (1998) note, "In short, it is likely that a sense of partnership, enhanced role conceptions, increases in public demands and greater informality in interactions will create conditions (and may affect motivations) which can lead to increases in the number of civil liability claims made against police when COP [community-oriented policing] is implemented with vigor" (p. 124).

Civil liability may help control specific behaviors of police officers as they enforce and apply the laws to others, but what about when police officers violate the law themselves? One of the oldest and most persistent problems in policing has been the existence of police officers whose behavior and activity violate the laws they are sworn to uphold. These violations have been most readily recognized as corruption.

THE ISSUE OF CORRUPTION

Newspapers around the country have featured headlines such as "Current and Ex-Cops Indicted: Detroit Officers Accused of Stealing Guns, Drugs and Cash," "5 N.Y. Cops Face Federal Charges in Haitian Torture Case," "Cicero Suspends Cop Chief, Top Aide," and "Busted Trust: 11 Current, Former police Officers Indicted on Federal Drug Charges." These headlines are mere examples of a phenomenon that has existed in policing since colonial times—**corruption.**

According to *Black's Law Dictionary,* "corruption" is defined as

> An act done with intent to give some advantage inconsistent with official duty and the rights of others. The act of an official or fiduciary person who unlawfully and wrongfully uses his station or character to procure some benefit for himself or for another person, contrary to duty and the rights of others (1991, p. 311).

In simpler terms, corruption is an act involving the misuse of authority to obtain personal benefits. As it pertains to policing, corruption is usually viewed as the misuse of authority by a police officer acting officially to fulfill personal needs or wants. For a corrupt act to occur, three distinct elements of police corruption— misuse of authority, official capacity, and personal attainment—must be present simultaneously (Sherman, 1974; Walker, 1999). However, depending on an individual's perspective, corruption can also be viewed as the attainment of goods, services, or any other personal benefits by a police officer by virtue of being a police officer. In other words, because a police officer's mere presence may be perceived to provide assistance or a service, the officer automatically becomes a viable target for goods and services not available to nonpolice personnel. For example, many restaurants and convenience stores offer free or discount drinks and meals to on-duty, uniformed officers. The same courtesy is not usually available to members of other occupations. Regardless of how it is defined, corruption has long been a part of policing.

EXPLAINING THE EXISTENCE OF CORRUPTION

Since its beginnings, many aspects of policing have changed; however, one aspect that has remained relatively unchanged is the existence of corruption. To eliminate corruption, police agencies have increased salaries, required more training and education, and developed policies that focus directly on factors leading to corruption. These changes have done little to eliminate the persistence of corruption's existence through the years. To understand why corruption persists, one must examine three perspectives that lend valuable insight into this phenomenon. These perspectives involve individuality, society, and the police environment.

Individuality

Every individual has a different set of morals, values, and norms under which he or she operates. These personal characteristics may be strong enough to combat the desire to commit a corrupt act, or not!

■ CASE IN POINT

A rookie police officer was dispatched on a call that required checking on the welfare of an elderly man. After forcing entry into the house the officer discovered the male subject, deceased. During his investigation, the officer found more than $1500 in cash on top of a dresser. No one else was around. The deceased subject appeared to have lived by himself. So, who would have known if the officer had pocketed the money? Considering that he was raised not to steal and strongly believed in the ethics of his job, the officer would have known. Needless to say, he did not take the money. Someone else might have taken it. As a matter of fact, some of his colleagues told him that he was crazy for not taking it.

The persona of the officer is extremely important; yet, sometimes other factors can override the "good" persona. Individual corruption can be the result of greed, financial problems, or peer pressure. The fact that there are numerous opportunities for personal gain during the course of doing police work does not help the situation.

Regardless of why an individual officer becomes involved in corrupt activity, it is much easier to defend a department's reputation and explain the corruption as an isolated event, or a "rotten apple." Although police departments systematically do all they can to ensure that an individual lacking in moral character is not hired as a police officer, it is not a perfect system and, thus, occasionally a "bad apple" goes undetected. Unfortunately, individuality does not account for the consistent appearance of "bad apples" in policing.

■ CASE IN POINT

In 1996 a former New Orleans, Louisiana, police officer was convicted for arranging the death of a woman who had filed a brutality complaint against him. In 1996 the firing of the Troy, Montana, police chief, accused of having sex on duty in his squad car, was upheld. In 1996 two New York Police Department officers were charged with criminal possession of a forged instrument, grand larceny, and theft of services in connection with "cloned" cellular phones. In 1997 eleven current and former Savannah, Georgia, police officers were indicted on federal drug charges. In 1997, eight current and former Detroit, Michigan, police officers were accused of stealing guns, drugs, and cash. In 1998 a New Orleans, Louisiana, police officer was arrested on three counts of extortion stemming from a sting set up to apprehend massage parlor owners willing to bribe police officers.

Society

In attempting to explain the persistence of corruption in policing, society's contributions must not be overlooked. Historically, corruption has existed in a variety of segments of our society. Nowhere has this been more noticeable than in politics. Patronage, payoffs, and break-ins are examples of corruption in politics. Policing is well known for its political connections. In Chapter 1 it was stated that, with respect to policing, corruption was once a direct product of political interference. This is still true. Politics can have a tremendous influence over policing, particularly among police agencies in which the top police executive is elected.

Politics is not the only societal factor contributing to corruption. The general community situation can have a direct impact on corruption. In a society in which illegal activity is accepted or promoted, corruption can flourish.

■ CASE IN POINT

New Orleans, Louisiana, is well known for Mardi Gras, days of nonstop partying and much alcohol consumption. Many years ago a police captain said that during these festive days it was not unusual to witness on-duty uniformed police officers consuming alcoholic beverages. Although this activity is not encouraged by the police department, officers apparently seldom fear disciplinary action because the community seems to accept such behavior during this time of year, even of police officers. Unfortunately, the drinking was merely one symptom of a department on the brink of chaos. The early 1990s was a tumultuous time for New Orleans because several of its officers had apparently become quite corrupt, participating in everything from theft to murder. The straw that finally seemed to break the camel's back was when one officer participated in a robbery of a restaurant, during which she killed several people including a fellow police officer. Since that time the New Orleans Police Department has been working diligently to clean up its image and rid the department of corruption, which includes no more drinking on the job, Mardi Gras or not.

Finally, a last societal factor that cannot be ignored is law. Many laws are criticized for being too broad, subject to uncontrollable officer interpretation and discretion, or too difficult to enforce fully. The result is the provision of opportunities for corruption. For example, the diverse array of traffic laws and the ability for officers to use their discretion has lead more than one officer to solicit money or sexual favors in exchange for not issuing a ticket.

Police Environment

Individuality and society provide ample possible explanations for the pervasiveness of corruption. The police environment provides an even greater amount of contributory factors for corruption. These include the general nature of policing, the other components of the criminal justice system, and the individual characteristics of the police agency (Walker, 1999).

Policing consists of a variety of tasks among which ample opportunities exist for corruption. As previously noted, because officers handle many tasks with little supervision or out of sight of anyone else, the ability to engage in corrupt activity is always present. Being faced with several temptations on a daily basis makes corruption extremely difficult for officers to avoid. In addition, ability to use ample discretion in many circumstances further enhances the possibilities of corruption, regardless of the lack of supervision or the individual officer's mores and norms.

A substantial part of the police environment includes other components of the criminal justice system that can breed pools for corruption. Political influences of a prosecutor or judge, a payoff from a defense attorney, or a kickback from a bondsman are examples of ways other parts of the criminal justice system can support corrupt activity.

Finally, the existence of corruption may be an outcome of the characteristics of an individual agency. Keys to limiting corruption are leadership and management. Well-trained and quality first-line supervisors have a direct influence on corrupt activity. The attitude of the agency toward corruption is extremely significant too; the police chief who sends a message that corruption is acceptable will find that corruption continues to exist. It is extremely important that the agency does not take corrupt activity lightly, or it may stimulate its growth. Unfortunately, the chief or top administrator of an agency can also be involved in corrupt activities.

■ CASE IN POINT

A former Newark, New Jersey, police director pled guilty to taking more than $29,000 from a police account for personal use, such the purchase of airline tickets, gifts for girl-friends, and vacations. He claimed that he was just following department tradition. In 1998 a man testified against the Logansport, Louisiana, police chief, claiming that the chief "shook him down" for more than $1000 after the man was stopped for drunk driving and arrested for possession of marijuana.

Because the existence of corruption remains pervasive in policing as a result of individual, societal, and police environmental factors, control is necessary. It is imperative that police corruption be controlled, simply because the costs can be tremendous, and it affects not only the individual, but also law enforcement as a whole, society, and the particular agency.

For the individual officer, participation in corrupt activity may lead to the ruining of career and family as well as the possibility of legal sanctions. Police agencies suffer when corruption occurs because this activity subverts and interferes with the general functions of policing, and makes law enforcement more difficult. From a community standpoint, corruption among police officers leads to a loss of respect and trust for all members of the police agency. An unfortunate phenomenon is that it only takes one corrupt officer to cause community distrust of the whole police agency, severely hampering the agency's effectiveness. Finally, within the agency itself, the existence of corruption can cause serious problems such as low morale, incompetent work, and image and authority problems. Obviously, corruption is not simply an economic liability, although the costs are varied and can be extensive. However, before we examine the controlling of corruption, an explanation of the types of corruption is appropriate.

● FORMS OF CORRUPTION

Corruption can be found in a variety of forms. However, it is easier to discuss corruption from a categorical perspective. For the discussion of corruption in this text, three categories are offered: **graft, criminal activity,** and **administrative practices.**

Graft

One of the more prevalent forms of corruption observed throughout the history of policing is graft. Graft is personal gains received by police officers for providing any obvious compensation or extra services to the giver while the officer is acting in an official capacity. Although graft in policing may include a variety of forms, the most common forms have been gratuities and bribery.

Police officers frequently receive gratuities from restaurants and small businesses. Although gratuities are considered a minor form of corruption that usually causes little concern to most police organizations, this minor corruption can eventually lead to major abuses.

■ CASE IN POINT

Many restaurants throughout the country provide free or discount meals to police officers who are in uniform and on duty. It is not uncommon for police officers to take advantage of this benefit, unfortunately, some to the extent of causing a scene. This author has witnessed several incidents in which officers, having been charged full price for their meals, yell at the waitress or cashier that they are police officers and are supposed to get the meal at half price. Although this in itself is embarrassing and gives police officers a poor reputation, what about the officers who put on their uniforms when they are actually off duty in an effort to receive the free or discounted meals? Another scenario involves officers who bring their family with them and insist that they also be fed free or at a discount price.

The supposed intent of these gratuities is to show police officers gratitude for the jobs they do. The real intent is to ensure that police officers frequent these businesses, allowing the businesses to receive extra service or protection. This is unfair to the rest of the public who do not expect to have to provide gratuities because they pay taxes and expect equity in services.

As a result of the abuses to which gratuities can lead, some police departments have taken a stronger stance on the acceptance of gratuities.

■ CASE IN POINT

In 1990 the New York Police Department reinstated its "no acceptance" policy of any type of gratuity. This means that any police officer accepting so much as a free cup of coffee is subject to disciplinary action. In early 1991 the chief of the Fort Worth, Texas, Police Department issued an order directing that gratuities from local convenience stores and restaurants could no longer be accepted by officers. Anyone caught violating this order would be appropriately disciplined. In Rhode Island the code of ethics sworn to by all police officers expressly prohibits accepting gratuities. In 1995 the Schuamburg, Illinois, Police Department also instituted an "no acceptance" policy. However, this policy garnered considerable criticism from officers and the businesses who would no longer receive additional "visits" from police officers.

The stance of police agencies toward the acceptance of graft in the form of gratuities can be hardline, as illustrated in the preceding Case in Point, or flexible (within limitations). However, flexibility does not appear to be the stance of any police agency with respect to another form of graft—bribery.

Bribery is one form of graft not accepted in any form or fashion by today's conscientious and professional police agencies. Bribery is defined as an arrangement requiring an officer's failure to enforce the law for financial consideration, sex, or merchandise. Although its existence in policing for decades is well documented, bribery really did not become a national issue until the early 1970s when the New York Police Department (NYPD) was investigated for alleged, rampant corrupt activity.

In 1972 the Knapp Commission, made up of five private citizens, submitted its report to then mayor and commission originator John Lindsay. The report culminated with more than two years of investigation into the alleged corruption of the NYPD. The commission found that bribery was rampant in many areas and took a variety of forms; the most active area involved narcotics officers. The report noted that officers participating in corrupt activity were making anywhere from $300 to $1500 a month above their salaries. NYPD acted on the commission's findings, and many officers lost their jobs; some were prosecuted. A mass reorganization of the NYPD occurred, and strict policies were implemented to avoid a recurrence of such overwhelming corruption. However, the 1990s were not good to the NYPD, which faced a variety of major corruption problems not seen since the Knapp Commission's investigation. It started in June 1992 when five officers were arrested on drug-trafficking charges. In 1996 four NYPD officers were charged with burglarizing two apartments while on duty and in uniform. Finally, in 1997 five officers were charged with violating an individual's rights when at least one officer brutalized the individual after he was arrested. Despite police departments' attempts to control corruption, it still occurs. Yet, it appears that there is little tolerance for the officer who solicits or accepts a bribe in any form, regardless of the level of policing in which the bribery occurs.

■ CASE IN POINT

In 1996 a Cincinnati, Ohio, police officer was charged with six counts of bribery and four counts of sexual battery. These charges arose from the officer's victimization of several women whose arrest warrants he agreed to overlook in exchange for sexual favors. In 1997 two Miami Beach, Florida, police officers were charged with racketeering and accepting bribes to allow certain nightclubs to remain open past curfew (5 A.M.). At the federal level, in 1996 a DEA agent was arrested and charged with attempting to solicit a bribe ($25,000) from a doctor in return for stopping an investigation of the doctor's alleged diversion of drugs for personal use; and in 1998 an FBI agent was arrested for taking a bribe from an informant in a drug investigation.

In sum, as long as there is no blatant misuse of police power, some police agencies allow their officers to accept gratuities. The acceptance or solicitation of bribes is never acceptable. This is also true of another form of corruption—criminal activity.

Criminal Activity

The idea of a police officer accepting money or other favors for failing to enforce or uphold the law is difficult for the average person to accept. It is even more difficult to accept the officer who commits violations of the law it is the officer's sworn duty to uphold. Criminal activity as a form of corruption may occur in one of two forms: the officer's appropriation of money or merchandise during the course of an investigation, or the actual commission of an offense.

Appropriation of money or merchandise during an investigation is the most common form of criminal activity. Most often referred to as theft, this type of activity includes retaining drugs or money during a seizure or arrest, failing to turn in a portion of confiscated goods, and removing items from any location to which the officer has access (legally or illegally), such as a burglary scene, the scene of a dead body, or an unlocked door to a closed business. Because of the nature of this activity, it is often difficult to discover unless the officer is observed and reported, or gets greedy.

■ CASE IN POINT

In 1997 the citizens of Savannah, Georgia, and Detroit, Michigan, along with their respective police agencies, were shocked and dismayed when several current and former police officers were arrested on drug-related charges. Eleven current officers or former Savannah police officers were charged with escorting and providing protection for shipments of cocaine. The arrests were the result of a twenty-month investigation by the FBI and a local narcotics team. Eight current and former Detroit police officers were alleged to have raided crack houses to steal drugs, money, and guns. They also allegedly planted evidence on innocent individuals and took money and drugs from dealers in exchange for no arrest.

Even though an officer encounters several situations on a daily basis that provide opportunities to steal, a few officers create their own opportunities.

■ CASE IN POINT

A police patrol sergeant, who had become addicted to pain killers after suffering an on-the-job back injury, created "burglary" investigations of pharmacies to support his habit. His method of operation was to set off the building's alarm by breaking or prying open a window. When the call was dispatched, the sergeant would be the first to respond. He would check the building before other officers arrived on the scene, during which time he would steal assorted pain killers. After other officers arrived, he would advise that the window had been broken and that it appeared that the perpetrator was unable to get into the building or had already fled the scene. He then would leave the scene before an owner could arrive, allowing him to escape without immediate detection of his theft of drugs.

Regardless of how it is accomplished, criminal activity by police officers has to be one of the worst forms of police corruption. When this type of activity is discovered and reported, it shocks and dismays both the citizenry and other police officers.

Administrative Actions

One of the most difficult forms of police corruption to discover is that which occurs as part of administrative actions. This type of corruption is both external and internal. External administrative corruption includes hindering investigations, making referrals to bondsmen and defense attorneys, making deals to stop or avoid investigations, and such politically motivated actions as employment of politicos' family members. For example, in 1996 a New York City police officer was charged with tipping off members of a drug gang about ongoing investigations and other activities that may have affected the gang's activities. The officer apparently did this from 1992 to 1994 but wasn't discovered until the 1995 trial of a gang member.

Internal corruption involves the "selling" of promotions or politically motivated promotions, or "selling" personnel assignments to special units, and shift and days-off preference. The use of money and sex have appeared to be the prevalent tools of internal corruption.

■ CASE IN POINT

A shift lieutenant for a midsized police department was well known for his tactics while riding with probationary female officers. During his "ride alongs" he would attempt to solicit sexual favors in exchange for the officer's choice of beat and days off. This activity finally ended when the lieutenant was caught in the middle of such an act by a field supervisor who had observed the vehicle parked in a dark location and went to investigate. However, only minor disciplinary action was taken. The lieutenant received a three-day suspension, and the female officer received a one-day suspension.

Whether it is in the form of graft, criminal activity, or administrative actions, corruption in policing is unacceptable. Isolated incidents are easier to cope with than widespread problems. The amount of corruption in a police agency is often referred to as level of corruption.

LEVELS OF CORRUPTION

An examination of local newspapers or the police-related newspapers finds that almost every day a police officer is caught committing some type of corrupt act. As the Knapp Commission discovered, this corruption is not limited to any one level of policing. From the patrol officer to the chief, corruption can occur. How much corruption occurs within a department depends on a number of factors. Sherman (1974) identified corruption as occurring at one of three organizational levels: rotten apples and rotten pockets, pervasive unorganized, and pervasive organized.

Rotten Apples and Rotten Pockets

If a police agency must suffer through an experience of corruption, the easiest level to deal with is "rotten apples and rotten pockets." The rotten apples level is when one or more officers are independently engaged in corrupt activity. Examples of this include a day-shift traffic officer who accepts bribes not to enforce a parking zone, and a vice officer who solicits sexual favors from prostitutes in lieu of arrest. Neither officer knows of the other's activities. In police agency lingo, these officers might be referred to as "meateaters," officers who aggressively participate in corrupt activities. Conversely, "grasseaters," are officers who may accept benefits from corrupt activity without having to seek it out or those who witness corruption, do not participate, but do not report the activity either. Rotten pockets occur when a few officers engage in corrupt activity as a group.

■ CASE IN POINT

As previously noted, the NYPD has had its share of corrupt activity over the years. In most cases, the situations seem to revolve around one or two officers working on their own. When more than one officer is involved, it definitely adds a different perspective. Such was the case in Manhattan's 34th Precinct. In 1996 four NYPD officers were arrested and charged with burglarizing two apartments while on duty and in uniform. In the first incident the officers allegedly broke into an apartment on which they had served a warrant the day before. From this apartment they supposedly took $2000 worth of sports equipment. In the second incident the officers allegedly forced an individual up to his apartment where the officers took approximately $1800 in cash.

Whether it's rotten apples or rotten pockets, it is easier for a police executive to explain away this level of corruption as isolated incidents. Society is also more accepting of this explanation. No one wants to believe that an entire police department is corrupt.

Pervasive Unorganized

The next level of corruption is not as easy to accept. Pervasive unorganized corruption takes the rotten apples level one step further by including many officers engaged in corrupt activity. Even though the number of officers involved has increased, pervasive unorganized corruption is identified by the unorganized and independent nature of the corruption. Officers are unaware that others are involved in corrupt activities, too. The NYPD during the 1990s is a good example of pervasive unorganized corruption. The various examples already provided demonstrate the types of corruption that have occurred; however, these acts of corruption were perpetrated by individuals or small groups, none of which were linked to the others except as NYPD officers. Yet, the number of events depicts a pervasive unorganized nature. When several officers discover that others are also involved and they band together, the police agency has a very serious problem.

Pervasive Organized

When corruption becomes well organized, the level of corruption has reached the pervasive organized level. This is the worst possible condition for a police agency. Pervasive organized activity usually will involve all levels of command and a number of officers. The activities can be limited or widespread. The NYPD before the Knapp Commission's investigation remains the best example of pervasive organized corruption. The following excerpts from the Knapp Commission report, concerning corruption and gambling, demonstrate the pervasive organization in NYPD:

In a highly systemized pattern, described to the Commission by numerous sources and verified during our investigation, plainclothesmen collected regular biweekly or monthly payoffs from gamblers on the first and fifteenth of each month, often at a meeting place some distance from the gambling spot and outside the immediate police precinct or division (1972, p. 74).

This pattern of collection and distribution appeared to Commission investigators to be quite standardized. It was evident in the four Manhattan divisions and the one Queens division which was the focus of the Commission's investigation (p. 75).

Although the NYPD remains one of the most prolific examples of pervasive organized corruption, it is no longer the only agency to bear the burden of such activity. For example, during the 1990s, police departments in Cleveland, Ohio; Savannah, Georgia; Philadelphia, Pennsylvania; and Detroit, Michigan, have all had disturbing episodes of organized police corruption with as few as five officers to as many as thirty officers (current and former) involved in drug-related corrupt activity.

Of course, police agencies should not want corruption at any level, yet, history indicates that corruption has been and continues to be pervasive in policing. What type or level of corruption exists often depends on the level of cooperation associated with the corrupt activity.

WHAT DO YOU THINK?

The Least of an Officer's Worries

Working undercover is not as easy or exciting as depicted on television or in the movies. Many long hours of surveillance or establishing a "cover" are often required to make a good bust. During these activities an officer is always aware of the possibility of discovery and what the consequences might be; however, the officer also knows that an assist is only a prearranged signal call away. Therefore, the last person you would be afraid of is a fellow officer. Then it happens. While sitting in an unmarked vehicle waiting to make a drug buy, the officer observes a marked patrol unit pulling in behind the unmarked vehicle. Before the officer can identify himself, the patrol officers order him out of the vehicle, grab him, and slam him against the unmarked vehicle. It is obvious these officers think he is a drug dealer and aren't worried about hassling him. Rather than identify himself or signal his backup, the undercover officer decides to let the officers continue their activities. During a patdown frisk the officers discover the "buy money," $625 in marked bills, but nothing else. They tell the undercover officer that they could arrest him as a drug suspect but decide to give him a break. However, they keep the money.

1. What do you think is the first thing the undercover officer should do after the patrol officers leave the scene?
2. What impact might this encounter have on the undercover officer's work in the future?
3. Would these officers have taken the money if they thought the undercover officer was a businessperson rather than a drug dealer?
4. Should the officer have identified himself up front?
5. If the officer had identified himself, how might the outcome have changed?

THE KEY TO CORRUPTION: COOPERATION

When the Knapp Commission's investigation exposed the degree of corruption in the NYPD, many people wondered how it could be so extensive. How was it that so many police officers and community members could be involved in such a large-scale operation for so long? The primary reason was the level of cooperation that existed. Although a corrupt activity may be a one-time event (e.g., stealing a VCR from the scene of a burglary), occasionally it becomes a continuing operation. How long the operation is able to continue depends on the type of existing cooperation. There are primarily two types of cooperative relationships that determine the duration of corrupt activity: **officer–officer cooperation** and **citizen–officer cooperation.**

Officer–Officer Cooperation

Trusting fellow officers has long been a key element of police officer relationships. When one's safety may depend on a fellow officer's support, it is extremely important to be able to trust that person. The importance of support for mutual safety extends throughout all aspects of policing. It sometimes contributes to corrupt activities.

When examining the officer–officer relationship, two levels of cooperation can be identified: active and passive (Sherman, 1974). Active cooperation consists of acceptance and agreement among the officers to be actively involved in corrupt activity. At this level, every officer is directly involved in the corrupt activity and receives a share of the proceeds.

Passive cooperation is somewhat more risky for officers involved in corrupt activity. This level of cooperation relies on the "code of silence." Although officers are not involved in the corrupt activity, they fail to report or acknowledge its occurrence. It is a "see no evil, speak no evil" proposition. In some respects, this passive behavior may be viewed as more reprehensible than the active involvement. When a police officer who is expected to enforce the laws allows fellow officers to violate those laws, it most definitely establishes a foundation for concern among police and nonpolice community members. Perhaps such ambivalence is partly a result of what officers perceive as corrupt or unethical conduct. For example, in a study of Illinois police officers it was found that the officers perceived the most serious form of misconduct to be the acceptance of a bribe; however, fixing a parking ticket was not so terrible. The type of punishment identified further supported officers' perceptions. For accepting a bribe, the first choice of punishment was prosecution, and the second was dismissal; whereas for fixing the parking ticket, the suggested punishment was a verbal reprimand or no consequence (Martin, 1994). No matter why or how they participate, any officer cooperation will encourage others to continue. Therefore, officer–officer cooperation must be eliminated if other forms of corruption are to be defused.

Citizen–Officer Cooperation

In isolated incidents of corruption, a citizen may not voluntarily want to cooperate but under the circumstances finds cooperation beneficial. These situations, by their nature, limit the duration of the corrupt activity. An example would be the police officer who once a week runs radar in a specific part of town, and inevitably stops a motorist who is considerably over the speed limit (for instance, fifty-five miles per hour in a thirty-mile-per-hour zone). The officer advises that a $25 fine paid directly to the officer eliminates the need for a citation and court appearance. To the average motorist this seems economically wise and so he or she pays the "fine." The relationship is mutually accommodating and of short duration. Conversely, there is the citizen who sees cooperating in corrupt activity for a long period as extremely mutually beneficial.

■ CASE IN POINT

The owner of a very popular nightclub is not able to provide the necessary number of legal parking spaces for customers. Therefore, customers park illegally. The beat officer recognizes the problem and offers the owner a deal: for $100 a week, the officer will not enforce the illegal parking. The owner realizes that if the officer began having cars towed away, it would hurt business and, therefore, agrees to the deal. This deal will last as long as it is mutually beneficial.

Whether corruption is mutually beneficial to police and citizens or only beneficial to police officers, its existence is dangerous and troublesome. As noted in several of the Case in Points, corruption can only lead to problems. Therefore, corruption must be controlled.

THE CONTROLLING OF CORRUPTION

It is obvious that corruption in policing has existed for years and will continue to exist. Regardless of this fact, it cannot simply be accepted. Continuing attempts to control and eliminate corruption are a necessity. This control must occur from within the police agency, and it requires support and assistance from the community.

Agency Controls

The behavior of the members of an organization such as a police agency often reflects its leadership. With respect to corrupt activity, a major element of control is the top executive's attitude and the quality of the administrative staff and line supervision. The top administrator must take a strong stance, and make it well known, against any type of corrupt activity. According to the 1973 Police Task Force, "A key to controlling police corruption is not necessarily agency procedures, but the integrity of the police chief executive and his ability to run his organization" (p. 473).

As previously noted in a Case in Point, when a police executive fails to take a solid disciplinary stance against corrupt activity, the message sent to the agency's officers is not very intimidating. This could be a catalyst for additional corrupt activity. Again, quoting from the 1973 Police Task Force report,

> Probably the most important factor giving rise to police corruption has been the general attitude of police administrators who fail to acknowledge that corruption does or may exist in the agency, resist self-examination, and are reluctant to change conditions that encourage police corruption (p. 473).

In addition to the stance of the top executive, establishing a well-educated, trained, and supportive administrative staff and line supervisors improves the ability of the agency to control corrupt activity (Bouza, 1990; Remesch, 1991).

A second aspect of agency control is training. During the initial stages of formal training (the academy), the agency must promote the ethical considerations of policing and the avoidance of corruption. Reemphasizing the need to avoid corrupt activity and activity that could lead to corruption, such as the regular acceptance of free meals from the same restaurant, should occur during periodic in-service training sessions. Sometimes this may mean having to go one step beyond the "normal" realms of training.

■ CASE IN POINT

In January 1998 Durham, North Carolina, was considering hiring a training consultant. This individual would provide specialized legal training to the city's police officers. Over a three-year period, the consultant would provide up to 1450 hours of training in such areas as use of force, civil litigation, searches, arrest, and probable cause.

The fact is that failing to make officers aware of the consequences of corruption only encourages its activity. Arrest and prosecution of corrupt police officers sends a clear signal to other members of the agency, "If you break the law, you face the same consequences as does any other alleged criminal." Finally, peer pressure can be a tremendous influence. Eliminating the "code of silence" would be a major step toward eliminating corruption (*Police*, 1973).

The existence of corruption in a police agency creates a very unpleasant situation. Training, education, and a competent administration make excellent tools for its control. Sometimes this is not enough, and corrupt activity still occurs. Many police agencies battle this problem using an IA Unit to investigate the improper activities of police officers. The presence of such a unit may be enough to prevent many officers from participating in corrupt activity, unless officers in this unit are part of the corruption as well. However, it is extremely rare to find today's IA unit officers involved in corrupt activity.

Community Controls

Although the primary responsibility for controlling police corruption is with the agency, the police agency needs assistance from its community. "The public is an essential ingredient in police corruption" (*Police*, 1973, p. 473). Therefore, it is important that the public be educated as to the effects of corruption. They should be shown how the simplest corrupt activity—gratuities—only promotes more corruption. The negative effects of corruption on the police agency and the community need to be emphasized. These effects include lack of trust, loss of respect, and police inability to be ineffective.

Education of the public is not always enough. One problem leading to police corruption is that several existing laws are too broad and ambiguous, resulting in ample opportunity for corruption. The decriminalization of certain crimes, or the changing or elimination of unenforceable laws, would assist in limiting the opportunity for corruption.

A final tool of community control is the establishment of community investigative bodies such as citizen review boards, commissions (e.g., Wickersham, Knapp, and Christopher [see Chapter 9]) and civil service. When the community recognizes that it has a stake in the outcome of corruption investigations, cooperation levels and interest generally rise. The downside to such investigative bodies is their lack of power to discipline.

When all else fails and agency and community controls are unable to limit or alleviate police corruption, there are always other police agencies. The FBI has become a valuable source for controlling police corruption (e.g., the investigations of corrupt police officers in Savannah and Detroit involved the FBI), particularly when the corruption is associated with civil rights, interstate commerce, or federal law violations. Police agencies do not enjoy having another police agency "clean their dirty laundry."

The complexity and nature of policing provide ample opportunities for corrupt activities to officers. Therefore, police executives must remain aggressive in the fight against corruption and not allow the prospects of its existence to overwhelm them. More than one source has claimed that corruption can be controlled. However, the effort must be made to gain the control. In the long run, that effort will be well worth it to both the agency and the community.

SUMMARY

The police have been empowered to enforce the law. This power is granted by state statutes based on the Tenth Amendment of the U.S. Constitution. In the enforcement of the law, the police deal with felonies and misdemeanors, traffic violations, and city ordinances. Each requires a specific action and observation by a police officer for enforcement. While carrying out their power to arrest, police officers must be sure not to violate rights guaranteed by the Fourth, Fifth, Sixth, and Fourteenth Amendments. Police officers must particularly be aware of rights surrounding arrest (probable cause), search and seizure (exclusionary rule), interrogations and confessions (self-incrimination), and the right of the accused to a lawyer. Established by the Constitution and upheld and enforced by decisions of the U.S. Supreme Court, constitutional rights violations are closely monitored. Violation of these rights by a police officer can lead to lawsuits. Civil liability is a growing area of litigation and concern for the police officer, agency, and governmental entity. Areas such as false arrest, negligent acts, and a failure to protect an individual are leaders in liability lawsuits. Improved hiring, training, supervision, and well-written policies and procedures will assist police agencies in eliminating the growing liability problem.

One of the oldest and most persistent problems in policing is corruption. It can take many forms: graft (gratuities and bribes), criminal activity (theft and burglary), and administrative acts (provision of information, and kickbacks from lawyers and bondsmen). Questions as to why this activity continues its pervasiveness in policing have led to several theories, whose bases are the individual, society, and the police organization. The type and level of corruption within a police agency are the result of the level of cooperation between officers and between officers and citizens. Its costs are not merely monetary but also the effects on the individual (loss of employment, family, and jail), the police agency (ineffectiveness and poor image), and the community (fear and suspicion). Controls must be established. These controls include agency tools such as a strict executive, quality supervision, discipline, training, and a special investigative unit. Community controls include educating the public, and community investigative bodies, such as civilian review.

DO YOU KNOW . . .

1. Whether there have been any recent constitutional attempts to limit police behavior?
2. In addition to those mentioned in this chapter, what other recent Supreme Court cases have been lenient toward police behavior?
3. If constitutional guarantees hamper police performance? have improved police performance?
4. What police agencies can do to limit their vicarious liability?
5. Whether your local police agencies have policies with respect to the acceptance of gratuities?
6. Other examples of police corruption?
7. What a police agency can do to eliminate all possibilities of corrupt activity?
8. Why corruption has been so pervasive in policing?
9. Whether corruption in other parts of the criminal justice system exists? If so, does it contribute to police corruption?
10. How police corruption in the United States compares with corruption in other countries?
11. Whether your city supports a civilian review board? civil service commission? other forms of community policing of the police?

REFERENCES

Asseo, L. (1998, December 9). Decision supports privacy rights in police-search case. *The Monitor*, 5a.

Black's law dictionary (6th ed.). (1991). St. Paul, MN: West Publishing Company.

Bopp, W.J., & Schultz, D.O. (1972). *A short history of American law enforcement*. Springfield, IL: Charles C. Thomas, Publishers.

Bouza, A.V. (1990). *The police mystique*. New York: Plenum Press.

Braziller, G. (1972). *The Knapp Commission report on police corruption*. New York: George Braziller.

del Carmen, R.V. (1991). *Civil liabilities in American policing*. Englewood Cliffs, NJ: Prentice Hall.

del Carmen, R.V. (1993). Civil liabilities in law enforcement: Where are we and where should we go from here? *American Journal of Police, 12,* 87–99.

del Carmen, R.V., & Smith, M.R. (1997). Police, civil liability and the law. In R.G. Dunham & G.P. Alperts (Eds.), *Critical issues in policing: Contemporary readings* (3rd ed.). Prospect Heights, IL: Waveland Press.

del Carmen, R.V., & Walker, J.T. (1997). *Briefs of leading cases in law enforcement* (3rd ed.). Cincinnati, OH: Anderson Publishing Company.

Ferrell, B.B. (1988). Duty to intervene: An officer's dilemma. *Journal of Contemporary Criminal Justice, 4,* 93–105.

Fyfe, J.J. (Ed.). (1985). *Police management today*. Washington, D.C.: International City Management Association.

Kalk, D. (1998). The rights stuff: Reviewing the *Miranda* warnings. *Police, 22,* 50–52.

Kamisar, V., LaFave, W.R., & Israel, J.H. (1990). *Basic criminal procedure* (7th ed.). St. Paul: West Publishing.

Kappeler, V.E. (1997). *Critical issues in police civil liability* (2nd ed.). Prospect Heights, IL: Waveland Press.

Kappeler, V.E., & del Carmen, R.V. (1989). Police civil liability for failure to arrest drunk drivers. *Texas Police Journal, 37,* 1–5.

Lewis, P.W., & Peoples, K.D. (1978). *The Supreme Court and the criminal process*. Philadelphia: W. B. Saunders Company

Martin, C. (1994). *Illinois municipal officers' perceptions of police ethics*. Chicago: Illinois Criminal Justice Information Authority.

McCoy, C. (1985). Lawsuits against police: What impact do they really have? In J.J. Fyfe (Ed.), *Police management today*. Washington, D.C.: International City Management Association.

Meadows, R.J., & Trostle, L.C. (1988). A study of police misconduct and litigation: Findings and implications. *Journal of Contemporary Criminal Justice, 4,* 77–92.

Neubauer, D.W. (1992). *America's courts and the criminal justice system* (4th ed.). Pacific Grove, CA: Brooks/Cole Publishing Company.

Police Task Force Report. (1973). Washington, D.C.: National Advisory Commission on Criminal Justice Standards and Goals.

Remesch, K. (1991). Police ethics. *Police, 15,* 28–30, 82–83.

Sherman, L.W. (1974). *Police corruption: A sociological perspective*. Garden City, NY: Anchor Books.

Stafford, A.R. (1986). Lawsuits against the police. *Journal of Police and Criminal Psychology, 2,* 30–35.

Walker, S. (1999). *Police in America* (3rd ed.). New York: McGraw-Hill.

Worrall, J.L., & Marenin, O. (1998). Emerging liability issues in the implementation and adoption of community policing. *Policing: An International Journal of Police Strategies and Management, 21,* 121–136.

THE USE OF DISCRETION 7

This chapter explores the concept of police officer discretion in great depth because it is a very important part of policing. For example, a patrol officer responds to a burglary in progress. When the officer arrives on the scene and begins to approach an open door, an indistinct figure appears in the doorway holding an object that appears to the officer to be a handgun. The officer yells for the individual to freeze. The individual begins to raise the hand with the object in it. Whether to shoot, issue a warning, or fire a warning shot requires use of discretion on the part of the officer.

As noted by the Police Task Force:

> The police in the United States exercise considerable discretion. The decisions they make largely define the limits of the criminal justice process and have a profound effect upon the overall administration of justice, particularly upon individuals. Police discretion is paradoxical. It appears to flout legal commands, yet it is necessary because of the limited police resources, the ambiguity and breadth of criminal statutes, the informal expectations of legislatures, and the often conflicting demands of the public (1973, p. 22).

Because of the broadness, complexity, and ambiguity of both policing and some parts of the law, one of the most important tools for police is **discretion.** According to *Black's Law Dictionary,* "discretion," as one would apply the term to police officers is, "The power to act in an official capacity in a manner which appears to be just and proper under the circumstances." It is the action an officer takes in correspondence to personal judgment, conscience, morals, attitude, and/or beliefs, as well as the officer's training, experience, and education.

Although the use of discretion is often denied (Davis, 1975; Doerner, 1998; Police Task Force, 1973), police officers use of discretion on a daily basis is quite evident. Some of the areas in which the use of discretion is practiced regularly include domestic disturbances, minor misdemeanors, use of force, and traffic enforcement. Other areas include juvenile contacts and general policy (Davis, 1975; Walker, 1999).

Domestic Disturbances

As noted earlier, one of the more frustrating situations for police officers is the handling of domestic disturbances. The nature of these situations often requires the officer's use of discretion. When violence is not part of the incident, and depending on the circumstances and the parties involved, it may be difficult for the officer to rely on laws or policies in making a cut-and-dried decision. Historically, it has been within the officer's discretion to separate the parties (by arrest if necessary), to suggest counseling, to mediate a peace agreement, or simply to threaten arrest if the behavior continues. The officer arrives at the action taken depending on the characteristics of the situation, and how they align with the officer's attitude and beliefs. However, recent changes in state laws and police agency policies are limiting the amount of discretion an officer uses in these situations by requiring specific actions to a certain circumstance, such as an arrest when an assault has occurred.

Misdemeanors

What constitutes a misdemeanor varies from state to state; so does the discretion an officer uses for these types of crimes. Minor misdemeanors can include public intoxication, disorderly conduct, trespassing, or simple assault. Like domestic disturbances, the action taken by an officer is often based on the circumstances. Whether an arrest, or even a report, is warranted depends on the officer's discretion.

■ CASE IN POINT

An officer is dispatched to a local nightspot on a "fight-in-progress" call. After arriving on the scene the officer learns the two combatants have quit fighting and gone back to drinking. It had been a mutual fight. Although neither combatant wants to press charges, the owner of the nightspot wants them removed. At this point, the officer could simply escort the individuals out, or could arrest them for public intoxication or disorderly conduct. The decision will depend on the attitudes of the individuals and the wishes of the complainant or victim, in this case, the owner as well as the officer's feelings or judgment.

Use of Force

A more in-depth discussion of use of force is found in Chapter 11, however, because it is a major topic of concern and criticism with respect to discretion, a brief discussion is necessary here. Police officers have traditionally had broad discretionary powers concerning use of force and how much force to use. It was not unusual practice for an officer to provide a little "curbside justice" when effecting an arrest (or, instead of an arrest). Over the years, the enforcement of citizens' constitutional rights and civil liability have caused officers to be more discreet in their use of force. Many police agencies are reducing the amount of discretion an officer has when using force through policies stating that only force necessary to effect an arrest may be used. Improved training and teaching officers methods of "control" using limited force or verbal commands have also been put into use by police agencies.

Two aspects of force that have recently received extensive attention, particularly in the media, are police pursuits and the use of deadly force. As discussed in Chapter 3, police pursuits, especially those that have ended in the loss of a life, have come under tremendous scrutiny by the media and the courts. Many police agencies have developed pursuit policies in an attempt to gain more control and lessen the officer's use of discretion. However, in most cases, the final decision to pursue is left to the officer because he or she is ultimately responsible for determining whether a pursuit is absolutely necessary and how safe the environment is in which the pursuit would occur. Although the discretion in initiating or ending a pursuit is often a difficult call for many officers, how much force one should use in a given situation is often even more difficult. In earlier times, officers were allowed to fire warning shots, shoot at fleeing felons, and use deadly force to protect a life. Today, many police agencies prohibit the use of force except in extreme life-or-death situations.

■ CASE IN POINT

Two police officers are executing an arrest warrant. In an attempt to avoid being taken into custody, the subject grabbed a table knife. Believing that his life and his partner's life were threatened, one officer shot and killed the subject. Based on policy statements, the officers' combined training, and the reported circumstances, the department decided that the officer's use of deadly force did not fall under policy. It was believed that the two trained officers should have been able to disarm and apprehend the subject without the use of deadly force.

One of the most discretionary decisions an officer will have to make: Do I shoot or not? Training is a very important part of the decision-making process. (Courtesy of the Scottsdale, Arizona, Police Department)

Traffic Enforcement

The one area in which discretion is most noted is in the enforcement of traffic laws. Officers have the discretionary power to issue a citation, give a written or verbal warning, or arrest the violator. The action taken depends on a variety of factors including the violator's attitude and demeanor, the actual violation, and the mood and attitude of the officer. Indeed, officers may sometimes simply choose to ignore the violation and act as if they did not see it occur.

Obviously, the use of discretion relies on a variety of unspecified factors. An effort to place limitations on the police officer's discretionary behavior has been underway for several years. Critics of police behavior, disgruntled citizens, academicians, and other actors in the criminal justice system who are not pleased with police performance suggest the police use of discretion has gotten out of hand. The result, they claim, has been a lack of equity in the application of the law and the provision of services.

Application of the Law

The broad use of police discretion seems to receive the most criticism in the area of equal application of the law. It is the argument of critics that broad use of police discretion creates or becomes a catalyst for discrimination (Visher, 1983). Contrary to popular belief, not everyone who is apprehended for violating a law gets arrested. This tends to lead to claims of discrimination. Critics claim that members of minority groups and the poor are not often recipients of the benevolent side of police discretion. Although the Fourteenth Amendment, in theory, guarantees equal protection of the law, in practice, there are no guarantees when discretionary enforcement occurs.

■ CASE IN POINT

Some police officers have demonstrated greater leniency when dealing with female law violators than male violators. Historically, the reason revolved around the fact that females need protection; female criminality had been viewed as a fluke or one-time mistake; and, because of the terrible conditions of jails and prisons, females were often shielded from arrest (Krohn, 1983; Visher, 1983).

Visher (1983) noted this phenomenon in a study in which he found that female suspects who deviated from general expectations of gender behavior lost the advantage often given to female offenders. The result had been an imbalance in arrest statistics. However, with the increases in female criminality and the "call for equality," the argument that women need to be protected is losing ground. Yet, some police officers are still lenient with female violators simply because they are female.

An imbalance in statistics from the use of police discretion is just one result of the application of law. The discretionary power of police officers in applying the law can also lead to police–community relations problems. When the police use of discretion tends to favor one class, ethnicity, or gender, the less fortunate segments of the community feel discriminated against. Even if the favored group is committing less serious offenses than the groups who believe they are being discriminated against, the discriminated group members voice their displeasure with the police. This sometimes may lead to a call for reforms, which may include a federal investigation.

■ CASE IN POINT

The 1990s were not a pleasant time for the city of Springfield, Massachusetts. Several incidents occurred in which many community members believed police actions were extreme and only because the alleged suspect or perpetrator was African American. Some of the major incidents included the shooting of a black motorist by a white police officer who thought the vehicle the motorist was driving had been stolen from a woman by gunpoint (the officer was cleared of any wrongdoings); police officers sprayed a 78-year-old black woman with pepper spray during a street altercation (the officers were cleared by the police commission of all charges brought against them); and about 50 city and state officers were involved in a melee outside an athletic club that caters mostly to black and Hispanic teens. Allegations of police misconduct arose from this incident. Although several of the 19 individuals arrested agreed to participate in a court-sponsored program, the inquiry into the actions of the officers had yet to be divulged. These and other such incidents lead the Springfield Branch of the NAACP to call for a federal investigation. As of the writing of this text, the Justice Department was still conducting its investigation.

Provision of Services

Although concerns over the police use of discretion in applying the law become the center of controversy as the result of specific incidents, such as a shooting or excessive police force, it is provision of services that invokes continuous concern with the use of discretion. Minorities and special-interest community groups have claimed that the services they receive are limited and are only made in response to specific complaints. Although there is little evidence of such limitations, the perception exists because of the discretion police officers have when responding to specific complaints as well as the discretion the police manager has in shift and beat assignments, and decisions about what needs the most attention at any given time.

■ CASE IN POINT

Throughout the 1990s increases in homicides occurred in many major cities (e.g., Detroit, Michigan; Miami, Florida; New Orleans, Louisiana; and Washington, D.C.). Police officials placed the primary blame for the increase on gangs and drugs. Other drug-related offenses also increased. As a result, more police personnel were and remain concentrated on these offenses. The ability to redirect resources to concentrate on these offenses is a result of the police manager's discretionary power to emphasize solving certain problems, usually at a cost to solutions of other problems. The casual observer who does not understand the budgetary or personnel problems in policing and the police manager's need to use discretion might perceive that the police are more interested in drug offenses than any other criminal activities. The concept of officer assignment based on priority crimes is again coming under scrutiny with the adoption and implementation of community policing. In several cities, the decision to implement a citywide effort or simply concentrate on certain areas has been the choice of the police leaders, a decision that may not always please everyone.

Police discretion plays an important part in the application of the law and the provision of services; yet, discussions of the use of discretion are often avoided by police managers and officers alike. A major reason for this avoidance revolves around the myth of police discretion.

POLICE DISCRETION: THE MYTH

The response of the police to the question of whether full enforcement is constantly practiced is usually affirmative; "policy" is offered as a response to the question of whether full enforcement is practiced. According to Davis (1975), the main ingredient of all law enforcement policies is a commitment to enforce all laws. Even though a shortfall in resources needed to enforce all laws exists and police officers' perceptions about prosecutors, judges, and the entire court system may influence decisions to enforce all laws, the failure to acknowledge the lack of full enforcement of laws by police officers remains. Nevertheless, the citizen who has been stopped for a traffic violation and has been given a warning instead of a citation knows that discretion in enforcement exists. Even when confronted with instances of discretionary practices, many police departments will not openly admit to them and, instead, adamantly continue to perpetuate the myth of full enforcement (Davis, 1975). Walker (1999) offers three possible reasons why the myth exists: **legality, the nature of the police organization,** and **the authoritative image of police.**

Legality

Every state's code of criminal procedure may be worded slightly differently, but the underlying notion is that the police are given a power to make arrests.

■ CASE IN POINT

"It is the duty of every peace officer to preserve the peace within his jurisdiction. To effect this purpose, he shall use all lawful means. He shall in every case where he is authorized by the provisions of this Code, interfere without warrant to prevent or suppress crime. He shall execute all lawful process issued to him by any magistrate or court. He shall give notice to some magistrate of all offenses committed within his jurisdiction, where he has good reason to believe there has been a violation of the penal law. He shall arrest offenders without warrant in every case where he is authorized by law, in order that they may be taken before the proper magistrate or court and be tried" (Texas Code of Criminal Procedures, Article 2.13).

Illinois Code of Criminal Procedures Statute 38, Article 2-12, defines a peace officer as, "any person who by virtue of his office or public employment is *vested by law* [emphasis added] with a duty to maintain public order or to make arrests for offenses, whether that duty extends to all offenses or is limited to specific offenses."

WHAT DO YOU THINK?

Using Discretion?

A uniformed patrol officer, while cruising his beat, observes an older model vehicle moving at a high rate of speed. The officer attempts to stop the vehicle, but rather than pulling over, the vehicle continues on its way. A pursuit is initiated by the officer. Despite being followed by several police vehicles, the driver of the vehicle not only does not stop but has started disregarding stop signs and traffic lights. Finally, as they get closer to the county hospital the vehicle slows down and eventually comes to a stop at the emergency room door. The officer observes the driver, a Hispanic male, jump from the vehicle and begin to run toward the ER. The officer jumps out of his vehicle, drawing his weapon, and yells at the man to stop. The driver ignores the command and continues into the ER. Several officers, including the lead officer, follow him in while others attend to the vehicle. The lead officer observes the driver screaming at hospital staff about his wife needing help, that she's in the car and is having a baby.

1. Simply because the vehicle was speeding and refused to stop, should the officer have initiated a pursuit?
2. After arriving at the hospital and seeing the driver get out of the vehicle and run toward the ER, should the officer have just followed him inside, or was drawing his weapon and yelling at the driver to stop a reasonable move?
3. Once the officer found out why the driver was speeding and refused to stop, what should the officer have done? Issued citations? Made an arrest? Or just lectured the man about yielding to police officers regardless of the situation?
4. What effect, if any, would the driver being Hispanic have on the officer's final decisions? If citations are issued, could a question of discrimination be raised?
5. Is there a difference between agency discretion and individual discretion?
6. What can a police department do to limit officer discretion?
7. How should the use of discretion by officers be controlled? By training? Laws? Departmental policies? Individual personalities?

There are no policies or laws that give police officers a right not to arrest. The result is that, from a legal perspective, police officers are governed by statute(s) requiring them to make arrests. Failure to arrest could be seen as a violation of the statutes. Considering that a duty of the police is to enforce the laws, blatant disregard—that is, publicly admitting to the use of discretion— would place police in a position of violating the laws they have sworn to uphold.

Nature of the Police Organization

A closed system operates with the intent of limiting access to internal happenings by anyone not immediately affiliated with the organization. By virtue of their bureaucratic structure and nature, police organizations have long been viewed as a closed system. It has been a common practice of police departments to provide limited information about their activities. Publicly admitting to the use of discretion exposes an important element of control for the police organization. Such an admission could lead to additional inquiries about other police practices. Ultimately, the police might lose the advantage they believe they have by being secretive; that is, the perception that police fully enforce the law, which is a potent tool in law enforcement.

Authoritative Image of the Police

Whether we want to accept it or not, the police are representatives of authority. The authoritarian image of the police is often the only edge they hold when dealing with the public. Although experience and opinion polls suggest that the level of respect for police authority has dwindled over the years, the police nonetheless have the authority to detain, investigate, arrest, and, when necessary, take a human life. This authoritarian image is an important element in successful policing. The police are expected to enforce and uphold the letter of the law. Failing to do so through the use of discretion, or admitting the use of discretion, could damage the authoritarian image and leave police vulnerable to an increase in discrimination lawsuits or claims of unequal protection.

It should be noted that the police are not the only users of discretion. The use of discretion is found in all components of the criminal justice system. For example, a prosecutor can choose whether to prosecute or what charges to file; a judge's discretionary power can influence the type of sentence imposed; and corrections' discretion is found in how inmates are classified, the types of programs offered to them, and whether parole should be granted.

It is, however, the use of discretion by the police that frequently receives more attention because of its impact on the rest of the system. The police use of discretion in enforcement can hinder the rest of the system's activities by (1) increasing or decreasing arrests and the need for incarceration, (2) creating backlogs of certain cases, and (3) failing to address other areas. In addition, it may mean that certain classes of offenders end up involved with the other parts of the system, whereas other offenders go free. Discretionary practice of the police affects everyone. Therefore, critics address the issue of controlling the use of discretion; however, before control can be established, sources of discretion must be understood.

SOURCES OF DISCRETION

To address controllability of police discretion, it is first necessary to explore the sources of discretion. Although there is a multitude of possibilities, three sources appear to be primary contributors to discretion: **environment; administration** (management, policies, and leadership); and **individuality** (Davis, 1975; Doerner, 1998; Krohn, 1983; Walker, 1999).

Environment

The general environment within which police officers work is a major impetus for the use of discretion. The police officer spends many hours handling a variety of situations alone. Supervision is limited. Many incidents are known only to those individuals immediately involved. The result of limited scrutiny is that the police officer is able to control individual behavior and the outcomes of the incident or situation with relative impunity. Therefore, use of discretion in an environment in which the police officer's freedom to operate is limited only by policy and law (and even these have been known to be bent, even broken, in the name of "justice") may not have immediately recognizable boundaries. A variety of outcomes can occur.

■ CASE IN POINT

An officer stops a vehicle to conduct an investigation of possible criminal activity related to prostitution. Initially, there are four suspects and the officer. There are no supervisors, other officers, or any other members of the general public involved. Thus, the officer's use of discretion has a direct impact on the outcome of the investigation. The officer decides to arrest the two suspected prostitutes and release the male occupants of the vehicle. Before this action can be completed, a supervisor arrives on the scene, conducts his own investigation, and advises the officer to arrest everyone. The patrol officer's discretion has been overruled by the supervisor, leading to a completely different outcome. In many situations there are no supervisors present, and the officer's decision, or use of discretion, stands.

The initial application of discretion in the preceding situation was partially the result of the immediate environment. Although visibility plays an important role in environmental discretion, so do the circumstances surrounding the incident. Circumstances that affect discretion include the type of offense, the outcome of the offense, and the desires of the victim or complainant.

■ CASE IN POINT

An officer responds to a complaint of a loud party. After arriving on the scene the officer observes several college-age individuals drinking and dancing in a fenced-in backyard. Although the music is loud, everything else is relatively controlled. The officer has the discretion to issue citations (disorderly conduct) or make arrests (minor possession of alcohol). However, the circumstances just don't seem to warrant these actions. So the officer requests that the music be turned down and issues a warning. If responding to the same call, the officer found people drinking, screaming, and hanging around all parts of the house, yard, and street—a generally rowdy, raucous situation—the results may be slightly different from the first set of circumstances.

Administration

Administration as a source of discretion for police officers consists of several elements. First, there are criminal laws. When one first examines a particular criminal law, the immediate reaction is there is only one application. Further study of the law or application begins to suggest a variety of possibilities. This phenomenon exists because of the broad scope of the law and the interpretative possibilities. In many instances, criminal laws are written in a fairly straightforward manner; the elements of the crime are quite specific, and, therefore, there is often little room for discretion based on interpretation. Still, with some laws, the distinctions between what a crime is and what it is not, are not as clear.

■ CASE IN POINT

The examination of several murder statutes in this country finds a similar trend: a person commits the offense of murder if he or she intentionally or knowingly causes the death of an individual or commits an act that is clearly dangerous to human life and causes an individual's death. During the first writing of this textbook, there was a debate in the state of Michigan as to whether Dr. Jack Kevorkian should be charged with murder for assisting individuals to commit suicide with a machine he designed that allows individuals to give themselves a lethal dose of drugs. The debate stemmed from how the murder statute was worded. Because there was no direct wording dealing with assisting suicides, the question arose as to whether a murder charge should be filed. However, this debate was quelled when Michigan's governor signed into law (December 1992) a bill that made assisting in a suicide a crime. This issue was further complicated in 1998 when Dr. Kevorkian himself actually gave the lethal shots to an individual. In March 1999 Dr. Kevorkian was found guilty of second-degree murder and was sentenced to ten to twenty-five years in prison.

A second element of administration is a combination of the police organization, the prosecutor's office, the courts, and overall resources. Every police agency, prosecutor, and judge has priorities. These priorities are often the result of a combination of the attitudes, goals, and resources available. Attitudes and goals are important, but when resources are limited, decisions must be made as to what should be emphasized. These decisions create discretionary behavior.

■ CASE IN POINT

The increase in drug-related crimes is causing problems for all parts of the criminal justice system. Increases in arrests means an increase in court cases. These increases coincide with increases in other areas. The resources available will not allow complete enforcement of all criminal offenses as well as the extra attention needed for the increase in drug-related offenses. Therefore, priorities are made, and it is initially left to the discretion of the police officer as to whether situations outside given priorities are handled officially or unofficially. The unofficial handling of the situation—warnings, threats, even physical coercion—has often been referred to as "curbside justice." Although not a recognized and accepted practice, it is a real result of the forced use of discretion.

The nature of the law and the general factors of the police, prosecution, and courts combine for an administrative source of discretion equal to that of the environment. The controllability of discretion as a direct product of both sources is possible. The same cannot be as easily said for the last source.

Individuality

Every person is different. Although it will be discussed in greater detail later in the text, it can be noted here that although there exist certain distinctive traits among police officers, there is no singular "police personality." The result is that officers who are different from one another cause completely different outcomes in the same situation as a result of an individual officer's personal values, norms, morals, biases, education, training, and experience (Doerner, 1998; Niederhoffer, 1969; Walker, 1999).

■ CASE IN POINT

Two veteran officers are dispatched to a disturbance at a local nightclub. On their arrival they discover the disturbance is between an individual who looked like a businessperson and his "date." Apparently the date was from an escort service to which the businessperson had paid several hundred dollars for a "full night of fun." When the escort advised that the "full night" would cost extra, an argument ensued. Both officers similarly assessed and recognized the situation. One officer, who is "religious," wanted to arrest both individuals for disorderly conduct and prostitution-related offenses. The other officer, who is more "liberal," found the whole situation amusing and simply wanted to send the individuals on their separate ways. Individual beliefs affect discretion.

In addition to the aforementioned individual characteristics of the officer, how the officer responds to the job creates discretion. Does the officer want to be promoted? Transfer? Work a particular area or shift? How the officer uses discretion is often a result of the answers to these questions. The ambitious, industrious officer may use less discretion in many circumstances, believing that the following of policies, procedures, and the letter of the law is the only way to achieve professional goals.

Among the three sources—environment, administration, and individuality—an abundance of opportunities and causes exist for the use of discretion. Again, the police critics claim there is too much discretion, and it must be controlled because failure to control discretion causes inequity in the application of the law and provision of services; not everyone who commits an offense is arrested and not everyone receives the same attention from the police. Therefore, controllability of discretion has become an issue of concern.

CONTROL OF DISCRETION

Considering the concern over the problems caused by the failure to control police discretion, critics have called for more intense control. The question is: How to control the use of discretion? There are three possible courses of action that might best be described as **actual full enforcement, pretend full enforcement,** and **selective enforcement** (Davis, 1975; Doerner, 1998).

Actual Full Enforcement

The most obvious way to control police discretion is through actual full enforcement of all the laws. This would require that everyone suspected of a crime or actually caught committing a violation of the law would be arrested. This action would alleviate any concern over inequity of the application of the law or provision of services. It would also be impossible to accomplish. Imagine how many more police officers, prosecutors, courts, and jails would be required. The reality is that the resources of the criminal justice system could not handle the strain actual full enforcement would cause nor would the public stand for it.

Although philosophically everyone wants laws to be fully and equally enforced, in practical terms that possibility is frightening. The general public is comfortable with the prospect of being given a break by the police, and the police enjoy the power this ability gives them. In many situations, it can be used to improve police–community interactions. Imagine societal response if there was no possibility of leniency for anyone, anytime.

Pretend Full Enforcement

The current practice of most police officers is pretending that full enforcement occurs while being selective. Considering that police departments would rather promote this action for reasons suggested earlier and that it is already a long-established practice, to do so requires little change. Yet, this option does nothing to eliminate the criticism currently voiced. However, it does appear to be a practical approach to feed society's general need to believe in full enforcement while offering a realistic approach to policing.

Selective Enforcement

What may be most beneficial to both policing and society is selective enforcement and admitting to its use, including the reasons why it is practiced. Most simply put, a police agency needs to be candid with its community (Davis, 1975; Doerner, 1998), an aspect not offered with pretend full enforcement. Selective enforcement is in fact what is practiced, although it is not currently admitted to. So, the question is: Why should police agencies admit to this practice?

First, police agencies are public agencies. Regardless of their desire to be "closed" in nature, the fact remains that as public agencies, they are open to scrutiny and criticism. Policies of public agencies, such as the police, must be shared with the public. This allows the public to form reasonable expectations of what behavior to watch for from these agencies. The failure to be open to the public assists in creating greater latitude for the use of discretion by police agencies and their members.

Second, fairness and truthfulness to the community are important for police agencies (Davis, 1975). As symbols and representatives of law and order, truth and justice, the police require truth and honesty from the community and the agency's members. Police agencies, too, must practice fairness when applying the laws. Failure to establish fairness and truth complicates their ability to perform and makes their discretionary practices more one-sided and open to criticism. Therefore, one might assume that the admission of selective enforcement could only improve the image of police in the eyes of the public. Yet such an admission could produce legal implications that neither the police nor the public should be willing to accept. For example, admitted selective enforcement could lead to documented charges of discrimination. Each incident would be scrutinized. The outcome of such an admission does not appear positive. However, rather than admitting to selective enforcement, a more sensible, candid approach might be for the police agency to share its policies and procedures with the public. Resolutions set in policy for handling various situations would provide the public with the knowledge of why police officers respond as they do. This knowledge could help alleviate the concern that there is too much discretion.

Being candid is only one way to control use of discretion. Another possibility is the clarification of laws. Many laws are written in a manner that leaves room for very broad interpretation. This broadness accounts for discretion in application. For example, the "open container" law basically gave officers the means to stop a motorist who appeared to be drinking from an open container. If the open container held an alcoholic beverage, a citation or arrest could be made. Initially, a problem with some states' laws was the lack of clarity as to what defined an "open container." This resulted in police officers stopping many motorists who were drinking from soft drink cans or juice bottles. Eventually the law was amended so that officers had to be able to recognize the container as being one directly known for holding an alcoholic beverage (e.g., a beer can). The passage of laws that are clear, concise, and of limited interpretation could help control the amount of discretion available to police. Finally, police departments themselves have tremendous influence over how much discretion an officer has in any situation through departmental guidelines, policies, or general orders. Most often these are referred to as standard operating procedures (SOPs).

The establishment of definitive SOPs that direct how an officer should perform in specific situations assist controlling the use of discretion. Areas in which discretionary control is limited by these orders and in which recognizable impact has been made include the use of force, high-speed pursuits, and the handling of domestic disturbances.

CASE IN POINT

The most common response of police officers to domestic disturbances in the past was separating the husband and wife, encouraging the husband to take a walk or drive until he "cooled off," or having the wife go to the home of a family member. History indicates that police officers failed to make arrests or insist that charges be filed. The police officer's discretion played an important part in the ultimate conclusion of the disturbance. This discretionary behavior did little for the long-term protection of the wife, and the result has been several civil lawsuits. In an effort to avoid further lawsuits and limit officer discretion in these circumstances, several police departments have written policies that require the officer to take specific action in certain situations, particularly when violence has been used. Recent policies require that the police officer make an arrest when violence has been used regardless of whether the victim wants to press charges. This requirement has stripped officers of discretion in these particular cases.

The implementation and enforcement of departmental policies that limit police discretion are admirable. However, an officer can encounter a variety of situations and circumstances. Can police departments, realistically, create policies that cover every possibility? Obviously, this is not possible. Policies will help, but the use of police discretion cannot ever be completely controlled. However, a greater understanding of its use by both the police and citizens could go a long way toward silencing criticism of its use.

SUMMARY

The use of discretion by police officers has a tremendous impact on police performance and behavior. Critics claim there is a need to control the use of discretion because of the unequal application of the law and provision of services. Although there is no one overwhelming source of discretion, most results from the combination of environment, administration, and individuality.

Reality forces use of police discretion; yet, because of legal reasons, the nature of policing, and the image of authority, experience indicates that the myth of full enforcement and few limits on use of discretion continue. Selective enforcement is common practice. Control of discretion is viewed as necessary. Candor, changes in laws, and departmental policies have been suggested as possible controls for use of discretion.

DO YOU KNOW . . .

1. How the use of discretion by police officers influences community perceptions? behavior?
2. Whether the use of discretion impacts political or governmental actions toward the police?
3. What areas of policing are obviously conducive to the use of discretion?
4. Whether equal application of the law and delivery of services can really exist given the status of today's police?
5. If the police use of discretion could be totally controlled?
6. What to recommend to a police agency looking for ways to control use of discretion?

REFERENCES

Black's law dictionary (6th ed.). (1991). St. Paul, MN: West Publishing Company.

Davis, K.C. (1975). *Police discretion*. St. Paul, MN: West Publishing Company.

Doerner, W.G. (1998). *Introduction to law enforcement: An insider's view*. Newton, MA: Butterworth-Heinemann.

Krohn, M.D. (1983). Is chivalry dead? *Criminology, 21*, 417–437.

Niederhoffer, A. (1969). *Behind the shield*. Garden City, NJ: Doubleday and Company.

Police Task Force. (1973). Washington, D.C.: The National Advisory Commission on Criminal Justice Standards and Goals.

Visher, C.A. (1983). Gender, police arrest decisions, and notions of chivalry. *Criminology, 21*, 5–28.

Walker, S. (1999). *The police in America* (3rd ed.). New York: McGraw-Hill.

RELATING TO
THE COMMUNITY

Although there is a variety of persistent problems in policing one of the more critical and controversial problems is how the police relate to the community, often referred to as police–community relations (PCR). Although PCR has been a popular term since the late 1970s, perhaps a more befitting term is police–community interaction (PCI). The interaction of community and the police has been the center of attention for many years, particularly when minority groups are concerned. Since the early 1960s, police agencies have been criticized for their relationship, or lack of positive links, with particular segments of the community.

According to poll information, the police tend to have positive standings nationwide. For example, Gallup poll results from 1997 showed that the police were among the top ten fields in terms of honesty and ethics, with 49 percent of the respondents giving the police a very high or high confidence vote (McAneny & Saad, 1997). This percentage has been relatively consistent since 1988, with the lowest confidence level (41 percent) recorded in 1995 (see Table 8-1). Furthermore, 58 percent of respondents in the same survey indicated they had a great deal or quite a lot of confidence in the police. Despite the percentage being slightly lower than the response to the same question in 1991, overall, confidence in the police is high compared to other institutions, especially the criminal justice system, which had only a 20 percent high-confidence rating in 1997 (*Sourcebook of Criminal Justice Statistics*, 1998). Although, as a whole, the public may have a more positive view of police, when viewed by the two larger racial categories in the United States—whites and blacks—a major difference in opinions become obvious.

Poll data indicate that specific community segments, particularly ethnic and racial minorities, are more displeased with many aspects of police agencies, such as enforcement, hiring, ethics, and use of force. Of particular interest is the difference in opinion about police behavior; black respondents were definitely more negative or critical about police behavior than white respondents. With respect to the question about honesty and ethics, 52 percent of white respondents rated the police very high, or high, whereas only 31 percent of black

TABLE 8-1

Citizen Ratings of Honesty and Ethical Standards and Confidence Levels of Police, 1997

Q: How would you rate the honesty and ethical standards of people in these different fields?

	Very High (%)	High (%)	Average (%)	Low (%)	Very Low (%)
Pharmacists	16	53	27	3	0
Clergy	17	42	31	5	1
Medical doctors	10	46	36	5	2
College teachers	11	44	35	3	1
Dentists	9	45	37	5	2
Police	10	39	40	8	2
Engineers	9	40	40	3	1
Funeral directors	7	29	45	9	2
Bankers	4	30	51	11	3
Journalists	2	21	53	17	4
By Race					
White	11	41	40	6	1
Black	10	20	38	20	11
Nonwhite	9	24	39	19	9

Q: How much confidence do you have—a great deal/quite a lot, some, very little, or none—in the police?

	Great Deal/ Quite a Lot (%)	Some (%)	Very Little (%)	None (%)
National	58	30	10	1
White	61	30	8	Less than .5
Black	34	38	25	1
Nonwhite*	40	33	24	1

*Includes black respondents.

Sources: Adapted from the *Sourcebook of Criminal Justice Statistics 1997.* (1998). Washington, D.C.: U.S. Government Printing Office. McAneny, L., & Saad, L. (1997.) Honesty and Ethics Poll. Gallup Poll Archives.

respondents rated the police on the same levels. A similar situation is found for the question of confidence: 61 percent of white respondents had a great deal or quite a lot of confidence in the police, yet only 34 percent of the black respondents could say the same. Although the police may savor a decent general public persona, the differences among groups is evident. There undoubtedly is a need for the police to heed these outcomes, especially when they reflect racial and ethnic differences.

■ CASE IN POINT

In a June 1994 Gallup survey of 1013 individuals, 43 percent of black respondents indicated that police overreaction to crime was a very serious threat to today's rights and freedoms, whereas only 24 percent of white respondents indicated the same. However, if the response "very serious threat" was combined with the response "moderate threat," the difference between and blacks and whites diminished considerably (from 70 percent to 66 percent, respectively). In the results of an August 1995 Princeton survey of 758 individuals, to the question of whether the improper behavior (racial overtones and implications of falsifying evidence) exemplified on tapes of former Los Angeles Police Department detective Mark Fuhrman were common among members of respondent's local police agency, 53 percent of black respondents indicated that it was common, whereas only 15 percent of white respondents indicated the same. A September 1995 Gallup survey found that 42 percent of black respondents thought that police treated blacks in their community worse than they treated whites. Only 11 percent of white respondents thought the same (Johnson, 1997).

National polls are just one source that tends to demonstrate the difference of perceptions between whites and minority group members. In a study of college students, it was found that a more negative perception of police existed, both overall and regarding specific behaviors, among black students in comparison with whites students. The difference was statistically significant (Dantzker & Ali-Jackson, 1998; Dantzker & Waters, 1999).

Apparently, there are differences in opinion between blacks and whites regarding the police. However, the polls and other research seldom indicate why the difference exists. Furthermore, it has become quite evident throughout the years that there are often problems between police and several different groups that may not appear in available data. Regardless of the group, a major cause of the problems between police and community is the **perception** the community, or specific segments of the community, have of police behavior or conduct, or simply of individual police officers (e.g., physical appearance, gender, or ethnicity).

Perceptions play a very important role in how well the police are received by community members. Unfortunately, perceptions of police brutality, corruption, racism, discrimination, laziness, and incompetence often lead a list of negative perceptions, many of which are perpetuated by the media (Dantzker & Ali-Jackson, 1998; Decker, 1985). However, the key to the source of these perceptions is to be able to provide proof or evidence of these notions. Proof that these perceptions are accurate may be found in such items as citizen complaints, grand jury indictments, IA investigations, arrest rates of specific groups, police-involved shootings, and the most recent form of evidence, citizen-made video tapes.

■ CASE IN POINT

Since the 1991 videotaping of LAPD officers and Rodney King, other such incidents of police force have been documented in the same manner. In 1992 a California Highway Patrol officer was taped beating a suspected sex offender (the tape was taken by the alleged suspect's wife). In 1996 a news crew in a helicopter recorded the beating of illegal aliens by two Riverside, California, deputy sheriffs at the conclusion of an 80-mile car chase. In separate incidents in 1997 video cameras captured the beatings of motorists by a Georgia Department of Public Safety trooper and by three Hartford, Connecticut, police officers.

Despite the type of evidence provided the perception problem will continue with or without it. Therefore, it is extremely important for the police to provide as positive a perception as possible for the existence of good police–community interaction. Before proceeding any further, it is important to understand what is meant by PCR and PCI. In general, PCR are viewed as being all aspects of the interactions between the community, as a whole, and the police. Although this is an important concept, more recently, PCI has been more appropriate. PCI concerns the results of any and all interactions between police and specific individuals. It becomes more of an issue when the interactions are between police officers and specific individuals from groups in which conflict occurs more regularly (Walker, 1999). Many groups may claim to fit this categorization, however, five classifications best represent those groups in which conflicts most often occur: **ethnic and racial minority groups, gays and lesbians, juveniles, elderly people,** and **women.**

Ethnic and Racial Minority Groups

One of the most controversial areas of both PCR and PCI is that of police–minority group member interactions. According to Cox and Fitzgerald (1983), "a minority group consists of people who receive unequal treatment from dominant members of the social unit, in the form of prejudice and/or discrimination" (p. 111). In this case, the social unit is the police, who are often perceived by members of racial or ethnic minorities as being representatives of the dominant social unit, "White America."

The number and variety of minority groups are rising in the United States (*U.S. Almanac and Fact Book,* 1992; 1995 U.S. Census). Although for centuries African Americans were the predominant minority, this is no longer the case. According to 1990 census data, Hispanics, Central Americans, Asians, Middle Easterners, and other European immigrants are expanding minority group communities. With these groups come a variety of languages, norms, cultures, and beliefs that differ from the U.S. culture the police have dealt with for years. The result is conflict that creates and sustains poor relations between the police and these groups.

For example, the primary language of the United States has been an Americanized version of English and was learned and used by most new immigrants and their descendants. However, many recent incoming ethnic groups have retained use of their own native languages, such as Spanish, French, Arabic, Vietnamese, and Japanese. With the exception of the few police officers who are fluent in one or more of these languages, police officers cannot readily communicate with victims or suspects who are not fluent in American verse, making the job more difficult and the establishment of a positive rapport nearly impossible. As a result many police agencies are seeking out alternative means to communicate with these groups.

■ CASE IN POINT

In 1990 San Diego County, California, had a population of approximately 2.6 million people. Of that number, more than half a million reportedly spoke a language other than English. Some sources report that there are at least 24 different languages spoken in that county. Obviously this diversity makes providing police services difficult. In response to this dilemma, the San Diego Police Department created the Volunteer Police Interpreters Program (VPIP). The volunteers in this program are either native speakers or have enough fluency in a language to be able to communicate effectively. When officers have to interact with non-English speaking individuals, a VPIP member is summoned to where he or she is needed. Undoubtedly it would be better if the lead officer could always interact directly with a suspect, victim, or withness; however, it would be impossible for any officer to be fluent in as many languages as one might need just in San Diego County (see Sanders & Caplan, 1998).

Although not considered an ethic or racial minority group, there is at least one other group in which communications can cause frustration and problems for the police and the group member—people with hearing impairments. Although technology has improved the ability for deaf people to communicate to someone in the police agency, there still exists a problem for officers on the street. One of the most common means of communicating with hearing-impaired individuals is through sign language, however, few police officers have that ability and must rely on interpreters or officers with those skills. For example, about 100 of approximately 40,000 New York Police Department officers know sign language. It is fortunate that there are not nearly as many deaf people as there are members in other groups, yet, the possibility exists that a police officer could need to communicate with someone who is hearing impaired.

In addition to language barriers, certain cultural traditions, such as the acceptance of male-over-female physical dominance in the family setting, which differ from mainstream U.S. cultural norms, are permissible in some groups. The striking of a female by her husband, boyfriend, or son is not as readily tolerated by mainstream American culture. However, police interference in a situation in which a male has assaulted a female, in a group in which this behavior is acceptable, is often viewed as meddling, and both males and females may take exception to the interference. This creates a poor bond between these groups and the police. Other culture-specific differences exist that assist in straining PCI, such as the belief in "revenge."

CASE IN POINT

For some minority groups, tradition and custom require that revenge be carried out by the victim's family, not the government. Therefore, rather than cooperating with the police in criminal investigations, group members typically do not give any information to police and then go out and handle the situation as tradition dictates, thus provoking more police intervention. For example, two Cuban brothers were shot and killed while sitting on the front porch of their residence. Although several other family members witnessed the shooting, they would not give the police any information. Three days later, relatives of the slain brothers fired several rounds from semiautomatic weapons into the house of the suspected killer's family. Although no one was injured, the incident caused further police intervention.

The multicultural population of this country is creating a variety of problems for the police who are expected to enforce a singular cultural–racial perspective. The result appears to be tense and strained relations between the police and many ethnic, racial, cultural, and social minorities. There has been some improvement over the years, however, primarily because of a variety of court decisions and civil rights legislation. For example, Title VII of the Civil Rights Act of 1964 prohibits discrimination based on race, color, religion, gender, and national origin. Section 1983 of the same act prohibits violations of constitutional rights.

This includes discrimination based on race. Despite these advances, further improvement is necessary. Police agencies need to improve training on race relations, cultural awareness, and public relations techniques. A technique that is gaining popularity among police agencies is the provision of multicultural training either as part of the basic training or as in-service training (Ford & Williams, 1999). Although the police have to take some control and responsibility for improvement, at the same time, society as a whole needs to do all it can to eliminate discrimination; education and intergroup activities may be two ways to begin the process.

Gays and Lesbians

Perhaps some of the more problematic interactions for police, among the five groups identified, have been and continue to be with individuals in the homosexual community—gays and lesbians. Although there are a number of reasons why these interactions are not very positive, one of the primary problems between the police and the homosexual community stems from the "machismo" of some police officers. Furthermore, the inability or failure of many police officers to try to understand the homosexual lifestyle and certain norms, such as those associated with sexual behavior, place additional strain on the forming of positive ties between the two groups.

Policing has traditionally been a "macho" occupation with very conservative ideas and beliefs about human sexuality. Homosexual practices go against everything some police officers believe in and feel that they represent. This in itself can cause tension and problems between the two factions. AIDS and its connection to homosexuality has driven a wider wedge between the two groups. Fear of contracting this disease has made some officers more cautious in handling or dealing with homosexuals. This attitude has incensed many homosexual groups and created even greater tensions. Adding to existing problems is the recent "outing" of homosexual police officers and the attempt by police agencies to keep homosexuals out of policing, a discriminatory action.

■ CASE IN POINT

The Dallas Police Department (DPD) maintained for years that because of a Texas law against homosexuality (the law refers to "deviant behavior," which was in the DPD policy as a reason for disqualifying, disciplining, or firing an officer), it would not hire homosexual officers. However, in February 1992 after the ban was challenged by an admitted lesbian who had been rejected by the DPD, a district court judge overturned the ban advising that the state law was unconstitutional. In May 1993 the Texas Supreme Court upheld the lower court's ruling that the law was unconstitutional. As a result, the DPD made the decision no longer to inquire of applicants' sexual practices. DPD is apparently not the only major city police agency to try to resist the hiring of homosexuals. A lawsuit filed by the American Civil Liberties Union against the Chicago Police Department in 1994 claimed that police officer applicants were tested for HIV, a disease strongly linked to homosexuals, and if test results were positive, applicants were found ineligible for the position. Furthermore, in 1997 a Chicago Police Department trainee filed a lawsuit claiming that he was fired because he admitted to a training officer that he was homosexual.

For many years, applicants for a police job who were identified as homosexuals were automatically disqualified from the hiring process; however, this began to change during the 1990s. Continued pressure from the federal government (e.g., the Clinton administration's policy on gays and lesbians in the military) and the courts to promote equal and civil rights, emerging political groups (such as California's Golden State Peace Officers Association, which is run for and by gay and lesbian officers, and the East Coast's Gay Officers Action League), a rescinding of a decades-old policy of opposing the hiring of homosexual officers by the International Association of Chiefs of Police, and discrimination lawsuits are all assisting to change policing with respect to homosexual police officers.

■ CASE IN POINT

In 1997 the New York Police Department settled a lawsuit filed by the Gay Officers Action League (GOAL) against the NYPD for refusing to allow the group to put up in the lobby of police headquarters an exhibit that honors gay and lesbian officers. The suit further charged that the NYPD failed to assign homosexual officers to its community affairs unit and repeatedly ignored GOAL's request for a recruitment van. Although the settlement does not admit any wrongdoing on the part of NYPD, the department did agree to consider several requests and to pay the group's legal bill of $15,000.

Despite the rising number of lawsuits against police departments, the expanding role of government, the courts, and political groups, there still appears to exist a negative attitude toward homosexuals by some police officers. However, the numbers and political strength of the homosexual community are slowly forcing a tentative change in attitude by police officers and society.

Juveniles

As previously noted in Chapter 3, an area of frustration for police officers concerns their interaction with juveniles. The problems between the police and juveniles tend to stem from a variety of factors such as physical appearances, use of drugs (e.g., crack, cocaine, and marijuana), and an increase in criminality. Again, the traditions of policing have tremendous influence on officers' perceptions. According to a traditional perspective, juveniles are supposed to be clean-cut, all-American youths who obey authority and do not openly reject tradition. However, many of today's youth are conforming to their own beliefs and ideas, which often are reflected in their physical appearance (e.g., spiked or unusually colored hair, deliberately torn or oversized clothing, tattoos, and body piercing), the music they listen to (e.g., rap or loud heavy-metal music), and how they dance (e.g., "mosh" and slam dancing). None of these are part of the acceptable image of youths in the minds of many police officers. Furthermore, some of these youths belong to street gangs or motorcycle clubs, or simply "hang out" at local establishments. Additionally, some of these youths are involved in criminality, and others plainly resent authority. This creates a variety of conflicts between the two groups, similar to those between parents and children.

One such conflict is the inability of some officers to communicate with today's youths at a level where good rapport can be established. Today's juveniles often have a unique language or communication style that the traditional officer does not understand. Attitudes of these youths also frequently differ from mainstream attitudes with respect to police authority and sometimes lead to an arrest in a situation in which only a verbal warning might otherwise be given.

■ CASE IN POINT

The city has a curfew ordinance that requires all youths under age seventeen to be off the streets by midnight on a weeknight. One night, a fifteen-year veteran and his rookie partner receive a disturbance call "reference youths and loud music" in a business parking lot. The officers respond and on arrival on the scene the officers observe several juveniles dressed in the current hip-hop fashion, some have tattoos and others have pierced navels and tongues, dancing to sounds the veteran officer does not consider anything close to music emanating from a large portable stereo. The veteran comments to his partner that if his kids came home looking like any of these youths, he'd disown them. Although the rookie is a little more current in his thinking, he agrees. As the officers approach the youths, several begin making rude and disrespectful comments; others simply want to know why they are being hassled. The officers advise them that they are violating the curfew ordinance and issue each one a citation.

Obviously, to improve the interactions between police and juveniles, officers will need to become more aware of youth trends. Increasing positive contacts between these two groups could assist in creating a more positive attitude by

Despite the debate over the effectiveness of D.A.R.E. programs, they provide good opportunities to develop positive interactions between police officers and youths. (Courtesy of the Scottsdale, Arizona, Police Department)

both groups' members toward each other. One possibility, which has been tested in one Ohio city, is the sponsoring of a "jam session" headlined by popular local disc jockeys where police officers and youth mingle. Prizes and awards are used as incentives for the youth to initiate a conversation with a police officer. Similar programs can only help improve police–youth interactions. Other helpful possibilities include creating a teen hotline (Leader, 1998), mentoring programs (Brann, 1998; Garcia, 1998), or sports programs. Although recently criticized for lack of effectiveness, D.A.R.E. (Drugs and Alcohol Reduction Education) programs are also good avenues for improving juvenile–police interaction. The reality is that dealing with juveniles can be as different or difficult as dealing with ethnic or racial minority groups, especially if the youths are part of these groups, too. Either way, police officers need to learn how to communicate and deal with today's youth.

Elderly People

Pundits have advised that the population of the United States is getting older, despite a slow growth in the number of individuals 65 and older (in 1990, this group made up 12.5 percent of the population; in 1996, 12.8 percent of the population). Support for this position may stem from the fact that the birth rates have decreased (from 1.5 births per 1000 people in 1993 to 14.8 births per 1000 people in 1996) while the death rate has remained stable at 8.8 deaths per 1000 people. If this condition is true, then those considered elderly (65 years of age and older) will increase in number. An increase will mean more chances for the police to interact with this group's members, especially if many elderly people continue to work, live on their own, and drive. Furthermore, this increase in numbers will also increase the number of elderly people involved in criminal activities, either as victims or as suspects.

According to various data sources (Uniform Crime Report and victimization studies), the number of individuals 65 or older arrested in 1997 was more than 67,000, with men constituting the majority of this number (84 percent). Among the index crimes, members of this group were arrested predominantly for aggravated assaults (mostly men) and larceny-theft. Although these arrests only account for about 1.2 percent of all persons arrested in 1997, it is a slight increase over previous years (refer to the 1997 Uniform Crime Report located at www.fbi.gov/ucr/Cius_97/Welcome.pdf). With regard to elderly people as victims, a 1996 report indicated that individuals age 65 and older were victims of a crime of violence at a rate of 4.9 per 1000. However, their overall chance of being a victim was 1 in 200 (Ringel, 1997). In either case, victim or criminal, the trend is toward growth, thus improving chances of police interaction.

In general, one might not think there should be cause for negative interactions between police officers and elderly people. Still, if one thinks of their interactions in similar terms of the police and juveniles, the possibilities for negative interaction become clearer. It may all begin with nothing more than a perception by the elderly person of the competence of the police officer simply based on the officer's age, a belief that the officer is too young to be a "real" officer. Other more serious problems might involve the need to arrest an elderly person who might remind an officer of his or her parents or grandparents; taking crime reports from those who may be suffering age-related physical problems, such as poor vision or hearing loss; trying to spend too much time being sympathetic; or just having to take time to respond to calls for service that are nothing more than calls for company.

■ CASE IN POINT

It is fairly common for police agencies to receive requests for police services from elderly complainants or victims. In many cases, the request is legitimate—a burglary, theft , or assault had occurred. However, not all such calls can be classified as "legitimate." For example, in this author's recollection of his experiences as a uniformed officer, one particular elderly woman comes to mind. Several times a week she called the police "reference a suspicious person" around her house. This woman was in her late 70s to early 80s and lived by herself. On the first few occasions, the calls were taken seriously, and at least two officers were sent to check the house. Eventually, it was realized that there was no prowler, only a very lonely woman who enjoyed having someone to talk with on occasion and all she could think to do was call the police. Once that fact was established, officers who worked her neighborhood would stop in every now and then just to see how she was getting along. If a few days fell between visits, a "prowler call" for that location would inevitably be given out.

Police interactions with elderly people tend to be the least hostile of interactions among the five groups in which conflicts most often occur. However, if the number of elderly people does continue to increase, so will the number of interactions and the potential for negative results. Therefore, it would be useful to police agencies to begin training their officers how to deal with the elderly, both as victims and as criminals.

Women

Women have long complained about their treatment by police officers. Two of the most common complaints have dealt with unequal or inadequate protection and sexual harassment. Much of the poor association with women is failure of

(Crankshaft © 1995 by Mediagraphics, Inc. Reprinted with permission of Universal Press Syndicate. All rights reserved.)

some police officers to practice equity in the provision of services to women. For example, an Oakland, California, Police Department internal investigation found that 90 percent of the sexual assaults reported to the police that were not investigated in 1989 and 1990 should have been. This meant that one of four women who had reported a rape or an attempted rape to the Oakland Police Department had been ignored (*Los Angeles Times,* February 4, 1991). These findings tend to support data suggesting that 23 percent of women decline reporting being sexually assaulted because of the perception that the police would be inefficient or uncaring (Harlow, 1991). However, changes in the law and the filing of civil suits have forced police departments and officers to change their approach toward female victims. For example, changes in departmental policies forcing provision of equal services, such as mandatory arrest of the primary aggressor in a domestic violence situation, are assisting in improving the relationship between women and police.

Sexual harassment of women, either as consumers, victims, or fellow officers has long been a problem area with police–women interactions. Again, increasing enforcement by the courts of the civil rights acts has forced police officers to become more aware of behavior that could be deemed sexual harassment and the consequences if accused of such behavior.

It has also been helpful that more women are becoming police officers. Their presence in uniform is forcing many police agencies and individual officers to change their attitude toward women. Of the five groups—minorities, gays and lesbians, juveniles, elderly people, and women—women have probably made

© 1997 United Feature Syndicate, Inc.

"Did you swipe some of their doughnuts?"

(Marmaduke reprinted by permission of United Feature Syndicate, Inc.)

the greatest strides toward a more acceptable and positive relationship between themselves and the police. However, it is not yet a perfect association, and both sides will need to continue working for improvement. (The following chapter offers more information on the status of women and their relationship to policing.)

Regardless of which group is the center of attention, PCI is based on the perceptions of individual group members, even though several individuals of the same group or many groups have a similar perception. For example, a very common perception among most groups is that all police officers have a fondness for doughnuts, and when an officer is needed a good tactic is to call the local donut shop. While this may be an overblown, almost humorous perception, it does exist. The key to improving PCI is to dispel the misperceptions. To do this, we must first identify the perceptions, which can be categorized into two broad areas: **street behavior** and **administration.**

STREET BEHAVIOR

The following are examples of some misperceived police behaviors and reality.

Harassment and Brutality

Perception.   Police are excessively brutal and harass people, particularly members of minority groups.

Evidence.   Isolated incidents of harassment and brutality do occur. Both, however, are a matter of definition; simply put, harassment is police interference into activities on a regular basis.

■ CASE IN POINT

Every day the same group of young men gather to play basketball at a specific spot. Every day the beat officer stops and requests identification from each individual, even though the officer already knows each one. This is harassment. The simple act of stopping an individual one time and asking for identification is not harassment. Unfortunately, some minority group members continue to perceive it as such.

Brutality, whether it is physical or verbal, exists when an officer goes beyond "standard" procedures when conducting a search, stop and frisk, an arrest, or any other activity conducted while acting as a police officer.

■ CASE IN POINT

In 1996 three Darby Borough, Pennsylvania, police officers were sued for allegedly dragging a trolley driver out of her trolley and using racial epithets against her just because she had blown the trolley's horn at them after officers had pulled their vehicle in front of the trolley, forcing the driver to make an emergency stop. An emergency stop apparently automatically sets off the horn. In another 1996 case a Fort Myers, Florida, patrol officer allegedly sexually assaulted a nineteen-year-old woman who had called the police to report a drug activity. The officer told the complainant/victim that she may be a suspect and was searched, then reportedly forced to perform an oral sex act on the officer. In August 1997 four New York police officers were accused of beating and torturing a Haitian immigrant. The victim was first beaten while in the squad car and then later in a precinct bathroom. In September 1997 two New York police officers were accused of beating a man after breaking into his apartment to search for drugs. In February 1998 the officers were charged with assault.

The result of these incidents and similar incidents is that citizens begin to wonder if all police officers act this way. Yet, available data from the FBI and the Department of Justice suggest that this behavior is not commonplace. Unfortunately, all it takes is one occurrence for all police officers to be branded as brutal.

Corruption

Perception.   All police officers are corrupt.

Evidence.   As with harassment and brutality, there are isolated cases of police corruption. This does not mean the whole department is corrupt, yet sometimes it takes only one incident, and the community believes that all police officers are corrupt. For example, although the investigations of police departments in Savannah, Georgia; Detroit, Michigan; Cleveland, Ohio; and New York City noted in Chapter 6 revealed that very small groups of police officers were involved, it would not have been surprising if a large percentage of citizens began to view the whole department as corrupt. Furthermore, as previously noted, certain types of discretionary police activity and differing ideas of what constitutes corruption does not help the situation.

Underenforcement or Selective Enforcement

Perception.   Police officers do not patrol minority group areas as much as "white" areas, and they enforce laws against members of minority groups more than against the white population.

Evidence.   When the patrol officer distribution of most police agencies is examined, one finds that the largest percentage of patrol units are assigned to the highest crime areas. In many cities these areas tend to be minority group members' neighborhoods. Therefore, it is difficult to accept the perceived notion of underenforcement. What does exist (and adds to the misperception) is a lack of friendly personal contact between the police and citizens of these areas. When an officer is observed or has contact with a citizen only when someone has done something wrong, the lack of pleasant personal interaction does little to change the negative perception. A focus of community policing is to establish better relationships so that community members do not perceive the lack of enforcement.

As for selective enforcement, the police are guilty of this; however, it is not limited to minority groups. It has been established that police officers use discretion in a variety of situations. For example, in a master's thesis study of arrests of individuals stopped for suspicion of drunk driving, this author found that white men were arrested more often than any minority group members or women. The simple fact is that citizens seldom see the officer perform assigned or mandated duties in other areas of the community. Therefore, the assumption is that police officers are only selective with minority group members.

Use of Deadly Force

Perception.   White police officers intentionally use deadly force more often against members of minority groups than against whites.

Evidence.   Although the use of deadly force is one of the most ominous powers of the police, national data on its use is scarce (Fridell & Pate, 1997). Part of the problem is that most of the available data has been provided by a variety of individual police agencies, which has resulted in unreliable depictions of police use of deadly force. However, as with other perceptions, this perception can stem from isolated incidents, such as the 1992 beating death of Malice Green by two Detroit, Michigan, police officers. Despite the fact that the number of African Americans killed by police has decreased considerably over the past twenty years, isolated incidents perpetuate the perception. Yet, it is relatively clear to see how a white officer may be more likely to be in a situation to use force against a black person than against a white person. A study of data for the past ten years finds that more blacks were arrested for violent crimes when a weapon was used than any other minority group or whites. In particular blacks were arrested at a greater percentage than whites for the crime of robbery. When one considers this type of information, one should see that the chances are greater that a police officer, regardless of his or her race, may confront a minority group member in a situation in which deadly force may be necessary. Regardless of perception, police officers, especially white officers, are not out gunning for minority citizens. (Further discussion on the use of force is offered in Chapter 11.)

Attitudes and General Behavior

Perception.   Police officers are lazy and avoid certain calls, generally ignore citizens, and are discriminatory.

Evidence.   Although there is little empirical support, honesty requires acknowledging that at some time or another some officers attempt to avoid certain calls, will not want to be bothered by John Q. Citizen, or demonstrate some discriminatory behavior. Because of the broad nature of police work and the broad range of characteristics of police officers, it is inevitable that situations will arise in which these perceptions are accurate. The interesting point is that although the race, ethnicity, or gender of the officer can be misperceived as the single cause for this behavior, almost all officers are guilty of such behavior at some point in their career regardless of their race, ethnicity, or gender. (As are people employed in other occupations.) However, when it occurs and if it is demonstrated to be a blatant attitude, police agencies need to respond in a positive and practical manner. Otherwise, the community may believe the entire agency harbors these attitudes.

The perceptions associated with street behavior will find limited evidence to support them. However, it may take only one incident to cause citizens to form their perceptions and apply them globally to all police officers. The same scenario applies to administrative practices.

ADMINISTRATION

As with street behavior of police officers, there are a variety of perceptions (or misperceptions) of how the police operate administratively. The following are three areas of mistaken perceptions of administrative actions frequently acknowledged in the PCR literature (see Carter & Radelet, 1999; Kelling, 1988; Walker, 1999).

Citizen Complaints

Perception. Police departments ignore citizen complaints, particularly those regarding an officer's behavior (i.e., that the police protect their own).

Evidence. Contrary to popular perception, police departments take citizen complaints seriously. Depending on the degree of severity of the complaint, the action taken may require only investigation by the officer's immediate supervisor, resulting in nothing more than a verbal reprimand to the officer. More serious complaints are usually directed to an IA investigator who conducts a fullscale investigation. In many instances the complaint is unfounded or does not warrant action (e.g., the citizen received a traffic citation and did not like the officer's attitude). In cases in which police misconduct is proved to have occurred, disciplinary action is imposed on the officer. Disciplinary actions include oral or written reprimands, suspension without pay, demotion, firing, and criminal prosecution. Despite this, the perception continues.

The problem with the handling of citizen complaints is the failure of the police agency to follow up with the complainant and advise him or her of its findings and actions. When an officer is disciplined, citizens seldom hear about it unless it is serious enough to be in the newspapers.

Recruitment

Perception. Police agencies purposely do not recruit members of minority groups or deliberately make hiring standards too high for minority applicants.

Evidence. Up to the late 1960s this perception was an accurate perception of many police agencies. Individuals most often recruited were white men. Depending on the city and the point in police history examined, it was not unusual for only certain ethnic groups to be recruited, such as early New York City and its largely Irish police population. In recent years, because of the civil rights movement, the Equal Employment Opportunity Commission, and affirmative action, recruiting of minorities for police agencies has become mandatory. Many police agencies are under court order to hire officers from minority groups in an effort to counteract the discriminatory hiring practices that continued into the late 1970s. Hiring criteria thought to be discriminatory has been examined by the courts, and criteria found to be discriminatory revised. Therefore, this perception should no longer exist.

Yet, the misperceptions continue. One reason is primarily because the number of minority group members in policing remains low; however, it is not necessarily because of discrimination in hiring. Many police agencies have a low number of minority group members, or are not meeting mandatory hiring "quotas" because qualified members of minority groups do not appear interested in law enforcement jobs because of the growing availability of better-paying and safer employment opportunities outside policing. As a result, the minority candidate pool is getting smaller. In addition, because of the mandatory hiring requirements, the competition between police agencies for police recruits, in general, let alone from minority groups, is fierce (Clark, 1998).

Granted, discrimination still exists and the demand for qualified minority group members continues. However, it seems that the demand may be greater than the supply. This makes it more difficult for departments to hire large numbers of minority group members. Thus, a police agency that does not have its quota of minority officers does not necessarily mean that it is discriminating against them, although that is how the community perceives the situation. It may simply mean that recruitment of individuals who meet community standards for police officers has been difficult.

Promotion

Perception. Police agencies do not attempt to promote officers who are minority group members.

Evidence. Civil service requirements, a growing condition for promotion among municipal police agencies, involves the taking of examinations and certain periods of service at each promoted level. Examinations are given only when there are openings; openings occur only when funding allows for the creation of new positions, or when retirements, resignations, or other promotions occur. Therefore, opportunities for promotion may be limited. When the opportunity does arise, it is up to the individual officer to prepare for and take the examination. If minority officers fail to do so, it is legally difficult for the police agency to promote them.

One of the biggest problems with the promotion of minority officers emerges from the lack of numbers. When there is only a small minority population within the agency, it is difficult for the agency to promote officers from minority groups. Therefore, it is not necessarily a question of the police agency failing to promote so much as the fact that there are very small numbers to promote. However, when there are qualified officers from minority groups available for promotion, they appear to be gaining promotions, especially to police chief. During the 1990s many police agencies particularly the larger urban agencies (e.g., Chicago, Los Angeles, Philadelphia, and Atlanta), hired or promoted minority group members to the position of police chief. Although the lack of numbers may be a legitimate excuse for some agencies, it does not apply to all. In some instances, several departments have come under fire for promotional processes that some

(Jump Start reprinted by permission of United Feature Syndicate, Inc.)

claim are discriminatory against minority group members (This discussion is continued in the next chapter.)

In sum, there are a variety of citizen perceptions about how the police operate that are not supported by evidence. Yet, the perceptions persist. One reason for this may be found in the portrayal of the police by the media.

MEDIA, POLICE, AND THE COMMUNITY

One of the most fascinating aspects of PCI is citizens' development of perceptions of police through the media. Both print and broadcast media provide stories detailing police actions every day. Often these are simplistic or incomplete explanations highlighting either a "crime-fighting" situation or alleged police misconduct. Seldom do the media promote the positive or less glamorous police action such as assisting a motorist, the solving of a residence burglary, or the arrest of a shoplifter. The result is that the public receives only a partial or unfair account of events. Despite the argument that the media has a right to information and a responsibility to report it to the public, a major impetus for the media is money. In most cases, the public is more willing to pay to read, see, or hear the negative aspects of policing. Unfortunately, the result is an unbalanced, uninformed perception of police behavior.

■ CASE IN POINT

It was the afternoon shift, approximately 4:30 P.M., when two relatively young and industrious officers stopped to investigate a gathering of black men at a location known for drugs and prostitution. During the course of their investigation, one of the individuals, a sixteen-year-old youth, was found to be in the possession of drugs. The officers proceeded to effect an arrest. The youth, rather big for his age, resisted and a struggle ensued during which the youth was able to get one of the officers' weapons. The second officer was forced to shoot the youth to protect both his partner and bystanders. Then, someone from the gathering crowd fired a shot and struck one of the officers. When the dust settled, there was one injured officer and a dead sixteen year old. The media, beginning that evening and continuing for the next few weeks, created the perception that two white police officers shot and killed an innocent black youth. Although the police agency, district attorney's office, and a grand jury declared that the shooting was "justifiable and according to police guidelines," many members of the black community viewed all white police officers with extreme suspicion and caution. Needless to say, community relations were rather strained for several weeks. The majority of the problem can be placed on the media's reporting of the incident.

Although the media play an important part in the creation and sustaining of misperceptions, policing itself must accept some blame as well. It has long been the nature of policing to be secretive or closed to public scrutiny. The existence of the police subculture and "code of silence" have been roadblocks to public understanding of how and why the police operate as they do. With the exception of those individuals who work for a police agency, are related to employees of police departments, or who have studied law enforcement in school, the average individual obtains a limited education about police matters from the media. Often, information provided by the media is limited to what the police have given them or will allow them to share. This secrecy only heightens curiosity and feeds perceptions. Therefore, if the police want to be better received by the community, it is necessary for police agencies to be more open and to help educate the public about the realities of policing. This is exactly what some departments have begun to do, many through the use of a citizens' police academy.

■ CASE IN POINT

The Austin, Texas, Police Department offers a citizens' police academy, a twenty-five-hour program designed to give the public a realistic view of policing. Instruction includes lectures, demonstrations, tours, ride-alongs, and hands-on practice. The topics covered include training, communications, investigations, and patrol. Attendees are a cross section of the community and include men and women of a broad range of ages, races, ethnicities, and occupations. This program also increases the rapport of the public with the police. Its positive results have encouraged the continuance of its use and have motivated other agencies to follow suit.

Because the nature of policing (authority, discretion, and so on) adds to the misperceptions, one should not overlook the police role itself. Policing has an extremely broad, complex, and ambiguous role in our society. How citizens react to this role plays a major part in PCR. This point is best supported by James Q. Wilson (1972), who attributes many of the problems between police and the community to the "police function" rather than to how police actually behave. According to Wilson, the "police function" is authoritarian, and many people resent authority. Therefore, because the police function projects authority, the police are just naturally resented. Thus, perceptions are created and accepted simply because of the police function and not because of what the police have done or do. Basically, it is what the police are asked to do and not what is done that chiefly leads to the problems and misperceptions. Yet, police function cannot be changed without completely overhauling policing as it currently exists. Ultimately, efforts must be made by police agencies to try to improve community relations.

Citizens learn about policing in their own academy class. (Courtesy of the Scottsdale, Arizona, Police Department)

THE POLICE–COMMUNITY RELATIONS UNIT

As restructuring the police function is extremely difficult, it is necessary for police agencies to find ways to create better relations. The citizens' police academies are a good start, but not every police agency can implement such a program. In past years, the alternative has been the creation of special units designed to focus on building good community relations. These units, often referred to as PCR units, are responsible for the creation of programs that develop cooperative efforts between the police and their community. Examples of such efforts include neighborhood watch programs, which encourage citizens and police officers to work together to try to prevent crime and various other problems within specific areas, or ride-along programs, which offer citizens the opportunity to spend an eight-hour shift with a police officer. Other programs emphasize relations with youths, such as the Officer Friendly school liaison program, in which an officer is assigned to a specific school, and the officer visits classes, talks with students, and eats lunch with them once a week. To date, one of the more successful youth programs, with respect to creating a more positive interaction between police and juveniles, is D.A.R.E. (Drug Awareness Reduction Education), a program in which police officers spend several weeks with students teaching them about the problems with drugs. This type of interaction appears to lessen the fear and animosity of the children toward police officers and often builds strong, caring relationships.

To encourage citizen interaction, one police agency displays its traffic unit at a public safety event. (Courtesy of the Scottsdale, Arizona, Police Department)

■ CASE IN POINT

This author once had the opportunity to attend a D.A.R.E. graduation ceremony for a fifth-grade class. Each child received a diploma and T-shirt from his or her police officer–teacher. As the children received their items, they shook hands with the officer and thanked him. One young man surprised everyone, especially the officer, when after receiving his diploma and shirt he wrapped his arms around the officer's waist and hugged him. It was obvious to everyone in the room that the youth felt comfortable enough to display his affection for the officer.

These programs and others similar to them are moderately successful efforts by the police agency to enhance and create better community relations. Yet, it is possible that the most effective and best tool for the agency in creating good relations is the officers themselves. Any people-oriented organization is only as good as its employees. If a police agency is going to support and strive for good community relations, its officers must be of the quality and character that promote the positive image the agency desires. This means recruiting and training officers so that their actions will positively reflect the image the department wants projected. Another action is the changing of the traditional police philosophy from one that limits citizen input to one that encourages citizen involvement. One way that police agencies are improving in this area is through **community-oriented policing.**

● COMMUNITY-ORIENTED POLICING

Kelling (1988) suggested that a "quiet revolution" reshaping policing in America was underway (p. 1). The revolution to which he referred was the change from a "traditional" police style to "community" policing. That revolution has taken a strong hold and is far from being quiet any longer (Dantzker, 1999). Undoubtedly, community policing is one of the most prolific concepts currently being employed in modern policing. Often referred to by a myriad of names, such as neighborhood policing, alternative policing, community problem-oriented policing, and the most regularly used name, community-oriented policing (COP), this concept has been fueled by the need for police to "rethink and restructure" their role in society (Rosenbaum, 1998). In particular, citizen dissatisfaction in the quality of interaction with police officers and concern about crime has prompted the police to explore new alternatives. COP has become that alternative, at least for now.

In the 1970s it was team policing, in the 1980s it was patrol decentralization, and the 1990s introduced COP. Team policing and patrol decentralization attempted to bring policing and the community closer together by providing community sectors where a variety of police services were available or by having the police officer live in the officer's patrol area. Both programs had a limited impact on community relations because they failed to seek assistance and input from an important element of the community, the citizens themselves (Goldstein, 1990; Hartman, 1988; Trojanowicz & Bucqueroux, 1994). Although COP was developed to fulfill the same goals, it is also hoped that it will take matters one step further—that is, solve the underlying problem leading to the call for the police so that additional calls will not be required. However, the problem is no longer expected to be solved by the police alone, but in conjunction with community members.

In recognizing and encouraging the need for change, Congress passed the Violent Crime Control and Law Enforcement Act of 1994. This act lead to the creation of Community-Oriented Policing Services (COPS), the office of which has overseen the distribution of more than $8 billion allocated to encourage and support the adaptation of COP. In particular, this office oversees grants to police agencies that have agreed to use the money to hire additional police officers with COP as the goal.

■ CASE IN POINT

In 1996 the Knoxville, Tennessee, Police Department had four of its thirty-three officers in a July graduation class funded through COPS; the Los Angeles Police Department increased its rank and file to more than 9000 officers when a June graduation class of eighty-six, all funded by COPS, joined its ranks; and seventeen of forty-eight Minneapolis, Minnesota, police officers graduated in June thanks to COPS funding. In 1997 COPS gave grants to the Delaware cities of Wilmington, Dover, and Georgetown to assist in their community-policing efforts; and Grand Forks, North Dakota, received $315,000 to hire three new police officers. In 1998 a new sheriff's substation in Jefferson County, Missouri, was established through a $1.9 million COPS grant. The substation will house eight officers serving a fifty-square-mile area; and Fairfield, Ohio, began receiving grant allocations to help offset the cost of hiring five new police officers to participate in COP. Overall, the goal of the federal funding was to assist in the hiring of 100,000 police officers throughout the country through the year 2000.

The stance taken here is that the popularity of COP is not because of what it might accomplish but because of the funding available. This position is a result of the manner in which COP is being implemented. More specifically, the concept of COP seems to differ from the application of COP. COP was first offered as a concept based on complete philosophical changes to how police agencies would approach providing police services (see Carter & Radelet, 1999; Kappeler, Gaines, & Buqueroux, 1998; Oliver, 1998; Trojanowicz & Bucqueroux, 1990, 1994; Trojanowicz & Carter, 1988). The success of this concept depended on three major characteristics.

1. *Involvement of the citizen.* Historically, citizens have been involved in policing in one way or another. Whether as volunteer or vigilante, some citizens have always wanted to be involved in law enforcement. In recent years, policing has, however, attempted to limit citizen involvement. COP requires citizen input and interaction. For example, during its preliminary phases of implementing COP in five experimental districts, the Chicago Police Department called on several community groups to assist in the program's development and implementation as well as to use some community activists as in-service training facilitators for police officers.

2. *Officer participation.* The participation of each officer in promoting the tenets of community policing is mandatory. The success or failure of such an effort is heavily determined by the officers' willingness to forgo traditional thought and accept sharing problem solving with the private citizen. If officers cannot accept the community-policing philosophy, the program cannot succeed.

3. *Reduction of fear and crime deterrence.* One of the biggest concerns or complaints about police agencies is their inability to control or deter crime. A high crime rate induces fear in many citizens. Citizens are believed to be more receptive to the police when crime is limited, and fear is at a "normal" level (Trojanowicz et al., 1998; *Understanding Community Policing*, 1994). To reduce crime it is important to examine what causes it. Citizens are excellent sources of information when attempting to determine why crime occurs. Using their input can lead to deterring crime and cause a reduction of fear. Community policing strives to reduce fear and improve crime prevention or deterrence by eliminating problems that lead to crime, such as abandoned buildings and poorly lit streets.

In general, COP was believed to be a complete conceptual and philosophical change required by the police agency and its officers toward how to provide services and incorporate citizen participation.

Community policing is both a philosophy and an organizational strategy that promotes a new partnership between people and their police. According to Trojanowicz and Bucqueroux (1994), "It is based on the premise that both the police and the community must work together to identify, prioritize, and solve contemporary problems such as crime, drugs, fear of crime, social and physical disorder, and overall neighborhood decay, with the goal of improving the overall quality of life in the area" (p. 2).

From an academic view, it is clear what originally was meant by COP. What the COP concept should mean to policing was presented quite formidably.

■ CASE IN POINT

According to Michael Heidingsfield, police chief emeritus, Scottsdale, Arizona, Police Department, community policing is

a philosophy shared by police officers who appreciate that they alone cannot ensure the safety of a community and must turn to the wisdom, resources, and support of the citizenry as a partner in that effort;

an attitude that each officer brings to work every day in which there is willingness to look beyond the situation at hand for all possible solutions and to treat each and every human being as we would wish to be treated;

a mindset that says when you are off duty, your concern for your beat and its residents and its issues aren't simply dismissed, but instead are remembered, pondered and brainstormed;

not programs but is, instead, a commitment by the community to support and understand its police department and a recognition by the department that the priorities and concerns of the citizenry we find, for the most part, allies and not enemies; and police recognition that prevention, interdiction, investment, treatment, and enforcement are equally important. (Heidingsfield, 1997, p. 12).

It is apparent that Chief Heidingsfield accepted and believed in the concept of COP as first introduced in the late 1980s and refined by Trojanowicz and others. However, it appears that more police agencies have ignored COP as a concept and embraced it as an approach.

■ CASE IN POINT

During the revision of this text, this author was assisting Macro International and the Police Executive Research Forum in a national study of COP implementation in the United States. More than 1600 police agencies responded to an in-depth questionnaire about their involvement with COP. All of the responding agencies claimed to be practicing COP. However, early data analyses found that many of these agencies had implemented programs, such as school liaison, drug awareness, or store-front substations, that they referred to as COP. In reality, what many of these agencies have done is create special programs under the guise of COP.

Although programs erroneously labeled as COP should not be considered completely negative, they do seem to contradict or shortcut the main concept. Instead of adopting COP as a philosophy or complete concept, it is being applied programmatically. This has lead to the creation of what is perceived as a more modern and legitimate description and employment of COP. As an applied approach, COP focuses on improving the quality of life in a community that requires police organizational restructuring, empowers officers, and improves police–nonpolice interactions because information and responsibilities are shared instead of delegated.

Regardless of the manner in which it is implemented, COP has become a popular approach to improving police services and police interactions. Complete acceptance and praise of this current commitment to policing must be held in check because the evaluation research is still relatively new and limited. However, the research that is available tends to be supportive of COP, regardless of the approach.

■ CASE IN POINT

In a report on COP researchers found that Indianapolis, Indiana, police officers were very proactive; officer-initiated encounters with the public outnumbered dispatcher-initiated encounters. During a typical shift, it was found that an officer spent approximately 71 percent of his or her time in self-directed activities. It was also found that police and citizens showed high levels of cooperation during encounters, many of which revolved around needing police assistance rather than enforcement of the law. Finally, researchers did find some differences in perceptions about COP by both officers and citizens, with officers being somewhat ambivalent about their roles and citizens not seeing the severity of problems as high in some cases as the police did (Mastrofski, Parks, Reiss, & Worden, 1998). [Author's note: For one of the better comprehensive looks at COP currently available, see Brodeur, 1998.]

A sign of the 1990s and beyond. (Courtesy of the Scottsdale, Arizona, Police Department)

WHAT DO YOU THINK?

Community Policing: Fix or Fad?

Today's police departments are trying to improve community relations as well as address a variety of societal problems with a concept referred to as community policing. Unlike the longtime traditional practice of policing, in which officers respond to a problem, solve it, and move on, community policing requires the officer to do whatever can be done to make sure that the problem doesn't recur. Unlike traditional practices that have kept the citizen out of the problem-solving loop, community policing invites and uses citizen input. Furthermore, community policing supports officer–citizen cooperation and communication on a more personal, congenial level than simply responding to a call for service. However, this is not the first time police departments have attempted to change their approach to policing. In past years such attempts have included patrol saturation, team policing, and directed patrol, none of which appeared to have been very successful nor did they last very long.

1. Adopting a community-policing approach requires a change in philosophy for many police departments and their officers; what might some of the concerns and problems be?
2. Why might some police officers not support a community-policing philosophy?
3. How do you think citizens view community policing?
4. Would the adoption of community policing require a change in how officers are recruited? trained?
5. What are some problems/advantages associated with the concept of community policing?
6. Do you think community policing is just another fad or will it last? Why?

Although a considerable amount of information is now available about COP, there is still much to learn. One thing does appear to be clear, COP can and does assist in improving the interaction between police and community members. (Internet information is available from COPS at www.usdoj.gov/cops or the Community Policing Consortium at www.community.policing.)

SUMMARY

One of the most persistent and perplexing problems for policing is its relations with the community. Part of the problem is caused by the perceptions citizens form about the police from isolated incidents. Therefore, it is pertinent that police departments provide the most positive impression possible. Although national polls have indicated that the police receive fairly positive support, it does not necessarily translate into good police–community interactions, especially among specific segments of the community such as minority groups, homosexuals, juveniles, elderly people, and women. A major portion of the problems arise from perceptions the community has about police street behavior such as brutality, harassment, and corruption and administrative practices such as recruitment, promotion, and handling of citizen complaints. Although there is little evidence to support many of the perceptions, they still exist. Both the media and the police feed the perceptions. As for the police, this is changing. The creation of community relations units and special programs that enlighten the community about the realities of policing are assisting in eliminating problems. The most recent attempt to improve relations is through COP, in which citizens and officers work together to solve the community's problems and improve their quality of life.

DO YOU KNOW . . .

1. Why perceptions of police behavior are more often negative than positive?
2. What specific segments of your community have poor relations with the police? Why?
3. Whether lack of evidence of police misconduct will ever override misperceptions of police behavior?
4. If your local police agency has a PCR unit? If so, what is its primary purpose?
5. Whether local police agencies in your area are practicing COP or problem-oriented policing?
6. What police agencies can do to improve the image or perception of policing?

REFERENCES

Brann, J. (1998). Police department invests its time in youths. *Community Links, 1,* 3.

Brodeur, J.P. (Ed.). (1998). *How to recognize good policing: Problems and issues.* Thousand Oaks, CA: Sage Publishing.

Carter, D.L. & Radelet, L.A. (1999). *The police and the community* (6th ed.). Upper Saddle River, NJ: Prentice Hall.

Clark, J.R. (1998, April 30). Is anybody out there? *Law Enforcement News, 24,* 1, 6.

Cox, S. M., & Fitzgerald, J.D. (1983). *Police in community relations.* Dubuque, IA: W.C. Brown Company.

Dantzker, M.L. (1999). *Police organization and management: Yesterday, today, and to-morrow.* Newton, MA: Butterworth-Heinemann.

Dantzker, M.L., & Ali-Jackson, N. (1998). Examining students' perceptions of policing and the affect of completing a police-related course. In M.L. Dantzker, A. Lurigio, M. Seng, & J. Sinacore (Eds.), *Practical applications for criminal justice statistics* (pp. 195–205). Newton, MA: Butterworth-Heinemann.

Dantzker, M.L. & Waters, J.E. (1999). Examining students' perceptions of policing: A pre- and post-comparison between students in criminal justice and noncriminal justice courses. In M.L. Dantzker (Ed.), *Readings for research methods in criminology and criminal justice* (pp. 27–35). Newton, MA: Butterworth-Heinemann.

Decker, S.H. (1985). The police and the public: Perceptions and policy recommendations. In R.J. Homant & D.B. Kennedy (Eds.), *Police and law enforcement* (vol. 3, pp. 89–105). New York: AMS Press.

Ford, M.C. & Williams, L. (1999). Human/cultural diversity training for justice personnel. In M.L. Dantzker (Ed.), *Readings for research methods in criminology and criminal justice* (pp. 37–60). Newton, MA: Butterworth-Heinemann.

Fridell, L. & Pate, A.M. (1997). Use of force: A matter of control. In M.L. Dantzker (Ed.), *Contemporary policing: Personnel, issues and trends* (pp. 217–256). Newton, MA: Butterworth-Heinemann.

Garcia, A. (1998). Saving our youths, one at a time. *Community Links, 1,* 4–5.

Goldstein, H. (1990). *Problem-oriented policing.* New York: McGraw-Hill.

Harlow, C.W. (1991). *Female victims of violent crime, 1990.* Washington, D.C.: U.S. Department of Justice.

Hartman, F. (1988, November). *Debating the evolution of American policing.* Washington, D.C.: U.S. Government Printing Office.

Heidingsfield, M.J. (1997, October 31). Dispelling old myths, a chief defines community policing. *Law Enforcement News, 23,* 12.

Johnson, J. (1997, September). Americans' views on crime and law enforcement. *National Institute of Justice Journal,* 9–14.

Kelling, G.L. (1988, June). Police and communities: The quiet revolution. *Perspectives on policing.* National Institute of Justice, Washington, D.C.: U.S. Government Printing Office.

Leader, E. (1998). Teen Line—More than a hotline. *Community Links, 1,* 2–3.

Mastrofski, S.D., Parks, R.B., Reiss, A.J., Jr., & Worden, R.E. (1998). *Policing neighborhoods: A report from Indianapolis.* A National Institute of Justice Research Preview. Washington, D.C.: U.S. Department of Justice.

Mcaneny, L. & Saad, L. (1997). *Honesty and ethics poll: Pharmacists strengthen their position as the most highly rated occupation.* Gallup Poll Archives. (www.gallup.com/poll_archives/1997/default.asp)

Oliver, W.M. (1998). *Community-oriented policing: A systematic approach to policing.* Upper Saddle River, NJ: Prentice Hall.

Police were wrong in rapes, chief says. (1991, February 4). *Los Angeles Times.*

Ringel, C. (1997). *Criminal victimization, 1996: Changes 1995–1996 with trends 1993–1996.* Washington, D.C.: U.S. Department of Justice.

Rosenbaum, D.P. (1998). The changing role of the police: Assessing the current transition to community policing. In J.P. Brodeur (Ed.), *How to recognize good policing: Problems and issues,* (pp. 3–29). Thousand Oaks, CA: Sage Publishing.

Sanders, J. & Caplan, N.M. (1998). Talk of the town: Policing in a multicultural community. *Police, 22,* 54–57.

Sourcebook of criminal justice statistics 1997. (1998) Washington, D.C.: U.S. Government Printing Office. (www.albany.edu/sourcebook)

Trojanowicz, R., & Bucqueroux, B. (1990). *Community policing: A contemporary perspective.* Cincinnati, OH: Anderson Publishing Company.

Trojanowicz, R., & Bucqueroux, B. (1994). *Community policing: How to get started.* Cincinnati, OH: Anderson Publishing Company.

Trojanowicz, R., & Carter, D. (1988). *The philosophy and role of community policing.* Flint, MI: National Neighborhood Foot Patrol Center.

Trojanowicz, R., Kappeler, V.E., Gaines, L.K., & Bucqueroux, B. (1998). *Community policing: A contemporary perspective* (2nd Ed.). Cincinnati, OH: Anderson Publishing Company.

Understanding community policing: A framework for action (1994). Washington D.C.: Community Policing Consortium.

Walker, S. (1999). *Police in America* (3rd ed.). New York: McGraw-Hill.

Wilson, J.Q. (1972). The police in the ghetto. In R. F. Steadman (Ed.), *The police and the community.* Baltimore, MD: John Hopkins University Press.

9 RECRUITMENT: QUALITY OF PERSONNEL

● WHAT ARE POLICEMEN MADE OF?

A policeman is a composition of what all men are, a mingling of saint and sinner, dust and deity. Less than one-half of 1 percent of policemen misfit the uniform.

He, of all men, is at once the most wanted and the most unwanted. He must be such a diplomat that he can settle differences between individuals so that each will think he won.

But, if a policeman is pleasant, he's a flirt; if he's not, he's a grouch. He must be able to start someone breathing, stop bleeding, tie splints, and above all, be sure the victim goes home without a limp—or expect to be sued. He must know every gun, draw on the run, and hit where it doesn't hurt.

He must be able to whip two men twice his size and half his age without damaging his uniform and without being "brutal." If you hit him, and he doesn't react, he's a coward; if he hits you, he's a bully. He must know where all the sin is and not partake. The policeman must chase bum leads to a dead end, stake out ten nights to tag one witness who saw it happen—but refused to remember.

The policeman must be a minister, a social worker, a diplomat, a tough guy, and a gentleman. And, of course, he'll have to be a genius—for he'll have to feed and clothe a family on a policeman's salary.

And, God help him if he is five minutes late for his shift's briefing . . .
—Anonymous

Many important aspects of policing have been identified and discussed to this point. Several are directly relevant to policing from an agency or organizational perspective. This chapter introduces a factor that is extremely relevant to the police organization because of its effect on the majority of aspects previously discussed—personnel.

The reputation of a police agency, how well it provides services, and its relationships with the community all greatly depend on the quality of its personnel.

"The quality of personnel selected for the police service determines the character of police performance and ultimately the quality of police leadership" (*Police Task Force Report,* 1973, p. 320). Public perception of the police is generated by the behavior, attitude, and general characteristics of police officers. For a police agency to sustain a good reputation, it must employ individuals whose actions will stimulate a positive response from the public. This is particularly important when citizens' perceptions are often the result of a one-time or first-time contact with a police officer.

■ CASE IN POINT

You just received your driver's license, and, for the first time, you are out driving by yourself. You are driving to a friend's house when you are stopped by a police officer. Never having had contact with a police officer, you are not sure what to expect. The officer approaches the vehicle and politely advises you that you were speeding and asks if he could please see your license. On examining your license, the officer observes that you just got your license. Rather than issuing you a ticket, the officer advises you to be more careful and lets you go. Your immediate reaction is, "That officer was okay." Conversely, if the officer had issued you a ticket, acted in a rude manner, and told you, "You shouldn't even have a license!," your reaction to or perception of the officer would be negative.

Obviously, it is beneficial to the department to employ individuals who promote a good image for the police agency; assuring itself of having such personnel is an important task. The first step is to attract and recruit individuals who will fulfill the agency's needs.

ATTRACTING PERSONNEL: RECRUITMENT

One of the most important issues affecting quality of personnel in policing is **recruitment.** Over the years policing has become a competitive job market, and in many cases this has forced police agencies to raise starting salaries. For example, in 1997 the Fulton County, Georgia, Police Department raised its starting police pay nearly 16 percent to $26,298, hoping to attract a suitable candidate pool. Also in 1997 the Albuquerque, New Mexico, Police Department increased its starting pay, a move that apparently proved successful for them, providing them with a sufficient candidate pool to be able to fill all positions. The previous year the department had 130 positions to fill and did not come close to filling them all. Although a competitive starting salary is a good beginning, it in itself does not guarantee a police agency the luxury of large, qualified applicant pools. This forces many police agencies to spend more time and money on recruitment than in previous times. They must seek out individuals who want a career in policing rather than just a job. In some instances, police agencies may have to convince individuals that policing is a great career choice, and this is causing some police agencies to work harder than usual to meet hiring needs. Therefore, they are taking advantage of several different arenas.

As a result of the rising level of educational requirements, one of the best arenas for recruitment are college campuses, especially if the college supports a criminal justice-related degree program. In a study by Langworthy, Hughes, and Sanders (1995), approximately 37 percent of the agencies they surveyed had recruitment strategies that targeted college graduates. Recruiting directly on the campus often gives agencies first choice of the more qualified students. It is no longer unusual to see police/law enforcement agencies at college career days or employing their own recruitment tactics, and distance does not seem to be an issue.

■ CASE IN POINT

In 1995 the Dallas, Texas, Police Department sent recruiters to several colleges and universities in the Chicago, Illinois, area. In 1997 the Glendale, Arizona, Police Department traveled all the way to Statesboro, Georgia, to recruit on the campus of Georgia Southern University. Although not traveling quite as far a distance as the other two agencies, in 1999 the Austin, Texas, Police Department recruited on the campus of the University of Texas Pan American, which is about 700 miles south of Austin.

On-site visits can be quite successful, however, they can also be expensive. Therefore, in lieu of recruiters, its common to see fliers posted on bulletin boards from police agencies located throughout the country. Like college campuses, military bases have also been good recruiting sites for police agencies.

Cities with high unemployment usually attract recruiters from other cities' police agencies. When police agencies cannot attract a sufficient candidate pool within their own community, they often seek out communities where jobs are scarce. In the middle to late 1970s, the Houston, Texas, Police Department often

Preparing for a recruitment fair. (Courtesy of the Scottsdale, Arizona, Police Department)

FIGURE 9-1   Internet Sites of Selected Police Agencies: Recruitment

Atlanta, Georgia   www.atlanta.org/career.html
Careers in government, links to minimum requirements, salary information, the police academy and where to apply

Austin, Texas   www.ci.austin.tx.us/police/pdrequir.htm
Brief description but offers necessary information

Berkeley, California   www.ci.berkeley.ca.us/bpd/join.html
Provides information on available positions, the police department, and the city

Dallas, Texas   www.ci.dalls.tx.us/dpd/rcrt.html
Extensive site with many separate links ranging from qualifications to career options

Fort Lauderdale, Florida   www. info.ci.ftlaud.fl.us/police/recruit.html
Recruitment and hiring site lists all available positions and requirements

Honolulu, Hawaii   www.co.honolulu.hi.us/depts/per/jobs/mprjune.htm
Offers all necessary information

Indianapolis, Indiana   www.ci.indianapolis.in.us/ipd/employ.htm
Offers all the minimum information necessary to apply

Los Angeles, California   www.ci.la.ca.us/dept/PER/recruit.htm#age
The personnel department public information service website lists job descriptions, minimum requirements, salary and benefits, testing dates and sites, and a description of the complete police selection process

New York, New York   www.ci.nyc.us/nyclink/html/dcas/html/police.html
Updated regularly, provides all relevant recruitment information, including application requirements, salary, and job descriptions

Tuscon, Arizona   www.ci.tuscon.az.us/police/recruit/recruit.html
Recruitment Web page links all requisite information

recruited as far away as Indiana, Illinois, and Ohio to develop a sufficient applicant pool. The drive was so successful that by the early 1980s the Houston Police Department began limiting recruitment activity to within a five-hundred-mile radius of Houston. A limited candidate pool in the early 1990s has again required agencies like the Houston Police Department to broaden their recruitment efforts.

If all else fails, print advertising is employed on a regular basis for recruitment by police agencies. They frequently advertise not only within their own cities, but also in surrounding cities and throughout the state. It is not unusual to see police agencies advertise in a national paper or trade journal, such as John Jay's *Law Enforcement News* and *Police* magazine, or by advertising in a statewide publication such as the Illinois Fire and Police Recruitment Commission's *Career Search Police Bulletin* or nationally available *Police Career Digest*. One of the newest methods for advertising or recruitment is through the Internet. Hundreds of police agencies now have web pages with links for recruiting (see Figure 9-1).

The ability to recruit on a national basis can obviously assist in increasing the candidate pool for many police agencies. However, a problem, for both potential recruits and currently employed officers, arises with residency requirements. Many agencies require that job candidates be prepared to become residents of the city in which the agency is located or at least live within an acceptable distance.

■ CASE IN POINT

For years the Phoenix, Arizona, Police Department required all of its police applicants to be residents of Arizona at the time of application, which tended to hamper its recruitment efforts. Today, the Phoenix Police Department residency requirement is that new officers have to be residents of the city of Phoenix within twenty-four months of the date of hire. The Fort Worth, Texas, Police Department requires its officers to live within thirty minutes of the designated report-in station, a regulation that must be met within six months of employment. For New York City police officers it is a state law that they must be a resident of the New York City or of Nassau, Westchester, Suffolk, Orange, Rockland, or Putnam Counties.

One may think that residency requirements would not present a problem. However, many police officers do not want to have to live in the city in which they work, and this requirement has resulted in controversy for more than one police agency.

■ CASE IN POINT

Since 1979 the Denver, Colorado, Police Department has required its officers to live within Denver city limits. In May 1991 a vote on a referendum to repeal this rule was defeated. A 1993 rule requiring Minneapolis, Minnesota, police officers to reside within city limits was challenged in 1998 by the Minneapolis Police Federation. A committee of city officials wanted to hold off the police union's effort to repeal the law. In 1994 the Boston, Massachusetts, city council approved a new ordinance that required all Boston police officers hired after July 1, 1994, to live inside city limits. Although officers hired before that date were exempt, they still had to live within 15 miles of the city. Legal battles challenging this rule continue.

Why do residency rules exist? Probably the most common underlying reason for residency rules is the belief that police officers would be more interested in the problems of the city in which they worked if they lived there too. This has become a particularly strong issue in light of community policing and has lead to the development of the Resident Officer Program (ROP), supported by both local and federal dollars. The ROP program offers economic incentives to police officers to live not only within city limits, but in the neighborhoods they police.

■ CASE IN POINT

One of the first ROP programs in the nation began in Elgin, Illinois, in 1991. In this program the city makes available rent-free housing to officers. In exchange for the free rent and utilities (except long-distance phone calls) police officers are expected to be available twenty-four hours a day to their neighbors. Other programs, such as those in Columbia, South Carolina, and Alexandria, Virginia, offer low interest loans to officers to purchase rehabilitated homes, many of which are located in low-income or high-crime areas. The federal government joined the ranks of programs in 1997 when President Clinton announced a plan to offer 50-percent discounts to police officers who would buy federally foreclosed homes located in low-income neighborhoods throughout the country.

Why the controversy? Although having its officers live within city limits would be beneficial to the city, many officers oppose being told where they can live and raise their families. In most instances, officers often find that economically it's better to live outside city limits. Taxes are lower, education is often better, crime rates are lower, and the overall quality of living is perceived to be better. Finally, just being able to have a choice is important to many officers.

Residency requirements have been somewhat controversial at times. The most recent data shows that approximately 50 percent of all municipal police agencies employing 100 or more officers have some type of residency requirement. Of these agencies, 26 percent stipulate that officers must live within the city or county of employment (Reaves & Smith, 1995). Still, requirements such as these have not been quite as controversial as the requirement of being a U.S. citizen. For many years, there was no question about this requirement: no one could become a police officer anywhere in the United States without being a U.S. citizen. However, this requirement has been challenged.

■ CASE IN POINT

In the early 1980s Maritza Vega-Gentry, a Nicaraguan native who had applied to the LAPD was rejected because she had not yet received citizenship status. Through her hard work and determination, Vega-Gentry convinced a California legislator to offer a bill that would allow non-U.S. citizens (who have applied for U.S. status) and alien residents to be considered for police service in California. The bill passed, and Vega-Gentry became the LAPD's first legally recognized noncitizen police officer. For several years, Officer Gentry was a national recruiter for the LAPD. Although there is support for hiring noncitizens, especially individuals from newly arriving ethnic groups, the change will be extremely slow (see *Lengthening the Stride: Employing Peace Officers from Newly Arrived Ethnic Groups*, 1995). California is still the only state that will allow noncitizens who have applied for citizenship to become police officers.

Locating potential candidates is only one of the problems facing police recruitment. In recent years, as a result of civil service and the taking over of recruitment by city personnel departments, the issue of who is to do recruiting has become even more important.

Who should handle recruitment? Who should set the criteria? The obvious answer to these questions is the police agency. As noted by the 1973 Police Task Force, "The police agency should administer its own recruitment program" (p. 312). Yet, many police agencies have lost the ability to control recruitment. Favoritism, patronage, and budget crunches have lead to changes in police recruiting. Civil service has assisted in the elimination of favoritism and patronage by forcing police agencies to follow the specific standards and practices for hiring set by the governing Civil Service Commission. Police executives whose agency is under civil service are no longer allowed any input in who is hired.

The lack of sufficient funding has also forced many police agencies to stop active recruiting. Instead, they must now rely on the city personnel office to do the initial attracting and testing of applicants. Because personnel departments

Officer Maritza Vega-Gentry, the first legally recognized noncitizen police officer. (Courtesy of Maritza Vega-Gentry)

have a variety of city departments to recruit for and limited funds with which to do so, policing needs do not always receive the attention necessary to recruit candidates. In many instances, a notice on a bulletin board outside the personnel office or an advertisement in the local newspaper is the extent of the recruitment effort. This may limit the number of qualified applicants. Those agencies that control and maintain their own recruiters have a tremendous advantage over less fortunate agencies.

Regardless of who does the recruiting, or how it is accomplished, it is a very important step toward establishing good personnel. However, even a strong recruitment effort may fail because the number of individuals who truly want to be police officers may be diminishing.

WHO WANTS TO BE A POLICE OFFICER?

Although whose responsibility it is to recruit remains an issue of debate, who is to be recruited is a greater issue. Historically, police officers have come from the ranks of white, blue-collar men. Although in 1997 police officers were still predominantly white (approximately 85 percent) and male (approximately 87 percent) (Harrington et al., 1998), there has been change, albeit slow. Despite population increases in minority group members, especially Hispanics, and women, the number becoming police officers still lags far behind. The reasons why policing has remained a predominantly white, male occupation for so long are twofold: the traditional image of policing and discrimination.

The traditional image of policing has kept minority group members and women from becoming police officers. This traditional image of policing views it as being representative of the racial majority's governmental structure, which historically has been white, and as being a masculine occupation. Both have kept minorities and women away. Discrimination has reinforced these traditional images. Even with the efforts of civil rights movements, the Equal Employment Opportunity Act (1972), the Crime Control Act (1973), the Local Government Fiscal Assistance Act (1979), and court-mandated hiring guidelines (affirmative action), minorities and women have not made tremendous progress in improving their status in policing (Doerner, 1998; Hale & Wyland, 1993; Harrington et al., 1998; Martin, 1993; Stalans, 1997; Stokes, 1997; Walker & Turner, 1992).

The traditional images and discrimination are not the only two reasons why women and minority group members do not overflow recruit applicant pools. Economics and career goals have had tremendous influence on who becomes a police officer.

For many years, police recruits came from "blue-collar" society in which policing was a family tradition or represented a career path better than that of the officer's parents. Policing was among the better-paying careers. This is no longer true. Today's recruits come from all walks of life and family backgrounds. With respect to salary, policing has not remained competitive with other occupations requiring similar characteristics in recruits (Table 9-1). However, just in a six-year span (1990 to 1996), the mean salary for a police officer had increased by almost

TABLE 9-1

Salary Comparisons

Occupation	Average Yearly Salary ($)
Policing	28,238
Other government	35,300
Finance, insurance, and real estate	44,629
Manufacturing	37,165
Communication	50,716
Wholesale trade	39,256

Sources: Statistical Abstract of the United States, 1998, and the Sourcebook of Criminal Justice Statistics, 1997.

$10,000 (from $18,910 to $28,238). Despite the increasing salary, many women and minority group members who are qualified to become municipal, county, or state police officers are foregoing such a career for positions in federal law enforcement, in which women make up slightly more than 14 percent and minority group members 28 percent of officers with arrest and firearms authority (Reaves, 1997), or for better-paying, higher-status, safer employment in other fields (Stalans, 1997; Stotland & Berberich, 1979).

Perhaps another factor that has influenced women and minority group members to avoid policing is the educational issue. For many years a high school education was sufficient for the police applicant, and is still the minimum requirement for about 80 percent of all municipal police agencies. Today, however, with more individuals receiving college degrees, it has been more difficult to persuade the better-educated woman, African American, or Hispanic to choose a police career when there are so many other employment opportunities for these individuals. The rationale behind this is that college-educated individuals may consider themselves overqualified for a career that only requires a high school education. Whether educational requirements are making a difference in recruitment of women and minority group members is still to be seen. However, it may already be benefiting at least one municipal police agency.

■ CASE IN POINT

In November 1997 in Chicago, Illinois, it was announced that the June police officers' entrance exam resulted in one of the most diverse and highly qualified groups from which the city has ever had to choose. What made this particularly important was that this exam was the first one given under newly established educational requirements (minimum of two years of college) and a new age minimum of twenty-three. In previous years white men had dominated the highly qualified group; however, among the 9030 individuals who took the June exam, 52 percent of those rated as "well qualified" were minority group members (32 percent were African American and 16 percent were Latino). Women constituted 27 percent of the "well-qualified" group. The Chicago Police Department hoped to be able to fill 2000 to 3000 vacancies from this group.

Our society is constantly changing. Policing must keep up with the changes. It must also be represented by qualified individuals, a task that has been difficult in years past (Dantzker, 1999; Doerner, 1997). Finding interested and qualified applicants has been a problem, but selecting the right individuals can be even more difficult.

SELECTION CRITERIA

Simply finding police applicants is not enough. Determining whether they are qualified and will represent the police agency in a positive manner is the key. According to Pugh (1986), the good police officer has, "common sense, mature judgment and reacts quickly and effectively to problem situations" (p. 5). Failure to implement stringent selection criteria could lead to problems.

■ CASE IN POINT

In the late 1980s the Washington, D.C., Metropolitan Police Department was forced into hiring hundreds of officers after Congress voted to withhold millions of dollars for 1989 and 1990 until approximately 1800 new officers were hired. Because the number of officers to be hired was staggering for such a short period and the candidate pools were not coming close, the department eased its hiring standards, which meant that about 1000 people were taking the entry exam every month. Eventually the department hired about one of four candidates (the national average is about one of ten). The results were disastrous. Drug dealers and other criminal types as well as those certainly unqualified for the position for various other reasons became police officers. Large numbers of these police officers ended up being arrested for everything from shoplifting to murder, and disciplinary problems doubled (Harriston & Flaherty, 1994). In more recent years the department has been able to weed out many of the individuals it should never have hired; unfortunately these unqualified officers often were only singled out because they got into trouble. For example, in March 1997 two officers hired in the 1989–1990 blitz were arrested on federal charges of conspiring to sell cocaine. Another police agency that suffered serious problems as a result of poor screening and selection of police officers was the New Orleans, Louisiana, Police Department, which like Washington, D.C., saw a rash of criminal activity—from selling drugs to murder—among its police force. The result was a complete overhaul of the selection process ("Becoming a New Orleans Cop Is about to Get Harder," 1996).

The question here is: How does a police agency make sure that it has selected a qualified individual? It is extremely difficult for a police agency to be 100 percent sure it has hired the right individual. Most agencies employ several criteria and methods to ensure as positive a selection as possible. These criteria can include physical factors such as height, weight, age, vision, and being a non-smoker. Selection procedures may include written examinations, oral interviews, medical examinations, psychological tests, physical agility tests, and background investigations.

■ CASE IN POINT

The selection process for the Nashville, Tennessee, Metropolitan Police Department requires applicants to pass a physical ability test, written service exam, polygraph test, background investigation, medical exam, and oral police board. Individuals who pass every exam are eligible for hire and are placed on an appointment list. (For more information, the Nashville Police Department can be accessed through the Internet at www.nashville.org/police_dept.html.) Want to be an Austin, Texas, police officer? The first phase includes an initial screening interview; a reading, comprehension, and vocabulary test; a writing proficiency test; a weapons compatibility test; and a personnel behavioral assessment analysis. If successful on all the preceding, candidates must provide an applicant history statement and then must still pass the following additional criteria: vehicle compatibility test, mini medical examination, physical ability test, written psychological test, background investigation, polygraph, oral interview, and a full medical exam. (The Austin Police Department is located at www.ci.austin.tx.us/police/pdrequir.htm.) Police candidates for the Scottsdale, Arizona, Police Department must pass a series of written examinations (multiple choice, spelling, writing, and aptitude), a physical fitness assessment, an oral board interview, polygraph, psychological exam, background investigation, physical exam, and substance abuse screening.

Despite the similarities in the selection criteria and methods of some police agencies, not all agencies have the same requirements. However, there is some commonality in recruitment criteria.

Education

Educational requirements for recruits are probably one of the most debated and longstanding (since around 1910) recruitment issues (see Langworthy, Hughes, & Sanders, 1995; Shernock & Dantzker, 1997). The majority of police agencies have certain educational requirement for its recruits. Current criteria range from a high school diploma to a college degree. Despite recommendations by a national commission that by 1982 all police departments should have required all applicants to possess at least a bachelor's degree, by 1993, 86 percent of all police agencies still only required a high school diploma, and only about 3 percent required any type of degree (Reaves, 1996; Reaves & Smith, 1995). However, higher levels of education appear to be gaining in popularity (Carter & Sapp, 1990; Dantzker, 1993; Shernock & Dantzker, 1997). Advocates of higher educational requirements argue that the complexity of the job, human nature, and the legal system demand a better-educated recruit than individuals with only a high school education (Carter & Sapp, 1990; Carter, Sapp, & Stephens, 1988; Dantzker, 1993). Opponents of higher education claim that it limits the number of applicants and is discriminatory against minorities (see Langworthy, Hughes, & Sanders, 1995; Shernock & Dantzker, 1997). Both sides continue to have trouble gaining support simply because there is not enough empirical data to support either side. Yet, the current trend appears to support raising educational requirements.

Surprisingly, although many police agencies are not officially changing their educational requirements for recruits, many are either hiring those with degrees or providing incentives to officers to obtain their degrees.

■ CASE IN POINT

The Boston, Massachusetts, Police Department provides an annual incentive depending on the level of degree held: $1000 for an associate's degree, $2000 for a bachelor's degree, and $3000 for a master's degree. The Nashville Metropolitan Police Department offers college incentive pay of 6 percent for a bachelor's degree and 3 percent for an associate's degree. The Dallas, Texas, Police Department not only offers monthly incentive pay for earning college credit and a degree, but also offers reimbursement for college tuition (up to 70 percent).

The reality is that despite not officially raising educational requirements, many police agencies are looking to hire individuals with a college education and encourage those already employed to pursue their degrees.

■ CASE IN POINT

In 1993 the Chicago, Illinois, Police Department, the nation's second largest municipal police department, changed its hiring policy (effective in 1997) to require new recruits to have a minimum of two years of college. Shortly after the Chicago Police Department announced this change in policy, a suburban police department in Palatine, Illinois, announced that police candidates would need a four-year degree. Following the requirement set by the Wilmette, Illinois, Police Department, this became only the second police department in Cook County, Illinois, which includes Chicago plus 115 other police departments, to raise its educational requirement for recruits to a bachelor's degree. The Tulsa, Oklahoma, Police Department jumped on the bandwagon when it announced that, effective January 1998, all recruits would have to possess a four-year college degree. However, unlike the drastic change implemented in Chicago, the previous requirement in Tulsa had been a minimum of 108 credit hours.

Physical Requirements

Many police agencies have certain physical requirements applicants must meet. Common requirements include a minimum age of twenty-one, weight proportionate to height, and correctable vision no worse than 20/100. These requirements have become generally acceptable. An area that continues to cause controversy is physical agility testing. A standard criterion of many police agencies is the ability of the applicant to complete successfully several physical exercises, which can include negotiating an obstacle course; running for time; dragging a weighted dummy; and doing a specific number of pull-ups, pushups, and sit-ups. The controversy is whether these exercises are truly job related and whether they are discriminatory against women and physically smaller men, such as some Asians. Critics agree that all applicants, regardless of gender, race, or ethnicity, must meet certain physical standards, but they argue that these standards should be based on what an average person can physically do, not the average man. Furthermore, the standards should be job related. For example, in 1996 the Milwaukee, Wisconsin, Police Department—under pressure from the Department of Justice—had to reexamine its hiring procedures, particularly the written and physical agility tests, which were said to be discriminatory and illegal because they were not "job related," a standard first upheld by the Court in 1971.

■ CASE IN POINT

The U.S. Supreme Court addressed the issue of job-related physical agility standards in *Griggs* v. *Duke Power Company* (1971). The Court advised that to eliminate discrimination employers need to study the job relatedness of all hiring and promotional requirements so that these requirements would measure the person's ability for the job and not simply the person in abstract.

As a result of cases such as *Griggs,* many police agencies have been forced to reevaluate their physical requirements to meet affirmative action guidelines and court-ordered hiring quotas as well as address the issue of task-related physical requirements. Today it is becoming more common for departments to employ

WHAT DO YOU THINK?

A Degree or No Degree? That Is the Question.

For almost eighty years the need for police officers to have college degrees has been debated. Despite the support by well-known police leaders and several national commissions, full support of such an idea as a requirement has yet to be obtained. The burning question is: Why is there a lack of support? Although several plausible answers have been offered, the answer that seems to make the most sense is that there is lack of evidence to support claims that an individual with a college degree would be a better police officer than a person with only a high school education. Some studies have shown that the college-educated officer does better in the academy, is more successful in promotions, and receives less citizen complaints than the non-college-educated officer. However, other studies claim that college-educated officers are more insubordinate (causing more problems), do not respond any differently in the field, and leave the police department with greater frequency. Yet, isn't a college education supposed to improve communication skills (oral and verbal); decision-making, critical-thinking, and problem-solving skills; understanding of societal problems; and maturity level of an individual? If so, aren't these the type of skills we would want a police officer to possess?

1. Why isn't a college-degree requirement for a police recruit more common than it is?
2. In thinking about the various assignments police officers receive, particularly rookie patrol officers, would a college degree be useful/beneficial in fulfilling their assignments? Why or why not?
3. What value, if any, do you see in requiring a college degree for a police officer? Problems?
4. Even if recruits are not required to have a college degree, should a degree be required for promotions?
5. If a college degree did become a standard requirement for police officers, should a specific major or area (e.g., criminal justice) be required?

"job-related" physical agility tests and to have separate standards for men and women.

CASE IN POINT

The physical ability test for Los Angeles Police Department applicants consists of tests for balance, agility, strength, and endurance. To test balance, the candidate must be able to maintain his or her balance for thirty seconds on a seesaw–style, moving platform. Agility is tested by counting the number of times a person can move from one side of a line to the other in ten seconds. To test strength, the person has five seconds to see how far he or she can pull apart a pair of handles on a cable. Finally, endurance is tested by counting the number of revolutions an applicant can pedal on a stationary bike in two minutes. Taking a different job-related approach, the Austin, Texas, Police Department's physical ability test starts in a patrol car where applicants are given a description of a "felony suspect." When told to go, the candidate starts a 440-yard run that includes an incline climb, obstacle run, barrier climb, ducking under the barrier, fence climb, stair climb, forced door entry, a second obstacle run, window climb, suspect identification, suspect takedown, and suspect move (a 165-pound dummy must be moved 15 feet). Passing the exam requires a candidate to complete all events within three minutes and eight seconds and to have correctly identified the suspect. Neither LAPD nor Austin Police Department differentiate by gender or any other characteristics. Conversely, the physical agility test employed by most of Arizona's police departments is approved by the Arizona Police Officers Standards and Training Board and does differentiate by gender and age. The four exercises are sit-ups, pushups, a 1.5-mile run, and sit and reach. Men between the ages of 20 and 29 must do 38 sit-ups in one minute; women in the same age group must complete 32. Men between the ages of 30 and 39 must complete 24 pushups in one minute; women in the same age group, doing modified pushups, must complete 19. Men 40 to 49 years old must run 1.5 miles within 14 minutes and 29 seconds; women in the same age group must run the distance within 16 minutes and 58 seconds. Finally, men between the ages of 50 and 59 must have a sit-and-reach measure of 13.3 inches; women in the same age group must attain a measure of 16.8 inches.

Ultimately, few could argue that it is not important for a police officer to be in good physical condition and be able to perform job-related physical duties. Job-related fitness tests have become bona fide selection criteria (Dantzker, 1999). However, there are some who ponder why an officer is required to be in good physical shape at the time of application, but then is not required to maintain that fitness (Doerner, 1997, 1998). With medical evidence to support the importance of continued physical fitness, police agencies are beginning to carry over physical fitness standards from initial hiring throughout the officer's career (McNickle, 1996). Making such a requirement mandatory is difficult, but making it voluntary with an incentive is a good place to start.

■ CASE IN POINT

As a result of a policy implemented in 1997, New York state troopers can receive cash bonuses of up to $1000 by meeting or exceeding prescribed fitness standards, including following nutritional guidelines. The fitness test includes pushups, sit-ups, and a 1.5-mile run. Everyone who participates regardless of how well they do is guaranteed $75. Good performances increase the bonuses.

Criminal Record

In the past, many police agencies automatically eliminated potential candidates if they had a criminal record. This generally meant either misdemeanor or felony convictions. In some instances, an overabundance of traffic citations was enough to eliminate the potential recruit. Today a misdemeanor criminal record does not automatically eliminate the individual from the process; in most cases, a felony record will keep an individual from putting on a police uniform. However, as agencies such as those in D.C., New Orleans, and New York have learned, sometimes individuals with criminal records slip through the process. Worse yet are those who are hired that have a strong potential toward criminality.

■ CASE IN POINT

Fulton County, Georgia, police officials began looking for ways to screen out potential sex offenders after a rookie officer was charged with raping a woman he picked up after responding to a disturbance call.

Obviously it is somewhat easy for a police agency to weed out applicants who have an established criminal history. However, not all criminal offenses may be a matter of record, which leaves the door open for someone who has committed a crime has never been arrested or prosecuted. Furthermore, what type of criminal record should automatically eliminate someone from an applicant pool? An answer to this question, and trying to become more cognizant of those who may have strong potential for criminality, are two issues facing police agencies, especially where drugs are concerned.

Drug Use

As with a criminal record, in the earlier years of policing any admitted sale or use of illegal drugs or misuse of a prescribed drug automatically eliminated a prospective police applicant.

■ CASE IN POINT

Several years ago a candidate for a large metropolitan police department (who was already a police officer in another state) was eliminated during the initial screening process because the candidate had admitted to selling $2 worth of marijuana seven years earlier as a college freshman. This department's policy was so stringent at the time that an experienced, highly educated (master's degree) police officer was eliminated as a potential recruit. However, such policies are changing.

Because of its popularity and availability, experimentation with marijuana and other illicit drugs by teenagers and young adults is not uncommon. Eliminating potential candidates who meet every other requirement but who tried marijuana once or twice, or have had some other minor experience with illicit drugs many years earlier (e.g., a one-time experiment with cocaine while in college but has not touched it or any other drug in ten years), has left police agencies with smaller applicant pools. As a result, many police agencies must now consider applicants with minor drug infractions, as long as the infraction it has not occurred within a specified time, such as within the past year. Again, this is one of those areas in which there has been little consistency among police agencies. For example, the Austin, Texas, Police Department, will disqualify a person who has within one year preceding date of application used marijuana or within three years preceding date of application illegally used any controlled substance or dangerous drug other than marijuana. In contrast, the Phoenix, Arizona, Police Department will disqualify anyone who unlawfully used dangerous drugs or narcotics within seven years of application to the department or used marijuana within three years of application. (In both cases, the Phoenix Police Department does have a caveat of "other than for experimentation.") The diversity of this criteria apparently became such an issue in one state (Maryland) that a bill calling to establish minimum standards on prior drug use was introduced and passed into law. Although the bill went into effect June 1, 1997, the state's training commission was given nine months to develop and finalize the minimum standards.

Undoubtedly it is important to have criteria about drug use. However, the size of the candidate pool may impact how strictly the policy is enforced. Of course, potential police recruits should avoid any illegal drug activity, but police agencies also need to realize that it is a sign of the times. President Bill Clinton even admitted to having tried marijuana (except he claimed not to have inhaled).

Testing and Preliminary Screening

It is in the area of testing and screening where police agencies begin to differ considerably. There are a wide number of procedures available to police agencies that assist in the applicant screening process. One of the most popular methods is a written, basic skills examination. This type of examination determines the basic reading and writing levels of the applicant. Other popular tests are written and oral psychological examinations. Additional tools include polygraph, assessment centers, oral review boards, and background investigations. The totality of these items make quite a formidable screening process. Even so, there are no guarantees that the individual selected will adequately represent the agency, or that the testing and screening process will accurately assess a candidate's qualifications (or disqualifications, as the case may be).

■ CASE IN POINT

In 1997 Cleveland, Ohio, police officials began to question the effectiveness of their applicant screening process. The question arose after a police officer pled guilty to charges that she fabricated an incident with a high-ranking city official. The issue of whether the police department's screening process is effective came about after attorneys on both sides of the case acknowledged that a psychological test the officer took before being hired indicated she had some problems, and, yet, the department did not rule her out as a suitable candidate.

Background Investigation

For most police agencies, the capstone of the applicant screening process is the background investigation.

> This inquiry typically results in a half-inch dossier of employment, school, military, and personal history. It is here that the agency really relies on weeding out the unfit, through discovery of behavior patterns in school, work, or personal life that presage failure in a job that requires optimal performance and superior personal characteristics (Bouza, 1990, p. 68).

During this process it is common for a police agency to try to gather all the information it can about the applicant by reviewing criminal history, credit history, and employment, education, and driving records. This investigation often includes interviews of references, employers (past and present), fellow employees, acquaintances, neighbors, friends, and family members. How extensive the background investigation is will depend on resources and how quickly the agency wants or needs to hire people. Again, using the example of the Washington, D.C., Police Department in 1989 and 1990, it is obvious that many problems may have been avoided with aggressive investigations. The results of this process will often seal the applicant's fate, be it positive or negative. If the results are positive, the applicant is usually hired. Once officially hired, the "probationary officer" begins the long climb toward veteran status starting with the training academy.

TRAINING

Obtaining qualified personnel is extremely important to the police agency; however, this alone is not enough. Every individual who is recruited, passes the recruitment process, and is hired by the agency receives specifically oriented training. The quality of the training is as important an element as the individual. Even extremely qualified applicants are often only as good as their training.

The formal training of police officers is a relatively modern idea. Although its beginnings are attributed to August Vollmer (the first police chief of Berkeley, California) who started training police officers in the early 1900s, an attempt to standardize training nationally did not come about until the late 1960s or early 1970s as a result of recommendations made by the National Advisory Commission on Criminal Justice Standards and Goals (Langworthy, Hughes, & Sanders, 1995; Shernock & Dantzker, 1997). Since that time many states have created **Police Officer Standards and Training** (POST) councils or commissions. These bodies establish and regulate training requirements, curriculum, and certification of instructors; issue licenses to those who pass the state exams; and monitor all issues related to certifications and training within the given state.

Although every police officer should receive some level of formal training, not every police agency requires formal training (Reaves, 1996). However, those that do, require their recruits to attend and successfully complete a basic police academy. The basic training phase is viewed as an integral part of establishing quality personnel. Thus, the training offered through the academy must be relevant and pertinent to the tasks the new police officer will face once out on the streets. Through the years the question has been raised as to whether training is appropriate and current (Marion, 1998), making police academies the targets of much criticism.

The major criticism involves the academy curriculum. Historically, police academies have offered such subjects as criminal law and procedures, arrest policies and practices, search and seizure, firearms, first-aid, and departmental policies (see Figure 9-2). These subjects are considered the practical-technical aspects of policing. Those who have criticized this traditional curriculum advise that the practical approach is no longer enough to establish well-qualified officers. The general complaint is that academies fail to address areas such as human relations, communications, cultural issues, and social or behavioral science-related topics. Actually,

FIGURE 9-2 Police Academy Curriculum

560-Hour Basic Peace Officer Course (Texas)

Subject and Course Hours

Introduction and orientation (2)

Fitness and wellness (6)

History of policing (3)

Professionalism and ethics (8)

U.S. and Texas Constitutions and Bill of Rights (10)

Criminal justice system (2)

Code of criminal procedure (16)

Arrest, search, and seizure (24)

Penal code (40)

Traffic (72)

Civil process and liability (12)

Texas alcoholic beverage code (4)

Drugs (8)

Juvenile issues—Texas family code (8)

Stress management for peace officers (8)

Field note taking (4)

Interpersonal communications/report writing (24)

Use of force—law (8)

Use of force concepts (16)

Strategies of defense—mechanics of arrest (40)

Strategies of defense—firearms (40)

Emergency medical assistance (16)

Emergency communications (12)

Problem solving and critical thinking (4)

Professional police driving (32)

Multiculturalism and human relations (12)

Professional policing approaches (6)

Patrol (40)

Victims of crime (8)

Family violence and related assaultive offenses (16)

Recognizing and interacting with persons with mental illness and mental retardation (6)

Crowd management (2)

Hazardous materials awareness (6)

Criminal investigation (45)

Source: http://geocities.com/CapitolHill/Lobby/5715/97index.html.

the most current study available on training curricula found that agencies were decreasing what time they did spend on such things as verbal communication, sensitivity, empathy, and problem solving (Langworthy, Hughes, & Sanders, 1995). The police response to this criticism usually includes a claim of limited training time and lack of qualified individuals who could instruct in these areas. A solution to this problem is requiring police recruits to possess a broad-based liberal arts bachelor's degree. This requirement would eliminate the need for police academies to offer anything but practically oriented material.

An issue related to the curriculum itself is the number of hours required in a basic academy. The average number of hours recruits currently spend in the classroom is 425 (Reaves, 1996). This number tends to differ based on the population size the department serves. The mean number of hours required in a classroom range from 352 (population under 2500) to more than 850 (population of 1 million or more). Does this mean that an officer from a small, rural police agency does not need to know the same thing as one from a large, urban agency? Based on the training averages the answer would appear to be yes. However, there are those who would argue that a police officer, regardless of the size of the agency for which he or she works, or the population size served, should have similar training and knowledge. Yet, even among the largest police agencies in the country, the number of training hours differs.

■ CASE IN POINT

The five largest municipal police agencies in the United States employ from 6600 to almost 40,000 police officers. They serve populations of no less than 1.5 million people. Much of what is required by way of police services is almost identical. Still, the number of basic academy training hours for each agency's police recruits is different, ranging from 700 to 1040. (The order of agencies are arranged according to size, largest to smallest.)

New York (NY)	915 classroom hours
Chicago (IL)	700
Los Angeles (CA)	971
Philadelphia (PA)	716
Houston (TX)	1040

The debate over curriculum and the number of training hours will continue, unless perhaps a national standard is eventually adopted.

Although the academy experience is an extremely important part of the recruit's training and has been the target of criticism, the training function that has received even more criticism is the field training experience, most often referred to as the **Field Training Officer** (FTO) program. The FTO program is considered the reality part of training; it is where recruits finally receive hands-on experience.

The basic format of the FTO program is assigning the newly graduated police recruit with a senior officer for a set period. During this period, the senior officer is charged with relating the academy experience to the streets. This program draws criticism because it often undermines many ideals taught in the academy. Many recruits on the first day of their FTO program are told by their training officer, "Forget everything you were told in the academy, because now you will learn what policing is really about." This tends to confuse the recruit. To make matters worse, reality is often different from the academy experience, in which "textbook" policing is emphasized rather than policing realities, or worse yet, academy instructors tell "war stories" that recruits accept as typical, when in many cases the incidents or situations reported are the exceptions rather than the rule. Furthermore, instructors in the academy may tend to establish the "us versus them" mentality (Marion, 1998) that the FTO has to discourage, especially in agencies in which community policing is employed. For some recruits reality is too much. Although it is unusual, there are times when a rookie officer will quit after only a few weeks "on the streets."

■ CASE IN POINT

Making it through the Houston, Texas, police academy was tough enough and had already begun to create doubts in the mind of rookie officer Duane DeBakery as to whether he would "make it" as a police officer. His first two weeks of field training convinced him he wasn't going to make it, especially when memories from his first day on the streets still bothered him. The first major call for this rookie was a "possible burglary." On arrival the officer and his FTO met a woman who advised that her husband was supposed to be home, but she found the patio door ajar after returning home. The officers went in and discovered that electronic equipment had been stacked by the door. They also discovered the husband's body in a back bedroom. He had been murdered. DeBakey apparently was shaken up simply by the nature of the crime. Having to break the news to the wife didn't help any. Although this officer had been among the top graduates of his academy class, the experience of the streets was more than he felt he or his family could handle. He quit. Six months of training had gone into this officer. As a result of this incident and reactions of other rookies to their first days on the streets, the Houston Police Department started a program aimed at giving trainees a taste of reality early in their training, a once-a-week ride-along program beginning with the second week of the academy (*Houston Chronicle*, September 16, 1990). [Author's note: Although this story is a decade old, it is still one of the best examples this author has come across in his 20 plus years associated with policing and criminal justice.]

Another problem, besides failing to provide an accurate perception of the job to recruits, is the failure of the police agency to promote continued training and updating of training officers. It is fairly common for the training officer to be a veteran of many years whose only training was his or her academy and FTO experience many years earlier. Often, laws, policies, procedures, and techniques change without the training officer being aware of them or schooled in their application. This is primarily the result of a lack of funds for continued training and a lack of concern for continuous training by the administration. Therefore, the recruit has been schooled in all the latest versions of law and policies, whereas the FTO is still practicing what was taught during the officer's own trainee days. This causes conflict between the two officers. It also creates conflict within the recruit; a decision must be made as to which method to follow. If the academy training is followed, the recruit faces the prospect of being downgraded by the training officer.

Conversely, if the academy is ignored and the officer is processed through the training program by learning to do things the FTO's outdated way there is a concern for problems with fellow officers, supervisors, or even the courts. This is one dilemma that policing needs to eliminate quickly, or the prospect of qualified representation will remain questionable. One solution is to provide FTOs with monthly updates on policy, law, or training news. A yearly two-day refresher course would also be beneficial. Finally, offering FTOs training on how to be "trainers" might also alleviate problems.

In all, training is an extremely important aspect of providing qualified personnel. Areas of concern include the academy curriculum and FTO programs. Obviously, both need to be addressed. Reforms must occur so rookie police officers are well trained. This is particularly true for police agencies adopting a community-policing approach. This in itself demands a different approach to training than that long associated with "traditional" police training. Requiring a college degree, updating curriculum, relating classroom to real-world experience, and keeping FTOs up to date will assist in preparing police officers for action in the field.

WHICH WAY DO I GO?

Making the decision to become a police officer is not always easy. It has generally not been the type of job one considers a "stepping-stone" or "something to keep me busy until something better comes along"; although it appears that for a growing number of college-educated officers, especially those interested in a federal law enforcement job, municipal policing has become a stepping-stone. Making the choice to enter into law enforcement is generally seen as a career decision: "I am here until I retire." With that in mind, the question is, What will I do for the next twenty or thirty years? Although other career choices may offer a more diverse array of career paths, policing does offer a suitably acceptable variety of career paths to follow. The career police officer has four choices: **patrol, management (promotion), specialization,** and **agency movement.** However, it must be recognized that in many police agencies these choices may be limited. Many police officers will remain in the area in which they all must start—patrol.

Patrol

To some police officers, the thought of spending twenty years as a patrol officer is a nightmare. For others, it is a dream come true. Because the first taste of policing the recruit usually receives is in patrol, it often has an initial advantage over other possibilities. Patrol offers a variety of situations and opportunities including choice of patrol area, shift assignment, and days off. For some police officers, the mix of these options provides enough differences and challenges that twenty years may not be enough time to experience all the possibilities. Patrol is also a very challenging career path because of the constant diversity. No two days are the same.

Management (Promotion)

For many officers, simply remaining a patrol officer for the duration of their careers is unsatisfactory. There are those officers who wish to move up the chain of command, perhaps becoming a chief someday. Many police agencies offer a promotional structure that includes the ranks of corporal, sergeant, lieutenant, captain, and deputy chief. Each promotion is accompanied by a pay raise and usually a chance to change from the current job assignment to another part of the agency. Eventually, the successful promotional climb can lead to key managerial positions such as a deputy chief or chief.

Specialization

Although limited by the department's size, specialization is a very popular career choice. Larger police agencies may offer a wide variety of specialty units such as vice and narcotics, SWAT, K-9, investigative divisions (e.g., homicide, burglary, robbery, theft), juvenile, records, and communications. Depending on the number of specialized units available, an officer may not be able to serve in all the units of interest during a career. Sometimes an officer finds a unit of particular interest and attempts to spend the duration of his or her career in only that unit.

It should be noted that an officer is not limited to making a single career path choice. Within most police agencies, a mixture is possible. Promotion is often available in specialized units as well as in patrol. Thus, an officer can experience a two-dimensional career path.

Agency Movement

Although some police officers are interested in a lifetime of policing, their current agency may not offer the variation or challenges desired. This often leads to changing agencies; movement from one agency to another is not uncommon in policing. There are primarily two ways to accomplish this type of movement: resigning from one agency and being hired by the new agency, and lateral transfer. However, the number of lateral transfers occurring is not well documented. Neither type of movement is particularly popular among police executives.

Resignation and new hiring is the simplest and most often used method of changing agencies. A common practice is the leaving of a smaller agency for a larger agency. Larger agencies tend to offer a greater variety of and more chances for upward movement or specialization. This attracts many officers who have spent a few years in a smaller agency and are now ready to move on. The negative side to this method is that officers are often required to attend the new agency's academy and must start again at the probationary rookie level.

■ CASE IN POINT

Having spent fifteen years with a smaller police agency and reaching the rank of lieutenant, a Colorado officer, knowing that further advancement in his current department was all but impossible, resigned and started over with a larger Texas police agency. Starting over for this fifteen-year veteran meant attending an academy again and being labeled a "rookie," a fifteen-year-experienced rookie. However, his experience allowed him to move up quickly in his new agency.

An alternative to having to begin as a "rookie" is a lateral transfer, which eliminates the requirement of "retraining." However, lateral transfers are not widely accepted in today's police community, with the one exception being police chiefs (Doerner, 1998). Lateral transfer or entry allows a police agency to hire a police officer or supervisor from another agency at a nonentry level. Use of this method allows the officer to retain seniority. However, a 1992 International City/County Management Association report noted that "less than 40% of responding jurisdictions with populations 100,000 and above permit lateral entry" (p. 7). A question that arises is: Why don't more police agencies have lateral transfer?

It might be assumed that police agencies would welcome lateral transfer simply because it improves their chances of obtaining well-qualified, experienced officers, such as the officer in the previous Case in Point; yet, it is often not a welcome proposition primarily because it is also a way for police agencies to lose their better officers. The adoption of lateral transfer also raises such issues as adequacy and quality of officer's previous training, morale problems caused by bringing an outsider into a position that a popular insider "should" have, and the prospective loss of time and dollars spent by an agency training an officer only to have that officer move to another agency. These issues are enough to cause skepticism among many police executives over lateral transfer. Lateral transfer might become more acceptable if training and salaries were more consistent. For example, states such as California and Washington support intrastate lateral transfer because all police officers in these states receive the same training, and all must pass a state-mandated licensing examination.

Generally speaking, police officers are not limited to a one-dimensional career. However, the options are not always readily available to all officers. There are situations that an officer may find himself or herself in that no matter how much the officer wants a diversified career path, individual and organizational factors may block that path. For example, the officer who works for a small police agency may have very limited access to promotion or specialization because of the amount of competition or the limited number of assignments or promotion slots.

■ CASE IN POINT

The Wilmette, Illinois, Police Department is a progressive, modern police agency that requires all its recruits to possess a bachelor's degree. Therefore, initially no one officer has an educational advantage unless he or she attains a graduate degree. Furthermore, in 1997 more than 60 percent of the officers were under the age of forty. A common problem for newly hired officers is that it could be ten years or more before they may be in a position for promotion. In 1997 there were only seven positions of rank (four sergeants, two lieutenants, and one deputy chief) and many of the current ranking officers were relatively young.

In comparison, although officers in a large agency may have greater opportunities for promotion or specialization, many may be held back from promotion because of poor testing skills or from specialization because of disciplinary problems. Despite these drawbacks, policing does offer the potential for a varied and interesting career.

NOTEWORTHY PERSONNEL ISSUES

The quality of police personnel raises many issues: where to search for applicants, who to search for, how to select applicants, and training. Yet, there are two distinct issues that deserve discussion: discrimination and women police officers.

Discrimination

Policing has long suffered the criticism of being discriminatory in its hiring practices. In particular, women and minority group members have had a difficult time entering the predominantly white, male occupation. In many cases the blame is placed on the selection and hiring process. For example, in February 1998 the Justice Department filed a lawsuit against the city of Garland, Texas, charging that the police examination lead to the exclusion of blacks and Hispanics in a disproportionate number. Along with discriminatory testing, the general atmosphere may be considered discriminatory, which may be evidenced by the use of racial or sexual slurs or the lack of promotions of women or minority group members.

■ CASE IN POINT

In 1996 the Houston County, Alabama, Sheriff's Department settled a sexual discrimination lawsuit filed by five women who claimed they were passed over for promotion. It was claimed that in some cases the promotions had been given to less qualified male employees. Also in 1996 the U.S. Department of Justice filed a lawsuit against the Canton, Mississippi, Police Department to force promotion of a female lieutenant to assistant chief. The suit charged that the lieutenant was passed over because she was a woman, despite being ranked as the most qualified. Again in 1996, a federal jury awarded a Pompano Beach, Florida, police sergeant $100,400. Her claim was that she had been called racial epithets by the acting police chief and retaliated against because of her complaints about racial and sexual discrimination in the department. In 1998 a black police lieutenant with the North Brunswick, New Jersey, Police Department was promoted to captain six months after filing a discrimination lawsuit against the police department. It charged that he was denied promotion because he was black.

An officer's race, ethnicity, or gender is often the reason linked to discrimination. Although on an individual basis discrimination must be supported by demonstrating past practices of the agency or establishing it through use of the agency's own hiring or promotion practices (often done statistically), discrimination is determined, with respect to policing, by the percentage of representation within the department of a particular group in relation to the percentage of that group in the community. For example, if the percentage of blacks in a given community's population is 30 percent, 30 percent of that community's police agency should be black. Failure to meet this criterion could allow a city to be cited for discrimination.

■ CASE IN POINT

In applying the "discrimination formula" to 1993 statistics, the following cities could have been cited as being discriminatory with respect to blacks represented in their police agencies.

City	% in Agency	% in Community
Atlanta (GA)	53.9	67.0
Baltimore (MD)	31.9	57.0
Chicago (IL)	24.7	39.0
Detroit (MI)	56.3	76.0
Memphis (TN)	35.1	55.0
Newark (NJ)	35.6	59.0
San Antonio (TX)	05.7	09.0

Sources: Adapted from Reaves and Smith (1995) and U.S. Census data for 1990.

One reason the agencies listed in the previous Case in Point have not been cited for discrimination is because the evidence shows that over the years they have made an effort to remedy the disparities (see Table 9-2).

Group discrimination in policing appears to be disappearing, albeit slowly. Unfortunately, there continues to be individual and small group discrimination claims that by this time should no longer exist. A main reason why these claims should not be necessary is the existence of the Civil Rights Act (1964) from which the Equal Employment Opportunity Commission (EEOC) was born. The EEOC is charged with monitoring discriminatory practices in all employment areas. When discriminatory practices are believed to exist, a complaint is often filed with the EEOC office. If evidence of discrimination is found to exist, the remedies include hiring (if previously rejected), reinstatement, back pay, promotion, policy or procedural changes, or jury-granted cash awards. Any type of restitution usually requires that a lawsuit be filed.

TABLE 9-2

Changes in Minority Representation within Selected Agencies, 1983 and 1993

City	Blacks			Hispanics		
	1983	1993	% Change	1983	1993	% Change
Atlanta (GA)	45.8	53.9	17.7	00.6	2.1	250
Baltimore (MD)	17.5	31.9	82.3	00.3	1.5	400
Chicago (IL)	20.1	24.7	22.8	03.4	7.9	132
Detroit (MI)	30.7	56.3	85.7	00.7	1.5	114
Memphis (TN)	22.0	35.1	59.5	00.0	0.0	—
Newark (NJ)	24.0	35.6	48.3	04.8	14.3	198
San Antonio (TX)	04.6	05.7	23.9	32.9	38.8	17.9

Sources: Adapted from the Sourcebook of Criminal Justice Statistics, 1990, and Reaves and Smith (1995).

■ CASE IN POINT

In 1996 a former LAPD officer was awarded $2.3 million after a jury agreed with her claim of discrimination. The officer, who had been a member of the LAPD SWAT team, claimed she was harassed to such a degree that she was forced to leave both the team and ultimately the department. Apparently she had been the first female SWAT member in its twenty-year history. In 1997 the only black member of the LAPD bomb squad filed a $5 million lawsuit claiming he was forced to take a stress leave as a result of racial discrimination. The officer claimed he was subjected to harassment, retaliation, discriminatory abuse, and denied advancement opportunities. In 1998 a former Wyoming Highway Patrol Officer sought lost wages and benefits and other compensation for alleged harassment and discrimination that occurred over a six-year period. The culmination of the discrimination was said to have been the failure of supervisors to send her backup during the apprehension of two escapees from the Wyoming Boys' School.

One of the most effective methods of combating discriminatory practices in policing has been **affirmative action,** a tool of the EEOC, which attempts to ensure equal employment through mandated quotas. Many police agencies have adopted affirmative action plans, some voluntary, some under court order.

■ CASE IN POINT

The following is a sample of cities that have implemented affirmative action plans either voluntarily or through a court order. It is believed that the increase in minority representation demonstrated in Table 9-2 resulted from these affirmative action plans.

City	Voluntary	Court Ordered
Birmingham (AL)		Yes
Boston (MA)		Yes
Buffalo (NY)		Yes
Chicago (IL)		Yes
Columbus (OH)		Yes
Dallas (TX)	Yes	
Detroit (MI)	Yes	
Jacksonville (FL)	Yes	
San Jose (CA)	Yes	
Tucson (AZ)	Yes	

Municipal and state police agencies have not been the only ones facing affirmative action; federal law enforcement has not escaped its impact.

■ CASE IN POINT

Both the FBI and the DEA were forced to reexamine their hiring and promotional policies after class-action lawsuits by Hispanic and black agents accused the agencies of discriminatory practices. The cases were settled out of court. As part of the settlements, both agencies agreed to make amends. The DEA agreed to pay Hispanic agents $275,000 (between $600 and $2500 to agents employed before January 1, 1985) and continue promoting them at the same rate as other agents. The FBI agreed to provide an unspecified amount of back pay, promotions, and better assignments. However, this pact was challenged by a group of white agents claiming the pact provides preferential treatment to black agents. In 1998 black agents threatened to file a new lawsuit claiming that the FBI had not yet fulfilled the agreements of the earlier lawsuit.

The intent of affirmative action has been to eliminate discrimination; yet, it has also appeared to some to have created discrimination. An issue that has arisen has been referred to as "reverse discrimination." Reverse discrimination is the belief that the discriminatory practices are being used against the "majority" to accommodate minorities. To meet federal quotas for hiring and promotions, some police agencies have found themselves defendants in reverse discrimination suits.

■ CASE IN POINT

In 1995 the Maryland State Police agreed to provide back pay to ninety-nine white, male troopers who claimed they were unfairly passed over for promotions. The agreement also resulted in promotions for seventeen of the troopers. Also in 1995 four white, male Indianapolis, Indiana, police officers filed a federal lawsuit claiming reverse discrimination after they were passed over for promotion to the rank of sergeant. The officers had been skipped over to allow the promotion of a woman and a black man. In 1998 the Illinois State Police was ordered by a federal judge to make an effort to contact and offer employment to all 5000 white applicants it rejected between 1975 and 1990 as part of its affirmative action program.

Affirmative action has had its impact on policing, as well as many other areas. In fact, many have questioned whether affirmative action should be discontinued. "The continued need for affirmative action programs is under renewed challenge from critics who contend that they have achieved their original goals of ending discrimination against minorities and providing parity with white males" ("Affirmative-Action Programs Looking a Little Black and Blue," 1995, p. 1). The first major step toward the elimination of affirmative action programs occurred in California in 1997 when voters agreed to Proposition 187, which effectively eliminated affirmative action programs. Affirmative action also was a campaign issue in the 1996 presidential election, and the U.S. Supreme Court has been reluctant to take a stance on cases in which reverse discrimination had been ruled against by lower courts. Whether this trend will continue is yet to be seen, but many of the supporters of affirmative action have vowed to continue fighting for its existence.

Discrimination, reverse or otherwise, is simply not going to go away. Police agencies need to hire more minorities to develop a sufficient promotional pool to give minorities an equal opportunity to be represented throughout the ranks. Discrimination in policing should not necessarily continue to be viewed as intentional; however, only when more of the groups currently underrepresented expand their numbers in the police ranks will the "air" of discrimination begin to lighten.

Women in Policing

Discriminatory practices in policing are not limited to racial or ethnic minorities. Women have been faced with a variety of obstacles in their attempts to establish themselves in policing. Although women have been connected to policing in

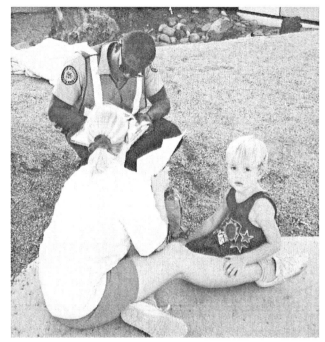

Although black officers have existed since the Civil War, it has only been since the 1970s that most black officers could provide police services to nonminority group members. (Courtesy of the Scottsdale, Arizona, Police Department)

some capacity since its formal beginnings, their usage and recognition as full-fledged police officers is relatively recent (since 1968), and their growth in policing remains slow. In 1972 women represented only 2 percent of all police officers in large police agencies, and in 1997 they represented 13 percent (Harrington et al., 1998); yet, despite these gains there is still plenty of room for growth, especially considering that women currently make up 50 percent of the population in the United States.

In the early stages of policing (1845 to 1890s), women were primarily used as matrons, or supervisors of women and children in correctional–type settings (Stalans, 1997). It was not until the early 1900s that the role began to expand. In 1910 the LAPD hired the first policewoman, Alice Stebbins Wells. Officer Wells' duties were to work primarily with women and juveniles. In 1912, the NYPD went one step further than the LAPD by hiring Isabella Goodwin as the first woman detective. Like her predecessor, Detective Goodwin specialized in handling women and juveniles. One of the most astounding moves of the time was in Milford, Ohio, where Dolly Spencer was made chief of police in 1914. Policing was beginning to change for women but not fast enough.

An effort to improve the status of women in policing led to the creation of the International Association of Policewomen (1915). Its first president was Officer Alice Stebbins Wells. Its intentions were to obtain greater recognition for and an expansion of the woman's role in policing. However, the group's success was rather limited. Until the late 1960s women police officers were assigned to general duties and social services. Of particular interest was the fact these women officers were often much better educated (many had bachelor's degrees in the social sciences or social work) than their male counterparts. Despite this fact, their opportunities for promotion and other duties were limited, and their pay was always less than that of the male officers.

It was not until the years 1968 to 1972 that the progress of women in policing made giant strides. In 1968 the Indianapolis, Indiana, Police Department (IPD) put the first two women on patrol. After several months of success, the officers had no problems outside those every officer experiences, IPD expanded their women patrol force to eight. As a result of the success of the IPD patrol women other police departments began to assign women to patrol. However, the IPD success was just a start.

The early 1970s was a politically active time for the whole country. This political activism opened many new avenues for women. Three elements that would have the most impact on women in policing up to this point were (1) recommendations from the National Commission on Criminal Justice Standards (Figure 9-3), (2) the extension of Title 7 of the 1964 Civil Rights Act, and (3) the FBI and the Secret Service appointed their first female field agents (Horne, 1980; Martin, 1993; More, 1992; Stalans, 1997).

More recently, women have gained other advocates who have assisted in increasing the number and role of women in policing: the National Association of Women Law Enforcement Executives; the International Association of Chiefs of Police (IACP) Ad Hoc Committee on Women in Policing; and perhaps the most ardent supporter, the National Center for Women & Policing.

Since its inception in early 1995, the National Center for Women & Policing has been a leading force behind increasing the numbers of women in policing. The positive impact of women in policing, including the reduction of police brutality, the increased efficacy in police response to domestic violence, and the increased emphasis on conflict resolution over force, mandates that we strive for gender balance in policing (Harrington et al., 1998, p. 1).

The center's 1998 report, "Equality Denied: The Status of Women in Policing," has been a catalyst for additional efforts to understand the problems and issues

FIGURE 9-3 National Advisory Commission on Criminal Justice Standards: Recommendations for Employment of Women in Policing

1. Institute selection procedures to facilitate the employment of women; no agency, however, should alter selection standards solely to employ female personnel.
2. Ensure that recruitment, selection, training, and salary policies neither favor nor discriminate against women.
3. Provide career paths for women, allowing each individual to attain a position classification commensurate with her particular degree of experience, skill, and ability.
4. Immediately abolish all separate organizational entities composed solely of policewomen, except those that are identified by function or objective, such as a female jail within a multiunit police organization.

Source: Police Task Force Report. (1973). National Advisory Commission on Criminal Justice Standards (p. 214).

of women and policing. On the heels of this report, the IACP conducted a national survey in 1998 to attempt to "provide a framework for inquiry into surrounding issues" ("Women in Policing," 1998, p. 36). Although the results were not available at the time of this writing, the areas that were being examined included the number of women currently in policing, recruitment efforts, promotions of women, female officers' skills, sexual harassment, discrimination, and the retention of women (1998, pp. 36–38). Both groups and their respective reports are instrumental in creating a better understanding of women and policing.

> As the 20th century comes to a close, policing remains a predominantly male profession . . . but the world of policing is much different now than it was when the IACP was founded over a century ago, and it requires a different workforce. Police departments can only benefit when they reflect the communities they serve and create supportive work environments for all of their officers. Therefore, chiefs must actively recruit, retain, integrate, and promote female officers (Polisar & Milgram, 1998, p. 42).

The fact that more women should be part of policing is quite clear. Yet, despite all the efforts currently underway to improve the situation, there are still several obstacles women must overcome (Harrington et al., 1998; Kranda, 1998; Polisar & Milgram, 1998; Stalans, 1997). These obstacles include the image of the job, selection criteria, training, and attitudes.

Image of the Job

The traditional image of policing is "macho." It began as a man's occupation and is still considered by many to be strictly a man's occupation. As noted by Hale and Wyland (1993), "The organizational culture of policing as man's work has been entrenched since the 19th century and is very evident today in the attitudes of male peers and supervisors" (p. 1). Women who become police officers are often forced to portray the macho image to obtain respect from male fellow officers; yet, this image is more a necessity in dealing with male officers than necessary for doing police work (Martin, 1993; Stalans, 1997; Wexler, 1985). Women who easily adapt to this role tend to find greater acceptance by male officers but are often snubbed by female officers who believe that they can be feminine and still be effective police officers (Berg & Budnick, 1986; Stalans, 1997; Wexler & Logan, 1983). Conversely, it has been noted that female officers who try to display a greater degree of femininity often must cope with overprotective male partners, sexual advances by both officers and citizens, and sexual harassment (Bennett, 1991; Berg & Budnick, 1986; Harrington et al., 1998; Stalans, 1997). Furthermore, women officers may find it difficult to obtain respect from some male citizens encountered through their work.

Despite the problems women police officers have had to face, they are a positive aspect of policing. In more recent years, with the police job description expanding to become more community-service oriented, "the growing presence of women may help burnish the tarnished image of police officers, improve community relations and foster a more flexible, and less violent, approach to keeping the peace" (McDowell, 1992, p. 70). Women have been found to have a calming effect in violent situations and certainly are far less likely to be violent when

Today's policewomen perform the same tasks as their male counterparts. (Courtesy of the Denver, Colorado, Police Department [top] and the Scottsdale, Arizona, Police Department [bottom])

performing their job as police officers (Women's Advisory Council to the Los Angeles Police Commission, 1993).

There is a growing belief that in some respects women make better police officers than men. Sherman (1973, pp. 384, 393) reported that with women patrol officers:

1. There was a reduction in the incidence of violence between police officers and citizens.
2. There was an increased quality of police service because women accentuate the service role of police work more than men.
3. There was improved PCR because women are more visible than men, make more contacts, and citizens will assist women on request.
4. Policemen can learn from the policewomen that an officer can be efficient without using force.
5. Policewomen are more effective than policemen in settling problems reported by women from low-income neighborhoods.
6. A police department becomes more democratic and responsive to the community by hiring personnel who are more representative of the community's population.
7. Lawsuits charging sex discrimination could be avoided by the police department that develops and implements job-related selection, recruitment, and promotional standards and tests.

These findings have been substantiated by several studies (see Grennan, 1987; Homant & Kennedy, 1985; Women's Advisory Council, 1993). Of particular interest were the findings of the Christopher Commission (1991), which was created after the LAPD–Rodney King incident. The commission reported, "that women on patrol communicate effectively without using physical force" (Hale & Wyland, 1993, p. 1). The result of the various reports convinced the Los Angeles, California, city council to pass a series of resolutions from 1992 to 1993, the goal of which is to increase the number of women on the police force to ultimately reflect the percentage of women in the Los Angeles area workforce (which was 43 percent in 1992). Despite their efforts, LAPD still has a long way to go to reach that goal; in 1997, only 17.3 percent of the sworn officers were women (Harrington et al., 1998), placing LAPD at number seventeen among the top one hundred police departments (by percentage of women officers). The Pittsburgh, Pennsylvania, Police Department had the largest percentage of women at 25 percent (Harrington et al., 1998). The fact is that women will increasingly become a part of policing, especially if the image softens and community policing shapes the new image: "Redefining law enforcement to a community-oriented model of policing would attract more women who reject policing's trademark aggressive, authoritarian image" (Harrington et al., 1998, p. 3).

Selection Criteria

The general selection criteria employed by police agencies—written examinations, polygraph, background investigations, and psychological testing—are becoming relatively unbiased with respect to gender. Although there have been some challenges to entry-level examinations, most selection criteria appears gender neutral. One criterion that has received tremendous criticism for its gender bias has been the physical exercises that test for agility and strength. According to Polisar and Milgram (1998), "Historically, women have been screened out disproportionately in the physical agility phase of the police selection process" (p.44). These exercises have been designed using the average man's physical abilities, not the woman's, as the norm. Therefore, women have had a more difficult time being successful, leading to their disqualification from the applicant process. It is not known how many female applicants today are eliminated because of unequal physical ability testing, but many were in the past. This resulted in lawsuits and changes in the process, in particular making the tests being more job related (as previously discussed).

Training

Police training, like most aspects of policing, has been male oriented. Self-defense, physical training, and firearms are just three areas in which the male orientation is extremely obvious. Academies have had to restructure training so that their application is gender neutral in such areas as self-defense, physical fitness, and firearms. This has included, in many instances, having to rebuild facilities to accommodate women's needs, restructuring physical fitness to meet the average female's physical prowess, and adjusting weapons and firearms training. Despite the changing atmosphere of training, it can still be quite difficult for even the best qualified woman.

■ CASE IN POINT

The following was related to this author through a letter from a former student who became a police officer in 1997 for one of the largest metropolitan police agencies in the country. The location of the department and the officer's real name are withheld by her request because she was concerned that she might suffer repercussions. However, be assured that the experiences are true and probably fairly representative of what other women have dealt with during academy training.

One of the first few things I remember about my academy days is the first week when you could discern the men from the women. During the first week you get to dress like a "normal" woman. You can wear make-up, earrings, skirts, etc. And then the change begins. No longer can you wear your hair down, have your nails painted, or wear any make-up. Women in the academy are basically expected to shed any hint of femininity. I cut my nails off, wore no make-up, and pinned my hair up because women could not have any hair hanging out of their caps. Eventually, I just cut my hair short because I was tired of certain instructors singling me out when my hair would come untucked. One of the guys in my homeroom exclaimed, "My god, Smith looks like Yentl." During my six months in the academy I felt like I lost touch with my feminine side, and some days I just didn't care because of the fatigue. However, one of the most startling changes I experienced in the academy was not my physical transformation but my emotional transformation.

The ratio of men to women in each homeroom was around 25 to 6. Consequently, the men had a tendency to harp on the women about everything. For example, the guys in my homeroom, during every gym class, would wager on which woman in our group would be able to keep up with the class during our run. The men would actually try to pit women against women by comparing our successes and our failures. Initially, I found this to be very degrading and annoying because I felt that the guys did not see women as their equals. Of course, the way the police department structured its power tests did not help because the requirements for the run, sit-ups, bench press, and sit and reach were age and gender biased. For example, as a woman at the age of 26, I only had to bench press 52 percent of my body weight, unlike a man the same age who has to press 98 percent of his body weight. I felt that the double standard was fair in that women generally are not as physically able as the average man. When I started the academy I could barely lift 85 pounds, but by the time I graduated I could lift 165 pounds. One thing that all the teasing and periodic harassment from my male counterparts taught me or brought out in me was my competitive spirit and ego. I worked hard during those six months to match my male classmates in terms of how fast I could run, how many sit-ups I could do, how much weight I could lift, and how hard I could fight in control tactics.

Perhaps my greatest moment came during an extremely long run on a particularly cold day when it was difficult to establish a steady breathing pattern. At the start of the run all the women were out front with the instructor, but as time wore on, one woman after another dropped back despite the cajoling of the men who made comments such as "I told you that none of our women can keep up with us," and "Women shouldn't be on this job if they can't run." Eventually, there were just two women left. The guys were cheering us on and trying to motivate us. Nevertheless, the other woman dropped out about six blocks from the academy, which just left me. I remember how badly I wanted to finish at the front—not just for myself, but to prove that women deserve to be police officers and that we can handle the physical challenges of the job. So, even though my sides were ready to bust and I felt like I was going to pass out, I kept running until we reached the academy doors. Despite feeling like I had been hit by a bus and on the verge of hyperventilating, I straightened myself out and began to accept the congratulations I was getting from the men. From that day forward, the guys in my class treated me with a newfound respect that I assume came from my "gutting it out" and not quitting. Amazingly enough, the only woman who congratulated me was the one who had almost made it with me. It was as if the other women couldn't share in my accomplishment because they were jealous (female rivalry, another topic for another time).

Attitudes

Changing the image, selection criteria, and training has not been easy. The most difficult area to change has been attitudes of both police and the public. What has been interesting with respect to public attitude is that, as a whole, the public has been very receptive to female officers. In some instances the public has been even more responsive to female officers than to male officers (McDowell, 1992). The difficulty has largely been with male officer attitudes (Hale & Wyland, 1993; Harrington et al., 1998; Stalans, 1997; Wexler & Logan, 1983).

Current literature tends to support the belief that many male police officers are not accepting of women officers. Hale and Wyland (1993) note that, "The presence of women in a traditionally male domain is threatening and they are perceived and treated as outsiders" (p. 5). However, the primary issue is whether women are capable of doing the job as well as men. Yet, evidence indicating that women officers do not appear as aggressive as male officers but are able to handle most situations as efficiently and effectively as their male counterparts is improving. Some evidence has shown that women officers are sometimes better than their male counterparts. Men simply have to accept the fact that most women can do the job as well as most men. Unfortunately, it is easier said than done and sometimes may lead to a very strong response from male officers.

■ CASE IN POINT

The Dayton, Ohio, police chief was appalled when in July 1998 fourteen members of the previously all-male SWAT team resigned from the unit. The resignations were in protest to the appointment of the first female officer to the SWAT unit, an officer the resigners contend was unqualified for the job. A sergeant who resigned from the unit contended that most of the SWAT officers believed the nine-year veteran female officer would have trouble handling the dangerous, high-stress situations the unit faced on a regular basis. Apparently the officer had applied for and been turned down for a spot on the unit several times in the past and eventually filed a grievance. However, her appointment to the team was said to be based on her merit, that she met all the requirements, and as a result of the grievance.

Even though they can do the job, women will continue to face more difficulties as police officers than men (minorities and white). Not only must they deal with the general stresses of being in law enforcement, but also with the additional burdens of being a woman police officer, which may include discrimination in training and promotion, and their roles as wives and mothers (Bennett, 1991; Hale & Wyland, 1993; Polisar & Milgram, 1998; Stalans, 1997).

There is no doubt that the status of women in policing is changing. Previous barriers that kept women out of policing are being moved aside, and the numbers of women police officers are slowly increasing (Harringon et al., 1998) (see Table 9-3). Furthermore, even though their numbers are increasing, high-ranking and administrative female officers, especially police chiefs, are still rare (see Table 9-3). However, some positive movement has been occurring.

TABLE 9-3

Female Police Officers by Percentage of Department and Percentage of Supervisors, 1992 and 1997

City	% in Agency			% of Supervisors		
	1992	1997	% Change	1992	1997	% Change
Atlanta (GA)	14.3	14.5	0.1	5.9	8.0	35.6
Chicago (IL)	16.0	19.2	20.0	3.5	13.1	274.3
Dallas (TX)	13.8	15.8	14.5	9.3	14.1	51.6
Detroit (MI)	20.4	21.6	5.8	10.0	22.0	120.0
Houston (TX)	9.6	11.9	23.9	1.5	7.6	406.7
Los Angeles (CA)	13.6	17.3	27.2	3.0	10.2	240.0
New York (NY)	13.8	15.0	8.7	6.3	8.8	39.7
Pittsburgh (PA)	23.0	25.0	8.7	7.9	25.6	24.1

Sources: Adapted from Walker and Turner (1992) and Harrington et al. (1998).

◼ CASE IN POINT

In January 1990 the Houston, Texas, Police Department (HPD) had appointed to its top spot its first woman chief, Elizabeth M. Watson, an eighteen-year veteran of the HPD. During her eighteen years with the HPD, Chief Watson served in a variety of positions as she climbed the managerial ladder. Chief Watson earned the distinction of having been the first female police chief of a top five (in size) municipal police department. In 1994 Chicago Heights, Illinois, appointed its first female police chief, thirty-seven-year-old Karla Osantowski, who had worked as an assistant state's attorney. In 1996 Trooper Lisa Taylor became the first female lieutenant in the Ohio State Highway Patrol. In 1997 the Savannah, Georgia, Police Department promoted its first woman officer, Captain Juliette Tolbert, a sixteen-year veteran, to the rank of major. An added first is that Major Tolbert is African American. Deborah K. Ness became the first female police chief in the state of North Dakota when she was appointed to head up the Bismarck Police Department. Chief Ness is a veteran police officer of more than twenty-four years, having started as one of the first three women hired as patrol officers by the Minot Police Department in 1974. In 1998 a twenty-one-year veteran became the first woman to head the Durham, North Carolina, Police Department. Like Chief Ness, Chief Teresa Chambers had been among the first female patrol officers in her agency (Prince George's County, Maryland).

To date, the rise of women to the position of police chief is obviously one of the greatest accomplishments for women in policing. Although most female police chiefs reached their rank in the 1990s, the road was first paved in 1985 when Penny Harrington became the first female police chief of a major police agency (one employing more than 100 sworn officers). Another major distinction among women police chiefs that requires recognition was the appointment of Chief Beverly Harvard, the first African-American woman to head a major urban police department. In both cases, the achievements of these women are definitely historical points of success for women police officers.

◼ CASE IN POINT

All things considered, women police officers have come a fairly long way in a short time. Every day a female police officer moves one step closer to becoming a police chief, and, although the appointment of most female chiefs is a 1990s' phenomenon, women's venture into the police chief realm, at least with respect to a police agency employing more than 100 sworn officers, began in 1985 when Penny Harrington was named chief of police for the Portland, Oregon, Police Bureau. Chief Harrington began her career in 1964 as a policewoman in the women's protective division. When she was hired, women could not work patrol; neither could they transfer nor promote. Furthermore, they received lower salaries than male officers. Harrington challenged this system and in 1970 became the first woman to be transferred out of the women's protective division. She added two more firsts to her list when in 1972 she became the first woman detective and then the first woman sergeant. In 1973 Harrington was successful in eliminating the height requirement (5' 10") that had prevented most women from becoming police officers. However, because of her continued challenges to the unfair employment practices, she suffered retaliation. It didn't stop her. She organized the women in the department, and together they filed more than 42 complaints of sex discrimination, most filed by Harrington herself.

A result of her strong stands, every area of the department was eventually opened up to women. As an ardent believer in problem solving, Chief Harrington worked closely with neighborhood and business people to solve crime problems. She taught these skills to other officers. Every place she worked, crime decreased, citizen complaints decreased, and morale increased—both in the department and in the community. Based on her stellar record, and support from the community, Harrington was named police chief in January 1985. As chief, Harrington implemented a variety of programs that assisted in reducing burglary, increasing drug arrests, reducing citizen complaints against police, and reducing crime overall. Chief Harrington retired from the Portland Police Bureau in July 1986. Today Penny Harrington is the director of the National Center for Women and Policing where she continues to work diligently on a national level to bring more women into policing and to help women reach the higher levels of command within their agencies. (For more information on the National Center for Women and Policing, access the Internet at www.feminist.org.)

Chief Penny Harrington, the first woman police chief of a major urban police agency. (Courtesy of Penny Harrington)

■ CASE IN POINT

When Penny Harrington was named police chief, making her the first woman chief of a major police agency, it definitely opened a door for women in policing, and was undoubtedly a proud moment. However, although the gender barrier had been broken, a racial barrier still existed for women. The racial barrier came down in 1994 when the mayor of Atlanta, Georgia, Bill Campbell, appointed as police chief Beverly J. Harvard, the first black woman to occupy that position in a major metropolitan police department. Harvard began her career in 1973 as a patrol officer. Through the years she steadily moved up through the ranks, serving in a number of positions: executive protection officer (breaking ground as the first woman to serve in the unit); affirmative-action specialist, director of public affairs; and deputy chief of police for the career development, criminal investigations, and administrative services divisions. Chief Harvard holds a bachelor's degree in sociology (Morris Brown College) and a master's degree in urban government and administration (Georgia State University). She also holds two honorary doctorate of law degrees. Chief Harvard has the distinction of being the first woman from the Atlanta Police Department to have graduated from the FBI's National Academy. As chief, Harvard has made community policing a part of Atlanta's growth as an international city and has expanded the juvenile section, domestic violence unit, gangs and guns task force, and jointly opened a state-of-the-art, citywide communications system with the fire department. Chief Harvard is also one of the few police administrators in the world whose city has hosted an Olympics (1996). Despite some difficult times, Chief Harvard has demonstrated that a woman, of any race or ethnicity, can be a successful police chief.

Although there are still barriers to conquer, the number of women in policing continues to grow. With growing numbers, the remaining barriers will eventually fall. Women may be expected to move up the promotional ladder and continue to become top executives of various police agencies in numbers commensurate with their numbers in the general population. Furthermore, women should begin to experience less discrimination and sexual harassment, especially because the courts are not tolerating or accepting this type of behavior.

■ CASE IN POINT

In 1996 a Philadelphia Pennsylvania, police officer was awarded $127,00 by a federal jury in her discrimination suit. She claimed that her refusal to date a supervisor ruined her career and caused her to be ostracized by fellow officers. That same year the Department of Justice filed its first sexual harassment lawsuit against the New York Police Department in support of a former officer who claimed to have been subjected to years of abuse from her male colleagues. In 1998 an inspector with the Philadelphia, Pennsylvania, Police Department, one of the department's highest-ranking women, settled her sexual harassment suit against the city for $150,000. In addition to the monetary award, the city was to expunge the inspector's record of a one-day suspension she claimed was retaliation for her filing a lawsuit.

Despite discrimination, and with the aid of the courts or just plain fortitude, women will continue to persevere in policing. However, not all the "firsts" will be pleasant.

Chief Beverly J. Harvard, the first black woman police chief of a major urban police agency. (Courtesy of Beverly J. Harvard and the Atlanta, Georgia, Police Department)

■ CASE IN POINT

The first Philadelphia, Pennsylvania, female police officer killed in the line of duty was Lauretha Vaird, who in January 1996 was shot during a botched robbery at a local bank branch. In 1998 Colleen Waibel became the first female police officer killed in the line of duty in Portland, Oregon. She was shot twice during a raid of a home said to be stocked with high-powered weapons. Also in 1998 Linda Huff became the first female state trooper killed in the line of duty in Idaho. A man on a bicycle shot at her seventeen times in the rear parking lot of the Coeur D'Alene, Idaho, police station.

In sum, women have come a long way in policing, but there is still much ground to cover.

SUMMARY

Because public perception of police officers is often based on initial contacts with citizens, it is important for the police officer to project a positive image. The reputation of the police agency and its ability to provide services is strongly dependent on its personnel. Therefore, the quality of personnel is extremely important, which means recruitment is a crucial component—particularly, locating and creating an applicant pool.

With competition increasing and applicant pools shrinking, police agencies have had to expand their recruitment to colleges, military bases, cities with high unemployment, and national advertising. However, an issue that has arisen in recruiting is who will do the recruiting, the police agency or the city personnel department? Funding plays a key part in making a decision as to who will recruit.

Despite who recruits and where, recruiting the most qualified individual is the most important element. Thus, certain requirements have been established to assist in screening out individuals. These requirements include, but are not limited to, education, physical ability, criminal history, drug use, miscellaneous testing and screening procedures, and a background investigation. Once an individual has cleared all the preliminary hurdles and is hired, the next step is training.

The training academy is a very important part of qualifying personnel. Although this phase has received its share of criticism—especially over its curriculum—it is still, nonetheless, a key facet to personnel development. Additionally, training includes a field training experience.

In making the decision to become a police officer or after becoming one, the individual has four primary career choices: patrol, management, specialization, and agency movement. Each choice has its own appeal and can be combined with others to allow for even greater diversity.

Finally, two issues of importance to personnel and recruitment are discrimination and women. As a result of several laws, administrative acts, and court cases, discrimination in policing is declining, allowing minority group members greater access to policing. This is true for women, too, who despite the advances still face problems of job image, selection criteria, training, and attitudes.

The respect granted to and the image of a police agency is strongly dependent on the quality of its personnel. Recruiting and selection criteria are important elements in providing quality personnel. Selection criteria and processes will continue to change and improve to ensure that the best personnel are employed. Hiring will be enhanced by training both in the academy and in the field. Elimination of discrimination will assist in diversifying the ethnic, racial, and gender composition of policing. In particular, women are making giant strides toward an improved stance in policing.

DO YOU KNOW . . .

1. How police agencies can improve recruitment efforts?
2. Whether simply improving the quality of personnel will improve the image of police officers?

3. Who recruits for your local police agency? federal police agencies?
4. How a police agency can persuade more women and minority group members to become police officers?
5. What the selection criteria of your city's police agency are?
6. Why lateral transfer is not more popular among state and local police agencies?
7. Why police agencies and colleges have not coordinated their training and educational efforts?
8. Whether "reverse discrimination" is a legitimate issue? Why or why not?
9. What women need to do to improve their status in policing?
10. What police agencies need to do to improve the status of women in policing?

REFERENCES

Affirmative-action programs looking a little black and blue. (1995). *Law Enforcement News, 21,* 1.

Becoming a New Orleans cop is about to get harder. (1996). *Law Enforcement News, 22,* 5.

Bennett, C. L. (1991). Interviews with female police officers in western Massachusetts. Paper presented to the Academy of Criminal Justice Sciences in Nashville, TN.

Berg, B. L., & Budnick, K. J. (1986). Defeminization of women in law enforcement: A new twist in the traditional police personality. *Journal of Police Science and Administration, 14,* 314–319.

Bouza, A. V. (1990). *The police mystique.* New York: Plenum Press.

Carter, D., & Sapp, A. (1990). The evolution of higher education in law enforcement: Preliminary findings from a national study. *Journal of Criminal Justice Education, 1,* 59–85.

Carter, D., Sapp, A., & Stephens, D. (1988) Higher education as a bona fide occupational qualification (BFOQ) for police: A blueprint. *American Journal of Police, 7,* 1–27.

Dantzker, M.L. (1993). An issue for policing: Educational level and job satisfaction. *American Journal of Police, 12,* 101–118.

Dantzker, M.L. (1999). *Police organization and management: Yesterday, today, and tomorrow.* Newton, MA: Butterworth-Heinemann.

Doerner, W.G. (1997). Recruitment and retention. In M.L. Dantzker (Ed.), *Contemporary policing: Personnel, issues and trends* (pp. 53–74). Newton, MA: Butterworth-Heinemann.

Doerner, W.G. (1998). *Introduction to law enforcement: An insider's view.* Newton, MA: Butterworth-Heinemann.

Grennan, S.A. (1987). Findings on the role of officer gender in violent encounters with citizens. *Journal of Police Science and Administration, 15,* 78–85.

Hale, D. C., & Wyland, S. M. (1993). Dragons and dinosaurs: The plight of patrol women. *Police Forum, 3,* 1–6.

Harrington, P., Besser, A., McAnneney, D., Terman, S., Smeal, E., & Spillar, K. (1998). *Equality denied: The status of women in policing,* 1997. Los Angeles, CA: National Center for Women & Policing.

Harriston, K.A., & Flaherty, M.P. (1994, August 29). D.C. pays price for easing police hiring standards. *Chicago Sun-Times,* 40.

Homant, R.J., & Kennedy, D.B. (1985). Police perceptions of spouse abuse: A comparison of male and female officers. *Journal of Criminal Justice, 13,* 29–47.

Horne, P. (1980). *Women in law enforcement.* Springfield, IL: Charles C. Thomas, Publishers.

International City/County Management Association. Police personnel practices, 1990. (1992). *Baseline Data Report, 23.*

Kranda, A.H. (1998). Women in policing: The importance of mentoring. *The Police Chief, 65,* 54–56.

Langworthy, R., Hughes, T., & Sanders, B. (1995). *Law enforcement recruitment, selection and training: A survey of major police departments in the U.S.* Highland Heights, KY: Academy of Criminal Justice Sciences—Police Section.

Lengthening the stride: Employing peace officers from newly arrived ethnic groups. (1995). Washington, D.C.: National Crime Prevention Council.

Marion, N. (1998). Police academy training: Are we teaching recruits what they need to know? *Policing: An International Journal of Police Strategies and Management, 21,* 54–79.

Martin, S. E. (1993). Female officers on the move: A status report on women in policing. In R. G. Dunham & G. P. Alpert (Eds.), *Critical issues in policing* (2nd ed.) (pp. 327–347). Prospect Heights, IL: Waveland Press.

McDowell, J. (1992, February 17). Are women better cops? *Time,* 70–72.

McNickle, R.G. (1996, October 15). Police fitness: Is there life after the academy? *Law Enforcement News,* 10–11.

More, H. W. (1992). *Special topics in policing.* Cincinnati, OH: Anderson Publishing Company.

Police Task Force Report. (1973). Washington, D.C.: National Advisory Commission on Criminal Justice Standards and Goals.

Polisar, J., & Milgram, D. (1998). Recruiting, integrating, and retaining women police officers: Strategies that work. *The Police Chief, 65,* 42–52.

Pugh, G. M. (1986). The good police officer: Qualities, roles and concepts. *Journal of Police Science and Administration, 14,* 1–5.

Reaves, B.A. (1996). *Local police departments,* 1993. Washington, D.C.: U.S. Department of Justice.

Reaves, B.A. (1997) *Federal law enforcement officers, 1996.* Washington, D.C.: U.S. Department of Justice.

Reaves, B.A., & Smith, P.Z. (1995). *Law enforcement management and administrative statistics, 1993: Data for individual state and local agencies with 100 or more officers.* Washington, D.C.: U.S. Department of Justice.

Sherman, L. J. (1973). A psychological view of women in policing. *Journal of Police Science and Administration, 1,* 383–394.

Shernock, S.K., & Dantzker, G.D. (1997). In M.L. Dantzker (Ed.), *Contemporary policing: Personnel, issues and trends* (pp. 75–98). Newton, MA: Butterworth-Heinemann.

Sourcebook of criminal justice statistics, 1990. (1991). Washington, D.C.: U.S. Government Printing Office.

Sourcebook of criminal justice statistics, 1992. (1993). Washington, D.C.: U.S. Government Printing Office.

Stalans, L. (1997) Police officers: A gender perspective. In M.L. Dantzker (Ed.), *Contemporary policing: Personnel, issues and trends* (pp. 1–30). Newton, MA: Butterworth-Heinemann.

Stokes, L.D. (1997). Minority groups in law enforcement. In M.L. Dantzker (Ed.), *Contemporary policing: Personnel, issues and trends.* (pp. 31–52). Newton, MA: Butterworth-Heinemann.

Stotland, E., & Berberich, J. (1979). The psychology of the police. In H. Toch (Ed.), *Psychology of crime and criminal justice* (pp. 24–67). Prospect Heights, IL: Waveland Press.

Walker, S., & Turner, K. B. (1992). *A decade of modest progress: Employment of black and Hispanic police officers: 1983–1992.* Unpublished report.

Wexler, J. G. (1985). Role styles of women police officers. *Sex Roles, 12,* 749–755.

Wexler, J. G., & Logan, D. D. (1983). Sources of stress among women police officers. *Journal of Police Science and Administration, 11,* 46–53.

Women in policing: IACP, Gallup assess recruitment, promotion, retention issues. (1998). *The Police Chief, 65,* 36–40.

Women's Advisory Council to the Los Angeles Police Commission. (1993). *A blueprint for implementing gender equity in the Los Angeles Police Department.*

THE PERSONALITY
OF POLICE OFFICERS

10

In Chapter 9 you were introduced to what is considered a key aspect of policing—the quality of personnel. Although several ideas and concepts were offered, two aspects receiving little attention were (1) who is the individual choosing to become a police officer, and (2) whether there is a certain personality or type of individual attracted to policing. The reason for the lack of attention in earlier chapters is because one of the more interesting aspects of police personnel is the concept of the police personality, which deserves more than a mere mention.

For years debate has focused on whether there exists a distinct personality type who enters policing or law enforcement. The type of individual who becomes a police officer and why has been the target of studies for several years; yet, the empirical data available has not assisted in establishing a definitive conclusion. This chapter examines a variety of issues surrounding this intriguing aspect of policing and should be read as being somewhat speculative in nature.

BECOMING A POLICE OFFICER

Policing is a job many individuals would never consider doing. When asked why, most people can identify many negatives of the job: physical danger, public apathy and hostility, health risks, rotating shifts, and the emotional toll (Bonifacio, 1991; Doerner, 1998). Yet, even being aware of all these negatives, there are many other individuals who energetically, enthusiastically, almost obsessively strive to become police officers (Bonifacio, 1991; Doerner, 1998; Herbert, 1998; Hernandez, 1989). Indeed, a question that every police officer is asked at some time is, "Why do you want to be . . . or why did you become a police officer?" For some, it is a family tradition. A study conducted by Arcuri (1976), which still has relevance today, found that "inheritance"—a police connection in the family—was a major reason many individuals became police officers. For others, it is a lifelong ambition.

In either case, there are two primary responses most often given to the question of why: **to help society,** and **the nature of the job** with its security and benefits (Arcuri, 1976; Bonifacio, 1991; Hernandez, 1989; Lester, 1983; Meagher & Yentes, 1986; Poole & Pogrebin, 1988). The first can be considered a philosophical, theoretical, or even altruistic response, which is more common among younger college-educated police officers (Doerner, 1998), and the second response is a more realistic approach.

To Help Society

Fighting crime and "cleaning up" society is a very worthwhile ambition. It is one that is not uncommon among policing students, recruits, and rookie officers. It is, however, a somewhat unrealistic—maybe even a little naive—but an admirable reason nonetheless. Although police officers are often viewed as civil servants or society's saviors, it is virtually impossible for them to fulfill such a role consistently. Police officers are only one facet of a complicated social structure charged with helping society and alleviating society's problems. The situation is that the police officers are often unable to do more than try to maintain society's status quo. It is not uncommon that, after a few days of the actual practice of policing, the officer who thought that he or she would help society as a whole, realizes that the best he or she can do is try to keep society from completely tearing itself apart. Yet, it would be unfair not to note that there are isolated incidents and situations in which police officers have assisted individuals in a manner that has helped improve their lives, such as delivering a baby in a taxicab, helping a burglary victim obtain replacements for stolen goods, or providing food baskets during the holiday seasons. Although these episodes might be few and far between, when they do occur they provide some positive feedback to officers and help fulfill some portion of the officer's desire to "help society."

Although this idealistic view of helping society, or the altruistic reason, might truly be a motivating factor for becoming a police officer, there are some who would argue otherwise. For example, Bonifacio (1991) suggests that the idea of helping society is, in reality, a search for recognition and power. Police officers want to be heroes. They want to save people from harm rather than just serve the public. Concentrating on society's ills and correcting them is a strong motivator for becoming a police officer. In either case, both are legitimate and acceptable reasons for becoming a police officer. However, neither seems to be as realistic as the nature of the job.

The Nature of the Job

An individual's belief that he or she can greatly help our society is a noble but not necessarily very attainable goal. Therefore, it is not always a good reason for becoming a police officer. What makes more sense as a motivator, and appears much more realistic, is the nature of the job.

Policing offers a variety of situations and possibilities that very few occupations offer: no day, no shift, no part of town is ever the same; there is no such thing as "routine." This kind of variety can be very intriguing and exciting. The authority and power accompanying the position can be compared with an addictive drug: some people just cannot get enough. For others, simply knowing that the job and its benefits will always exist is enough reason to become police officers—that is, there will always be a need for police officers.

The reason a person becomes a police officer is not as fascinating to consider as is the type of individual who becomes a police officer. As a way to identify those individuals willing to wear gun and badge, concepts of recognizable personality type or distinct traits have been suggested.

PERSONALITY TRAITS

It has been noted that the individual who, historically, most often enters policing is the blue-collar, white male. However, identifying who becomes a police officer by race, gender, or socioeconomic status is just one method of examining who becomes a police officer. Through the years, the notion of recognizing prospective police recruits by their personality has arisen; the question is whether a distinct police personality exists. The attempt to answer this question has led to two conflicting viewpoints.

The first viewpoint, **unique traits** (referred to by some as the predispositional personality), insists that policing/law enforcement attracts individuals who possess certain personality traits. Some of the traits identified are authoritarianism, cynicism, racism, hostility, secretiveness, and loyalty (Bonifacio, 1991; Niederhoffer, 1969; Walker, 1999). The other viewpoint, **socialization and experience** (or occupational personality), suggests that these personality traits are developed through the socialization and experiences of policing. Both views can be pervasively argued.

Unique Traits Viewpoint

Considering the general authoritative role of the police officer, authoritarianism is a pertinent personal element. Some individuals may become police officers because of the authoritarian image. It is not difficult to believe that such an individual may possess authoritarian tendencies and wishes to expand them by becoming a police officer. Because of the nature of law enforcement, its attractiveness to some persons may include the power of authority. To argue that the individual willing to wear a badge, gun, nightstick, and handcuffs and who is legally charged with the power to take away liberty, or in some instances life, does not have some degree of an authoritarian characteristic before entering law enforcement seems foolish. Yet, although becoming a police officer automatically makes the individual an authority figure, not everyone who becomes a police officer may initially be authoritarian; however, chances are better than not the person will be (Austin, Hale, & Ramsey, 1987; Doerner, 1998; Niederhoffer, 1969; Tenerowicz, 1993). Bonifacio (1991) points out that many police officers see themselves as being dominant and having power—two very strong elements of authoritarianism; however, the question still remains whether this is a predispositional factor.

As for cynicism, racism, and hostility, it is difficult to believe these personality traits universally exist among potential police officers before their entry into policing/law enforcement. It is not uncommon for police agencies to use some type of psychological testing, such as the Minnesota Multiple Personality Inventory (MMPI), the California Personality Inventory, or the Sixteen Personality Factors, during the recruitment process to screen out such traits as hostility, cynicism, racism, lying, low self-concept or self-confidence, and high dominance. Individuals who blatantly or overtly demonstrate these traits, or score high in these areas on the examinations, are generally identified and often disqualified. Carpenter and Raza (1987), in a study of personality characteristics of police applicants, based on the MMPI, suggested that police applicants can be identified as possessing the personality characteristics that are within the normal range necessary for the demands of police work.

Cynicism, hostility, and racism are not the kind of characteristics police agencies want in their officers. Yet, it may be argued that there are those who are able to conceal these traits better than others during the hiring process, eventually enter policing/law enforcement, and then are not "discovered" until after a series of incidents or complaints that indicate the existence of these traits.

■ CASE IN POINT

A white, male officer who, when assigned to work in minority-group areas, consistently is the subject of complaints of brutality, hostility, or racist actions; however, when the same officer is reassigned to a white area he receives no complaints. Another example is the African American in a leadership position who constantly attempts to keep white officers off his patrol team. When a white rookie officer is assigned to an FTO on his team, this sergeant does not hesitate to say derogatory, racist statements in front of the rookie in an effort to get the rookie to ask for a transfer to another team.

One could argue that both scenarios in the preceding Case in Point demonstrated traits that probably existed before the officers' entry into policing but were not discovered during the hiring process. However, there are those who will argue that these traits may have been formed during the police experience or the socialization process.

Socialization and Experience Viewpoint

Although the empirical data may be limited, it is easy to argue that identified personality traits such as cynicism, racism, and hostility (authoritarianism may be a possible exception) are the result of the policing experience (see Bonifacio, 1991; Tenerowicz, 1993; Topp & Kardash, 1986; Wellman et al., 1988). Some individuals even suggest that the socialization process begins before the person actually becomes a police officer (Roberg & Kuykendall, 1993). In either view, the authoritarian trait, if preexistent, is reinforced through the police experience. When the police officer puts on badge and gun, that sense of authority is enhanced many times over. There is no doubt that there is an intimidation factor in the policing role that allows the authoritative characteristic to grow. It has been argued that authoritarianism and cynicism are pertinent parts of the police personality (Doerner, 1998; Lyman, 1999; Niederhoffer, 1969; Skolnick, 1994). As for being preexistent, the authoritarianism is generally acceptable, but the cynicism is not.

A cynical police officer is an individual who believes that human conduct is motivated solely by self-interest. This attitude often becomes part of the police persona after years of police experience (Bonifacio, 1991; Herbert, 1998; Lyman, 1999; Niederhoffer, 1969; Walker, 1999; Wellman et al., 1988). When one considers that police officers frequently deal with the negative side of life, as well as with the seeming ineptness of the criminal justice system, it is not difficult to understand how officers become cynical. Some officers recognize this condition and leave policing, as demonstrated in the following Case in Point. Others learn to live with it. The unfortunate part is that the cynicism does not remain on the job at the end of the shift. It becomes a very real part of the officer's complete life.

■ CASE IN POINT

Before becoming a police officer, a soon-to-be rookie had studied religion and was very active in his church. It was difficult for him to get angry at people, and he was always trying to find ways to improve a negative situation. This did not last for long. Academy classmates with prior police experience knew what was going to happen to this individual's gentle disposition and tried to warn him. He just smiled and said, "Not to worry." After a little more than one year on the job, he quit because he did not like what he was becoming and how it was affecting his family. No longer was he tolerant and believing. In his eyes, everyone had become untrustworthy and self-centered, including his wife and children. It was a world he no longer wanted to contend with, at least not as a police officer. Having to arrest his own sergeant for burglary seemed to be the last straw. If he could not trust the people he worked with, whom could he trust? As a police officer, it is difficult not to become cynical.

It is almost as tough not to become racially or ethnically biased. At some point in every officer's career, an incident reflecting what could be perceived as a bigoted or racist attitude occurs. Furthermore, to spend an entire career in policing without struggling to avoid forming and demonstrating certain racial or ethnic biases and attitudes, positive and negative, is extremely rare. The major issue is how or when these attitudes appear. Logic requires the admission of pre-existing biases in some cases. According to social psychology, all people are biased to some extent (Baron & Byrne, 1991). The policing experience can be a catalyst for the growth of negative biases and racial attitudes. When an officer spends several years working with a particular class, ethnicity, or race of people, it is extremely difficult not to form certain biases that tend to be projected toward all individuals of the specific group. Even though the officer may not often demonstrate the bias, it sometimes shows up in specific incidents.

■ CASE IN POINT

A white, male officer who considered himself a fairly unbiased, unprejudiced individual, who had many black friends, and had worked in a predominantly black section of town for many months, found himself one night demonstrating an action that the casual observer would instantly have labeled as bigoted and racist. This officer had to restrain and arrest a black man who, while high on drugs, assaulted his parents and then insisted on fighting the officer. An altercation ensued. Attempting to avoid an arrest, the suspect broke free and tried to flee after observing additional officers arriving on the scene. In his adrenaline-excited state, the officer trying to make the initial arrest began shouting to his fellow officers derogatory remarks about the suspect that could have been construed as racist, even though the officer was not normally considered a racist individual.

Like cynicism and racism, hostility sometimes grows within police officers after years of dealing with the problems and unlawful activities of society. It is not difficult to understand that, after numerous occasions of dealing with the downside of life, a police officer can become hostile, particularly toward certain groups.

■ CASE IN POINT

The officer was assigned to a predominantly Hispanic section of town. Although he knew enough Spanish to ask specific questions such as the person's name, address, and place of business, his Spanish was not fluent. Contacts with Hispanics who claimed to speak no English were frustrating, particularly when the officer realized that many individuals actually understood and spoke more English than they claimed. After several months of these types of contacts, the officer became quite hostile toward all Hispanics when it came to their language abilities and had difficulty accepting their claims of "No se ingles."

It appears that certain personality traits do exist among police officers. Studies have been contradictory in determining whether these traits preexist or become part of the officer through socialization. For example, using the Edwards Personal Preference Schedule, studies have shown that police officers score higher than the norm on needs for achievement, exhibition, and heterosexuality, whereas they score lower on needs for affiliation, abasement, nurturance, and order (Butler & Cochrane, 1977; Lester et al., 1980). These results would indicate that certain personality traits occur as a result of police experience. Yet, studies by Carpenter and Raza (1987) and Klopsch (1983), using the MMPI, found that certain traits preexisted and remain stable after five years on the job. Butler and Cochrane (1977) may best summarize this issue.

The literature does clearly demonstrate that there are no unique factors within the police officer's working personality; where it differs from other people is in emphasis. For example, police officers are not alone in being self assertive, but they are likely to be more self assertive than other groups (p. 442).

This issue remains debatable. Yet, common sense suggests that we consider the nature of the job itself and the effect it can and often does have on an officer's personality. However, this approach paves the way for perhaps a third way of viewing the police personality, as a distinct "working personality" (Skolnick, 1994). The working personality is based on a police officer's need for two elements: danger and authority. Skolnick (1994) suggests that police officers develop a personality that requires danger or the consistent exposure to hazardous situations, and the authority or the need to be able to use force in appropriate situations.

An area that has yet to receive critical attention is the effect personality has on job performance (Thompson & Solomon, 1991; Topp & Kordash, 1986; Wellman et al., 1983). An exception to this has been the continuing study of personality and police officers who work undercover. Since 1981, psychologist Michel Girodo has studied the impact of personality traits of officers with respect to corruption, an area that has long plagued policing.

The results of Girodo's research could assist police departments to decide who should work undercover, and also shed some light on why officers may become corrupt. Girodo (1991) identified impulse control, neuroticism, a desire to experiment with new experiences, a disinhibited attitude, and an undisciplined self-image as personality traits linked to officers who have a propensity toward corruption. Although these traits are presently associated with officers working undercover, particularly narcotics officers, the potential implication of searching for these traits among other police officers is not without merit. Although the question of personality traits with respect to preexistence or socialization is an important and interesting topic of research, how personality affects behavior and performance requires more attention and research in the future.

WHAT DO YOU THINK?

Police Personality Traits: Preexistent or Created?

The police literature routinely addresses the debate over whether a distinct police personality exists. This personality is said to include such traits as racism, authoritarianism, cynicism, and hostility. One side says that these traits preexist in the individual who becomes a police officer; the other side says these traits are formed during the policing experience. Although neither side has provided strong empirical support for their positions (although some social psychologists will argue that authoritarian types drift toward police work), research and anecdotal and observational experiences lend credibility to both arguments. Some recruits have been observed from day one of the academy to possess many of these traits, whereas others have spent several years in policing before these traits have been observed. In either case, with the possible exception of authoritarianism, these do not appear to be traits society would want police officers to possess.

1. Are certain personality traits apparent in all police officers?
2. Does policing attract a certain type of individual? How would you describe this individual?
3. What effect might policing have on an individual's personality?
4. Is the identification of personality traits important to policing?
5. Generally it is believed that the police personality is negative, whether preexistent or created. Can policing have a positive effect on personality?
6. Should police departments assess personality traits of recruits? veterans?
7. Other than the psychological tests currently used to screen the personality of potential police officers, what else might a police department do to evaluate a recruit's personality?

The question of a distinct personality type or traits is just one of the intriguing issues of the police personality. The concept of attitude, preexisting and developed, also lends some interesting aspects to the study of the police personality. As Bonifacio (1991), points out, "What may set the cop apart from the civilian is his opportunity to actualize his unconscious wishes through the reality of his job, an opportunity few civilians may have" (p. 148).

ATTITUDE

An important element of any people-oriented occupation is the attitude of the personnel toward the job and the people they serve. Policing in particular must be concerned with the attitudes of police officers. A poor attitude is not acceptable to the police agency because it can reflect poorly on the police agency the officer represents. The attitudinal component of the police personality invites two questions: Do predisposed attitudes such as racism or sexism carry over to the job? Are there any differences in attitude by gender, race, or ethnicity?

Gender

Considering that women have been active in all areas of policing for a relatively short time (approximately thirty years), the research on gender attitudes in policing is relatively limited. However, an examination of the literature advocates that there is little difference in attitudes between male and female applicants or officers. A study by Carpenter and Raza (1987) found that there was little psychological difference between male and female police recruits. They found that attitudes of both genders were positive, with a balance of optimism and pessimism. They did find that female applicants were actually more assertive and nonconforming, had a higher energy level than male applicants, and were less likely to identify with traditional sex roles.

Other studies have found that both genders sought a career in policing for similar reasons: to help society and for job security (Meagher & Yentes, 1986). In addition, attitudes toward the job were significantly similar. One study even found that male and female officers had similar perceptions about women police officers (Lord, 1986). Based on available literature, it would appear that there is little difference in attitude between genders before and after entering law enforcement. However, more research is required before these findings can be readily accepted.

Race and Ethnicity

The ethnic and racial composition of policing is still changing; thus, as with gender, there is a limited amount of research available that offers insight into the effect of race and ethnicity on attitude before entry into policing/law enforcement. There is, however, some literature focusing on attitudes of black officers after entry into policing/law enforcement.

In the available research, it has been noted that black officers generally have a much more difficult time as police officers than their white or Hispanic colleagues. Black officers who enter policing with an attitude geared toward helping all of society, not just a specific segment, often find a need for change. Black officers often face limited or no acceptance from fellow white and Hispanic officers and guarded acceptance from the black community. Available research indicates that although some black officers prefer to work in black areas, others prefer not to. It has also been found that black officers are both more likely to arrest black offenders and to arrest other blacks with less negotiation than white officers.

■ CASE IN POINT

On several occasions, a white police officer had the opportunity to observe how black officers acted and reacted in settings in which the victim or alleged offender was black. It was noted that some black officers went easier on black offenders, whereas others were harsher on black offenders. It was also interesting that some black officers would take offense when black complainants or suspects tried using a "brotherhood" attitude with the officer. As a matter of fact, several black officers advised that they would rather not work in all-black areas and did not like having to deal with many blacks. Their reasoning ranged from having little empathy for those who wouldn't help themselves to the belief that those who broke the law degraded the black race.

In all, it would appear that there are some differences in the basic attitudes of groups of police officers. Black officers appear to be more punitive with black offenders than whites. There is also, albeit limited, research indicating that race may be associated with personality traits (Austin et al., 1987; Tenerowicz, 1993). As for preexisting attitudes, there is little or no empirical evidence to demonstrate that they carry over to the job.

What has been found is that elements associated with policing affect attitude and sometimes cause preexisting attitudes to change. Job assignment (including time and shift), supervisors, departmental policies, court decisions, societal changes, and the nature of the job all tend to affect police attitudes.

Regardless of what an individual's personality or attitude is before becoming a police officer, there is almost certain to be a change once the individual is introduced to the world of policing. Therefore, it is important to understand the effect that being a police officer tends to have on individuals.

CHANGE OF PERSONALITY

As noted earlier, such traits as cynicism and hostility can become part of the police personality. Isolation, distrust, elitism, egotistical observations, and introverted behavior (except toward other police officers) may also become part of the police personality (Billings & Moos, 1982; Cortina et al., 1992; Girodo, 1991; Kroes, 1985; Lyman, 1999; Niederhoffer, 1969; Skolnick, 1994; Territo & Vetter, 1981; Topp & Kardash, 1986).

Considering the nature of the job, it is often difficult for police officers to retain the personality with which they started. The constant barrage of other people's problems, people hurting each other, stealing from one another, and death resulting from a variety of causes all can begin to affect the officer negatively. It is not uncommon for police officers to become drug users or alcoholics, or get married and divorced several times at an early age (Dantzker, 1989; Dash & Reiser, 1978; Martin, 1987; Violanti, Marshall, & Howe, 1985).

Additionally, police officers often become isolated from the rest of society and socialize only with other officers because they believe that no one else can understand what they do, except another officer (Herbert, 1998). Although this is an unfair assessment, it comes to be accepted by many officers within a very short time on the job (Graf, 1986). The fact that police officers are expected to solve everyone's problems and not have any of their own, be model citizens, and deal with situations or incidents that many others would choose to avoid is a very heavy burden to bear. For some officers it is too much.

■ CASE IN POINT

In 1996 a New Jersey state trooper shot and killed his wife with his service revolver. He then took his own life. An Oklahoma City, Oklahoma, police sergeant, who was to receive a medal of valor for his efforts during the rescue of victims from the 1996 bombing of the Federal Building, apparently committed suicide. Also in 1996 a Royal Palm Beach, Florida, police officer admitted himself to a hospital after stealing a squad car and threatening to commit suicide. In June 1997 a New York City police officer shot and killed his ex-girlfriend and then took his own life. How much being a police officer influenced the decision to commit murder and/or suicide is speculative, but it is believed to play a major role.

Fortunately, murder and suicide are not typical responses of police officers. A more typical response is to turn to drugs, excessive alcohol consumption, or sexual activity (Dantzker, 1989). Ultimately, the impact of the job and the changes in the officer's personality can be linked to stress.

STRESS

Stress is a phenomenon that every occupation experiences. Policing/law enforcement has been viewed and identified as an extremely stressful occupation. Yet, it has only been since 1972 that there has been a formal interest and concern with stress and its effect on police officers. Although police stress may have, at times, been exaggerated, it is an issue with which both officers and agencies should be concerned.

LAPD psychologist Marty Reiser (1974) observed that, "Police work is a high stress occupation that affects, shapes and also scars the individuals and families involved" (p. 156). Others have pointed out that police work is particularly stressful because of the psychological, sociological, and physiological problems police officers experience, and that the perception of the stressfulness of situations encountered affects performance (Dantzker, 1997; Gaines & Jermier, 1983; Terry, 1983). The stress associated with policing requires recognition because of the personal and work-related consequences that result (Dantzker, 1989, 1997; Maslach, 1976; Wexler & Logan, 1983).

The most easily detectable area that stress affects involves physiological problems. Through the years, stress has been found to be related to such illnesses as ulcers, migraine headaches, hypertension, backaches, asthma, and heart problems. It has even been suggested that the effects of stress may be linked to systemic diseases, such as cancer, lupus, and arthritis (Asterita, 1985). The truth is that stress has been found to play an important role in the causation of physical disorders. What this means to policing is that medical retirements and time lost because of illness may be related to stress-induced illnesses (Blank, 1987).

Physical problems are only one possible effect of excessive stress. Sociological problems may also occur. One of the most common sociological problems among police officers has been divorce. Because of the nature and stress of the job, police officers often have a difficult time establishing and maintaining a "normal" family life. The daily activity of dealing with others' personal problems makes handling the officer's own personal and family problems that much more difficult. Unlike many other occupations, after the shift has ended the stress of work cannot be left at work. Ultimately, it affects most officers' family lives (Bell, 1988). Some researchers have discovered that it is not unusual in larger urban police agencies to find a higher than normal proportion of officers under the age of thirty who are in the midst of their third (or more) marriage (Territo & Vetter, 1981).

Another sociological problem for police is socialization. It has been recognized that many police officers find it difficult to socialize outside the ranks of policing. Thus, there appears to be a tendency toward isolation from anyone outside policing/law enforcement, even family members. The common belief among police officers is that no one else can understand the stress of the job other than another police officer. This perception frequently leads police officers to socialize only with other officers. Unfortunately, this often only increases the level of stress in the officer because conversations among police officers ultimately focus on the job, which offers little relief from the stress. Officers who attempt to build social relationships outside policing/law enforcement find that, because of elements of the job such as rotating schedules, overtime, and working on holidays, it is difficult to plan social activities. In addition, even in the most casual off-duty circumstances it is difficult to stop thinking and acting as a police officer.

■ CASE IN POINT

Personal experiences and observations of police officers have found that, even when off duty and out with family or friends, many police officers refuse to sit with their backs to the door and constantly watch the activity around the cash register and the door. Also, when off duty and driving in personal vehicles, it is common for police officers to point out vehicular violations, suspicious persons and vehicles, and possible criminal activity (e.g., drug deals or prostitution).

Regardless of the difficulty, police officers need to establish outlets for sharing their stress outside policing, such as with family members. Many police officers will not share the experiences of the job with family members, believing that they are shielding them from the ugliness of the job. This may best be summed up in this quotation from the wife of a former police officer:

> I think that a lot of the problem with intrafamily communication is due to police officers' belief that they shouldn't bring the "ugliness" or the "filth" of the job home to the bosom of their family. I think that this is often symbolized by the changing into/out of the police uniform at work. I think that this also has a lot to do with police family divorce—i.e., that the home should be the sanctum sanctorum, managed for the cop in his absence by a virgin/whore wife, where worries never intrude and the cop is clean, honored, and his word is "law."

Many officers fail to share the stress of the job with family members; yet, someday it may be really necessary to share, and no one will be available or will want to hear it.

■ CASE IN POINT

A veteran police officer never shared the stresses of the job with his spouse even though in the beginning years of their marriage she tried to get him to share. For twenty years, the officer would share nothing of the job with his spouse. One day the officer was involved in an incident in which he shot and killed someone. For the first time in his career he needed to share how he was feeling with his wife. When the officer began to discuss the incident with his wife she advised him that after all these years of being "shut out," she had no interest in his work-related problems.

Although the physiological and sociological effects of stress contribute their share of problems for police officers, the most devastating effects of stress appear to be the psychological problems. Three major problems are alcoholism and drug dependency (which are also physiological addictions) and suicide. Like divorce, these three problems seem to appear at a high rate among police officers. One explanation sees these problems simply as a consequence of the inability to cope with the stress of police work. Joseph Wambaugh probably provided the best depiction of these problems in his book *The Choirboys*. Group drinking and sexual activities, drug usage, and even suicide are sometimes acceptable modes of behavior for police officers in their efforts to cope with stress; police officers themselves are their number one killer ("What's Killing Americas' Cops?," 1996). Yet, these are not, and should not be, acceptable behaviors.

Physical, social, and psychological problems are the result of excessive stress in police officers. The ultimate effect of stress has been identified as "burnout." Burnout is viewed as an exhaustion—physical, emotional, or mental, or a combination thereof—resulting from a compilation of job stress with no acceptable or healthful avenue of release. Burnout in police officers has been found to lead to attitudinal problems such as cynicism, judgment and decision-making problems, and the impairment of reflexes (Maslach, 1976). Burnout can be extremely dangerous for the police officer.

■ CASE IN POINT

Having been a patrol officer for several years, an officer was feeling mentally fatigued with the job. Everything was boring, mundane, or frustrating. The officer's cynicism was becoming more noticeable. One day the officer was dispatched to a local convenience store in reference to "a man with a gun." Under normal circumstances, on arriving at the scene the officer would have parked to the side of the building and waited for an assist. On this particular day the officer pulled right up to the front door, observed that the suspect was still inside and, not seeing a gun, went in. As the officer approached the suspect, the suspect began to back away from the counter and started to reach under his jacket. This movement finally caused the officer to think. He grabbed and restrained the suspect quickly enough to prevent him from reaching a .357 Magnum hidden under his coat. Needless to say, this incident was enough to make the officer realize that something was wrong and seek advice. The conclusion was that the officer was suffering from burnout. The remedy was a transfer out of patrol into a specialized investigative unit. Not all burned-out officers are lucky enough to be alive for a remedy.

Considering the serious effects of stress on police officers, it is important to recognize what causes it. The causes that lead to stress have been referred to as stressors (Dantzker, 1989, 1997; Reiser, 1974; Terry, 1983). Although many occupations share similar stressors—such as shift work, supervisory problems, and inadequate equipment—there are those that are inherent to policing. These include responding to unpredictable situations, periods of work that range from inactiveness to extremely stressful activity back to periods of less stressing activity, instantaneous decision making, the court system, and the use of force (Dantzker, 1989, 1997; Doerner, 1998; Reiser, 1974; Wexler & Logan, 1983).

The research on police stressors has identified numerous stressors. In all, what constitutes police stress is generally dependent on individual perceptions. Therefore, it is important for police agencies to educate officers on the various facets of stress and how to cope with it.

Because of the rising costs associated with stress—stress-related medical retirements, related illnesses, and civil liability lawsuits that have held police departments responsible for their officers' behavior and psychological well-being—police departments have begun to make a concerted effort to promote awareness of stress and provide assistance to police officers in dealing with it. As a result, stress management is rapidly becoming a part of the academy training curriculum. By introducing rookie officers and their spouses to the elements associated with stress, police agencies hope that recognition will occur much sooner and assistance will be sought. This assistance is primarily found in special units or programs created within the police agency that are staffed with a full-time psychologist and peer counselors. For example, the Boston, Massachusetts, Police Department is credited with creating one of the first police stress programs. Its services include counseling, "rap sessions," and referrals to outside agencies. Many other police departments have followed the lead of Boston and have created similar in-house programs or have contracted with outside agencies for available services. Stress management is becoming such an important issue that the federal government has made money available for the development of model programs.

Although it's only a training exercise hanging upside down with smoke bombs going off cannot be too relaxing. Imagine this same situation with lives on the line. (Courtesy of the Scottsdale, Arizona, Police Department)

■ CASE IN POINT

In 1997 the National Institute of Justice awarded eight grants to help develop programs aimed at becoming models for stress management programs throughout the country. Among the agencies and organizations that received the grants were the Vermont Department of Public Safety, which established a state police peer support team and state police spouse peer support team; the New York Bureau of Municipal Police, which created a statewide "train the trainers" course that would train several individuals who could then provide stress-management training in academies; the Arkansas State Police, which used the grant to conduct an eighteen-month project that focused on providing stress-reduction skills to the agency's thirty-three volunteer chaplains; and Iowa State University, which developed and evaluated a comprehensive model stress-management program for university, municipal, and county police officers and their families in rural areas.

In all, it is extremely important that police officers and police agencies continue to recognize, address, and deal with the stresses of police work.

The nature of policing can affect an officer's personality; generally, the change leads the officer to seek companionship and understanding from fellow officers or to become a loner. Historically, the fellowship appears to have won out more frequently and has been identified as the **police subculture.**

THE POLICE SUBCULTURE

A phenomenon not uncommon to our society is the formation of subcultures (Herbert, 1998). A subculture is viewed as any ethnic, regional, economic, or social group demonstrating particular patterns of behavior that may distinguish it from the rest of society. Policing has been identified as a subculture, often referred to as "The Blue Brotherhood."

The existence of the police subculture was first formally identified in a 1950 study of the Gary, Indiana, Police Department by W.A. Westley. As a result of his research, Westley argued that a distinct subculture existed among police officers. He found that there was an evident lack of trust by police of the general society that caused officers to lean on each other for support. The subculture appeared to stress secrecy ("code of silence") and support the use of violence in certain situations. Even though this appears to still be an existing trait of policing, it is becoming less acceptable outside of policing.

■ CASE IN POINT

In fall 1992 a federal jury in Indianapolis, Indiana, ordered six police officers to pay $1.5 million to a man who was allegedly beaten by officers after firing his shotgun (which he claimed was accidental) at an officer who had allegedly forced his way into the complainant's home and began to beat him with a nightstick. Two of the officers, who were sergeants, were ordered to pay $400,000 for failing to intervene during the beating that followed the shooting. The most interesting part of the verdict was the ordering of all six officers to pay a total of $300,000 for following the "code of silence" by attempting to cover up and protect one another after the incident.

An obvious result of the police subculture has been the "us versus them" mentality that is still fairly common today (Bouza, 1990; Herbert, 1998). First officially recognized in Westley's research, the "us versus them" mentality has appeared to be an important part of the police subculture. This mentality includes a belief among police officers that only other police officers can share and understand the problems and stress of the job. It is a mentality that assists in creating problems between police and citizens because its underlying basis is that

(Jump Start reprinted by permission of United Feature Syndicate, Inc.)

citizens neither understand nor care about police officers and only want to cause officers problems. More recently, Herbert (1998) noted that the police subculture exists of six normative orders—law, bureaucratic control, adventure/machismo, safety, competence, and morality (p. 347)—which "fundamentally structure the social world of police" (p. 361). Current models of police subculture usually indicate a very cynical approach to dealing with citizens and a strengthening in the bond among officers. Yet, this may be changing.

Since Westley's study, policing has undergone changes that appear to have had a significant impact on the police subculture. First, the ethnic, racial, and gender composition of policing have changed. For years, policing was primarily a white, male occupation, the members of which shared similar morals, social values, and religious beliefs. The diversity of today's police population offers a variety of social, ethnic, racial, and religious backgrounds often with only one common link—policing.

Another factor that may be responsible for causing a change in the police subculture is education (Dantzker, 1997; Doerner, 1998). In previous years, most police officers were at a common educational level. Today, it is not uncommon for a police agency to have levels of education among police officers that start at the high school graduate level and end with the doctoral level. This diversity in education has assisted in separating officers. Furthermore, it appears that some officers are no longer willing to accept their fellow officers' limitations nor willing to "cover" for them when they make mistakes.

■ CASE IN POINT

Several police departments contacted during the past few years have advised that a larger percentage of complaints against their police officers are coming from other police officers. For example, one midsized Texas police department reported in 1997 that among the complaints against police officers filed with the IA unit, most were initiated or made by fellow police officers. This is extremely interesting considering that in years past, less than 25 percent of all complaints came from police officers.

Why individuals become police officers and what happens to them after doing so are interesting aspects of the police personality. Yet, how a police officer performs his duty on the job is linked to personality. In addition, the relationships established with community members are also interesting and an important element related to the officer's personality. These issues are further understood through the examination of an officer's style of policing.

● STYLES OF POLICING

With the exception of the citizen who has a personal relationship with a police officer, most citizens rely on those isolated incidents when contact between them and a police officer occurs to establish an attitudinal perception of the officer. The citizen's perception of the officer's attitude or personality may be based solely on what occurs during the contact; the outcome of that contact often depends on the style of policing practiced by the officer.

Over time, several styles of policing have been identified. Many are identified as the "traditional styles": the **crime fighter, social servant, law enforcer,** and **watchman.** These styles were first identified by Wilson (1968) and have been further established through the literature and years of practical observations.

The crime fighter is the officer whose goal and objectives focus on capturing the felony offender. This officer is always looking for felony-in-progress calls and will respond whenever possible, whether the call is in this officer's beat or not. Fighting crime is this officer's sole reason for being a police officer. This officer has an extremely aggressive nature, has little tolerance for law breakers, and may often be very authoritarian with little room for negotiation. An ultimate goal may be to remain as a "street cop" for all the officer's career.

The social servant is somewhat more restrained than the crime fighter. This officer's attitude is, "It's my job to help people whenever and however I can." The social servant is more accepting of the social welfare aspect of policing and considers it a useful part of policing (Greenberg & Ruback, 1982). Although he or she sometimes attempts to make the promotional climb, there does not appear to be an intense drive for promotion. Overall, the attitude of the officer who practices this style of policing reflects an "Officer Friendly"–type individual.

Writing traffic citations, enforcing city ordinances, and apprehending misdemeanor violations appear to keep the law enforcer satisfied. The officer who approaches policing with this style appears as a semiaggressive individual whose attitude dictates enforcing all aspects of the law. No one area of law receives more attention than another. Being a patrol officer for life is satisfactory; there is no great drive for a promotion in rank. The officer's attitude toward an individual generally is a reflection of the attitude of the individual. Adaptability to all personalities and attitudes is the key for this officer.

The watchman is simply doing no more than is required: enforcing the law when absolutely necessary. The most passive of the four, the watchman simply appears to be biding time until something better comes along. This officer often conveys an indifferent, nonchalant, and uncaring attitude, or is relatively content performing order maintenance chores rather than law enforcement (Greenberg & Ruback, 1982).

The traditional styles of policing are one way of examining police behavior. Walsh (1977) identified three styles of policing. These included the **street cop, action seeker,** and **middle-class mobile.** The street cop views policing as a secure work environment. The attraction to the job is the security and benefits. The action seeker is interested in policing because of the potential excitement it offers. This officer is constantly looking for something to do. Extreme aggressiveness makes up a major part of this officer's attitude. Finally, the middle-class mobile sees policing as a career, an opportunity for advancement and respectability in a profession that has required minimal levels of education.

A third perspective of police styles is offered by Broderick (1987), who has labeled officers as **enforcers, idealists, realists,** and **optimists.** These styles can be divided into two main aspects of the officer's occupational outlook: due process (individual rights) and social order. The enforcer is more concerned with social order and keeping society safe than individual rights or due process. The idealist places a high degree of value on individual rights and due process as well

FIGURE 10-1   Police Officer Style Typology

	Due Process	Social Order
Enforcer	Low	High
Idealist	High	High
Realist	Low	Low
Optimist	High	Low

Source: Adapted from Broderick, J.J. (1987). Police in a time of change (2nd ed., p. 5). Prospect Heights, IL: Waveland Press.

as social order. The realist places little emphasis on either social order or individual rights, accepting society at face value. Relatively similar to the social servant, the optimist sees the job as being people oriented, providing a variety of opportunities to help people. Individual rights are highly valued, whereas social order is not as much of a concern (see Figure 10-1).

The style of policing practiced by an officer depends greatly on the officer's personality. Traits such as authoritarianism, cynicism, racism, and hostility can negatively influence the style practiced. Therefore, it is important to policing, as well as to society, for police officers to possess personality traits conducive to establishing an effective and efficient police agency. However, the personality issue is not just about how police officers view their role within society; an institutional issue has also been identified.

MANAGEMENT VERSUS RANK-AND-FILE PERSONALITIES

Before concluding this chapter, the existence of a personality conflict within the departmental structure of the police agency should be acknowledged. Because the literature on this is limited, the following discussion is primarily based on experience, observations, and discussions with both line officers and police managers.

The conflict is viewed as the management personality versus the rank-and-file personality. Although personality may be determined by a variety of individual factors as well as environmental factors, one's position within the police agency may also have an impact.

The management personality refers to those individuals who are part of the police command-management structure. Their personality often revolves around the requirements of their position. For example, they must now enforce the guidelines or policies they disliked as officers. This has a tendency to cause movement away from a certain camaraderie with "the troops" and begins to isolate police managers. Eventually, the police manager must accept that his or her role requires cooperation and support of departmental policies and guidelines regardless of how he or she is accepted by line officers (Bouza, 1990).

The other side of the coin is referred to as the rank-and-file personality. Those individuals not part of management wonder why things happen as they do, such as why certain policies are created or enforced, whereas others are ignored. It becomes an "us versus them" mentality similar to that which police officers often have with citizens. The rank and file may not believe management knows what it is doing or cares about how management decisions affect the "guys on the street" (Swanson, Territo, & Taylor, 1993).

The struggle between management and rank and file seems to reflect the traditional bureaucratic structure of the police organization. This structure has been found to cause a division among organization members that, in turn, often assists in creating a conflict of organizationally recognized personalities.

SUMMARY

The existence of a distinct police personality has yet to be documented. There is support for the existence of distinct personality traits. Whether they preexist or are a result of the police socialization process is debated and still requires substantial empirical support.

With respect to race and gender, there appears to be little attitudinal difference before entry and after acceptance into policing. However, it appears that black officers are more punitive toward other blacks.

Policing is known to cause changes in one's personality. A major component of policing that impacts personality is stress. The effects of stress are linked to physical, sociological, and psychological problems among police officers.

The nature of policing is often blamed for the closeness of police officers to each other. A police subculture exists to assist in socialization, yet, this limits the type of interpersonal relationships to those inside policing.

The style of policing is often the result of the officer's attitude and ambition. Several styles have been identified, and, although personnel changes, styles remain consistent.

Finally, the nature of the police organization causes a personality division in its members, best viewed as management versus rank and file. One personality is more concerned with policy and procedure, whereas the other is concerned with activities.

DO YOU KNOW . . .

1. Other reasons why individuals might become police officers?
2. What types of incidents officers handle that help fulfill the "need to help society"?
3. What preexistent traits can be identified in police officers? What traits can be learned after joining the police force?
4. Why some black officers are harsher on black citizens than their white or Hispanic peers?
5. Whether stress management training should be a mandatory part of police recruit training?
6. Whether the collapse or weakening of the police subculture is a positive or negative factor for the future of policing?
7. What the best style of policing is?
8. What might be done to eliminate the management versus rank-and-file personality differences?

REFERENCES

Arcuri, A.F. (1976). Police pride and self-esteem: Indications of future occupational changes. *Journal of Police Science and Administration, 4*, 436–444.

Asterita, M.F. (1985). *The physiology of stress.* New York: Human Sciences Press.

Austin, T.L., Hale, D.C., & Ramsey, L.J. (1987). The effect of layoff on police authoritarianism. *Criminal Justice and Behavior, 14*, 194–210.

Baron, R.A., & Byrne, D. (1991). *Social psychology: Understanding human interaction* (6th ed.). Boston: Allyn and Bacon.

Bayley, D.H. (Ed.). (1977). *Police and society.* Beverly Hills, CA: Sage Publications.

Bell, L.M. (1988, June). The unfair family affair. *Police,* 29–31.

Billings, A.G., & Moos, R.H. (1982) Work stress and the stress-suffering roles of work and family resources. *Journal of Occupational Behavior,* 215–232.

Blank, D. (1987, October). Workers seek payment for job-related stress. *American Banker,* 19, 26, 28.

Bonifacio, P. (1991). *The psychological effects of police work.* New York: Plenum Press.

Bouza, A.V. (1990). *The police mystique.* New York: Plenum Press.

Broderick, J.J. (1987). *Police in a time of change.* Prospect Heights, IL: Waveland Press.

Butler, A.J.P., & Cochrane, R. (1977). An examination of some elements of the personality of police officers and their implications. *Journal of Police Science and Administration, 5*, 441–450

Carpenter, B.N., & Raza, S.M. (1987). Personality characteristics of police applicants: Comparisons across subgroups and with other populations. *Journal of Police Science and Administration, 15,* 10–17.

Cortina, J.M., Doherty, M.L., Schmitt, N., & Kaufman, G. (1992). The "Big Five" personality factors in the IPI and MMPI: Predictors of police performance. *Personnel Psychology, 45,* 119–140.

Dantzker, M.L. (1989). *The effect of education on police performance: The stress perspective.* Ann Arbor MI: UMI Dissertation Information Service.

Dantzker, M.L. (1997). Stress and the badge. In M.L. Dantzker (Ed.), *Contemporary policing: Personnel, issues and trends* (pp. 99–126). Newton, MA: Butterworth-Heinemann.

Dash, J., & Reiser, M. (1978). Suicide among police in urban law enforcement agencies. *Journal of Police Science and Administration 6,* 18–21.

Doerner, W.G. (1998). *Introduction to law enforcement: An insider's view.* Newton, MA: Butterworth-Heinemann.

Gaines, J., & Jermier, J.M. (1983). Emotional exhaustion in a high stress organization. *Academy of Management, 26,* 567–586.

Girodo, M. (1991). Personality, job stress, and mental health in undercover agents: A structural equation analysis. *Journal of Social Behavior and Personality, 6,* 375–390.

Graf, F.A. (1986). The relationship between social supports and occupational stress among police officers. *Journal of Police Science and Administration, 14,* 178–186.

Greenberg, M.S., & Ruback, R.B. (1982). *Social psychology of the criminal justice system.* Belmont, CA: Wadsworth Publishing.

Herbert, S. (1998). Police subculture reconsidered. *Criminology, 36,* 343–369.

Hernandez, J., Jr. (1989). *The Custer syndrome.* Salem, WI: Sheffield Publishing Company.

Klopsch, J.W. (1983). Police personality changes as measured by the MMPI: A five-year longitudinal study. Unpublished doctoral dissertation.

Kroes, W.H. (1985). Society's victim—the police. Springfield, IL: Charles C. Thomas, Publishers.

Lester, D. (1983). Why do people become police officers? A study of reasons and their predictions of success. *Journal of Police Science and Administration, 11,* 170–174.

Lester, D., Babcock, S.D., Cassisi, J.P., Genz, J.L., & Butler, A.J.P. (1980). The personalities of English and American police. *Journal of Social Psychology, 111,* 153–154.

Lord, L.K. (1986). A comparison of male and female peace officers: Stereotypic perceptions of women and women peace officers. *Journal of Police Science and Administration, 14,* 83–97.

Lyman, M.D. (1999). *The police: An introduction.* Upper Saddle River, NJ: Prentice Hall.

Martin, R. (1987). Stress and police work: An overview of general responses. Paper presented at the Academy of Criminal Justice Sciences Annual Conference. St. Louis, MO.

Maslach, C. (1976, September). Burned-out. *Human Behavior, 16*–22.

Meagher, M.S., & Yentes, N.A. (1986). Choosing a career in policing: A comparison of male and female perceptions. *Journal of Police Science and Administration, 14,* 320–327.

Niederhoffer, A. (1969). *Behind the shield: The police in urban society.* Garden City, NY: Anchor Books.

Poole, E.D., & Pogrebin, M.R. (1988). Factors affecting the decision to remain in policing: A study of women offenders. *Journal of Police Science and Administration, 16,* 49–55.

Reiser, M. (1974). Some organizational stresses of policemen. *Journal of Police Science and Administration, 2,* 156–159.

Skolnick, J. (1994). *Justice without trial: Law enforcement in a democratic society* (3rd ed.). New York: Macmillan Publishing Company.

Swanson, C.R., Territo, L., & Taylor, R.W. (1993). *Police administration* (3rd ed.). New York: Macmillan Publishing Company.

Tenerowicz, C.M. (1993). A longitudinal study of personality change in urban police officers: Educational implications (Doctoral dissertation, Cleveland State, 1992). *ProQuest-Dissertation Abstracts, 53,* 6027.

Territo, L., & Vetter, H.J. (1981). *Stress and police personnel.* Boston: Allyn and Bacon.

Terry, W.C. (1983). Police stress as an individual and administrative problem: Some conceptual and theoretical difficulties. *Journal of Police Science and Administration, 11,* 211–216.

Topp, B.W., & Kardash, C.A. (1986). Personality, achievement, and attrition: Validation in a multiple-jurisdiction police academy. *Journal of Police Science and Administration, 14,* 234–241.

Violanti, J.M., Marshall, J.R., & Howe, B. (1985). Stress, coping, and alcohol use: The police connection. *Journal of Police Science and Administration, 3,* 106–110.

Walker, S. (1999). *The police in America* (3rd ed.). New York: McGraw-Hill.

Walsh, J.L. (1977). Career styles and police behavior. In D.H. Bayley (Ed.), *Police and society* (pp. 149–176). Beverly Hills, CA: Sage Publications.

Wellman, R.J., Kelly, R.E., & Trapasso, P.A. (1988). Predicting "accident proneness" in police officers. *Journal of Police Science and Administration, 16,* 44–48.

Westley, W.A. (1970). *Violence and the police.* Cambridge, MA: MIT Press.

Wexler, J.G., & Logan, D.D. (1983). Sources of stress among women police officers. *Journal of Police Science and Administration, 11,* 46–53.

What's killing America's cops? (1996, November 15) *Law Enforcement News,* 1.

Wilson, J.Q. (1968). *Varieties of police behavior.* Cambridge, MA: Harvard University Press.

11 ISSUES: TODAY AND TOMORROW

The first ten chapters introduced and illustrated myriad elements associated with the structural and functional existence of policing. This chapter concludes the text with a discussion of a variety of important issues for policing both today and in the future.

To begin, being a police officer at any time in U.S. history has been, and will continue to be, a difficult task. If today's and future police officers are going to be able to carry out successfully the duties of the job and survive, awareness of a variety of issues is vital, such as offenders' rights, new technologies, civil liability, and health-related issues. Although each of these deserves attention, it is impossible to address every issue crucial to policing. However, such issues as use of force, AIDS, legalities (especially police officers' rights), technological changes, and professionalism are extremely relevant topics worthy of discussion.

USE OF FORCE

Police officers are granted a power few people ever have—the legal and moral right to use force during the performance of their duties, even if it means taking a life. Use of force is a main characteristic of policing, and its inappropriate use is often a central problem in many police misconduct allegations (Kerstetter, 1985). Fridell and Pate, (1997) argue that "the history of policing has been characterized by a dynamic search for the means by which to optimize the use of legitimate force: utilizing it as necessary to maintain order, but not to the extent that it is excessive and abusive" (p. 217). The use of force by police officers often receives mixed reviews from the public.

■ CASE IN POINT

On a yearly basis, the Roper Center for Public Opinion Research conducts a national social survey. A question asked of respondents is, "Under what conditions would you approve of a police officer striking a citizen: if the citizen was attacking the police officer with fists; was attempting to escape from custody; had said vulgar and obscene things to the police officer; or was being questioned in a murder case." Respondents' approval of such use of force appears to be on a downward trend. In 1996, 91 percent (compared to 94 percent in 1986) said they would approve of an officer striking a citizen who was striking the officer with fists, 68 percent (compared to 72 percent in 1986) said it was okay during the escape attempt, only 7 percent (compared to 14 percent in 1986) approved when vulgar or obscene language was used, and 5 percent (compared to 9 percent in 1986) approved of striking a citizen during questioning in a murder case. Respondents are also asked, "Are there any situations you can imagine in which you would approve of a police officer striking an adult male?" In 1996, 67 percent (compared to 72 percent in 1986) gave an affirmative response (*Sourcebook of Criminal Justice Statistics, 1997*; http://www.albany.edu/sourcebook/1995/pdf/t229.pdf).

The use of force by police officers is just one side of this issue. Police officers also find themselves likely to have force used against them more often than the average citizen. According to a recent national study, policing is the most victimized occupation in the country. From 1992 though 1996, more than one million police officers were "victims of a nonfatal violent crime" while on duty (Warchol, 1998). In 1994, 157 officers were fatally wounded (*Sourcebook of Criminal Justice Statistics, 1994*).

Citizens do not like to hear about police officers being assaulted or killed; they like even less hearing about officers who use excessive force against citizens. They believe that risking personal assault is part of the officer's job, as is the training that limits excessive use of force. The issue of the police use of force is two-dimensional: (1) **nonlethal excessive force** and (2) **deadly force.**

Nonlethal Excessive Force

The nonlethal excessive use of force by a police officer while performing the duties of the job are most often referred to as cases of brutality. Brutality may be either verbal or physical; however, it is the physical use that receives more attention from the media, community members, and the police agency. The beating of a handcuffed or uncooperative prisoner or the use of unauthorized items as weapons to subdue a suspect are examples of nonlethal excessive force. Departmental policies, improved training, and liability lawsuits have assisted in the limiting of episodes of excessive force (del Carmen, 1991; Fridell & Pate, 1997).

Many police department policies explicitly indicate that excessive force is unacceptable. These policies often define "excessive force" and what constitutes "excessive." Excessive force is any force used beyond what would be reasonable to effect the arrest; "when it is used for other than lawful purposes or when it is used out of proportion to the need" (Chen, 1995, p. 234). For example, striking an individual on the head several times with a flashlight is considered excessive force. Violation of such policies leads to disciplinary action by the department as well as possible criminal and civil sanctions.

■ CASE IN POINT

The following incidents occurred in 1997 and 1998. Two Riverside, California, sheriff's deputies were caught on videotape beating two occupants of a pickup truck after they engaged the officers in a pursuit. At the time of this writing, both deputies face criminal and civil actions.

A Savannah, Georgia, police officer was fired and indicted for sexually assaulting a man in custody. A Georgia state trooper was caught on videotape beating an individual he stopped for an alleged traffic violation. The officer faces criminal and civil charges. Five NYPD officers face criminal and civil charges for the alleged beating and torture of a Haitian man in custody for minor offenses. Five Houston, Texas, officers face civil charges and one officer faces both criminal and civil charges in what appears to be a wrongful death case. A Springfield, Massachusetts, officer was not indicted on charges of excessive force after a videotape showed the officer kicking an individual in the shoulder during an arrest. However, he still faces the possibility of a civil lawsuit.

The key to fewer incidents of excessive force continues to be training (del Carmen, 1991; Fridell & Pate, 1997; Garner, Schade, & Hepburn, 1996). Most police academies now require several hours of self-defense, arrest-control techniques, and nonlethal weapons training in an effort to keep to a minimum the use of excessive force. Some of the nonlethal weapons being implemented are the baton, or PR24; dispensers of chemicals, such as pepper mace; and the taser, a weapon that discharges 10,000 volts of electricity into its target. Some agencies are experimenting with other types of nonlethal weapons as they become available. For example, in 1997 the Portland, Oregon, police started using "beanbag" rounds, which are shot from a shotgun, in situations that require less-than-lethal

Nonlethal force training has become a constant in today's police training. (Courtesy of the Scottsdale, Arizona, Police Department)

force. Other nonlethal items designed for the police include "ooze guns" that fire a sticky, glue-like substance and nets for capturing and restraining aggressive subjects. In addition, nonlethal self-defense training includes verbal judo, take-down techniques, control holds, and pressure-point immobilization. However, some departments have had to reevaluate their policies on the use of specific forms of nonlethal force. For example, in 1992 the Albuquerque, New Mexico, Police Department seriously began to reconsider its policy on officers' use of martial-arts techniques, and in 1996 the Cincinnati, Ohio, Police Department started reviewing its policies after an officer was videotaped kicking an individual during an arrest. Regardless of what specific techniques are taught and used, training remains the key to fewer incidents of excessive force (Fridell & Pate, 1997).

One of the most common training sources is the FLETC (Federal Law Enforcement Training Center) use-of-force model. According to Graves and Connor (1992), "The model supports the widely accepted practice of progressive application of force, which applies the appropriate selection of force options in response to the level of compliance from the individual to be controlled" (p. 56). This model is divided into five levels of enforcement. Each level matches the officer's perception of suspect resistance to how much force should be used (Table 11-1).

Level 1 is compliant and cooperative suspect behavior requiring only verbal commands from the officer. In level 2 the amount of resistance from the suspect is passive (e.g., simply doesn't respond to verbal commands), which requires the officer to use some form of psychological rather than physical contact control (e.g., advising suspect of the additional consequences for failing to cooperate, such as additional charges). When level 3 is reached the suspect's resistance becomes active, physically defiant (e.g., pulling away from officer) but not yet assaultive, and the officer must use some form of compliance technique equal to the force being used to defy the officer (e.g., wrist lock). In level 4 the suspect is being assaultive toward the officer, causing the officer some bodily harm (e.g., kicking or punching officer). The officer's response to this resistance should be some form of defensive tactics (e.g., use of nightstick or chemical spray). Finally, when the resistance enters level 5 the suspect is being extremely assaultive (e.g., has some form of a club, knife, or gun) and the officer faces serious bodily harm or even death. This will often require the officer to respond with deadly force.

TABLE 11-1

Use of Force

Level of Resistance	Level of Enforcement	Response
Assaultive (serious bodily injury)	5	Deadly force
Assaultive (bodily injury)	4	Defensive tactics
Resistant (active)	3	Compliance techniques
Resistant (passive)	2	Contact controls
Compliant (cooperative)	1	Verbal commands

Source: Adapted from Graves, F.R., & Connor, G. (1992). The FLETC use-of-force model. The Police Chief.

Using this model as a training device should assist officers to determine the appropriate response to suspect resistance.

Training will continue to be an important aspect of the police use of force. Generally, nonlethal excessive force is found in isolated incidents that seldom receive much public attention.

■ CASE IN POINT

Officers responded to a "fight in progress" at a local nightclub. On their arrival, the officers separated the fighting individuals and began attempting to gather information. The primary officer had taken control of the alleged instigator; however, before he was able to properly arrest the suspect, the suspect broke away and began running from the officer. A foot pursuit ensued, which included the primary officer and two assist officers. Less than a block from the scene, the officers caught up with the suspect near an empty house. During the course of effecting the arrest, the suspect was the recipient of some "curbside justice" and advised he should never run from the police. No one but the three officers and the suspect ever knew about the excessive force used.

Although training is an extremely important factor in limiting the use of excessive force, lawsuits against police agencies have also played an important role in limiting excessive force. For example, in *Graham* v. *Connor* (1989) the U.S. Supreme Court ruled that, "Police officers may be held liable under the Constitution for using excessive force. Such liability must be judged under the 4th Amendment's 'objective reasonableness' standard, rather than under a 'substantive due process' standard" (del Carmen & Walker, 1997, p. 174). The potential of facing a liability lawsuit has caused police agencies and officers to be more aware of the use of excessive force.

Incidents of excessive force cause considerable concern among police and the public. However, it is when the excessive force goes from nonlethal to lethal that it receives extensive attention and criticism.

Deadly Force

The use of deadly force by police officers has long been a concern of the general public. When there is no clear evidence of its necessity, the public often questions police use of deadly force. Every year there are several cases of police use of deadly force that are ruled as justifiable homicides. This means the use of force was determined to have been within departmental policies and not in violation of an individual's constitutional rights.

■ CASE IN POINT

In 1996 three Sterling, Colorado, police officers were found to have been justified in shooting a man after he hit two police cars and a neighbor's car with his vehicle then slashed an officer with a knife. An autopsy revealed that the subject's blood contained a "lethal level" of Ritalin (a drug chemically related to amphetamine). Also in 1996 it was determined that an Annapolis, Maryland, officer was justified in his use of deadly force trying to protect a man who was being beaten and cut with broken bottles by two men during a robbery attempt.

Even when the use of deadly force is considered to be justifiable, the public is still concerned about such incidents. In recent years, the issue of deadly force has gained so much attention that some practitioners and scholars are concerned with the negative effect the criticism has on police officers. Harold Christensen (1989), former deputy attorney general of Texas, illustrated how scrutiny of police deadly force may affect police officers.

> Their ability to respond freely as a rapidly deteriorating situation might dictate has been hampered. Aware that every action will be the subject of intense scrutiny, and that the slightest deviation from what is perceived by some as appropriate, could cost him his reputation and his job, he may be disposed to hesitate. And perhaps long enough to get himself killed (p. 12).

The use of deadly force has become such a publicized issue that any "unusual" amount of police force attracts an amount of attention that may lead to changes in policy.

■ CASE IN POINT

Police policies on the use of deadly force allowing officers to shoot warning shots or shoot at escaping or fleeing felons were not uncommon in the past. However, in 1984 a police officer in a city in Tennessee shot a teenager (who later died at the hospital) fleeing from the scene of a burglary. The case went to the U.S. Supreme Court, which in 1985 ruled that although the officer had acted within departmental guidelines, departmental policies were too broad and inappropriate. The decision in this case, *Tennessee v. Garner* (1985), has led many police departments to create stricter guidelines for the use of deadly force as it pertains to fleeing or escaping felons.

It should be noted that not all public scrutiny leads to changes or finds anything negative about department policies.

■ CASE IN POINT

After fourteen fatal shootings by New York police officers by the end of March 1990, then–Police Commissioner Lee Brown created a five-member committee of law enforcement experts to review the department's existing guidelines on the use of deadly force. The policy allowed for (1) only the minimal amount of force necessary to protect human life, (2) no firing of warning shots, and (3) no shooting at fleeing felons unless the felon poses an immediate danger to the officer or to others. After months of examining the shooting incidents, the committee approved retaining the deadly force policy "as is," noting that there had been a steady decrease in incidents since the policy was implemented in 1980. The committee also recommended the continued use of nonlethal weapons and commended the department's comprehensive training.

Police use of deadly force is an important issue to both the police and the community because of growing use of force against the police and citizens, and the need for the police to respond to this increase. Although police should work hard at limiting use of deadly force, neither the public nor the police should ever lose sight of the fact that sometimes the only choice is to use deadly force. Unfortunately, such recognition frequently seems to stem from an officer being hurt and using deadly force to save his or her own life or the life of another officer.

■ CASE IN POINT

In 1996 Denver, Colorado, police officers shot a naked nineteen year old who reportedly advised officers he was on a "bad acid trip." When officers called for an ambulance the teen allegedly became violent, attacking the officers and grabbing for their guns. It took five officers to subdue the teen even after he was shot in the stomach. Fortunately, the teen survived. Not so lucky was a Bloomfield, Connecticut, man, who in 1997 was fatally shot by a police officer during a drug raid. Upon entry into the residence, officers were confronted by the suspect who was carrying a firearm and allegedly refused to drop it. Fearing for his safety, an officer shot the man. Also in 1997, a murder suspect was wounded by a Roanoke, Virginia, police lieutenant after a standoff of several hours, punctuated by brief chases, during which the suspect refused to drop the semiautomatic weapon he had pointed at several officers.

The police use of deadly force may often be justified. An officer never knows when he or she may have to shoot someone. Because this is such a critical issue, training for when to use deadly force has become an important part of police academy training. To improve training, many police agencies have started using computerized programs in addition to the traditional "role playing" model. The computer programs simulate "shoot–no shoot" scenarios. Early versions of these programs actually allowed officers to fire a projectile at a paper screen, after

Although it is the last thing an officer ever desires to do, the need to use deadly force may arise. Training is very important in knowing when and how to use it. (Courtesy of the Scottsdale, Arizona, Police Department)

which scores and analyses were done by instructors. Newer programs make use of a laser weapon that automatically advises trainees of the results almost immediately after the shooting. Although computers have assisted in the training, they have not replaced target recognition during "live firearms" training and "role playing" exercises, during which officers must act out possible deadly force scenarios. As with nonlethal force, the use of deadly force training is a key part of police use of force.

Most often, police officers have found themselves in a position to have to use deadly force to stop a crime from occurring. However, some situations that require the use of deadly force involve taking the life of an individual who apparently wants to die but is unable to take his or her own life. This phenomenon has become known as "police-assisted suicide" or "suicide by cop" (Huston et al., 1998; Parent, 1998; Scoville, 1998). The number of these cases has been difficult to determine; yet, recent studies of police-related shootings have indicated the number may be higher than expected (Huston et al., 1998; Parent, 1998). In many of these cases, the ruling of police-assisted suicide is based on information learned after the shooting has occurred. However, sometimes the mere nature of the incident made it quite clear that suicide was the goal.

■ CASE IN POINT

A nineteen-year-old New York man used the Nassau County police to help him commit suicide in April 1998. The teen, after being stopped for speeding, pulled out what officers thought was a handgun. The subject was shot after he refused to lower the weapon and continued to advance on the officers. It was later discovered that the "gun" was a toy, and an envelope addressed to "the officer who shot me" was found in the teen's vehicle. The envelope contained a neatly written note that read: "Officer, it was a plan. I'm sorry to get you involved. I just needed to die. Please remember that this was all my doing. You had no way of knowing." Apparently, the teen had been depressed over gambling debts in excess of $6000.

Regardless of the nature, determining whether the use of force is required is a difficult dilemma for police officers, and all officers hope to avoid having to use deadly force in particular. However, having to use deadly force against someone who wants to die but is unable to take his or her own life presents police with a whole new dilemma, one that comes with little training or warning. Obviously, if these types of incidents continue, police officers will need to find ways to be better prepared (Parent, 1998; Scoville, 1998).

Deadly force, whether in response to a criminal situation or a suicidal individual, often is ruled justifiable or necessary. Yet, it only takes one unjustifiable shooting to cause concern about later shootings. McCarthy (1989) stated, "A major necessity is trust between police and community—if no trust exists, all incidents of deadly force may be viewed as improper" (p. 12). Therefore, it is imperative that police departments are open in their investigations, allow public scrutiny, evaluate policies, and maintain high standards of training. Otherwise, every incidence of police use of force—deadly or not, justifiable or not—will come under severe criticism. This, in turn, may be detrimental to officer behavior and community safety because it causes officers to hesitate in situations in which hesitation could be the difference between life and death. Furthermore, it creates an atmosphere of hostility and distrust in the community.

Finally, although the use of deadly force by the police is a concern, deadly force against police officers cannot be ignored. Because national statistics on all police-related shootings (lethal and nonlethal) are not readily available, it is difficult to know just how many citizens are injured or killed by police officers each year. Yet, this is not the case with regard to the number of police officers who are injured or killed. The FBI annually reports on the number of police officers assaulted and killed in the line of duty. Although the number of officers killed seemed to decrease during the 1990s, every officer killed in the line of duty is one too many.

■ CASE IN POINT

In October 1997 Atlanta, Georgia, police officer John Richard Sowa was killed while responding to a domestic violence complaint. Hundreds of uniformed officers from several states attended his funeral. In July 1998 Helena, Arkansas, police captain Richard Wyssbrod became the first officer in the department's history to die in the line of duty. He was shot and killed while responding to a domestic disturbance. His assailant then shot his girlfriend and himself. In March 1999 Chicago Police Department tactical officer James Camp was shot and killed with his own weapon during an investigation into a possible stolen vehicle.

In conclusion, regardless of the scenario, the use of force by or against a police officer, whether nonlethal or deadly, is a current, as well as future, issue of concern. Police officers must be aware of all the implications surrounding the use of force against others or themselves.

Training for a potentially dangerous situation may mean the difference between life and death. (Courtesy of the Scottsdale, Arizona, Police Department)

AIDS

Although the deadly virus AIDS (acquired immunodeficiency syndrome) is no longer a new issue of concern for policing, it remains a prevalent issue. AIDS results from a virus referred to as HIV (human immunodeficiency virus), which infects and destroys the white blood cells that assist in combating infection. One reason this virus is such a concern is that a person can be infected with it for years without developing AIDS and its related symptoms, yet can transmit the virus.

The concerns for policing stem from the fact that many individuals police officers come into contact with, such as prostitutes and drug addicts, are considered "high risk" for AIDS. Because there is no vaccination for its prevention or a known cure and its active infection results in death, police officers have become extremely leery of handling these high-risk individuals and are often very cautious during searches and arrests.

■ CASE IN POINT

Most episodes of the television series *Cops* feature at least one or two incidents in which officers make an arrest. Inevitably, the officers either ask the individual to empty his or her pockets or inquire whether the individual has anything sharp on his or her person that may cut the officer. This precaution is taken because of the fear that the person may have a needle or razor blade or some other sharp object that could possibly injure the officer and transmit HIV.

Despite the extensive information provided by the medical community, there still appears to be a lack of real knowledge about AIDS among police officers. As a result of their ignorance of the subject, police officers have voiced their concerns over the threat of AIDS. These concerns include being bitten or spit on by an HIV/AIDS carrier; contact with any body fluids or dried blood, urine, or feces; contact with a dead body; administration of first-aid; and open wounds, cuts, or sores (Hammett, 1989). The fear of contracting HIV has risen to such heights that it has lead to legislative reforms in some states. For example, in 1995 the governor of Utah signed into legislation a bill that permits public safety workers, such as police officers, who fear that they may have been exposed to HIV or any other blood-borne pathogens to obtain a court order that forces the individual suspected of exposing the worker to undergo blood tests. ("Utah Seeks Extra AIDS Peace-of-Mind for Police," 1995)

The following is what police officers should know about HIV/AIDS according to current research on its transmission. Because this information may change as new reports become available, police officers and police agencies should remain informed on current research.

Bites and Saliva

Research continues to advise that the transmission of HIV through saliva is rare. Tests have found that the virus has been isolated in saliva only in very low concentrations, and the risk of infection is highly unlikely. However, there is evidence that the possibility for transmission of HIV through saliva may be higher than initially believed, particularly through intimate exposure of saliva, either through prolonged kissing or oral sex. As for bites, it is usually the person who does the biting who is at a greater risk of being exposed to blood and the virus than the person who was bitten. However, a self-inflicted bite to expose someone to AIDS-infected blood is possible.

■ CASE IN POINT

A Texas city grand jury indicted a man in connection with intentionally exposing a police officer to AIDS. During an attempted arrest, the suspect advised officers he had AIDS, bit his lip, and spit blood on the officers. The indictment is based on a seldom-used 1989 revision of the Texas Penal Code covering the intentional exposure of another to AIDS. This law is a third-degree felony, and, if convicted, the man faced two to ten years in prison.

Contacts

During most officers' careers it is inevitable that they will come into contact with a variety of body fluids, dried blood, a "leaking" dead body, or urine or feces. Current information advises that there is little risk of infection from contact with any of these. Low concentrations of HIV have been found in urine, and none has been found in feces. The wearing of gloves is recommended when contact with a dead body, dried blood, or other body fluid is necessary. However, the risk is extremely limited. In addition, there have been no cases of HIV infection resulting from simple casual contact, the handling, searching, or arresting of individuals.

Administration of First-Aid

An initial function of every police officer arriving first at the scene of a crime is to check for injuries and, if necessary, administer first-aid. The threat of AIDS has made many officers fear providing this type of assistance. In general, the use of airmasks minimizes the risk of HIV transmission when cardiopulmonary resuscitation is necessary. As for bleeding wounds, avoiding contact with the blood with the use of rubber gloves minimizes the risk of infection. Avoidance of contact of the victim's blood with open wounds or cuts on the officer's body will also minimize risk.

Cuts and Punctures

When searching or frisking a suspect or arrestee, or having to fight with an individual, there is no guarantee that an injury will not occur. Hidden sharp objects, needles, razor blades, or knives may be present. The possibility of both the officer and the arrestee suffering injuries that could expose the officer to blood also exists. Although extreme caution should always be used, regardless of the risk of HIV, transmission of the virus from a cut or puncture by any of these objects is extremely rare, but may occur, and, therefore, the officer should always use caution when having to remove or deal with such objects. The risk does increase, however, if there is infected, active blood on or in any of these objects, and it comes into contact with the officer's blood. Therefore, the use of extreme caution cannot be emphasized enough when conducting searches and frisks.

The risk for police officers is rather limited, and this needs to be communicated to the police not only for their benefit but for society's. Considering that the police come into contact with high-risk individuals, policing needs to serve as an educational source to the community. Yet, before this is possible the police must be educated on the subject. In the future, police departments should require mandatory training on AIDS as well as frequent testing of officers for HIV. Then again, it may not be a question of choice. Some states have begun adopting statutes requiring individuals who are in policing/law enforcement, corrections, fire prevention, and emergency medical services to be trained in the handling of high-risk persons to AIDS.

■ CASE IN POINT

In 1989 the 71st Texas legislature adopted Article 4419b-3, which mandated that the Texas Department of Health (TDH) develop a model policy for the handling, care, and treatment of HIV/AIDS-infected persons in the custody of or under the supervision of

WHAT DO YOU THINK?

HIV and Policing

The topic of AIDS came to forefront in the late 1970s but it became a paramount issue in the 1980s and 1990s. AIDS is the result of HIV, a virus identified primarily among intravenous drug users and homosexuals. An individual who tests positive for HIV will not necessarily develop AIDS, but the chances are more likely than not. Because HIV can be spread from one person to another through the transmission of body fluids such as semen or blood, its accidental contraction is possible for a police officer who must deal with an individual who is HIV positive, despite precautions. Training has helped to make police officers more aware of the risks of contracting HIV. However, a dilemma currently facing police agencies is the hiring of police officers who are already HIV carriers. The American Disabilities Act (ADA) protects individuals who are refused employment because of their HIV status. Therefore, a police agency cannot reject an applicant simply because of HIV.

1. How should police agencies approach the HIV hiring dilemma?
2. Does the fear of HIV cause police agencies to refrain from recruiting homosexuals?
3. Would a police agency be held responsible if an HIV-carrying police officer infected another officer or a nonpolice person?
4. What kind of training should be given to officers who are HIV positive? What types of assignments?
5. How might a police agency be able to "get around" the ADA and not hire HIV-infected individuals?

specified correctional, law enforcement, and emergency services agencies. In addition, these entities are to develop policies that are based on and similar to those developed by TDH. The policy must include HIV/AIDS education; infection control supplies, equipment, and training; occupational exposure; and, when applicable, testing, segregation, and isolation.

The issue of AIDS is important to policing. However, with the proper training, education, and testing it should not be as frightening as originally believed. In fact, police officers are at higher risk of exposure to hepatitis or tuberculosis than they are to HIV. Still, it is one more inherent risk associated with law enforcement.

LEGALITIES

The prospect of changes to the amendments of the U.S. Constitution applicable to policing are extremely slim. However, court decisions affecting applications are always a possibility. Since the "due process" revolution of the 1960s, changes in the application and enforcement of the law have restricted police action as well as held police liable for failing to uphold the law or for violating the law themselves.

Recent court decisions have eased restrictions on police activities in some areas (search and seizure) and have become more restrictive in others *(Miranda)*. Although the current U.S. Supreme Court is considered more conservative than its predecessors and appears to be "propolice," its composition and focus are never guaranteed. Future police officers will need to be well versed in constitutional and criminal law, both substantive and procedural. More and increasingly complex statutes and new laws will require police officers to be almost as well educated on the law as attorneys.

The public's awareness of its right to sue the police for a police officer's or agency's failure to provide equal protection or violation of civil rights has led to a dramatic increase in lawsuits against the police. Civil liability is a growing topic of concern for policing. In coming years, the police agency will want all of its members to be aware of the ramifications of a civil lawsuit, and will want to train and educate officers adequately to keep liabilities at a minimum.

Finally, police officers will need to be aware of their own constitutional rights. Contrary to popular belief, police officers are afforded the same basic civil and criminal rights as anyone else. For years police officers have been subjected to treatment as second-class citizens whose civil rights were restricted while they were expected to behave above the norm. In some instances, lawsuits or court motions have been filed on behalf of police officers. For example, in April 1998 the National Association of Police Organizations filed an amicus brief with the Colorado Court of Appeals on behalf of two Denver police officers who were forced to testify in an internal affairs investigation despite having invoked their constitutional rights.

U.S. constitutional guarantees, as well as individual state constitutional guarantees, apply to all citizens regardless of creed, race, ethnicity, gender, or occupation.

In addition to constitutional protections, police officers are also afforded equality from such sources as the 1964 Civil Rights Act and its 1972 extension of Title 7 Title 42, Section 1983; and Equal Employment Opportunity guidelines. Police officers can no more be discriminated against or harassed than any other citizen of the United States. Yet, there is still a tremendous concern that police officers have limited rights. The result of this concern has been the continued offering of federal legislation that would create a bill of rights for police officers. (This bill is not supported by the International Association of Chiefs of Police and has been defeated on several occasions.) The primary focus of the bill is to protect officers from arbitrary discipline and from invasion of privacy (search and seizure rights).

For example, random drug testing of police officers is becoming a growing issue. Some individuals believe police officers should be randomly tested for drug use, especially officers who spend a large quantity of time around narcotics. However, an issue raised is whether this is a violation of an officer's rights. The apparent trend in lower federal appellate courts to approve random testings found support from the U.S. Supreme Court.

■ CASE IN POINT

In *Skinner* v. *Railway Labor Executives' Association* (1989) the Court ruled that drug testing because of safety-sensitive tasks was justified and did not violate search and seizure requirements. In *National Treasury Employees Union* v. *Von Raab* (1989) the Court ruled that suspicionless drug testing was constitutional pertaining to promotions or transfers to positions involving drug interdiction or the carrying of a firearm, because of the government's interest in public safety (del Carmen & Walker, 1997).

As a result of the legal support for such testing, many police agencies have established some type of drug testing program or policy (see Table 11-2).

Regardless of personal belief, police officers are citizens and retain the same rights as any other citizen. Expecting the behavior of police officers to be somewhat above the norm is not completely unacceptable; however, requiring them to give up their constitutional rights is unacceptable. In addition, it is not acceptable that families of police officers are expected to be better behaved than the norm and that police officers are disciplined when a family member's behavior is in question.

TABLE 11-2

Percent of Municipal Police Agencies with Drug Testing Policies, 1993

	Mandatory of All (%)	Random Selection (%)	Use Suspected (%)
Civilian employees	7	9	44
Applicants for sworn positions	67	2	7
Probationary officers	14	18	46
Regular field officers	4	21	52
Officers in drug-related positions	14	23	45

Source: Adapted from Reaves & Smith (1995).

■ CASE IN POINT

An officer's son is involved in a fight at school. Instead of the officer being called by the school and advised of the incident, the police department is called, and the officer's supervisor advises the officer of the incident along with a "friendly suggestion" to make sure this kind of problem does not happen again.

In all, police officers and their families have the same rights as other citizens and should be afforded the right to make mistakes just like other citizens without being exposed to excessive punishment.

■ TECHNOLOGY

Although a future of "Robo-Cops" is intriguing, it is at least decades away. However, advancements in other types of technology for policing are not as science fiction–based as once thought. With the exceptions of the automobile and the two-way radio, technological advances in policing have been historically rather limited in initial acceptance, and changes to a more technological approach to policing have been relatively slow. However, beginning with the adoption of the mainframe computer, computer technology has played, and will continue to play, an extremely important role in policing.

When the use of a computer was first introduced to policing, the skepticism was overwhelming. Today, the computer has been successfully implemented in a variety of ways. The primary use has been for accessing databases to conduct "wanted" checks on individuals, examining driver's license histories, or making "stolen" checks on vehicles. The linking of the National Crime Information Computer (NCIC) and similar state systems provides broader and quicker access to information for police officers. Originally, this information had to be accessed from permanent terminals located in the communication centers of police agencies.

Computer innovation now allows police officers to access computer information directly from a police vehicle. The mobile data terminal (MDT), although available for the last twenty years, is a technological innovation that gives officers immediate opportunity to access mainframe computer systems. This eliminates the need for officers to request the information from already overburdened communication officers. This type of technology seems to be gaining popularity on a daily basis, especially in the form of laptop computers.

■ CASE IN POINT

In 1997 Brandon, Vermont, police officers were the first in the state to use laptop computers in their police cars, which allowed officers to check driver's license records and car registrations; more than 460 Charlotte–Mecklenburg, North Carolina, police vehicles were equipped with laptop computers, which provided officers with immediate access to a variety of information, including motor vehicle records, police reports, geographic information systems, and criminal warrants; 60 Pueblo, Colorado, police cars were equipped with laptop computers, which enabled officers to access background information on vehicles before making traffic stops; the police force in Philadelphia, Pennsylvania, installed 120 laptop units believed to be the latest and most durable line of computers designed for the inside of a police car; the Los Angeles Police Department plans to install laptops in all police cruisers, which will be linked to all district computers and main agency computers. In 1998 the Corrales, New Mexico, Police Department acquired 15 laptop computers thanks to a federal grant; the Missouri Highway Patrol requested $15 million over a 5-year period to be able to equip its 700 police vehicles with laptop computers, which would be linked to various state and national databases.

In addition to the ability to make information checks, some of the newer mobile systems allow officers to enter reports directly into a mainframe computer. A growing number of police agencies have implemented this type of computer-generated report system, most often referred to as the "Decor System." Initially, this system allowed officers in the field to telephone reports to a Decor operator, who would type the information into the computer. The advanced mobile terminals provide officers the opportunity to enter their own reports. Future mobile systems will give officers access to mug shots, fingerprints, and any departmental criminal history database without having to leave the police unit.

The use of computers for fighting crime is a growing trend in policing. Although initial uses had been limited to accessing statewide computers for license and warrant information and national databases, such as the NCIC, some departments are finding other ways to enhance crime fighting through computers. The latest trend has been referred to as "crime mapping." Crime mapping has been defined as a "system where large amounts of crime data can be analyzed and made useful to police" (Fortner, 1998, p. 16). Like laptops, crime mapping is growing in popularity.

■ CASE IN POINT

Loyola University sociologist Richard Block first introduced crime mapping as a means of assisting the Chicago Police Department in tracking gang activities. Crime mapping became well publicized through its use in New York and its application in community policing. Known in New York as Compstat (compare statistics), this computer program keeps track of all the reported crime in each beat and gives officers access to up-to-date information about what is happening in their areas. This information gives officers an opportunity to create strategies to fight crime. Crime mapping is becoming extremely popular in police agencies across the United States and in other countries such as Canada (Fortner, 1998).

In addition to general information searching and crime mapping, the computer is currently being used to search and compare fingerprints. Often referred to as AFIS (Automated Fingerprint Identification System), this computer system is fed all the fingerprint information a police agency has gathered on suspects and arrestees. When a "latent" (a fingerprint that is not apparent to the eye) is located at the scene of a crime, it is entered into the AFIS database. If the fingerprints are in the database, the system will then identify several possible suspects. Although current systems require trained latent examiners to find the exact match among those identified by the computer, future systems are expected to be able to identify the exact print match while requiring nothing more than human validation of the selection. Either way, AFIS has definitely aided the police in solving numerous crimes.

■ CASE IN POINT

AFIS technology is slowly proving itself extremely effective for solving crimes. The Dallas Police Department has had more than an 80 percent success rate for identifying suspects from prints found at crime scenes since installing AFIS in 1989. In 1990 Oregon state police arrested a suspect for a 1978 murder with assistance from AFIS. Other successes include the identification of a deceased person in Utah that lead to the arrest of a murder suspect in Portland, Oregon; in a one-year period in California CAL-ID (the statewide fingerprint identification system) helped identify suspects in thirty-two homicides, thirty-three narcotics cases, thirty-three robberies, ninety-two grand thefts, nine sex crimes, and nine assaults; and in Connecticut the state's AFIS matched prints in one hundred cases in just the first fourteen months it was available.

Computer technology assists in matching fingerprints with a suspect. (Courtesy of the Los Angeles Police Department)

Other available computer systems aid in the development of suspect sketching/drawings and provide an electronic mug book. Similar to AFIS, the newest innovation is the Combined DNA Index, also referred to as CODIS. Developed by the FBI and as of December 1998 operated in "94 laboratories, 41 states, and Washington, D.C" (Sandoval, 1998), CODIS is a database of DNA profiles that can be accessed by police computers equipped with the authorized software. This system gives police the opportunity to search for potential suspects in crimes in which DNA samples were available (e.g., sexual assaults) in the same manner as the fingerprint searches. Computers have also aided police departments to apprehend suspects and find missing persons through websites on the Internet. For example, the website for the Tustin, California, Police Department has more than one hundred pages of information "ranging from the phone number for a graffiti hotline to warnings about credit card scams to detailed neighborhood maps displaying locations of armed robberies and car thefts" (Cohodas, 1996). (To access the Tustin Police Department website, go to www.tustinpd.org.) Although computers, once considered an intrusion in policing, will become more progressive and reliable tools for policing, particularly if they provide such enhancement to solving crimes as the AFIS has and CODIS is expected to, the reality is that computers have also increased problems for policing.

With the growth in computer technology has come the growth of computer crimes. Theft, stealing services, smuggling, terrorism, and child pornography (Sussman, 1995) are just a few of the types of computer crimes the police must learn to investigate. The FBI was the first law enforcement agency to create a special unit to focus only on computer crimes. Because the growth is both national and statewide, other agencies will need to follow suit. For example, in 1998 the Florida Department of Law Enforcement created a fifty-agent task force to help battle "cyber" crime ("Taking Cue from FBI, Florida Launches Cyber-Crime Squad," 1998). Whether used to investigate and solve crimes or to stop crimes committed through their use, computers are a vital part of the police future.

For the criminal investigator, technology has provided a useful tool in the development of the laser. A device currently used to locate "hard to see with the eye" evidence, the laser assists in locating physical evidence such as dried blood, fingerprints (latent), and trace evidence (e.g., hair and fibers).

■ CASE IN POINT

With the help of a laser, which was used to search for fingerprints not found through traditional means, investigators located two bloody prints. After the prints were entered into the AFIS databse, a possible murder suspect was identified.

Other investigative technological devices include a variety of scanners that aid in the identification of handwriting and voices, and detect residual amounts of drugs. A scanner in use in some FBI offices even identifies individuals by the pattern of their retinas. This device is said to be able to recognize the blood vessel patterns at the back of an individual's eye. In all, future police investigations may become more technologically geared.

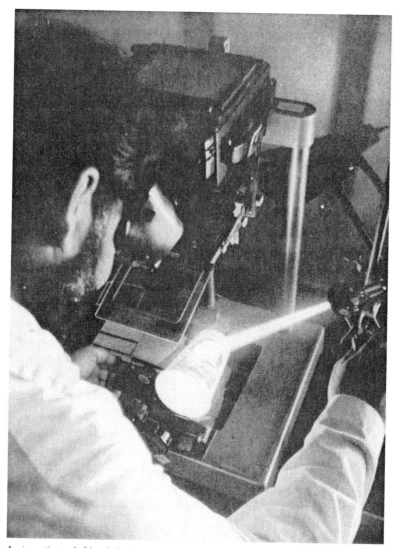

An investigator's friend: the laser. (Courtesy of the Los Angeles Police Department)

Beginning with the first two-way vehicle radio, police communications systems have experienced numerous changes. Current technologies offer the 911 system for emergency contact with police services, the hand-held and the voice-activated two-way radio and portable scanners, vehicle tracking devices, and surveillance devices that allow long-range eavesdropping on conversations. The future offers miniaturized two-way, scrambling or encoded, and voice-activated radios. The latter of the three will give officers an opportunity to communicate with each other or the communication center without having to use their hands. This will be especially useful in those situations in which the officer needs the use of both hands, such as in a high-speed pursuit, a fight, or when using a weapon. Although not limited to policing, the cellular phone is a technology that is becoming more commonplace in police departments.

■ CASE IN POINT

In 1997 forty cellular phones were donated to the Hoffman Estates, Illinois, Police Department. The phones were placed in all the department's police vehicles and some were given to neighborhood watch groups. The purpose of the phones was to assist in the community-policing efforts by allowing officers to speak directly to callers instead of relying on information from dispatchers.

The future of technology for policing will also offer innovative weaponry. For example, a nonlethal weapon such as the taser when discharged emits 10,000 volts of electricity into a suspect without causing severe injury and makes arrest more manageable. Handguns will be lighter, more compact, yet powerful and laser sighted, which should improve an officer's ability to handle a situation when deadly force is a necessity.

In addition to the changes in weaponry are the technological changes in training using computers to teach officers when to use their firearms. For example, the latest technology is a system that uses laser disk–projected images controlled by computer. Officers must interact with the projected images as if the scenario were actually occurring. After each simulation exercise the computer advises the officer how many shots were taken, number of hits (lethal and non-lethal), and grades the officer's performance as good or poor judgment. This type of technology can only improve police recognition of and performance in possible deadly force confrontations.

Police vehicles will continue to change. The needs of police will be met with vehicles that are faster, smaller, and electronically equipped with computers and video cameras. Video cameras are now being used to record pursuits, suspected drunk driving violations, traffic stops, and other police interactions.

Cellular phones have added a new dimension to communications for patrol officers and supervisors. (Courtesy of the Scottsdale, Arizona, Police Department)

The use of video cameras in police vehicles is just one of its technological advances. Because relatively small cameras are available, other uses have been found.

■ CASE IN POINT

The Denver, Colorado, Police Department employs a video camera device for handling bombs. K-9 units in New York City now use a miniaturized camera called RECON (Remote Canine Optical Navigator) that attaches to the leather harness around the dog's neck and transmits images back to a television screen. East Spencer, North Carolina, police have made use of a robotic camera in situations in which it's better not to send officers. For example, in November 1997 the camera was sent into a house in which two officers had been shot while trying to serve a warrant. Westbook, Maine, police officers started wearing tiny, pendant-like cameras that clip onto their shirt pockets. These cameras allow the recording of all interactions with individuals regardless of the reason or location.

Video camera technology is of great assistance to policing, and the use of video recordings as evidence in criminal cases has been tested and upheld by the courts.

■ CASE IN POINT

In early spring 1991 an eastern Texas constable, whose vehicle was equipped with a video camera, was killed during a traffic stop. Before exiting his police vehicle, the constable turned on his video camera, which recorded the actions of the stopped vehicle's occupants,

Handling bombs is left to "Robi" in Denver, Colorado. (Courtesy of the Denver, Colorado, Police Department)

including their attack and murder of the constable. During the trial, the defense argued against the validity and admission of the videotape. The tape was admitted, and the defendants were convicted. The results of this case and others like it will have far-reaching impact on the use of video recordings as evidence of alleged criminal activity.

Of course, although camera technology is useful to police officers, it can also document their own censurable behavior. For example, an Atlanta, Georgia, police sergeant was suspended for thirty days without pay after being videotaped beating a man who drove through a police roadblock.

Technology has had, and will continue to have, tremendous impact on police performance. Therefore, it will be critical for police officers to be trained and knowledgeable in specific technological areas. It will also be important for police to receive support in the use and development of new technologies ("Applying Technological Advances to Criminal Justice," 1997; Walker, 1997). Furthermore, the continuing growth of technology is one more element associated with the debate over policing and its growth toward the status of a "profession."

POLICING AS A PROFESSION

Although the previously discussed issues are undoubtedly important to officer survival and success, the professionalization of policing has been a consistently debated topic since the early 1900s, and is very much an issue today and for the future of policing (Dantzker, 1997; Rechtschaffen, 1998). Police officer behavior, such as corruption and brutality, have led to charges of unprofessionalism among police officers and arguments for the professionalization of policing. Commissions, such as Wickersham and the President's Commission on Law Enforcement and Administration of Justice, were formed to study the problems associated with policing. The findings of these commissions ultimately suggested that the lack of a "professional" standing was a major reason for the problems in policing.

Since the establishment of this country's first official police department, policing has experienced numerous changes. Among these changes are technological advances, improved administrative practices, formal training, and requirement of higher levels of education. It can be said that all of these changes have assisted in the development of policing toward becoming a true profession. When incidents occur, such as those witnessed in the past few years in which officers' behaviors are not consistent with societal expectations (e.g., inexplicable deaths of suspects in police custody, excessive use of force during an arrest that sometimes has led to the death of the arrestee, or police involvement in criminal activities such as drug dealing, theft, or rape), citizens ask, "Why does this happen?" Again, the debate on whether policing should be considered a profession is fueled. The following sections focus on several of the issues associated with the recognition of policing as a profession.

Defining Profession

To better understand this issue, one must first define the term *profession*, particularly as it relates to policing. Undoubtedly, one of the biggest difficulties in the police profession debate is reaching a consensus on the definition. If the standard definition of profession is applied to policing, in its current state, policing is not a true profession (Dantzker, 1997).

Webster's Collegiate Dictionary defines profession as, "an occupation, especially one requiring extensive education in a branch of science or liberal arts." *Black's Law Dictionary* defines profession as, "a vocation or occupation requiring special, usually advanced, education and skill; e.g. law or medical profession." *Black's* definition continues with, "The labor and skill involved in a profession is predominantly mental or intellectual, rather than physical or manual." Neither definition is particularly fitting to policing. Swanson, Territo, and Taylor (1993) compound the issue by advising that no singular definition really exists—rather a collection of elements. These elements include (1) an organized body of theoretical knowledge, (2) advanced study, (3) a code of ethics, (4) prestige, (5) standards of admission, (6) a professional association, and (7) a service ideal. An additional element that can be added is autonomy. The application of each of these elements to policing will be offered shortly.

The issue of defining *profession* is not the only problem with police professionalism. The term *professionalism* creates an additional problem. In reality, the heart of the profession issue may be the problem of profession versus professionalism. Application of the definition of profession will usually eliminate policing as a profession. Yet, many police agencies consider themselves professional or products of professionalism (Dantzker, 1986, 1997).

Again, current definitions enhance the problem. A professional is often recognized as an individual who engages in activity professionally. Professionalism may be best viewed as the conduct, aims, or qualities that characterize or identify a profession or a professional person. The application of these terms to policing creates a dilemma. Police officers may act professionally and police agencies promote professionalism; yet, policing has not yet received recognition as a true profession. However, to gain a better understanding of the police profession debate, a brief historical examination is helpful.

A Historical Perspective

A historical review of policing finds that formal policing in this country began in the 1830s. However, it was not until the early 1900s that the terms *professional* and *professionalism* would be attached to policing. This primarily resulted from the efforts of one man, August Vollmer (Carte, 1973).

August Vollmer was a self-educated individual who first became involved in law enforcement when he was elected marshal of Berkeley, California. This position evolved into the first chief of police for the Berkeley Police Department, as which Vollmer would serve from 1905 to 1932. It was Vollmer's belief that technology combined with honest and efficient officers would bring professionalism to policing. Vollmer argued that because of the changes in society, policing would also have to change and that this change would require more educated individuals with greater skills.

In 1908, breaking from a tradition of giving a physically strong individual a gun and badge and telling him to go out and enforce the law, Vollmer introduced the first formal police training school. Curriculum in this school included general police subjects, criminal law and procedures, police psychiatry, criminal identification, and police organization and management (Carte, 1973). By 1930, recruits attending this school received more than three hundred hours of police-related study.

The formal training school was only Vollmer's first move toward professionalizing his department. Even though his own formal education had been limited, Vollmer was a strong advocate of a college education for police officers. Therefore, in 1919 he began hiring college students as police officers. This was the first time that any police agency hired individuals with an advanced education. It would not be the last.

During his association with policing, Vollmer served as the president of the International Association of Chiefs of Police (1922) and as a member of the Wickersham Commission (1931). In both instances, Vollmer's educational beliefs and genuine concern about the need to professionalize policing throughout the country would be influential. The basis of today's push toward professionalism in policing is the direct result of Vollmer's beliefs and efforts.

The Police Profession

The problem of applying the formal definition of profession to policing was previously noted. The standard dictionary definitions simply cannot readily be applied to policing. The concept of the elements of a profession offered by Swanson et al. tend to provide the clearest path to the examination of policing as a profession.

An Organized Body of Theoretical Knowledge

A prevalent element of a true profession is a well-developed, complex, theoretical body of knowledge. Law and medicine are examples often referred to as true professions. Individuals interested in joining either of these professions must absorb and prove their understanding of the body of knowledge. Failure to demonstrate a complete comprehension of the required body of knowledge bars the individual from the profession.

Policing uses a very broad body of knowledge that incorporates both training and academic studies. The major problem is that there is no commonly agreed-on body of knowledge that every officer should possess. Each police agency is allowed to define what it deems an appropriate body of knowledge. This is also true of colleges and universities that offer a law enforcement curriculum. This fragmentation makes it difficult to establish a "professional body" of police knowledge. As noted by Price (1985), for policing to be considered a profession "it must exhibit a unique and specialized body of knowledge that is written down and can be transmitted abstractly" (p. 320). Although a consensus has yet to be reached, movement toward meeting this element cannot be too far off because when one examines various academy curriculums, there are numerous similarities.

Advanced Study

To become a lawyer or doctor takes years of study. On the average, it takes a minimum of seven years of college study for lawyers and eleven years for doctors just to enter the profession officially. After entry is gained, a continuing course of study is often required. Although most federal police agencies and some local agencies require some type of college curriculum, policing as a whole requires no advanced study. As a rule, the only requirement (above a high school diploma or equivalency) is the training academy most recruits are required to attend, which averages from eighteen to twenty weeks, and the occasional in-service training program.

Code of Ethics

According to Davis (1991), "A code of ethics is a formal statement of a group's ethics, whether a description of a preexisting practice (like a dictionary definition) or a formula creating the practice (like a definition in a contract)" (p. 17). All professions have a code of ethics relating to the moral action, conduct, and characteristics of the professional. Although it has yet to be determined whether policing is a profession, policing does appear to support a code of ethics. However, there does not seem to be just one code for all of policing.

■ CASE IN POINT

The following is an example of a code of ethics (Caldwell & Nardini, 1977).

Law Enforcement Code of Ethics

AS A LAW ENFORCEMENT OFFICER, my fundamental duty is to serve mankind; to safeguard lives and property; to protect the innocent against deception, the peaceful against violence and disorder; and to respect the constitutional rights of all men to liberty, equality and justice.

I WILL keep my private life unsullied as an example to all; maintain courageous calm in the face of danger, scorn, or ridicule; develop self-restraint; and be constantly mindful of the welfare of others. Honest in thought and deed in both my personal and official life, I will be exemplary in obeying the laws of the land and the regulations of my department. Whatever I see or hear of a confidential nature or that is confided to me in my official capacity will be kept ever secret unless revelation is necessary in the performance of my duty.

I WILL never act officiously or permit personal feelings, prejudices, animosities or friendships to influence my decisions. With no compromise for crime and with relentless prosecution of criminals, I will enforce the law courteously and appropriately without fear or favor, malice or ill will, never employing unnecessary force or violence and never accepting gratuities.

I RECOGNIZE the badge of my office as a symbol of public faith, and I accept it as a public trust to be held so long as I am true to the ethics of the police service. I will constantly strive to achieve these objectives and ideals, dedicating myself before God to my chosen profession, law enforcement.

The preceding example notes a variety of actions and behaviors that a police officer should attest to uphold when accepting the role of a police officer. Yet, this code (and others similar to it) are not necessarily mandatory. The use and acceptance of a code of ethics is still relatively limited to individual agencies attempting to enhance their professional status.

Prestige

At one time policing had a considerable amount of prestige; police officers could often rely on the respect and influence their position held among the general public. Since the 1960s the prestige of policing has dwindled. Lawyers, doctors, and even accountants command a certain amount of respect and prestige. Being a police officer in today's society often means receiving little respect and appears to no longer be viewed as a very prestigious occupation, especially at the local level.

■ CASE IN POINT

In a 1989 survey of several hundred criminal justice college students, among the 60 percent who indicated that their job goal was a law enforcement position, more than 75 percent were interested in a federal police job instead of a local police position. When an inquiry was made as to why so many wanted to be federal officers, the number one response was that federal officers received more respect, and it was more prestigious to tell people, "I am a federal agent" instead of a state trooper, county sheriff, or city police officer. This author has consistently observed this attitude, especially among women, in class after class when students are asked about their job goals. Policing is still a major goal, however, students tend to choose federal law enforcement over local policing.

Standards of Admission

The true profession carries with it universally accepted standards for admission. State or nationally certified requirements and licenses are found in the true professions; both lawyers and doctors must meet certain educational requirements and pass a certified examination before being allowed to practice the profession. Although many states require state licensing for police officers, this license is usually good only in the issuing state. This means that if a police officer licensed in California moved to Texas, the state of Texas would require the individual to pass the Texas licensing examination. Usually this requires having to go through a state recognized training program before the test can be taken. Doctors, lawyers, accountants, teachers, and other such professionals can more frequently plan on being able to practice their professions anywhere in the country without having to retrain, recertify, or license. However, they may have to apply for certification, licensure, or take a state examination for which previous preparatory schooling or training is often sufficient. This is seldom the case for police officers. However, as more and more states have increased their training requirements and require licensure some states are providing a means for an officer certified in one state to become licensed in another state without having to attend a full training academy.

■ CASE IN POINT

In 1984 this author moved from Indiana, where he had been a state licensed police officer, to Texas, where he was required to complete another training academy before he was allowed to take the state examination for licensure as a police officer. In 1996, as an applicant for a police license in Georgia, he was again required to complete a full academy before being allowed to take the licensing exam. Now back in Texas, he will be allowed to take the exam to reactivate his Texas license as a result of his previous Texas certification and recent Georgia licensing. However, should he fail it on three attempts, he would have to complete a full academy once again.

In addition to licensure or certification, unlike other professions, policing has no nationally consistent entry standards. Age, education, residency, and physical/mental test results are some of the elements used to determine entry into policing. These differ from state to state, even from agency to agency within a given state. Although a general consensus on age and physical characteristics exists, each police agency sets its own standards.

A Professional Association

The American Bar Association watchdogs the legal profession; the American Medical Association caters to the medical profession; the American Psychiatric Association provides guidance to the psychiatric and psychological profession; policing has no such national association. The International Association of Chiefs of Police (IACP) would argue that they are such an association. However, this association has yet to establish national standards for knowledge or admissions to entry-level positions that all police agencies would be required to follow.

In addition, there are several other national organizations that provide input, such as the Fraternal Order of Police, the National Organization of Black Law Enforcement Executives, the National Sheriffs' Association, and others. The fragmentation problem in policing continues to hamper the formation of one national association and professionalization. However, there is some speculation as to whether one national organization is really necessary, and whether it might hamper the growth of policing as a profession, an issue that led to the creation of the American Police Association and the Law Enforcement Credential Board (more on both organizations appears later in the chapter).

A Service Ideal

The service ideal is the obligation of a profession to serve the best interests of its clientele and its acceptance of a formal code of ethics. It is within this element that policing rests as a borderline profession. Regardless of the criticisms it receives, policing as a whole and many individual agencies appear to operate in a manner that best fits the needs of the public. Critics will argue that it is an extremely limited service ideal; nonetheless, a service ideal does exist.

Autonomy

It is difficult to argue that policing suffers from the lack of autonomy. Yet, from a professional standpoint, policing has yet to become autonomous. Autonomy in a profession relates to the manner in which the members of the profession are allowed to conduct their own affairs. It is the ability to control who gets into the schools, licensure requirements, professional recognition, and definition of the base of knowledge. Policing has not yet been able to obtain this autonomy. However, the question arises of whether policing actually ever can be autonomous because of its public nature, as opposed to the private nature of other professions (e.g., law and medicine).

Based on the preceding elements, policing cannot be viewed as a profession. However, there is debate as to whether it is fair to apply these elements to policing because it is a public and governmental entity (Dantzker, 1997). Perhaps in all fairness, the effort to professionalize policing should take another avenue, one more befitting its nature.

Keys to Police Professionalization

Policing has made great strides toward establishing itself as a true profession. Yet, there is still a long way to go. Meeting the criteria previously noted will be difficult, if not impossible. For policing to reach a status of a true profession several elements must be met. The four most fundamental elements that, if met, can assist in categorizing policing as a profession are **education, training, lateral transfer,** and **accreditation** (Dantzker, 1997).

Education
If there is one element that separates policing from all other true professions it is education. There is no other true profession willing to rely on a high school education as an adequate entry-level requirement. Currently, more than 80 percent of today's police departments require a recruit to possess no more than a high school diploma or its equivalent (Carter, Sapp, & Stephens, 1989; Reaves & Smith, 1995). The need for higher educational levels has been and is continually debated. Beginning with August Vollmer in the early 1900s, and followed by several national commissions including the Wickersham Commission (1931), the President's Commission on Law Enforcement and the Administration of Justice (1967), and the National Advisory Commission on Criminal Justice Standards and Goals (1973), it has been suggested that higher levels of education are a necessity to policing if it is to be established as a true profession. Caldwell and Nardini (1977) stated, "If a police force is to become professional, it must require higher educational degrees. That this is essential is evidenced by the development of other professions such as teaching, social work, chemistry, medicine, law, psychology, and many others" (p. 89). More (1985) noted, "The need for police officers who are intelligent, articulate, mature, and knowledgeable about social and political conditions is apparent" (p. 306). Mecum (1985) advised, "Education is an integral part of gaining the status of 'professionalism,' and if the police are to become professional, they must accept the requirements of some formal, higher education as a minimum standard for their occupation" (p. 316). Finally, Carter et al. (1989) advised that, "The college-educated force sets higher professional standards and goals, which, in turn, command public respect and help shape public opinion" (p. iv). These views have been supported by various forums and groups, including the American Police Association.

In 1996, through the collaboration of ex-New York Police Commissioner Patrick Murphy and longtime criminal justice professor Louis Mayo, the American Police Association (APA) was created. The major goal of the APA is to require all police officers to have college degrees. Membership and chapters are built on officers with bachelor's degrees. As of August 1998, APA membership was at 485 members. Although still in its infancy, the APA is continuing to push for members and to encourage college education requirements in policing. Its efforts helped to convince the Police Executive Research Forum (PERF) and the International Association of Directors of Law Enforcement Standards and Training (IADLEST) to pass resolutions supporting college-graduated police officers. The resolutions will establish "a task force to assist in accomplishing the goal of four-year degree entrance requirements for all police" (*American Police Association Newsletter*, 1998). (More on the APA can be found at its website, www.apai.org.)

Another means for increasing the number of college-educated officers has been through the Police Corps, a national college scholarship program funded by Congress since 1996. The focus of the program is to recruit and train college students to serve four years as community-policing officers. Although the IACP demonstrated a lack of support for the program, during the program's inaugural year six states were selected to receive funding. In 1997 the Mississippi Department of Public Safety was given a $1.36 million grant to launch a Police Corps program.

Despite the continuous push for higher educational standards among police officers, where scholars, academicians, and commissions have failed in their continuing quest for higher education in policing is in their inability to reach a consensus as to what level of education is necessary, and what the contents of that education should be. The National Advisory Commission suggested that by 1982 all police agencies should require a minimum of a bachelor's degree for its recruits, and groups like APA, PERF, and IADLEST are pushing for the same requirement. As of 1994 approximately 2 percent of all police agencies (excluding federal agencies) appear to require such a degree. Perhaps there is a legitimate reason for the lack of a higher-education requirement; for example, the empirical evidence supporting this requirement is still very limited (Dantzker, 1997). Additionally, the contents of the degree still lack a consensus.

There are more than one thousand criminal justice degree programs in this country, many of which offer a concentration in policing. No two have the same requirements or offer the same curriculum. Even those states, like Texas, whose institutions of higher learning have agreed on a "transfer core" of courses are unable to say that every student who takes a course with the same title at different places or times receive the same information. The result is a fragmentation of knowledge and a debate over what is relevant and what is not.

Of course it is difficult to reach a consensus on a core curriculum when an agreement cannot even be reached over what type of degree is necessary, or even *if* a degree is necessary. Arguments over this issue include debates about associate versus bachelor's degree, criminal justice versus criminology, and criminal justice related versus liberal arts. However, because police agencies continue to struggle with the concept of higher educational requirements, states may have to step in and try to assist in solving this dilemma. Some states are doing just that.

■ CASE IN POINT

In June 1991 the governor of Minnesota signed legislation that would establish the state's first higher-education institution devoted to the law enforcement profession. The legislation would require schools, colleges, and universities that offer professional peace officer education to integrate curriculums into a single, state-accepted law enforcement degree program. The purpose of this legislation is to be able to raise the state's current requirement for entry into law enforcement from a two-year degree to a four-year degree. Minnesota is presently the only state to have a statewide educational requirement for entry-level police officers. Although as of this writing the degree program has been designed and a site designated to offer the degree, funding to implement the program has been unavailable.

As the debate over the education requirement for entry-level officers continues, it should become fairly obvious to the most casual observer that higher levels of education for police officers are becoming a necessity. Modern technology, laws and the legal system, and the nature of our society are all beginning to dictate a need for better-educated officers. An accord between police practitioners and educators must be reached. Once a consensus on education has been obtained, policing will be a giant step closer toward being recognized as a true profession.

Training

Education is not the only element over which police and educators lack consensus; they disagree about training as well. Before education became the issue it has in policing, there was training. As noted earlier, Vollmer was the first to introduce any formalized training into policing. Since that time, training has grown in some areas and stagnated in others (Shernock & Dantzker, 1997).

Training is viewed as the method of developing practical or "hands-on" knowledge of policing. Education focuses on the social and behavioral sciences, and training focuses on techniques and procedures. In general, policing techniques and procedures do not differ greatly from agency to agency. Yet, there has not been any nationally standardized method of training; what is taught, how it is taught, and how much is taught still vary greatly.

■ CASE IN POINT

The legalities associated with policing is probably one of the most important areas of training. Arrest, search and seizure, interrogations, and confessions are important elements of enforcing the law. Police officers should be well trained in these areas. However, in examining current curriculum from several states' training academies, the number of hours of training in law-related topics ranged from a low of 20 hours to more than 150. The three different academies this author attended devoted a low of approximately 30 hours to a high of approximately 85 hours to legal issues.

The setting for training has traditionally been the "police academy" where a cadet/recruit is supposedly schooled in all necessities for working the streets. Although the street necessities differ very little from street to street, academies differ, in some instances dramatically. The difference is usually in the number of hours required, which in 1993 ranged from a low of 24 hours (Plantation, Florida, Police Department) to a high of 2000 (Providence, Rhode Island, Police Department) (Reaves & Smith, 1995). The average number of training (classroom and field) hours required is about 1100 hours (Reaves & Smith, 1995). Again, the problem is the inability for police practitioners to agree on how much training is truly required.

Inability to agree on the number of training hours is only part of the problem. What should be taught, how much should be taught, and who is going to teach it create most of the training differences. Traditionally, subjects such as arrest procedures, firearms, self-defense, penal code, patrol procedures, and search and

326 / Chapter 11 Issues: Today and Tomorrow

seizure make up most of the content taught in the academy. These courses have traditionally been taught by veteran police officers, who, more often than not, spend a large quantity of time telling "war stories." This is not training; yet, it is accepted as such (Marion, 1998). What should be taught and who should teach it continues to cause debate. Until this problem is solved, policing will continue to suffer from a lack of training standardization associated with a true profession. Fortunately, there has been and continues to be some activity toward solving this problem. Minnesota's effort, as noted in an earlier Case in Point, is one example of such activity toward eliminating the problem. Other examples include state-mandated licensure of police officers that is achieved after candidates pass an examination, the contents of which are state approved and taught in all training facilities.

Lateral Transfer

An element that truly separates policing from other professions is the inability of trained police officers to transfer laterally. Although it is not completely impossible, especially at the federal level, lateral transfers are rare. Lateral transfer is the opportunity for an officer to leave one police agency to work for another, within the same state or in another state, without having to retrain or lose seniority.

Again, the current practice for most police agencies, when an individual with previous policing experience is hired, is to require the individual to attend their "sanctioned" academy and start as a probationary officer with no seniority. The primary reason for this practice, as previously noted, is the lack of standardization in training. Standardization would help eliminate this problem. It would also help eliminate another concern associated with accepting training from another agency—liability.

The question of liability of a police agency with regard to training has already been established by the courts. As discussed earlier in the text, a police agency can be held liable if inappropriate or no training in certain areas leads to an injury of a citizen or a violation of rights. Thus, a concern with lateral transfer is whether previous training was sufficient and would be defensible if a civil suit arose from the transferred officer's actions. Because the agency did not originally train the officer, and accepted in good faith previous training, the question of liability arises. Therefore, rather than take a risk, a police agency would rather "retrain" the officer. This is another reason standardization of training is necessary.

■ CASE IN POINT

States such as California and Washington have eliminated the training concerns associated with lateral transfer by requiring that every police officer pass statewide mandatory training. Regardless of where in the state the officer is employed, he or she must pass the state licensure test. Because it is a state-required, standardized training curriculum that leads to the license, there is little concern throughout the state with regard to training liability. The accepted practice of lateral transfer in these states is often evident in recruitment ads. For example, in the July 1998 issue of Police magazine the San Jose, California, Police Department advertised a position opening for a police officer who desired a lateral transfer. The qualified candidate had to be currently employed as a full-time sworn officer and have a valid Police Officer Standards and Training certificate issued by the state of California.

Although standardized training can assist in eliminating the concerns of training in implementing lateral transfer, other issues arise. One such issue is that of seniority and promotions.

The stance of the average police administrator with respect to lateral transfer is not to allow it. When asked why, the response often includes a concern over the expense of training and employing an individual only to have him or her leave the agency for another, taking the expensive training already provided. Furthermore, as budgets continue to tighten, more police agencies will begin to advertise for officers who completed training or state certification. This could lead to a bidding war for trained officers that many police departments may not be able to fight, let alone win.

Additionally, problems surrounding promotion can arise. If an officer with ten years' experience comes to an agency and is credited with those ten years of seniority, this officer is in a much better position to promote than officers with less seniority but who may have been in line for a promotion. Promotion of this officer over someone who has been with the department for eight or nine years can lead to morale problems. Therefore, to eliminate unnecessary expenditures or promotional problems, most police executives prefer not to grant lateral transfers. A possible solution to the problem of lateral transfers may be the standardization of training and educational requirements, as well as parity in salaries and available opportunities for promotion and specialization. A national pension and retirement system would also help.

Accreditation

The profession-related issues previously discussed are individual oriented, as the concept of a profession tends to dictate. This has resulted in the creation of the Law Enforcement Credential Board (LECB). The LECB was created in 1996 as a means to further the individualistic drive for police professionalism. The LECB helps officers interested in demonstrating their knowledge and skills to attain national recognition through certification. In 1997 the LECB issued its first set of certificates to ninety-four police officers from across the United States. To receive the credentials, individuals must be full-time officers with at least five years of experience and a college degree, or eight years of experience and no college degree. They must be able to demonstrate firearms proficiency, have a clear disciplinary record, have taken at least fifty hours of post–basic training courses directly related to policing, perform at least one hundred hours of community service per year, have a propensity for instilling professionalism in others, and pass a two hundred–question multiple-choice exam.

Individual accolades, credentials, and/or accreditation are a positive move toward profesionalization. However, because of the diversity of issues and their application to policing, it appears that an agency or occupation-oriented approach may be more critical and appropriate for policing and the quest for professional status.

Accreditation is no stranger to professionalism. Hospitals, school districts, colleges and universities, and many other institutions that employ professionals have followed mandatory agency accreditation for years. The failure of an agency to meet accreditation criteria would result in the loss of accreditation. The loss of accreditation leads to a loss of standing in the profession as well as economic problems. Therefore, accreditation has extremely powerful implications.

In 1979, because of the efforts of several groups such as the International Association of Chiefs of Police, the National Organization of Black Law Enforcement Executives, the National Sheriffs' Association, and the Police Executive Research Forum, one of the stronger moves toward police professionalization since the days of Vollmer occurred with the creation of the Commission on Accreditation for Law Enforcement Agencies (CALEA). The commission was formed to develop a set of standards that could be applied nationally. Agencies that accomplish these standards are granted accreditation; they have met the professional criteria. The criteria address nine major areas (CALEA Online, 1998):

1. Role, responsibilities, and relationships with other agencies
2. Organization, management, and administration
3. Personnel structure
4. Personnel process
5. Operations
6. Operational support
7. Traffic operations
8. Prisoner and court-related services
9. Auxiliary and technical services

These areas are based on 436 standards to which police agencies must comply to attain and maintain accreditation (CALEA Online, 1998). These standards are believed to assist police agencies in the following areas.

1. Crime prevention and control capabilities
2. Essential management procedures
3. Fair and nondiscriminatory personnel practices
4. Service delivery
5. Interagency cooperation and coordination
6. Citizen and staff confidence in the agency

The process is voluntary with no current legal mandates. As of September 1998, 434 agencies (an increase of 129, or 42 percent, since March 1994) had completed and received accreditation (this includes agencies that have had their accreditation renewed). Hundreds more are in various phases of pursuing accreditation. The efforts of these agencies to achieve accreditation is a giant step toward community recognition of policing as a profession.

Although many of today's practitioners and academicians see accreditation as the key to police professionalization, others see it as the beginning of a national police and question whether accreditation is truly beneficial (Doerner, 1998). There are also those who believe it is too costly (Carter & Sapp, 1994). Considering the novelty of the process in policing, a verdict has not yet been reached. However, in the meantime, it appears that accreditation will continue to be one of the more popular means for police agencies to gain recognition as a profession.

Finally, while agencies wrestle with the elements that could propel policing into the status of a profession—higher education, lateral transfer, standardized training, and accreditation—we cannot ignore individual efforts to become

The Scottsdale, Arizona, Police Department is just one of many police agencies that proudly displays its certificate of accreditation. (Courtesy of the Scottsdale, Arizona, Police Department)

professional. The attainment of higher education by an individual is a positive step toward individual professionalization. Yet, recognition of this achievement by the police agency and the community is still limited. However, there is an educational or training achievement that not only receives tremendous recognition but is often touted as a major step toward individual professionalization—attendance and completion of the FBI academy.

For many years the FBI has invited a select group of local and state police officers to attend its academy. The select few are chosen from a pool of candidates whose names have been submitted by police executives throughout the country. The group chosen often represents the more outstanding officers. Selection to and completion of the academy are highly regarded by fellow officers as well as community leaders. For example, it is no longer unusual to see an advertisement for a chief of police requiring the applicant to have graduated from the FBI academy. This is because of the professional aura that has surrounded the FBI since its movement into the professional status many years ago when a college degree became a requirement and training became standardized.

The concept of professionalism with policing has garnered attention. Although individual agencies and individual officers continue to strive for the "professional" status, policing as a whole still has a way to go.

● ISSUES TO PONDER

Each of the previous issues—use of force, AIDS, legalities, technology, and professionalism—is a relevant topic of discussion for today's police officer. A variety of other issues probably could be identified and discussed. Although not all of them can be covered in this text, a few more topics that are viewed as being somewhat more applicable and relevant to the future of policing deserve, albeit brief, mention before concluding this text. Their offering should be considered "something to ponder" or "food for thought." They are personnel, administration, and community relations.

Personnel

At the end of October 1997, there were more than 650,000 individuals employed in policing in the United States. Each year the numbers grow. The future of police employment includes a growing number of ethnic minorities and women and their increasing roles in policing. In addition, police agencies are faced with the potential problems associated with recruiting individuals who previously had not been considered "ideal" candidates for policing—homosexuals. EEO, affirmative action, and court-mandated quotas will continue to force policing to be a "melting pot" of humanity. Furthermore, the enactment of the Americans with Disabilities Act will pose a new set of problems and challenges for police recruitment.

Selection criteria will continue to change, particularly concerning education. The high school–only educational requirement is slowly giving way to minimum levels of college hours. Higher levels of education, primarily bachelor's and master's degrees, will become requirements for promotions. The simple passing of an examination will no longer be enough in many agencies.

Training will continue to improve. Applications of the law, human relations, nonlethal use of force, civil liability, and community relations, especially in the form of community policing, are topics of growing importance and will be addressed in training as well as through educational requirements. The quality of training is an important element for effective policing. The police officer of the future will need to be constantly updated in areas of concern. The initial training in specific areas must be more than a meager few hours. Future training will be incorporated with college programs, allowing the police recruit to obtain a degree while completing the required training. Practical application and theory will become more intertwined. New technologies should also improve training. For example, shoot/no shoot simulators use realistic videos for firearms training, microcomputer simulators provide exercises and solutions for real-life scenarios, and the use of satellites keeps officers up to date on a variety of issues. In sum, the recruitment of personnel and its related issues will be major factors in the success of policing.

Administration

From an administrative perspective, future policing will find an increase in college-degreed individuals employed in top managerial positions. It will no longer be extraordinary that a police chief possesses a master's or doctor's degree. The fifteen- or twenty-year veteran without an advanced degree who climbed the promotional ladder will no longer be as attractive a candidate for chief. In addition to the degree, management training will be a necessity.

A major issue facing the future top police executive is a shrinking budget. As more cities find themselves in a precarious economical situation, police funding will be affected. Police administrators will need to key in on such factors as effectiveness, competitiveness, and productivity (Dantzker, 1999; Sutton, 1991). No longer will complacently ineffective officers be carried by the police agency. The ability to get the most out of a dollar will be an important skill for administrators. Police agencies will have to begin operating more like a business or corporation, with an eye to the total cost or profit, to deal effectively with the financial crises ahead.

The budget is merely one area in which the future administrator will need to be well versed. Improving race relations, dealing with labor disputes, recruiting qualified officers from a shrinking recruit pool, promoting qualified officers, and building good community relations are areas that the police administrator will be required to address. The simple fact is that the future police administrator will have to be a true administrator rather than just "the head cop."

Community Relations

A continuing criticism of policing has been its community relations. Historically, policing has been criticized for its less than adequate methods of dealing with the community as a whole. The approach of the late 1980s and early 1990s for improving the relationship is community-oriented policing, a method that brings the police and the community together to determine the needs of the community. The question for the future of this approach is, "Is this approach just another flash-in-the-pan attempt to please community critics as its predecessors, team policing and direct patrol, were?" Although the jury remains out, open-mindedness and acceptance by both policing and the community concerning each other's shortcomings could aid in the implementation, success, and survival of community-oriented policing.

Regardless of the success of community-oriented policing, police departments must address their relationships with their communities and find an acceptable position. Improvement in race relations and understanding cultural values and differences are necessary elements. Communities are becoming more culturally and ethnically diverse. To avoid both intertensions and intratensions on two fronts—within the community and among themselves—police officers must learn to deal with all the multicultural elements of their community. The future requires the recognition and acceptance of community changes; otherwise, the police task will become even more difficult.

Probably the biggest issue of concern with respect to community problems is the handling of increasing crime. As crime rates rise, the community naturally turns to its police agency for answers as to why this happens and, of course, to put a stop to it. The police do not have all the answers; nor do they have the complete power or ability to stop all crime. In general, lowering of crime rates requires cooperation between the police and the community. For the police to be able to have greater success in the controlling of crime, the community will need to be of greater assistance. Neighborhood watches, crime stoppers, and cooperation with investigators by providing information when it is available will be of tremendous help to the police. Furthermore, the police will need to be more open with the community. Mutual trust is a necessity for future cooperation. Police and communities must forge stronger bonds—which is believed possible through community-oriented policing—or accept the consequences.

In all, policing has gone through and will continue to experience many changes. The role has gone from an untrained, limitedly educated responder to a multifaceted, better-trained, and educated individual. Some might even refer to today's police officers as social workers with firearms. The fact remains that police officers and policing are an integral part of our society. Without their existence anarchy and chaos would probably be the order of the day. However, they need to be recognized for what they are and what they can legitimately, realistically accomplish. In turn, they must recognize and accept their roles as defined by society. Being a police officer is no easy task; both today and tomorrow a police officer requires much more than just a badge and a gun.

● SUMMARY

Policing involves a variety of issues, some more important for the future than others. The use of force will continue to draw critical reviews. Police officers have a right, even an obligation in some instances, to use force to protect themselves and others as well as necessary to effect an arrest. The force used, deadly or nonlethal, must not be excessive.

During the past ten years, the threat of AIDS has grown. Police officers are especially concerned because of their contact with high-risk individuals. Policies supporting proper education, training, and testing will help lessen the concern.

Law changes, new laws, and the decisions of the U.S. Supreme Court will continue to dictate changes in police behavior. Current trends tend to be more supportive of the police. Civil liability and personal rights will be an increasing problem for police officers. Furthermore, police officers are citizens too. As such, they are afforded the same rights under constitutions and specific statutes as any other citizen.

Technology will grow and improve communications, investigations, and completion of the daily tasks of the job. The computer will become an even greater asset to policing. New nonlethal weapons, along with improved lethal weapons, will improve the police use of force.

If policing is to rise from a quasi-professional state to that of a true profession, it must meet the elements attached to being a profession. Currently, a few elements, such as a code of ethics and a service ideal, are already in place. There is even a growing, recognized body of knowledge. The raising of educational levels and an agreed-upon body of knowledge, standardization of training, lateral transfer, and accreditation are four key components to the police professionalism movement.

Personnel issues will focus on quality of personnel with selection criteria increasing and improving along with training. Racial and ethnic minorities, women, and homosexuals will increase their numbers within policing as well as their roles. Education and training will become more dependent on each other.

Administrators will be better educated and more experienced in management skills. This is a necessity, particularly with rising budgetary problems, increasing racial tensions, and community-relations problems.

Finally, police–community interaction is an important facet of the future of policing. The current efforts of community-oriented policing are an attempt to improve the status of the relationship. A cooperative effort is a necessity.

DO YOU KNOW . . .

1. Whether cases of excessive police force are exaggerated for the public's benefit?
2. Whether the use of deadly force can be completely avoided by police officers?
3. What other methods of restraint and control can be used by police officers in situations in which excessive force may result?
4. How much impact AIDS has had on police officer performance?
5. Why police officers and their families are expected to be "better behaved" than everyone else?
6. Whether police officers should have the right to sue citizens who have violated the officers' civil rights during a course of legal action taken by them against the citizen?
7. Why policing has continued to have such a difficult time being recognized as a profession?
8. Whether police officers really need a college degree to perform their duties?
9. How much training is required of police officers in your state? Is it required of all police officers or does the training level differ from agency to agency?
10. What other reasons limit greater acceptance of lateral transfers?
11. Who benefits the most from accreditation? The agency? Its members? The community?
12. What new technologies are on the horizon for policing?
13. How effective technology has been in improving police performance? safety?
14. What policing will need to do to recruit a more culturally/ethnically diverse population?
15. Whether laws and court decisions will continue to favor law enforcement or individual rights? Which is more important?
16. If college-degreed police executives will become a necessary part of the police future?
17. Whether community-oriented policing is just another fad or a realistic step to improving PCR?

REFERENCES

American Police Association Newsletter 3. (1998, August).
Applying technological advances to crimnal justice. (1997, June). *National Institute of Justice Journal,* 11–15.
Black's law dictionary (6th ed.). (1991). St. Paul, MN: West Publishing Company.
Brancato, G., & Polebaum, E.E. (1981). *The rights of police officers.* New York: Avon Books.

Caldwell, R.G., & Nardini, W. (1977). *Foundations of law enforcement and criminal justice.* Indianapolis, IN: Bobbs-Merrill Company.

CALEA Online (1998). http://www.calea.org.

Carte, G.E. (1973). August Vollmer and the origin of police professionalism. *Journal of Police Science and Administration, 1,* 274–281.

Carter, D.L., & Sapp, A.D. (1994). Issues and perspectives of law enforcement accreditation: A national study of police chiefs. *Journal of Criminal Justice, 22,* 195–204.

Carter, D.L., Sapp, A.D., & Stephens, D.W. (1989). *The state of police education: Policy direction for the 21st century.* Washington, D.C.: Police Executive Research Forum.

Chen, M.M. (1995). Are lawsuits an answer to police brutality? In W.A. Geller & H. Toch (Eds.), *And justice for all: Understanding and controlling police abuse of force* (pp. 233–259.) Washington, D.C. : Police Executive Research Forum.

Christensen, H.G. (1989). The use of deadly force. *Texas Police Journal, 37,* 11–12.

Cohodas, M.J. (1996, September). The cybercops. *Governing,* 63–64.

Coyle, J. (1987, August). The future of law enforcement. *Police,* 43–44, 61–64.

Dantzker, M.L. (1986). Law enforcement, professionalism and a college career. *The Justice Professional, 1,* 1–18.

Dantzker, M.L. (1997). Being a police officer: Part of a profession? In M.L. Dantzker (Ed.), *Contemporary policing: Personnel, issues and trends* (pp. 127–144). Newton, MA: Butterworth-Heinemann.

Dantzker, M.L. (1999). *Police organization and management: Yesterday, today, and tomorrow.* Newton, MA: Butterworth-Heinemann.

Davis, M. (1991). Do cops really need a code of ethics? *Criminal Justice Ethics, 10,* 14–27.

Deadly force policy OK'd. (1991, February-March). *CJ the Americas,* 5–6.

del Carmen, R.V. (1991). *Civil liabilities in American policing.* Englewood Cliffs, NJ: Prentice Hall.

del Carmen , R.V. & Walker, J.T. (1997). *Briefs of leading cases in law enforcement* (3rd ed.). Cincinnati, OH: Anderson Publishing Company.

Doerner, W.G. (1998). *Introduction to law enforcement: An insider's view.* Newton, MA: Butterworth-Heinemann.

Felkenes, G.T. (1984). Attitudes of police officers toward their professional ethics. *Journal of Criminal Justice, 12,* 211–220.

Fortner, R. (1998). Computer technology: Mapping the future. *Police, 22,* 16–21.

Fridell, L. and Pate, A.M. (1997). Use of force: A matter of control. In M.L. Dantzker (Ed.), *Contemporary policing: Personnel, issues and trends* (pp. 217–256). Newton, MA: Butterworth-Heinemann.

Garner, J., Buchanan, J., Schade, T., & Hepburn, J. (1996). Understanding the use of force by and against the police. NIJ research in brief. Washington, D.C.: U.S. Department of Justice.

Graves, F. R., & Connor, G. (1992). The FLETC use-of-force model. *The Police Chief, 59,* 56, 58.

Hammett, T.M. (1989, August). AIDS and HIV training and education in criminal justice agencies. *NIJ-AIDS Bulletin.* Washington, D.C.: National Institute of Justice.

Huston, H.R., Anglin, D., Yarbrough, J., Hardaway, K., Russell, M., Strote, J., Canter, M., & Blum, B., (1998). "Suicide by cop." *Annals of Emergency Medicine, 37,* 665–669.

Lutz, C.F. (1985). Overcoming obstacles to professionalism. In H.W. More (Ed.), *Critical issues in law enforcement* (4th ed.) (pp. 326–342). Cincinnati, OH: Anderson Publishing Company.

Marion, N. (1998). Police academy training: Are we teaching recruits what they need to know? *Policing: An International Journal of Police Strategies and Management, 21,* pp. 54–79.

McCarthy, R. (1989). Real issues and answers on police use of deadly force. *Texas Police Journal, 37*(6), 12–16; *37*(7), 18–20.

Meagher, M.S. (1985). Police patrol styles. *Journal of Police Science and Administration, 13,* 39–45.

Mecum, R.V. (1985). Police professionalism: A new look at an old topic. In H.W. More (Ed.), *Critical issues in law enforcement* (4th ed.) (pp. 312–318). Cincinnati, OH: Anderson Publishing Company.

More, H.W., Jr. (Ed.). (1985). *Critical issues in law enforcement* (4th ed.). Cincinnati OH: Anderson Publishing Company.

Nowicki, E. (1992). Simulated reality. *Police, 16,* 40–43, 97, 98.

Parent, R.B. (1998). Suicide by cop: Victim-precipitated homicide. *The Police Chief, 65,* 111–114.

Price, B.R. (1985). Integrated professionalism: A model for controlling police practices. In H.W. More, Jr. (Ed.), *Critical issues in law enforcement* (4th ed.) (pp. 319–325). Cincinnati, OH: Anderson Publishing Company.

Reaves, B.A., & Smith, P.Z. (1995). *Law enforcement management and administrative statistics, 1993: Data for individual state and local agencies with 100 or more officers.* Washington, D.C.: U.S. Department of Justice.

Rechtschaffen, O.H. (1998). CRIM-I-KNOWLEDGE: Upgrading police professionalism. *Texas Police Journal, 46,* 10.

Regoli, R.M., Crank, J.P., Culbertson, R.G., & Poole, E.D. (1987). Police professionalism and cynicism reconsidered: An assessment of measurement issues. *Justice Quarterly, 4,* 257–275.

Regoli, R.M., Crank, J.P., Culbertson, R.G., & Poole, E.D. (1988). Linkages between professionalization and professionalism among police chiefs. *Journal of Criminal Justice, 16,* 89–98.

Report outlines issues for automated fingerprint system. (1991). *Criminal Justice Newsletter, 22,* 2, 3.

Sandoval, E. (1998, December 10). High-tech help: DPS soon to link up to DNA database. *The Monitor,* 1c, 5c.

Scoville, D. (1998). Getting you to pull the trigger. *Police, 22,* 36–44.

Shernock, S.K., & Dantzker, G.D. (1997). Education and training: No longer just a badge and a gun. In M.L. Dantzker (Ed.), *Contemporary policing: Personnel, issues and trends* (pp. 75–98). Newton, MA: Butterworth-Heinemann.

Sourcebook of criminal justice statistics, 1994. (1995). Washington, D.C.: U.S. Department of Justice.

Sourcebook of criminal justice statistics, 1997. (1998). Washington, D.C.: U.S. Department of Justice.

Stotland, E., Pendleton, M., & Schwartz, R. (1989). Police stress, time on the job, and strain. *Journal of Criminal Justice, 17,* 55–60.

Sussman, V. (1995). Policing cyberspace. U.S. News OnLine. http://www4.usnews/com/usnews/nycu/policing.html.

Sutton, J. (1991). Policing challenges for the 90s. *CJ the Americas, 4,* 1, 12–13.

Swanson, C.R., Territo, L., & Taylor, R.W. (1993). *Police administration* (3rd ed.). New York: Macmillan Publishing Company.

Taking cue from FBI, Florida Launches cyber-crime squad. (1998, September 30). *Law Enforcement News,* 9.

Toder, H.A. (1987). The necessity of taking an interdisciplinary perspective in CJ education. *The Justice Professional, 2,* 92–99.

Utah seeks extra AIDS peace-of-mind for police. (1995). *Law Enforcement News, 21,* 1, 6.

Walker, J.T. (1997). Re-blueing the police: Technological changes and law enforcement practices. In M.L. Dantzker (Ed.), *Contemporary policing: Personnel, issues and trends* (pp. 257–276). Newton, MA: Butterworth-Heinemann.

Warchol, G. (1998). *Workplace violence, 1992–1996.* Bureau of Justice Statistics Special Report. Washington, D.C.: U.S. Department of Justice.

Witkins, G., Gest, T., & Friedman, D. (1990, December 3). Cops under fire. *U.S. News and World Report,* 32–44.

INDEX

337